JOEY

Jacobson's War

Peter J. Usher

A Jewish Canadian Airman in the Second World War

JOEY Jacobson's War

Wilfrid Laurier University Press acknowledges the support of the Canada Council for the Arts for our publishing program. We acknowledge the financial support of the Government of Canada through the Canada Book Fund for our publishing activities. This work was supported by the Research Support Fund.

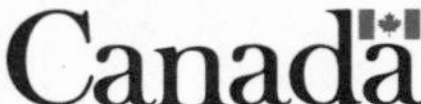

Canada Council for the Arts
Conseil des arts du Canada

Library and Archives Canada Cataloguing in Publication

Usher, Peter J., 1941–, author
Joey Jacobson's war : a Jewish Canadian airman in the Second World War / Peter J. Usher.

Includes bibliographical references and index.
Issued in print and electronic formats.
ISBN 978-1-77112-342-6 (pbk.). – ISBN 978-1-77112-344-0 (epub). – ISBN 978-1-77112-343-3 (pdf)

1. Jacobson, Joey. 2. Flight navigators – Canada – Biography. 3. Airmen – Canada – Biography. 4. Great Britain. Royal Air Force. Squadron, 106. 5. World War, 1939–1945 – Aerial operations, British. I. Title.

D786.U84 2018 940.54'4941092 C2017-904632-2
C2017-904633-0

Cover design by Blakeley Words + Pictures. Front cover: top – Joe, Regina, 1940 (courtesy Janet Jacobson Kwass); bottom – A Handley-Page Hampden Mk. I of No. 455 Squadron RAAF, based at Leuchars in Scotland, May 1942. © Imperial War Museums (COL 182). Back cover: Air observer pupils and Anson trainer, No. 3 Air Observer School, Regina, 1940. Joe Jacobson is second from left (Canadian Jewish Archives).
Text design by Mike Bechthold.

Waterloo, Ontario, Canada
www.wlupress.wlu.ca

This book is printed on FSC® certified recycled paper and is certified Ecologo. It is made from 100% post-consumer fibre, is processed chlorine free, and is manufactured using biogas energy.

Printed in Canada

Contents

List of Illustrations

Preface

Four black horse-drawn carriages led the funeral cortège to the cemetery under leaden skies and light snow. Each bore the coffin of an unidentified flyer recovered from the wreckage of a Royal Air Force bomber. Several hundred Dutch townspeople and a platoon of German soldiers followed. The pastor who conducted the funeral service at Lichtenvoorde General Cemetery declared that the four unknown men had fallen for a cause they knew was just. His eulogy would soon be rewarded with a term in concentration camp. A few men surreptitiously recorded these events on film, at risk of their own arrest. In this second winter of the occupation, the airplane that had dropped from the sky was a harbinger of help from afar. The funeral, which the townspeople had insisted on organizing, was their first act of collective defiance. Active resistance, notably by assisting downed Allied airmen to evade capture, would follow.

One of those coffins contained the body of Flight-Sgt. Joseph Alfred Jacobson of Westmount, Quebec. He was the sole Canadian of the bomber crew that had crashed short of its target at Münster on 28 January 1942. He had had no doubts about the justice of the cause for which he fought. He had taken his copy of Thomas Paine's *The Rights of Man* on his fatal flight.

Joey, as his family and friends called him, was a privileged and ambitious son, a university graduate, and an accomplished athlete. He was the only Jew on McGill University's 1938 league championship football team. In June 1940, he left behind a bright and secure future to enlist in the Royal Canadian Air Force (RCAF). Like many new recruits, he wanted to become a pilot, but he was selected for air observer training – navigating a bomber aircraft to the target and bombing it. That seemed like office work compared to flying the aircraft, but it was office work of the most dangerous kind.

Even before he left Canada, Joey was convinced that he would be engaging in a mortal struggle for civilization: a total war in which there could be no partial or limited victory. When he arrived in England in May 1941, the British Empire stood alone against Germany, the depth of American commitment was as yet unclear, and the Soviet Union watched from the sidelines. The precariousness of the situation served only to fire his appetite for the struggle.

Like so many young Canadians who volunteered for air force duty as spring turned to summer in 1940, Joey Jacobson did not survive. Unlike most of them, he recorded what he saw and did, who he met, what was happening around him, and how he interpreted and judged events as they unfolded, in over two hundred letters to family and friends and in several personal diaries and notebooks that did survive. His father Percy, a Montreal businessman, author, and playwright, also kept a diary throughout the war. Separated by four hundred miles after Joey left home in September 1939 for a factory job in Ontario, father and son began a weekly correspondence that would continue until that January night in 1942 when Joe failed to return. Over that time, their relationship changed from that of a youth still in passage to adulthood and needing fatherly guidance, to one of grown men confiding in each other their hopes and fears in uncertain times. Joey, the boy from Montreal, became Joe, the man in combat over Europe.

The letters exchanged between a young man, who would be buried in Europe before his twenty-fourth birthday, and his family and friends in Montreal, testify to the struggle of war as experienced on the front line and in Canada. They reveal the state of mind that fuelled Joe's convictions, and how those convictions inspired his actions. His letters home while training in Canada and England were full of amazement and discovery. Even during his most intense months of combat, Joe continued to write long letters home and keep detailed diaries that conveyed the immediacy of his experience. Joe lived his life with an intensity that burns through his letters. Percy was lit by that intensity for the time that Joe wrote home, and he was crushed by its absence. For Joe, his father's counsel and understanding was his anchor in rough waters. Reading Joe's diaries, discovered after his death, left Percy humbled by his son's life and courage.

It is those letters and diaries that lay claim on our attention today. None of their authors was of independent or enduring fame. Virtually all of those who knew and loved and mourned them are now dead. Hardly anyone now remembers the sound of their voices and their laughter, their mannerisms and expressions, their jokes, pranks, or preoccupations. It is through their letters and diaries that they wrote themselves into enduring visibility, and enabled us to put human faces and personalities on names carved in stone long ago.

Letters are rarely bulletins from the deepest reaches of the writer's soul, nor can they reveal more than a fragment of the writer's thoughts and actions. Yet what is truly exceptional about Joe's record is how much it does reveal. We know how he experienced and understood the execution of the war in the air, how he responded to the inevitable battle stress, and how he became both an idealist and a deadly serious warrior, because he told us.

Also exceptional about Joey Jacobson's account is the detail of his experience and the depth of his comprehension of the strategy, tactics, and effectiveness of Bomber Command's attempt to destroy the nerve centres of Germany's war-making capacity. In order to understand his story, therefore, I have also related in parallel the nature and progress of Bomber Command's training and operations during that most discouraging time in 1941. Joey's experience was shared by hundreds of Canadians who served in that early stage of the air war. His story, at least in part, is also theirs.

Believing his views on air force operations would never pass the postal censors, Joe Jacobson recorded them in his private diaries and notebooks that were secreted home after his death. Both Joe and his father considered that their letters and diaries could serve as rough drafts of history. Letters were their forum for discussion and debate, and their means to challenge each other to live each day to the fullest in accord with their ideals. Joey expected much of his friends, and Percy expected much of him. Joe's letters and diaries brought news of things far beyond the experience of those at home in Canada. More than a record of daily life in air force service, they addressed existential questions of purpose and perseverance in the face of danger and death. He made no attempt to conceal the risks, even as he reassured his family of the rightness of his task and his dedication to it. He had a gift for letter writing. He could tell a good story about events and exploits, and paint a deft character sketch. More than that, setting out his hopes and fears was a means for Joe to push himself to carry on night after night to face whatever fate he had volunteered to encounter and still get the most out of life. Writing was the means by which Joe sought to understand his life.

Servicemen's letters may be questioned as reliable indicators of attitude and emotion because they are normally written (under the watchful eye of the censor) to minimize distress and sustain morale at home. Joe Jacobson's letters, however, made little effort to please or dissemble. Personal wartime diaries, because they are necessarily kept secret, are thought to offer better access to the actuality of experience and mood. Joe and Percy's letters and diaries, in combination, provide exceptional insight to the state of mind of their authors. Joe's attitudes, actions, and outlook emerge unreconstructed by subsequent reflection or events. The record is remarkably complete, and without mysterious gaps. Joe wrote letters home at least weekly, and virtually all were received and preserved. He made entries in his personal diary, kept not only as a record of events but also of self-reflection and self-improvement, every day for the last year of his life. He also kept an operational diary, and several notebooks on his views of the air war and the books he was reading.

Yet even such a richness of sources only hints at some things and reveals nothing about others. I have speculated about some of the inevitable missing spaces, but I have avoided attributing dialogue or thoughts for which there is no evidence. When Joey was nineteen he confided to his diary that he had a strong tendency to exaggerate: "I improve upon and often distort facts. I shall try to be more precise." Keeping this self-admitted proclivity for embellishment in mind I have sought, with the aid of both official and unofficial sources, to distinguish among what may be true, what cannot be true, and what is undoubtedly true, to the extent that those distinctions matter.

As readers will divine, these are men's letters. Women are spoken of, but rarely speak for themselves, mainly because so few of their letters have survived. I have omitted the mundane, along with the family news and gossip (important as that was in sustaining the connection with home and family), although those elements have grounded my description of Joey's home life and background, especially in Part One. Where dates are unrecorded in the original (or are apparently incorrectly recorded), I have tried to reconcile them with or infer them from other sources, so far as is possible. I have taken the liberty of correcting obvious typographical, spelling, and grammatical errors. These were few in the original, mostly the consequence of haste and immediacy at the time of writing. Otherwise I have not edited the authors' particular styles of writing, which convey both their personalities and their time. To distinguish among the source materials, a three- or four-letter code precedes the date of each item: PJD for Percy Jacobson's diaries and PJL for his letters, JJD for Joe's diaries (except for his operational diary, which is denoted as JJOD), JJL for his letters, and JJN for his notebooks. Other writers are identified by their full name.

The air offensive against Nazi Germany began on the first day of the war and continued until a few days before its end. Bomber Command's objectives, capabilities, and strategies evolved rapidly during those years, as did the training and capabilities of the aircrews charged with carrying them out. Those Canadians who volunteered at the outset went into action when the bombing war brought little to cheer about. Rarely were Germany's industries and railways brought to a standstill, despite well-publicized bombing attacks on them. When they were it was not for long. Germany's battleships and submarines continued to prowl the seas in 1941. Unknown to those reading and listening to news bulletins at home was that on any given night, more of Bomber Command's flyers were killed in the air than were Germans on the ground. Bomber Command's learning curve would be steep, its losses high, and its successes few. The popular heroes of those early years were the Spitfire pilots who had turned the tide in the Battle of Britain. Bomber Command's spectacular successes, like the dam-buster raid and the attack on the V-2 rocket facility at Peenemünde, were another two years off. Those who served in the early years of the strategic air offensive did so with no less courage and determination than the pilots of Fighter Command, but with far less tangible reward. Nor was their cup sweetened by postwar controversies about the effectiveness and morality of the bombing of Germany.

Those early Canadian volunteers went largely unsung for another reason. On arrival in Britain they were attached to Britain's Royal Air Force (RAF), whereupon they were dispersed among its training units and operational squadrons to serve alongside British and other Dominion flyers. Those Canadians became the Royal Canadian Air Force's orphans. Those who were killed before the formation of 6 Group – the Canadian squadrons in Bomber Command – in 1943 went unnoticed in the official histories of the RCAF and the RAF. They are barely mentioned in Canada's War Museum, and their stories are largely untold in the many popular histories and accounts of the RCAF published after the war.

The veterans of the air war have by now written their last accounts. No one alive and alert today can relate from his own experience a night run to a German industrial target in a Hampden bomber in 1941, undefended through cloud and darkness against anti-aircraft fire and enemy fighters, with the aid of only a map, a compass, and an airspeed indicator. The young Canadian airmen whose first experience of the air war was London in the Blitz are all gone.

How those veterans told their stories changed over the years. Memoirs written shortly after tours of duty were long on excitement and derring-do, but short on reflection. The first accounts of the bomber war told of exceptional deeds performed under exceptional danger, but little of the day-to-day experience of the tens of thousands of men who performed those deeds. Memoirs written twenty and thirty years later tended to be more reflective, and reveal more of the fear, though no less of the courage, that accompanied dangerous and exhausting night bombing runs over enemy territory. If recall of the details faded or seemed less important, the intensity of the experience did not. As the decades passed, veterans' stories became filtered by the accumulation of life's experience and reflection, and coloured by a mix of gratitude and guilt for having survived when so many others did not. Some were motivated by the desire to set the record straight in response to the steady flow of popular and professional histories of the bomber war. Some just wanted to tell their stories to a public that had forgotten or never knew what they had done and why.

This account returns to the time when the daily events of war actually happened. Seventy-five years later, the lively, articulate, and intimate conversation between father and son, and among close friends, has lost none of its freshness and immediacy. It is a record of their time and place, now beyond living memory, told as they experienced it, without the memoirist's reflection, revision, or hindsight. They could not know the outcome. Joey never got to read the history books. I have accordingly let their writing take centre stage in this book. Father and son speak for themselves, even after all these years.

⊙

Joey Jacobson died when I was six weeks old, and he remained at the outer edge of my consciousness for most of my life. His father Percy died when I was ten. His mother May, my great-aunt, kept Joey's uniformed portrait on her living-room wall, and she wore his operational wings on her lapel every day. I don't recall her ever speaking of him, though, and I never asked. Nonetheless I came to understand that Joey had been a very special member of our family, and that his loss, even if unspoken, had left a hole in many hearts.

Growing up in the shadow of the Second World War shaped my sensibilities in ways I saw very clearly at the time, and in others that took me much longer to comprehend. The war took the youngest of my parents' generation. They were the men I never knew.

In 1992, a Canadian television documentary about that increasingly forgotten war suggested that the bomber crews were led to their deaths unknowing of what they were destroying below or of the risk to themselves. The program attracted substantial ire among veterans. One of them, Joey's cousin Ray Silver, decided to write his own book in response. It was in those years that I began to ask myself what my relatives who had served in Bomber Command had really done and experienced so many years ago. Periodic visits to Joey's sisters Edith and Janet in Montreal prompted the discovery of letters, diaries, and photographs long stashed away in cupboards and basements.

In 2004, not long after I read Joe's daily diary, I had lunch with his best friend, Monty Berger. On parting, Monty handed me a bundle of letters that he had kept for sixty years. Anticipating my interest, he had brought them to entrust in my care. I would become Joey's biographer, he said, and it was then that I realized that I had taken on the obligation to write this book. Shortly after I came across a news item about the son of Joe's wireless operator in England, and about their wartime funeral in Lichtenvoorde. In the months following I visited England and the Netherlands to find out more. So began my voyage of inquiry in England, the Netherlands, and Canada.

By virtue of my undertaking, Joey came alive and immediate to me in a way that my other uncles, middle-aged men when I was a boy, never had. I liked them, of course, but a generation stood between us. Joey's letters and diaries revealed a vibrant young man in whom I could recognize something of myself at that age. But he had been confronted by circumstances that my generation had not. And so I came to see and also to wonder about what I too had lost, and to grieve for the man I never met.

Acknowledgements

This book is based on the letters and diaries of Joe Jacobson and his father Percy, and the letters Joe received from his friends. I first became aware of them through his sisters, Edith Jacobson Low-Beer and Janet Jacobson Kwass, and his closest friend, Monty Berger. I am deeply grateful for their assistance and encouragement along the way. I am also grateful to their children, Jo-Ann and Peter Kwass, and Susan and Jane Low-Beer, for their co-operation and assistance in organizing the donation of Joe's letters, diaries, and photos to the Alex Dworkin Canadian Jewish Archives in 2012.

Over the fifteen years since I first imagined this book, I have had the opportunity to visit or obtain the assistance of numerous libraries, archives, and museums. In Canada, these included Library and Archives Canada, the Directorate of History and Heritage (Department of National Defence), the Canadian War Museum, the Canadian Aviation and Space Museum and Library, Carleton University Library, and the Ottawa Public Library (in Ottawa); the Alex Dworkin Canadian Jewish Archives and McGill University Archives (in Montreal); the Toronto Public Library (in Toronto); the Royal Canadian Air Force Museum (Trenton, Ontario); Cambridge City Archives (Cambridge, Ontario); Kitchener Public Library (Kitchener, Ontario); Debert Military Museum (Debert, Nova Scotia); and the Canadian Museum of Flight and Transportation (Langley, British Columbia).

In the United Kingdom, I benefited from visits to or assistance from The National Archives, the Imperial War Museum, the Royal Air Force Museum, the British Library, the Jewish Military Museum, and the Air Historical Branch (RAF) (in London); Cambridge University Library (Cambridge); the National Meteorological Archive (Exeter); the Commonwealth War Graves Commission (Maidstone); the Woodhall Spa Library (Woodhall Spa, Lincolnshire); the Metheringham Airfield Visitor Centre (Metheringham, Lincolnshire); the Lincolnshire Aviation Heritage Centre (East Kirkby, Lincolnshire); and the RAF Museum at Cosford. I was also assisted on visits to the AVOG Crash Museum in Leivelde, Netherlands, and the National Archives and Records Administration in College Park, Maryland, in the United States. The staff at all of these institutions were invariably helpful, but I must single out a few for special recognition: Janice Rosen at the Canadian Jewish Archives, Stephen Harris at the Directorate of History and Heritage, William Spencer at The National Archives, John Marshall-East at the Aviation Heritage Centre, and Jan Geerdinck at the AVOG Crash Museum.

Site visits to Lincolnshire and Yorkshire, and to the Lichtenvoorde area in the Netherlands, provided me essential grounding for the events described here. I owe my deepest thanks to Wim Rhebergen of Hoevelaken, NL, without whose meticulous investigations of Allied bomber crashes in the Achterhoek area of the Netherlands, and whose dedication to communicating his findings to the families of the lost airmen, I would never have learned of the events of early 1942 in Lichtenvoorde. He guided me on site visits, provided me with records and translations, and steered me through the complex story of occupation and resistance there.

I am also indebted to many friends, colleagues, and others who graciously provided me with encouragement, advice, and information over the life of this project. In Canada, they include Chris Burn, Ted Chamberlin, Tim Cook, Michael Cristofaro, John Godwin, Jack Granatstein, Jim Lotz, Ian McKendry, Sietze Praamsma, Hulbert Silver, Gerald Smith, Norm Snow, John Stager, Ron Verzuh, Randall Wakelam, Robert Willinsky, and (in the United States) Yvette Kale (née Kostoris) and Herb Ross. My special thanks to Gerald Tulchinsky for his encouragement and sage guidance along the way, and to my editor at Wilfrid Laurier University Press, Mike Bechthold.

In Great Britain they include Phil Bonner, Mark Connelly, Linzee Duncan, Simon Elmer, Marilyn Farias (née Selfe), Stuart Hadaway, Dave Harrigan, Andrew and Janette Hodgkinson, Mike Hulme, Brian and Denise (née Michaels) Infield, Andy Marson, Margorie Sargeant, Des Richards, Rod Sanders, Margo Schwartz, Peter and Zena Scoley, Martin Sugarman, and Derek Thomas. In the Netherlands, I owe a debt of gratitude to Henny Bennink, Henk Heinst, Theo and Hannie Leemreize, and John Griffiths.

Several of those who inspired and assisted me over the last twenty years did not live to see the result. They include Joey's sister Edith, his best friend Monty, and three men who also served as navigators in Bomber Command: my mother's (and Joe's) cousin Lionel (Ray) Silver, my father-in-law Al White, and my mentor and dear friend Moose Kerr. Had our conversations not been terminated before I really knew what to ask them about, this would have been a better book.

I am grateful to those who read and commented on drafts, in whole or in part, including Hugh Brody, Gillian O'Reilly, Wim Rhebergen, Diana

Schwartz, George Thompson, and Tony Usher. My greatest debt is to my wife, Pamela White, whose unstinting support, close reading, and incisive observations have sustained me throughout.

Most of the photographs in this book were originally provided by the Jacobson family. Some of them are now in the Percy and Joe Jacobson collection at the Alex Dworkin Canadian Jewish Archives, and are credited accordingly; the others are credited to Janet Jacobson Kwass. Other photographs were obtained from Library and Archives Canada, the Laurier Centre for Military Strategic and Disarmament Studies, the Imperial War Museum, the Metheringham Airfield Visitor Centre, the AVOG Crash Museum, Marilyn Farias, Mrs. Leo Passhuis, and Robert Willinsky.

Part One

Father and Son

We have taken the very cream of the youth of Canada. These boys are … bred in Canada, schooled in Canadian schools and with an intensely Canadian viewpoint.

– Charles Power, Minister of National Defence for Air, 6 November 1941

The honour of our race is in the keeping of but a fraction of her people.

– Lord Moran, *The Anatomy of Courage*, 1945

One

September 1939

On the day that news of the German invasion of Poland arrived in Montreal, Percy Jacobson rolled a blank sheet of paper on to his typewriter carriage, noted the date at the top, and began to write. He would do this most days for the next six years of war, recording his observations on daily events at home and abroad, not least on what they might mean for his only remaining son, Joe. Percy had expected war and dreaded it. He knew it would bring disruption and sorrow to his family circle at 635 Grosvenor Avenue, just as it would to his city, to Canada, and to the nations of Europe. Yet on this day he was relieved that the necessary struggle would finally be engaged.

Joe Jacobson was an ambitious young man and an accomplished athlete. He was the only Jew on McGill University's 1938 intercollegiate champion football team. He had graduated in commerce in the spring of 1939. He had set course to enter his father's office furniture business, which supplied many of Montreal's corporate headquarters. To that end, he had a factory job lined up with one of his father's business associates in Ontario. But when Joe returned to Montreal from summer camp at the end of August, troops were already on guard at railway yards, bridges, and power stations, and the Red Cross was training ambulance drivers and nurses.

> For several days now, in fact ever since the war, I have had Joe on my mind. He is twenty-one and must make his own decision. I know that he can't keep out of it. First of all we are Jews and Hitler's persecution of the Jews will go down into history along with the stories of the Spanish

> Inquisition. Second of all even if he felt war was wrong and realized the wickedness of destroying the youth of the world he couldn't stand by and see his friends fight for him. And third as a graduate of McGill with a fine record in the classroom and on the field, he would lose caste in his own eyes as well as with his fellow men. Then again he is just the right age and his physical fitness is par.
>
> I told him to think it out and if he decided to join up to select the work he is best fitted for. It is going to be very hard on his mother. I am desperately sorry for my boy, I know he hates war and hates fighting. He is a gentle nature and has an awfully lot of good sense. God Bless the boy. (PJD 13 September 1939)
>
> Joe's two best friends, lads about his age, came over in the afternoon and of course talked about the war. They are both intelligent and wide minded.... They are quite disillusioned about everything but they know that they are trapped, they know they must do their duty and they agree that the menace of Hitlerism is not mere propaganda but is borne out by actual facts. They feel, like I do, that when Hitler began his persecution against the Jews the civilized nations of the world attempted no interference. And when the purge of Jews was at its height and they were flung out into the world no country went on record as being willing to afford asylum for them. (PJD 14 September 1939)
>
> What a difference between the young men of 1914 and the young men of today. What a happy go lucky crowd of lads they were full of gaiety and keen for adventure. They would march along the streets singing little knowing what they were in for. They would shout "We're on our way to Berlin." They visualized a tour of Europe at their country's expense. We all know what happened. Now our boys know what they are up against, know what they are going into, and although they perhaps realize that there is a job to be done, they don't like the business. But they will fight and if they have no stomach they have guts and backbone. One thing I notice particularly that they won't stand for any cant or even idealisms. They are not to be fooled by high-sounding empty phrases. They are completely disillusioned and completely cynical about the whole affair. (PJD 15 September 1939)

The declaration of war did not immediately deflect Joe from his intended path. Even if he could step into his father's business whenever he liked, he wanted to get some real work experience under his belt.

> Tonight Joe left for Preston to work in a furniture factory. I am afraid he will not be there for long because the war news is so bad that it will not be long before every young man will be in the army. The reason Joe is still a civilian is due to my persuasion. I want him to carefully consider what branch of work he is best fitted for. At present the Government is unable to handle the men already enlisted.
>
> Joe has the makings of a first class man. God grant that he may be allowed to be of more use to this Canada of ours than holding a rifle. That he may be called upon to do something better for his Alma Mater than stick some poor devil in the belly with a bayonet.
> (PJD 18 September 1939)
>
> There is no question that at present he is not needed and I am sure that the Government (although they dare not say so) are embarrassed about how to deal with the men they already have. (PJD 19 September 1939)

Yet Percy also knew that this state of suspension could not and must not last.

> Those of us who have English blood in our veins, who know and love England, must be prepared to make every sacrifice that England and the British Empire may continue a factor in civilization. It is our one safeguard against the law of the jungle. I know England has made mistakes, terrible mistakes.... But I still love England. I don't want to live under German rule. (PJD 22 September 1939)

Percy, although born in Montreal, spent his early childhood years in Liverpool and Manchester, where his mother's family had long prospered in the tobacco manufacturing business. Some time after his father abandoned them, Mrs. Jacobson and her only son Percy returned to Canada, where the Montreal branch of the family saw to the boy's welfare. Percy was sent to board at Lower Canada College, and by the age of twenty he had been set up in the office furniture business. Some years later he met May Silver, who was studying library science at McGill University, and married her.

In 1939, Percy and May were living halfway up the slopes of Westmount, in the heart of upper middle-class English Montreal. They had had four children: Edith, twenty-three years old when the war began, Joey, two years younger, Peter, who died of leukemia in 1937 while still in high school, and Janet, aged sixteen. The Thirties had brought Percy his share of business anxieties, but the family was always able to afford what mattered to them. They eschewed ostentation, but their house was spacious and comfortable, they employed a live-in maid as was common to their station, and they sent their children to summer camp.

Percy and May built an emotionally stable and nurturing household for their children, as well as a financially secure one. Much was given, much was accepted, and much was required of each member of the household. On Monday nights parents and children met to discuss family issues and plan the coming week. Joey was fiercely protective of his sisters despite some competitive but good-natured squabbling. He was the golden boy of his family. They were generous with him, as he was with them. Joey drew his ideals of family life from this background, observing that "of all the homes I have ever been in or all the families and gatherings I have been in, none have the warmth, informality or the vigour of ours."

The Jacobsons were very much a part of Montreal's established uptown Jewish community, and they were active in its affairs. They were members of the city's Reform congregation, but they wore their Judaism lightly, being minimally observant in practice, and skeptical in their faith. They did not keep a kosher house, they decorated a tree and exchanged gifts at Christmas, and they observed Friday nights as a stay-at-home family evening, but without prayer or ceremony. They were outward-looking Jews, and shunned any self-imposed mental or occupational ghetto. May's father had managed to combine the presidency of a prominent Montreal synagogue with his Masonic lodge membership, his atheism, and his devotion to the writings of philosopher Thomas Carlyle. Her brother, who scorned religion and put his faith in science, had been a geologist, prospector, and mine manager in northern Ontario. Yet if the Jacobsons were not entirely typical of the uptown community, they shared many of its sensibilities, not least its unswerving loyalty to Britain and to the Liberal Party of Canada. In November 1938 they opened their house to a family of Jewish refugees from Austria.

Percy and May were high-minded and public-spirited, and not without a touch of intellectual and social snobbery. Percy was a businessman by day, but he was a writer and playwright in the evenings. Several of his scripts were performed as radio dramas on the national broadcasting system. Percy was chair of the Montreal chapter of the Canadian Authors' Association, which concerned itself as much with civil liberties as the development of a national literature. English Montreal's literary notables were familiar visitors to the house. May, attracted to the ideals of progressive education, ran a children's bookstore on fashionable Sherbrooke Street. It was as much a vocation for her as a business.

Montreal's established Jewish community had high expectations of its sons. They should do well in school, make something of themselves, raise a family, and be good citizens. They should succeed in the professions and prosper in business, they should not marry without prospect of doing so, and they should marry within the faith. By all accounts Joey, as he was called by family and friends, would fulfill these expectations. He was quick to assert his individuality but was not by inclination a nonconformist. Ambitious to get ahead, he was alert to the importance of self-improvement, getting to know the right people, and putting his best foot forward. He had had a good start, as he was engaging and gregarious, sturdy and handsome with brown eyes and hair, admired in his own social set and highly thought of in his parents' circle.

Joey's chief passion as a youth was sports. After a childhood bout of pneumonia, he dedicated himself to developing his strength and fitness. The athletic staff at Westmount High characterized Joey as "a sure tackler in football and one of the few Jewish boys who stood out in hockey," and he continued to excel at both at McGill.[1] On any good winter weekend, Joe and his friends would board the ski train at Westmount Station for the Laurentians. At summer camp he played tennis and baseball. Whatever the sport, he loved to compete. The pinnacle of Joey's athletic career came in his final year at McGill, when the Redmen won the intercollegiate football championship. One of the team's smallest players, at five foot ten and 160 pounds, he was admired for his grit, agility, and determination as a tackler, and he was undeterred by pain and injury.

> All the players on the winning football team are heroes, I have been walking on air. Every Saturday after the game I get high wide and handsome, last night was no exception. Mom & Pop are pretty proud, take a lively interest in the game, and discuss football learnedly. As a result of football, I have done no studying, spent money freely, get tight and generally let matters important and otherwise slip. I will be glad to settle down after next week when we hope to win the championship.
> (JJD 6 November 1938)

Joey began his first diary on New Year's Day 1936, the year that Europe slipped irrevocably toward war. He kept it almost daily for three months, so that in future he would be able to see his "ideas, accomplishments, failures, [and] shortcomings in a clear light." Character assessment of both himself and his schoolmates played no small part in his diary entries. He could be mercilessly critical and, in equal measure, lavish in praise.

He began a second diary at the beginning of 1937, intended as a weekly review of events "with a little philosophizing and pondering and observations on the side." His entries often described family or social events from which he drew lessons about character, family life, and self-improvement. His New Year's resolutions for 1937 were to be more decisive, to stop making excuses for himself, and to keep his tendency to exaggerate things in check. In February his younger brother Peter fell ill of leukemia and died within weeks. Most of Joe's diary entries that winter concerned the response of family and friends to this dreadful development. It was the first time Joe had been confronted with the death of someone close to him. Steeling himself for what was to come in Peter's last days, Joe wrote:

> I don't mind taking the inevitable and seeing a beloved brother who I was just beginning to consider as an equal go, and it's bad enough watching my family heartbroken but I am going to hate to see friends and relatives weeping and moping around. But I guess that can't be helped. That's life. (JJD 12 March 1937)

Again Joe let his diary slide in the spring, and his entries are sporadic thereafter. Joe's early diaries were not only a record of his day-to-day activities. They illustrate the development of his thinking and attitudes, reveal much about his character, and in both style and theme presage his subsequent letters home. He used his diaries to focus his thoughts, and to develop his skills as a storyteller and in drawing character sketches, also evident in those later letters.

Joey had elected to complete his senior matriculation at Westmount High, which enabled him to enter second year at McGill University in the fall of 1936. His scholastic efforts continued to take a back seat to his athletic and social life. If Joe was inspired by any of his professors, he made no record of it in his diaries. He observed self-critically at the end of his second year:

> I have been going to college all year presumably to learn to think. Most of my thinking has been done on the ice, football field, ski trails, or dance floor. But very little real thinking, reasoning and concrete original deductions. I have spent an extremely enjoyable year, but perhaps a little too stationary. I don't feel I am going ahead.... I met a lot of people, but I doubt if I gave anything to any of them (except a few laughs) or got anything worthwhile in return (outside lipstick).... there are many things that worry me. Little things, habits, customs that I should correct and the all important one of using the old bean. (JJD 17 April 1938)

Frivolous as his university years may have been by his own account, Joe had a serious and introspective side. It was during that second year at McGill that Joe encountered three young men with whom he would develop an intense and enduring fellowship. They were of modest circumstances, and had attended West Hill High in suburban Notre-Dame-de-Grâce. Joe had known Monty Berger from summer camp, now they were fraternity brothers at McGill. Monty, a rabbi's son, was the intellectual of the group. It was through Monty that Joe met Herb Rosenstein and Gerald Smith, neither of whom could afford summer camp or fraternity membership. Herb went to work after leaving high school, and soon afterwards changed his surname to Ross. Gerald's father, who had jumped ship from the Czar's navy during the Russo-Japanese war, and started a small clothing business after coming to Montreal, had fallen into penury during the Depression. The family was reduced to moving from one apartment to another ahead of the rent collector. Gerald nonetheless managed to enter McGill, where he and Monty became editorial staffers on the *McGill Daily*. All three knew better than Joe, from their own experience, that being Jewish made finding work and a place to live more difficult than it otherwise was.

Their friendship soon provided the intimate space for comparing their experiences and challenges. They were at the critical time of their lives when both bridges and barriers were beginning to crystalize – not least for young Jews in English Montreal – around career opportunities, friendships, women, and social life. The foursome thrived on thoughtful debate, friendly rivalry over sports and women, and pranks. In September 1939, they were confronted with the first really serious decision of their lives.

The question of when to enlist, and for what, would preoccupy the four young men for the first winter of the war. Like Joe, his friends wanted to establish themselves in the workforce so that they might have a job to come home to when the fighting was over. But unlike Joe, their futures were insecure, and job prospects were still scarce in that last year of the Great Depression. Monty, having been accepted in a one-year journalism program at Columbia University, spent that winter in New York City. Gerald Smith stayed in Montreal to look for work, and signed up for Officer Corps training. Herb Ross had gone to New York the previous year to find a job. Joe did not have to look for work, because Percy had already secured him a job for the coming winter in his supplier's furniture factory in Preston, Ontario. Joey, Monty, Gerald, and Herb styled themselves that fall as "the Pony Club," an anagram for Preston, Ontario, and New York. Once separated, they kept their conversation going by circulating their letters to each other in a chain. So began a vigorous discussion of the war situation in Canada, and the question of enlistment.

Percy had high expectations for Joe. He believed that his son had the right stuff to take a leading place in the national life of the Dominion, by which he meant Canada's business, governing, and opinion-leading circles, and so contribute to the public good. Percy would have been pleased enough for his son to take over his office furniture business, but he would have been even more pleased if Joe managed to succeed in public service or industry.

Joe for his part was anxious to live up to his father's high expectations. Many in Joe's circle were content to become doctors, lawyers, and accountants – opportunities that had only recently opened up to better-educated young Jewish men. Joe, seeing himself as a man of action and a builder, had no desire to confine himself to this milieu. He had different ambitions and wider horizons, even if he did not as yet know much about the life of the Dominion beyond the confines of English Montreal. Joe seems to have shared his parents' idealism and public-spirited values, which would find expression in his own writings two years later in wartime England.

Yet both father and son knew that there was a barrier to those ambitions. It would be harder for a Jew to gain a place on that larger stage. Neither Joe's university degree (which only a tiny fraction of Canadians then had), nor his sporting achievements were enough to provide him with the ready connections in higher places. Without them, the bastions of Canadian industry, government, and society were not easily prised open, and Joe was still figuring out how to address that problem.

Joey with sister Edith and brother Peter, ca. 1922. (Janet Jacobson Kwass)

Percy with Peter and Joey, ca. 1929. (Janet Jacobson Kwass)

Left: Joey at Twin Lakes summer camp, Vermont, 1933. The camp catered to Jewish youth from the northeastern states and Montreal. (Janet Jacobson Kwass)
Right: Joey and May, Twin Lakes summer camp, ca. 1935. (Canadian Jewish Archives)

Joey at 635 Grosvenor Avenue, Montreal, ca. 1938. (Canadian Jewish Archives)

Joey in McGill Redmen practice jersey, ca. 1938. (Janet Jacobson Kwass)

Two

Preston

On the morning train from Toronto, Joe

> decided to get a better sampling of Ontario public opinion [regarding the war] so I started a chat with the trainman – a burly looking fellow. He got wound up in short order and told me that he was at a veterans' meeting the other night where they numbered 1200. They decided that the Jews would not be allowed to be left behind to profiteer and that they would [be] rounded up by the soldiers themselves and be forced to fight. He went on in that vein in such strenuous fashion that I was extremely glad to break up his story of only 3 Jews out of 10,000 volunteers joining up in Ontario last week, by leaving the train as we arrived in Galt. (JJL 19 September 1939)

Evidently the burly trainman was not alone in his views. Joe was an avid reader of *Saturday Night*, the national weekly current affairs magazine. So he was unlikely to have missed the full-page article entitled "Will the Jews Enlist?" that appeared a couple of weeks later, by the United Church's Dr. Claris Silcox, a leading advocate of better understanding between Christians and Jews. Dr. Silcox acknowledged both the reputedly low rate of Jewish enlistment in the previous war and the resentment that had aroused among Gentiles, but he asserted that contrary to common expectation, Canada's Jews would most certainly enlist in the current war.

Joe knew that his fellow citizens were watching. Very likely it was then, within the first month of the war, that Joe saw clearly that he must before long enlist, and that he must do so not only as a Canadian, and not only to fight against Hitler, but to give a good account of himself as a Jew. The issue of enlistment was never far from his mind, but he took a cautious approach. Joe was not without income or employment as many young Canadian men then were, nor did he rush to army recruiting centres at the outset as many did. Within days of his arrival in Preston, he discovered that he could take a Canadian Officer Training Corps (COTC) course in nearby Guelph (where hundreds of men were already responding to an army recruiting drive), or apply for the navy, which he preferred. "If conscription comes and my application is in – I am not conscripted for the army," but he thought that would be a matter of months. In October Joe learned of an officer training course in Galt, but commented:

> It's only for infantry – run by the Royal Highlanders – and – you have to buy your own uniform which is like buying a commission since an outfit cost around $100.... Besides you have to be sponsored by somebody in the Highland Regiment – so that's out. Other disadvantages for me – 7–10 o'clock two nights a week – until New Years – probably meaning no Christmas holidays for me. I will still wait which means doing nothing over the winter. (JJL 15 October 1939)

So Joe let the issue ride during his winter in Preston.

Preston was in 1939 a small manufacturing town in the agricultural heartland of southern Ontario. It was situated at a sulphur spring by the Grand River, where several hotels catered to those seeking the restorative powers of the waters. The Preston Furniture Company, owned by Percy Hilborn, was one of the town's main industries, and Percy Jacobson's office supply business was one of its leading customers.

Joe's year in Preston was his first extended time away from home, and his first regular job. He was twenty-one years old. He had until then lived a privileged life in Westmount, Canada's most prosperous and influential community, and he knew little of the rest of the country. Like many such young men, he was only just beginning to understand that his good fortune was not shared by all. Preston was a world apart from Westmount, and a novelty for Joe. Eight months of living on his own in small-town Ontario, working in a factory, and mixing with people of ordinary circumstances broadened Joe's social and political perspectives, and his awareness of Canada.

Joe worked ten hours each weekday and nine on Saturdays. He took to learning about wood furniture manufacturing from the bottom up with alacrity. He worked in all parts of the factory, from lumber scaling to furniture finishing to production line management. He was doing men's work, physical labour that left him satisfied that he had put in a day's work, and he liked that. Percy Hilborn took Joe under his wing, inviting him for supper from time to time and, before long, sending him on business trips and finding opportunities for him to observe other southern Ontario factories.

For self-improvement, Joe spent two evenings a week in the town library. Putting his new reading glasses to work, he devoured trade and business magazines, current affairs magazines (especially *Saturday Night* and *The Atlantic Monthly*), and books such as *The Life of Edison*, *The Prince*, and *The Grapes of Wrath*.[1] He also began to write letters. He wrote to his family and to the Pony Club every week about life in Preston, with acuity and sometimes amazement, and in considerable detail. He took writing as a craft, and his letters home that fall bore little resemblance to the one-pagers he used to write from summer camp. He asked his parents for a typewriter, and he was highly pleased to receive one at Christmas. Percy followed Joe's progress with satisfaction:

> Letter from my son Joe today from Preston Ont. made me feel rather proud of the lad. He has adapted himself so quickly to hard manual labour and seems so eager not only to learn the desk business but to understand the various types of men he comes in contact with. He seems to like them all which I guess means that they like him. He is probably the only Jewish factory worker in the whole district. I think he will prove a good ambassador of our people. In his letter he talks about joining the navy. I have a friend, Commander of the district. I intend to discuss the matter with him. In the meanwhile Joe is getting excellent training for either peace or war duties. He says he is as fit as a fiddle and his muscles are like iron. Joe sure writes a good letter and his sense of humour should help him a whole lot in the trying times ahead.
> (PJD 3 October 1939)

> Joe is full of his job at Preston. He is not lazy and I am sure if he ever has to earn his living by hard manual labor he will make the grade. He is off to a football match between McGill and Varsity. This time last year he was playing and playing well for McGill. I remember one Saturday afternoon in particular, his mother and myself went to the game full of pride at having a boy on the senior team. I never enjoyed a game more. It was a lovely day and Joe did well, McGill won and there was much rejoicing. (PJD 7 October 1939)

After a couple of weeks at the Sulphur Spring Hotel, Joe went to board with the Grahams, an elderly couple who lived at Kress Hill on the edge of town, where they kept a garden, chickens, and a small orchard. They took to each other with enduring affection. Two years later Mrs. Graham was still sending food parcels to Joe in England. Joe related, in a letter home:

> Yesterday morning as old Bill woke up with a slight hangover after drinking away his week's pay check, Mrs. G took the occasion to do a little preaching and pointed out how well she and I felt after a good night's rest. Then looking at me with admiration in her kind eyes she said "look at Mr. Jacobson there's a young man that always acts decent like and reads his books instead of wasting his time and money – oh yes we're glad we got to bed early aren't [we] Mr. Jacobson?" I managed to mumble a "yes" thinking to myself – what I wouldn't give for a real good binge and to hell with the early hours and books.
> (JJL 5 November 1939)

Different as the social life of Preston was, Joe didn't lack for companionship. One of the office workers at the factory introduced him to Clara Bernhardt who, he told Percy,

> writes poetry, has a write up in who's who in Canadian Poetry. She is really keen, intelligent, literary and has heard of you and wants your plays to read. She has a nice sister – my age. (JJL 22 October 1939)

That Saturday he took "the nice looking sister," Kathryn, out skating, which led to another discovery about small-town life:

> It seems my innocent skating date easily spread around. I am practically engaged to the girl they tell me (everybody finds out who you go out with) even though I only took her out once. If I take her out twice in a row it is tacitly understood that the marriage will take place shortly – so I am steering clear for a while. (JJL 29 October 1939)

Although Joe continued to visit the Bernhardts, he must have exercised discretion, saying "I consider myself extremely fortunate to be still free and boss of myself."

The next weekend he went to Toronto to watch McGill play Varsity and get together with his old teammates at the football banquet. Joe was quickly recruited to play on the town's hockey and basketball teams. In January, he scored eight goals and six assists in five games for the Preston Riversides, the town's entry in the Ontario Hockey Association. Although the team got knocked out of the playoffs at the end of February, Joe wrote that:

> Thru my hockey I became acquainted with everybody in the surrounding countryside. I think I had more fans in the arena and scattered around the numerous towns than any other player on the teams. I can now walk into any store in town and speak with the managers, clerks and helpers. The policemen, firemen, grocers, factory workers and everybody else, say hello to me and always stop for a little chat. I feel thoroughly at home here. Around the factory hockey gave me a tremendous boost and in the neighbourhood and amongst Mrs. G sons, family and relations, my career is closely and carefully followed. So I feel it was worth a little extra effort and a little loss of sleep.
> (JJL 3 March 1940)

Percy observed of this news that Joe "finds the natives are impressed … not by his learning but by his sports record."

Joe found the local factory workers generous and hospitable, and that many relied on their own gardens for food. He reported that there was little talk about the war in Preston, although it had brought work to the town's factories and railyards. Of the sixty-odd men alongside whom he toiled every day at the furniture factory, almost half were foreigners – Poles and Germans – none of whom in his estimation would voluntarily enlist. Of one man from Austria he commented: "he is definitely like most of the foreigners here not much of a Canadian although he has his papers. He is good material for agitators."

Yet he soon developed a liking and respect for the Ontario factory workers he met, and came to appreciate that they hadn't over-much to live on and that medical bills could be a particular worry. Such injustices, he commented, could make people "easy meat for a communist." A month later he wrote home about the Red Cross campaign:

> Our factory workers decided to donate a day's pay. Since most of the fellows live pretty close to the belt the amount is going to be paid over a 12 week period … when workers getting 34c per hour, as I am, and supporting families of up to seven with it offered one full day's pay of $3.40, I should at least offer three days pay … so accordingly I gave ten bucks in one shot.… when I think of the money being flung around for social entertainment which will do nobody any good I wonder why anybody should offer comment when I decided that those fellows who were fighting so that I might have a good job, should in return get a paltry few dollars from my salary to make life a little more comfortable for them when they get blasted into the hospital.
> (JJL 26 November and 10 December 1939)

Reflecting on his first three months in Preston, he wrote home:

> As far as the experience to be gained up here is concerned I feel I am in a particularly fortunate position, not only because of the reference and knowledge to be gained on the job, but because of the type of life I have been forced to live up here. I really feel that although my schooling has ended, my education has just begun. In the city there is always so much to do to take up your time, and such excitement and commotion at all times that it is extremely difficult for the average fellow to do any real concentration and thinking and get a fairly accurate perspective of things. On the other hand things are so quiet and dead around here that the average fellow brought up here does not want to do any thinking or studying but tries to dig up excitement. However, this little stay in the wilderness so to speak is ideal for me, and the longer I stay here the more I like it. I have all the time I want for myself. I am finally getting down to good solid reading and have lots of time to ponder on what I read. I do a good day's work and have time to ponder on what I learn during the day and what I heard and saw and to give the information its due importance. At the same time I have lots to keep me busy with basketball, hockey shortly and attempts to get the right amount of sleep needed for a good day's work. I am fortunate in having a marvelous home with kind-hearted keepers and splendid neighbours. So although I at all times get lonely for home and for the boys, I am too busy mentally and physically to ponder on my solitude during the week. (JJL 10 December 1939)

Not least of what Joe discovered in Preston were different (if not necessarily more sympathetic) attitudes toward Jews. Only two or three Jewish families lived there when Joe arrived, and whatever Prestonians thought about Jews was more likely based on rumour and myth than on personal experience. Evangelical Christian piety prevailed in Preston, and Jews were seen more as a target for conversion and salvation than of suspicion for shirking or sharp business practices. Joe's presence was thus not only noteworthy, but for some at least, a challenge. Much of this he regarded with good humour or at least equanimity because he was generally received with kindness and friendship.

He told his family how he was charting his course as a Jew in a strange town, not least how he was dealing with the reactions – expected or unexpected – of others.

> Since by now my religion is known by most everyone and still looked upon with mingled feelings by many, I gave my good barber 50¢ and told him to keep the change and calmly walked out as they revived him with smelling salts. It's amazing what the old nickel will do when it's well placed.... However, I know only too well what I am doing. From the stories the fellows tell me, the only Jews they know are the accented junk dealers. I will change that notion in Preston at least before I leave.
>
> So you see I am becoming either a missionary in a new community or a salesman on introducing a new religion in an old territory. That, however, produces numerous disadvantages. I have to show a broad mind and spoil a good Sunday by going to the Barracos Sunday school class in the very near future. Their most devout member reminds me of it every day. Then a fanatical [and persistent] rolly polly insists that the only way I can be saved is thru Jesus Christ – backed up of course by biblical quotations. He fails to agree with me when I tell him that Christ was a Jew and Jews were saved long before he ever appeared, so I now have to dig up some quotations from the bible to prove my point. (JJL 5 November 1939)

Yet Joe did take the opportunity to find out about his neighbours' beliefs, and found the Sunday school class a "non-sectarian and exceedingly broad-minded group" in which he got "a surprisingly warm reception."

Overall, Joe wrote home that:

> It is comforting to feel that I have at last found a community that can really appreciate my true worth. No longer am I subject to insulting criticisms or barbarous insults such as I have received in certain cities. (JJL 5 November 1939)

What insults, and in which cities, remain opaque in Joe's record. Was he referring to the casual anti-Semitism of the street or the locker room, or slurs and insults directed to him personally? Was he referring to Ontario cities where he had played football? His native Montreal? Whatever and wherever, they had stuck in his mind and evidently rankled.

In December, Percy discerned from Joe's letters that he was:

> forming many friendships amongst all classes perhaps he will give the natives a more liberal minded attitude toward the Jews than they now have. After all Joe went to college, played on all the teams, has read quite a little and besides has a nice appearance and pleasant manners. He is by no means unique in his own environment but he evidently is unique in Preston. (PJD 4 December 1939)

Joe cannot have been unaware of his father's vision of him as an ambassador for his people. But what did this role require of him? Who was he representing, and what was his message? Was he an ambassador for all Jewry? Or only those who shared and acted on his conviction that Jews could redeem their standing in public opinion by their behaviour and their deeds? A man of action, Joe was out to change the image of the Jew, not reinforce it. So he saw himself as an exemplar, who would demonstrate, rather than an ambassador who would represent.

What might changing the image of the Jew have involved? For Joe, anti-Semitism was the product of ignorance and so could be combated by reason and example. Jews therefore needed to adhere in exemplary fashion to the moral and ethical standards of their fellow citizens. Likewise they should avoid behaviour that might offend other sensibilities and reinforce degrading stereotypes. This strategy of demonstration and reason presumed that prejudicial stereotypes could be successfully combated through one's own efforts. In wartime, the implications were clear.

In April Joe wrote his father that he would like to get a management position at the furniture factory and remain there for the summer. But Percy didn't think that Joe could continue on that course:

> All is quiet in Canada, no recruiting as yet but I fully expect that when large scale operations start on the western front (this may be occurring even now) there will be a call for more Canadian troops.
> (PJD 13 April 1940)

News of those large-scale operations by Germany was arriving even as Percy wrote. Joe saw that the war situation was changing quickly that spring. He told his family in his regular Sunday letter:

> I follow the war situation very closely via my radio and a dozen odd maps which I have posted on the walls. I shall look into the situation more closely over the 24th of May if I get home. I might decide that it was about time I swung into full gear and get into a bit of action. The Navy is my first love but the air force will do in a pinch. However, we will follow developments until then.... I am getting to feel very much as if I would like a couple of nice little pot shots at these loud mouthed Germans. (JJL 12 May 1940)

Percy noted Joe's turn of mind with interest:

> So far he has not been keen about going to war. Like the Americans he thought he could be an isolationist and that this war was just another imperialist war of grab. (PJD 18 May 1940)

By the next Sunday, the Netherlands had capitulated, and Belgium was barely holding out. It was time to enlist. Joe wrote home:

> This decision naturally will result in my giving up a business career for a military one, at least for the present and possibly for the future as well. Since the outbreak of war there have been but two considerations kept me from joining up immediately:
>
> 1. The total unpreparedness of the Canadian govt to cope with the problem of recruiting and training volunteers. I had no desire to waste a year in the fighting forces with nothing to show for the time put in. I decided to wait until such a time that I thought the forces would be well enough organized to be able to accept and efficiently train young men who wanted to join up.
>
> 2. I saw a wonderful opportunity for myself to study a profession at first hand and see for myself the full scope and possibility of the Office Equipment field. I have managed in the short period of eight months to get a fairly technical understanding of one branch of this profession, the furniture line, and a fairly good idea of how extensive the industry is, what has to be learned to make a success of it and also some of the mental and physical equipment that is essential to sound business organization. Unfortunately the field is so extensive that I have only scratched the surface and would still have to continue working from the bottom up if I wish to continue in this field in future years. (JJL 19 May 1940)

On the other hand, Joe continued, there had been many reasons to join up long before, not least

> the type of civilization the Germans are trying to introduce. It's all right taking the U.S. attitude of "let the other fellow do the dirty work." But the fact remains that somebody has to do it. If you are prepared to let Germany's challenge go unchallenged, then you sit back and do nothing about it. If you think your own system of society is worth maintaining at any cost against that of the alternative one, then you have to be prepared to take all the risks and suffer all the consequences. The U.S. for example wanted her American civilization but thought that

> she could maintain it by leaving it coast along on its own accord. Her people were not willing to make any sacrifices to ensure its existence. They depended on Great Britain. Now that Great Britain is seriously menaced, they are slowly realizing the nasty facts, that they are going to have to make sacrifices and heavier ones than they would have had to make had they taken action sooner.
>
> Assuming that I feel it my position and desire to join up, I naturally want to make as good a job of it as possible. I intend going into the thing in the same thorough manner as I started learning the Office Equipment field. I shall start from the bottom (which is my only choice in this case) and proceed to learn as much about naval tactics etc. as I can. I feel that some of the qualities I possess are best suited for this branch of military service which is why I have incidentally decided upon the Navy. But what is far more important, I have learned from reliable authority that one can get a much better training in the Navy than in any other Canadian fighting force. It is unfortunate, but true, that the army and their leaders and officers and equipment are hopelessly disorganized, ill prepared, poorly trained and generally seem stymied. The air force is little better. Naturally I am seeking the best training possible. If you are going to fight you want to be as well prepared, trained and equipped as your opponent, if not more so. The Navy does just that.
>
> My reasons for deciding that now is the time are obvious. There is still time to train recruits thoroughly, which is especially necessary for sea warfare. Even if Hitler's Blitzkrieg does fail the war has a lot longer to go, especially if the other nations get involved. If the allies should on the other hand be defeated, then Canada would have to join with the U.S. for our mutual safety, which would require two tremendous fleets, one on the Atlantic, the other on the Pacific. We are indeed fortunate in Canada that we at least have a second chance should we lose the war. For Great Britain and France, there will be no second chance.
>
> (JJL 19 May 1940)

Joe had finished the first phase of his business training, pleased with his progress. Now it was time to move on, not to another factory, but to war.

Three

Enlistment

Joe returned to Montreal on 24 May, Empire Day, as Percy observed:

> God Grant that it may not be the last. God Grant that this coming year may not see the disintegration of the British Empire. The crisis is upon us. The next few days will be vital to our continuation as free men....
> (PJD 24 May 1940)

Percy did not exaggerate the crisis. Neither had he exaggerated the earlier confusion about what the war might bring. Since Poland's defeat in September, the war had become one of threats more than acts. Contrary to what Percy and many others had expected and feared, Germany did not bomb London or Paris. There had been no engagement on the Western Front, and the Canadian army units sent overseas were still training in England. There had been no set-piece naval battles, only sporadic submarine attacks on Atlantic shipping. In Canada, air force recruiting offices told interested young men to go home and wait. In the meantime, local armouries conducted drills and marches without boots or uniforms and with only a few rifles left over from the last war.

This standoff had come to an abrupt end when Germany invaded Denmark and Norway in April, and the Low Countries and France in May. More alarming was the rapidity of the German advance. Winston Churchill, prime minister for only two weeks by Empire Day, was confronted with the prospect that France would shortly fall, leaving Britain with no allies in Europe, and Germany poised to attack Britain itself. Could Britain stand alone against Germany, or would it negotiate a peace that would inevitably leave its citizens, and those of its Dominions, vulnerable to Nazi encroachment and domination? The five days beginning 24 May, during which Churchill prevailed on the War Cabinet to carry on the struggle against Hitler to the end, whatever it might be, were a crucial turning point in the war.

Joe wrote to Monty and Herb in New York:

> I came to Montreal Friday morning to survey the war situation.... over the weekend I had a long interview with Commander Brock of Navy. There is practically no chance of getting in as officer altho I have my name in. Then I went to the air force and received applications which I will send in and might possibly be accepted. Finally I went to C.O.T.C. and signed up, being the last one to be accepted and only thru a little pull of my own. Drill has started already and going up to summer camp on June 13th for a week.... I am determined to get a military training without wasting further time.
>
> Now that brings us to the war situation.... Here again is the situation as I see it.
>
> 1. We are all definitely menaced. Of that there can be no argument.
>
> 2. There can be no sudden ending of the war either way. If we lose Canada will still have to keep preparing for the next war. The allies can't possibly win before 1942 at best. They need that much time to get the equipment necessary for a large scale offensive.
>
> 3. If you agree with the above two assertions then you will also agree that some steps have to be taken to organize our industrial and physical resources to meet and combat and defeat the menace. The fairest way of course would be conscription. That might possibly come. I will go further and say it will *have* to come. The seriousness of the situation will bring that. I can realize the necessity more than you since where I was working, a factory made up mostly of foreigners, you could not raise a volunteer on a bet.
>
> 4. Now here is where my position veers from the rest of you.... When I say I have nothing to lose by going to war I mean that when and if I get back, I still have the same jobs, the chances for training and the same opportunities waiting for me, unless of course something unforeseen occurred. If Gerald goes, he has to start looking for jobs all over again. Since he has had a hell of a time getting his present one, naturally nobody in his position would want to give it up

for somebody else to take over. But nobody can take my job from me. I have something to come back to.

If point four is clear and accurate then I have dozens of reasons for going to war.

a. to protect the business if for no other reason. You will say it makes no difference which way the war goes, that business will go on as usual. I think you are mistaken. This is not like the last war. We are in for big changes regardless of what happens.

b. as a Jew I feel it my position to accept my share of the dirty work and take the same risks as our gentile friends. I don't give a hoot what the unemployed are doing or what the other guys are doing. I think it is my particular duty to accept my responsibility and uphold our side which I am in complete agreement with.

c. I feel it is important to have a military training. These are times when every young fellow should be in a position to defend his country. The ones that are in the greatest danger are the civilians, not the army men. I think you will agree with me there.

… But don't get the idea that I am trying to pick a soft touch or a safe place. There are no safe places in war and I do not give two hoots in hell whether I am blown sky high by a bullet or live to rot away at the rusty age of ninety. There are lots worse ways of dying than by a bullet and there are lots worse things go on in this world than a little war. I am honestly itching for some real action. I have seen enough of our sloppy civilian life to make me look for a change. (JJL 29 May 1940)

⊙

Canada had been ill prepared to go to war in 1939. There had been little public support for maintaining the armed forces after the armistice in 1918, and during the Depression even less money for doing so. Successive governments believed that the military needed to consist of no more than a small core of professionals who could train the militia, and a small air and naval force. In September 1938, when Britain's Prime Minister Chamberlain thought he had secured peace with Hitler at Munich, the Royal Canadian Air Force consisted of less than one thousand men equipped with a few 1920s-era biplanes. Its role was envisaged largely as coastal defence, with no plans for overseas engagement. It could train fifty pilots a year at best, few of whom could expect to be taken on by the RCAF upon graduation. Those keen on being military pilots went to England and joined the Royal Air Force.

Prime Minister Mackenzie King's defence policy in the late 1930s looked like isolationism, and in hindsight, appeasement. There was no joint planning with Britain, no military mobilization, and no commitments about future action. If war came, King preferred to go in late, limit military action to the defence of Canada and its sea lanes, minimize casualties, and above all avoid conscription, which a generation before had been so divisive of national unity.

Two weeks after the war started, twenty RCAF recruiting centres were opened across the country. They had no trouble attracting young men looking for glamour and adventure. The freedom to fly like a bird above the banalities of daily life, along with the aviator's prestige and charisma, held wide appeal during the Depression years. Mindful of the stories from the previous war and of the maimed who returned, many young men thought it better to fight in the air than on the ground, and better to die in an airplane than in the trenches. The air force also seemed to place more emphasis on skills than drills. And if one survived the war, a career in civil aviation might be on offer. Without a training system in place, however, most of the willing but thoroughly inexperienced applicants were simply given an interview and a medical exam, and told to get on with their civilian lives until further notice. Recruiting was temporarily suspended in November, except for civilian aviators who were needed as instructors.

In December 1939, Britain concluded an agreement with Canada, Australia, and New Zealand to establish the British Commonwealth Air Training Plan (BCATP).[1] Under this plan, Commonwealth aircrew would be trained in Canada, and then proceed to Britain to serve with the Royal Air Force. The plan, although directed by the RAF, would be operated by the RCAF and largely paid for by Canada. The BCATP met Prime Minister King's political objectives perfectly: Canada could contribute to the war effort on her own territory, and the program would promote the domestic aircraft and armaments industry and generate much-needed employment. For Britain, Canada provided uncrowded air and ground space, better flying weather, and immunity from enemy air attack. Under these conditions, it was expected that far greater numbers of aircrew could be trained faster than would be possible in England.

Like Canada's other armed services, the Royal Canadian Air Force looked to Britain for technology, professionalism, and direction, not to mention the training syllabus. Canada was quite unprepared to train large numbers of men, let alone actually engage in the battles that were to come.

Participating in the European war, and manning the fighter and bomber aircraft that would become critical to it, would require instructors, schools, aircraft, and airfields far beyond what Canada had in place. Pre-war civil aviation had consisted mostly of bush flying in the North, hobby flying in local clubs, and a fledgling national airmail service. Thousands of Canadians had flown for the Empire during the Great War, but few had the opportunity or the means to sustain those skills after they came home. During the hard times of the 1930s, Canada had done little to establish a network of aerodromes with paved runways, navigation aids, and radio communication that would provide a national infrastructure for night and instrument flying.

Nonetheless, the BCATP was ready to open its doors on schedule, in mid-April 1940, with the objective of turning out fifteen hundred aircrew every four weeks by 1942 – more men every day than the RCAF had trained each year during the Depression. The air force started calling up the backlog of applicants in the spring of 1940, none too soon in view of the events in Europe. The Air Training Program was a monumental achievement. It became the largest national project in Canada since the transcontinental railways had been completed decades before. Sixty-four flying schools and thirty-two air observer, wireless, and bombing and gunnery schools were established, most of them in the first two years of the war. Each school required an aerodrome and accommodation for hundreds of pupils, staff, and ground crew. The total cost was in the order of $2 billion.

When France fell, so did Mackenzie King's limited war effort strategy. Other than Britain itself, Canada was now the largest unoccupied nation at war with Germany. The National Resources Mobilization Act of June 1940 provided for universal conscription for the defence of Canada, but there remained no conscription for overseas service. That was for volunteers.

For those volunteering in the early summer of 1940, the choice of service was not difficult. It was the air force that was actively recruiting, and that now had a training program in place. The navy had not yet begun its expansion. Allied armies overseas were in retreat or defeat. Only air power could carry the fight to German territory, so joining the air force was the quickest way to get into action.

Although many young men were enthusiastic to join, not all would qualify. But who did the air force really want? In the Great War, suitability for military aviation was assessed on the basis of medical and physical characteristics on the one hand, and character on the other. Character was judged largely on the basis of proper personal background, preferably of British extraction. The applicant should be clear-headed, keen, and daring, with such sporting interests as riding, hockey, and motoring. In short, as pilots were normally commissioned, if you were going to be a pilot, you should also have the qualities of an officer and a gentleman. The association of officer qualities of courage and leadership with race and breeding ran deep in the British military tradition, and inevitably these views were also found in Canada's Anglo-Scots officer class.

In April 1940, 166 men had been recruited from across the country for aircrew. Two months later, recruiting quotas were sharply increased, which brought in eight times that number of aircrew in June, and many more ground crew. There was now an urgent requirement for large numbers of men who could be trained quickly, not only as pilots but as navigators and wireless operators, with bombing and gunnery skills as well. An old school tie and a daredevil attitude would no longer be good enough without some math and science. The needs of 1940 found earlier air force traditions wanting, in Canada as in Britain. New ideas about the skills, intelligence, and performance under stress required of airmen would contest with the old in the coming years of the war, as would the means of testing for and measuring these characteristics.

The regulations then in place specified that aircrew quotas were to be filled by single men aged eighteen to thirty-one, British subjects, of good education, with a sufficient level of physical fitness determined by an initial medical exam. As in Britain, candidates for a commission had to be of pure European descent. Pilots and air observers required a minimum of junior matriculation, presumed, in the absence of any other test, to be a sufficient indicator of aptitude. Officers in charge at recruiting centres were instructed to satisfy themselves that applicants were of good appearance and good character, with the capacity to absorb training. The interviewing officer, often a Great War veteran, was also required to provide his subjective rating of selected personal characteristics. Flying experience was not a requirement. Few Canadians had ever been in an airplane at that time, let alone piloted one.

After nine months, Joe knew what he wanted, and made sure he got it. He had never doubted that he would enlist. He had known that in his mind, if not in his heart, since September, but he watched and waited for the right opportunity, knowing he had that luxury so long as conscription was not imposed. Although the army had been first off the mark in recruiting, Joe wanted to be a sailor or an airman, not a soldier. The crisis on the Western Front was Joe's trigger, and in May 1940, the air force became his target.

Why had his resolve hardened over the last three months? As a Canadian, Joe shared the motivations of so many others: that if Britain was in danger, then Canada would stand with her, and he must play his part. The self-ascribed British Imperial characteristics of manly virtue – resolution, decency, forthrightness, and physical courage – still had traction in English Montreal. Deciding to enlist was perhaps above all, and as it must have been for many young men, a test of his inner resolve, and the means to overcome his own doubts and fears.

But there was more for Joe than serving King and country, or fighting against Nazi Germany. At a time when Jewish loyalty and character were publicly maligned, military service offered the ultimate opportunity to vindicate one's place as a citizen. Doubtless mindful of his conversation with the burly trainman in September en route to Preston, perhaps followed by the Silcox article and much else he seems to have learned about Jewish reputation along the way, he would personally show up all those who questioned Jewish resolve and fighting abilities.

In June 1940, Joe was responding to a personal call to honour and sacrifice, to apply not only his courage but also his skills to a higher purpose. He had indeed waited for the right opportunity, not only for advancement but to acquire the skills he would need. The air force would provide that opportunity. That it arrived at the same time as the crisis on the Western Front put any lingering doubts to rest.

Having resolved to apply for the air force, Joe obtained letters of reference from his father's business associates, and from his high school principal, who recommended him as an above-average scholar, a strong athlete, and a leader. He went to the Montreal recruiting office on Monday, 3 June to fill in his attestation paper, stating his preference for training as a pilot. The next week he passed his medical board examination, and was declared fit for all air and ground duties. The interviewing officer rated him "above average" and characterized him as:

> Very good player in all kinds of sports, strongly built, good character, good education. Speaks French quite fluently. Keen to join though he doesn't need it to live. Knows what he wants. Good material and highly recommended.[2]

Joe had come a long way since 1936, when he had written "I don't want to go to any war, neither do the people," and asserted that "war is a racket and those that gain by it are pulling for it."

Percy and May knew that Joe had to go. They kept their forebodings to themselves.

> Our own little world at 635 Grosvenor is rapidly changing. Joe goes to military camp for a week tomorrow. He has his application registered with the Air Force and may be called at any time. (PJD 13 June 1940)
>
> May and I went to St Bruno to see Joe at Military Camp. It is visitors day. Joe looks fine. Likes the life but is anxious to get in the air force. He does not like the infantry.
>
> Six hundred (mostly young men) training to defend their country. Some of them will go overseas. Nice looking youngsters. Was sore at heart. (PJD 19 June 1940)

Joe's enlistment was not the only change at 635 Grosvenor Ave. Percy's wealthy English relatives had inquired whether the Jacobsons might provide a safe haven for their children, now that England itself was under threat of bombing or invasion. During the first days of July, boatloads of English children began arriving in Canada, among them teenagers Lillian and Yvette Kostoris of Manchester, accompanied by their aunt Rebecca Michaels and her daughter Denise of Liverpool. Percy was delighted to have them in the house, but also observed:

> six hundred [children] strong to be guests until after the war of Canadians who have guaranteed they will not be charges on the country. Children of high degree, offsprings of the bluest blood of England were on the boat: coming here without a penny (England to protect the pound will not allow any export of capital). These youngsters must exist on the bounty of friends and strangers. (PJD 10 July 1940)

Lillian and Yvette, however, were not strangers. Their Aunt Rebecca was married to Percy's favourite cousin Alfred. The Jacobson children had already met them during their family trip to England and Belgium in the summer of 1930. Liliane and Yvette would stay with the Jacobsons for the next two and a half years. Alfred was soon posted to the censor's office in Bermuda, so Rebecca and Denise left Montreal in October to join him there.

> Our only remaining son Joe has been called up for the Air Force and leaves Monday night destination unknown. He is a free man no longer. He is just a cog in a huge war machine in rapid state of formation for defence and attack.

May worries me. She takes things apparently in her stride but there are always after effects. I know she will feel terribly about Joe going away Monday. She won't show it to me. And I won't show it to her … and there you are … we'll both try and fool each other and neither will succeed. (PJD 29 June 1940)

Joe sworn in to the air force yesterday leaves tonight for Toronto to train. So this birthday of mine [54th] is of particular significance. With good luck Joe should become after this war one of Canada's leaders. He has had and will continue to get the training that will provide him with the necessary qualifications. He has a good head. Lots of sense. Imagination and a sense of values. Also he has a saving grace of humour. While his brains may not be premier grade the intelligence he has coupled with these other qualifications mentioned, should take him a long way. But there is the question of luck … fate or if you like the will of God …

And the war … Chamberlain broadcasted yesterday that the Cabinet was unanimous in the resolve to fight for victory or extermination. No compromise is possible with the Germans. Britons realize that compromise or appeasement would merely mean that Britons would be slaves. God grant (again my prayer) that we will be victorious or have the courage to die rather than allow evil to prevail. (PJD 1 July 1940)

Letter from Joe today. Sad to say he will be sent to either Saskatoon or Vancouver. However, it is a good thing for the lad as he will see something of his country. However, we had hoped to see him home on leave every month until he sees active service. He writes in good spirits and says he looks forward to the adventure ahead of him. He says the other boys of the Flying corps are a nice bunch. I can quite understand it … the Flying services get the pick of the youth. I don't think it is just a father's partiality that sees in the boy certain exceptional qualities. Young as he is (and although he is a real outdoor fellow) he is a good deal of a philosopher. He has a grand sense of humour. I am sure that if Please God he is spared whole he will become one of the National leaders of this country. He has the stuff in him that will win him a following: personality, intelligence, good appearance, integrity.

It is heartbreaking but what can we do about it. I don't say that life is over for us but I feel that in the dark days to come we will not forget that life has been very good to us. (PJD 3 July 1940)

Four

Toronto

On arriving at Toronto's Union Station on Tuesday morning, Joe proceeded directly to Number 1 Manning Depot on the Canadian National Exhibition grounds. There, he joined a thousand young air force recruits assembled from all across Canada for their initiation to military life. Each was issued a kit and uniform, and vaccinated for typhus, tetanus, and diphtheria. Recruits were instructed on the fine art of making beds, shining brass buttons and boots, and pressing pants to military standards. They learned the rudiments of military discipline: how to salute, march, and take orders. They were warned about the dangers of venereal disease by way of lectures, graphic films, and "short arm inspections"; learned of the rough justice meted out to anyone caught stealing; and watched inspirational films about Canada's war effort. Several hours a day were devoted to physical training and to rifle drill on the parade square.

Manning Depot was many a young recruit's first experience of living away from home and looking out for himself, in close quarters with men from all parts of the country. Not for Joe, however. Air force training, he soon reckoned, would be like a giant summer camp with plenty of opportunity for team sports. Joe was quick to form opinions about his new situation, which he embraced with unbridled enthusiasm.

> Here begins another diary a war time diary. Volunteered and called up in the R.C.A.F. Arrived in Toronto manning depot today. Very exciting getting your outfit – letting army take over all your problems – meeting new fellows from all over the country. Impossible to realize great change that has taken place in my existence – my life in govt's hands.

> Doesn't feel like war anymore – too busy preparing to fight – I only have one regret – that is that Monty, Herby and Gerald didn't join up with me. We would have all had a riotous time and stuck together – we won't have much time or chance to think of each other from now on. We will all be in different branches of the services – … but such is the way of friendship. (JJD 2 July 1940)
>
> With the type of fellows on hand here and the system that is developing there can be no question of defeat – we have started to roll and will start turning the tide of battle in a year or so. The problem for the govt is to get everybody busy doing something, directly or indirectly connected with the war – once you are doing something you never think of defeat. (JJD 3 July 1940)
>
> Not much chance to write as lights are about out. Should write essays on the efficiency, thoroughness and marvelous spirit of air force – entirely different than that of other armed forces – corporals get work out of men by treating them with respect, humour and above all with decency. They aren't interested in how they get results, they are only interested in the results whether attained thru originality informality etc. – that is its greatest strength – that will be the deciding factor in beating Germany – we can't lose. (JJD 5 July 1940)
>
> Life in the service is extremely nice – we are treated as gentlemen inside and outside the barracks – we are receiving the best training possible for the job in hand and without a doubt we will carry on the tradition of our branch of the service.
>
> Whether we come out with our skins on is immaterial. The point is that we will act with courage as our predecessors are acting – we shall set an example and inspiration for our successors – a National pride and feeling shall evolve, the enemy will eventually be defeated, and we shall set about building a better society of our own for the future – all very interesting. As far as the war is concerned we think and talk about it very little – it is not important to us at the moment. We are primarily interested in becoming the best pilots in the world – the larger issues depend on our success. (JJD 7 July 1940)

Not only had the once reluctant soldier had become an enthusiastic warrior for his country, he was also very much enjoying his off-duty time with friends and relatives in Toronto. For three weeks at Manning Depot, every night was party night.

> we … eat at the best restaurants, visit the golf club – ride in nice cars and generally insist on the best – we are looking for some nice girls with cars class and inexperience – we do everything on a high level. (JJD 7 July 1940)

Joe also encountered his cousin Lionel Silver from Windsor, whom he had rarely seen since childhood. Lionel had been a reporter for the *Windsor Star* when he first sought to enlist in the fall of 1939, by his own account to see first-hand the biggest story going. He had been called up two weeks before Joe.

It didn't take long for Joe to resume hectoring the Pony Club about enlisting. Joe's decision to enlist, made abruptly during the third week of May while both Monty and Herb were still in New York, had set the Pony Club's conversation on a new course. The day after he got to Toronto Joe wrote:

> Naturally the question has to do with the war – and signing up.… The angle I wish to emphasize is the idea of doing something together.
>
> Most of the odd thousand fellows at Manning Depot are from out west. The most apparent thing is the number of pals that joined up together. And there is no greater chance for pals to have a marvelous time than in the air force.
>
> You can bunk, eat, play, go out and do everything together – the officers are all young clean cut – efficient. There is almost total lack of red tape, prejudice and formality and routine which was so apparent in the army. It would be better than a summer vacation here for guys that go around together – everything possible is done for your health, comfort and enjoyment.… Mind you I am not saying you should all immediately apply in the air force – there are lots of ways in which your applications can get separated and in which you yourselves can get weeded out and separated. But that is one of the risks you will have to take.
>
> But if you were skillful or lucky enough to stick the whole thing out from beginning to end together – think of how much you can actually get out of the war in the way of real friends. For no matter where you are, or what you do, it will seem a thousand times pleasanter, a thousand times more interesting and a thousand times more important if the balance of the Pony Club acts together. (JJL 3 July 1940)

Monty reminded Joe that the rest of the Pony Club could not leave civilian life behind as casually as he.

> From Joe's reasoning, the only way we can all do our duty properly is to all join the air force. He is right in a way – we would be combining duty with pleasure. All other factors ruled out, I would gladly be in the Air Force today. So would Smith, likely so would Herbie. BUT the whole of Canada and United States cannot enter the air force....
>
> All this, we know, does not entirely answer Joe whose accusing finger points at the issues at stake, we Jews, the future of the world, and so on –
>
> We are fully conscious of the issues at stake; agree wholeheartedly with Joe on the necessity of winning the war.
>
> In fact, quite obviously, it is our feeling that there will be some kind of a world left for us to come back to when it is all over. It is our feeling that whatever we can do toward our life's work now is worth ten times any rehabilitation that will come about after the war. Quite obviously, too, we know we will be in it soon. The armed services are being kept plenty busy until we come along. In the meantime the next few weeks can be valuable to Gerald and me in our regular work. Conscription awaits me if I wait too long; Gerald has no alternative. He is in training, is not subject any longer to the conscription and in the meantime continues his work. Herb has made his choice to stay in New York.
>
> Joe's letter is a masterpiece, a marvelous effort. We have not meant to criticize it one whit. We just feel that he has lost the perspective for the moment of our personal positions and has started to talk in broad generalities – possibly forgetting that the bulk of the Canadian people still has not come to realize the situation as acutely as he and even we do. Our position, instead of being laggards, is amongst those out in front. (21 July 1940)

Joe had all along been enthralled by the prospect of a happy-go-lucky band of brothers in the same branch of service, sharing excitement, adventures, and danger at the sharp end of the coming struggle. Joe's enthusiasm was, unfortunately, matched by his naïveté. No such scenario could possibly have unfolded in the air force, even if all four had marched arm in arm down to the recruiting office on Dorchester Boulevard. The air force was organized very differently from the army, which commonly recruited men into locally based regiments, so that those who signed up together might well stay together for the duration. Such a "regiment of chums" is what Joe had imagined would happen if his friends had signed up with him. As he soon learned, however, air force recruits were quickly separated by trade and assigned to any one of several schools, where they trained with men from all across the country. They went overseas unattached to any territorial unit.

As Monty noted with annoyance, Joe had made his decision on his own, and had returned to Montreal to enlist when he and Herb were still in New York. Taking a shot at Joe's claim that his work and career were no longer important to him in light of the wider issues at stake, Monty remarked to the Pony Club:

> With all due respect … that is the way everybody feels just prior to signing up. Very few people sign up until they reach that stage. In Joe's case that feeling came before it came to Gerald, to you, Herb, or to me. It came about, as has been pointed out so many times to us guilty Ponyites in New York, as a result of different circumstances. Joe's position, his work in Preston, his general sensitiveness about anything that smacks of duty, and his particular enthusiasm for adventure – all these things permitted him to see "the wider issues" and face them squarely before we did. (21 July 1940)

In Monty's more sober view, if the issue was serving one's country, there were many ways to do so. Each had his own skills, talents, and inclinations to bring to the struggle. More to the point, Monty reminded Joe of his good fortune and circumstance that the others did not share. Joe had his father's business to return to, and thanks to his father, he had secured employment over the winter. Monty, Gerald, and Herb had all struggled that winter to find work or to qualify themselves for it. They had nothing to return to except what they could secure for themselves, and so had to think about how and when to enlist without unnecessarily jeopardizing their chances to make a living when it was all over. Joe could afford to be idealistic – as his interviewing officer had noted: "keen to join though he doesn't need it to live."

In a mood to goad rather than inspire, Joe fired off a jeremiad to the Pony Club.

> Mr. Walker told Bernie Tritt to join up a home defense course because the govt were going to force firms to fire all single guys who are not doing anything. Naturally, the Jews here are all flocking to the Non Permanent unit.[1] It's a scandal – they are sluts – I would like to run them thru. Whatever you guys do – do it voluntarily. I would hate to see you guys classified with these yellow bastards here. It really makes

> my blood boil to see how the Jews are behaving here. Win, lose or draw 80% of them deserve what they get – and they will get it.
> (JJL 20 July 1940)

Joe's letters from Preston make clear that he took seriously his father's view that Jews had to do better than others to vindicate their place in Canadian society. By actions not words, Joe would show the world that Jews were as good as anybody else in any endeavour, and no less willing to risk their lives for their country and their freedom. So he was absolutely insistent that his best friends redeem the honour of the Jewish people, and earn respect by getting off the sidelines and into the game without regard to comfort or risk.

The next stage in becoming aircrew was Initial Training School (ITS). There recruits would be selected for training as pilots, air observers, wireless operators, or gunners: the trades that would make up the bomber crews needed for the war in Europe. Most of Joe's fellow recruits had wanted to be pilots, some had wanted to be air gunners. Few expressed a preference for air observer, perhaps because the majority hadn't a clue what it involved.

No. 1 Initial Training School, located on the former Eglinton Hunt Club grounds on Avenue Road in Toronto, opened its doors on schedule at the end of April 1940, again with the lingering smell of horses. The buildings were still under renovation, the water mains and drains still being installed, and the parade ground was not yet paved. Yet the school was soon processing several hundred men every four weeks. Joe Jacobson was in the fourth intake, arriving on 22 July. As at Manning Depot, military discipline and parade square drill were an essential part of the program. But in view of the urgency of technical training, rather less time was spent on these matters than in the other services.

Joe wrote home about ITS in glowing terms.

> This is a swanky joint of the first order. Meals are dished up piping hot, varied, well cooked and of good quality. It is similar to a classy restaurant. Then we have a swimming pool here, a bowling alley, ping pong tables, tennis courts and various other attractions. The sleeping accommodations are excellent. We even get sheets and pillow cases here. Of course we sleep where the horses once passed their evenings but I feel highly honoured to be allowed to sleep in the same stall as the fine horses once occupied. I am sure the beasts were rare specimens with a high price tag on them. Naturally I wangled the most comfortable

> bed in the joint, right beside a door which allows a refreshing breeze to pop in.
>
> We are here for about an 8 week course. No weekend leaves until around August 10th and then only for 36 hours, starting Saturday noon. Unless I can talk the P.O. into giving me a 48 hour pass that week I won't be home until the end of September. The last gang here abused their privileges and they are taking it out on us. Moe Usher and his gang probably. My only chance of getting home will be after my course is over here and before I go on to the next stage. Unless of course I am in as a gunner and wireless operator, in which case I take a 16 week course in Montreal. (JJL 23 July 1940)

Over the next four weeks of ground school, the aspiring airmen would study math, armaments, drill, and air force law and discipline. Joe soon realized that party time was over, and he was effectively a university student again. The key challenge facing the new Air Training Program was to determine how to direct recruits into the trade for which they had the greatest aptitude and the greatest likelihood of meeting the required standard in the limited training time available. At the outset, the answer was based largely on physical testing not much changed since the First World War, and a mélange of stereotypes about race, empire, and class that permeated both the military establishment and society in general.

A few weeks before the school opened, a senior RAF officer arrived at the Hunt Club with some University of Toronto psychology professors to address the problem of determining aptitude for training in the different aircrew trades. These men would pioneer the use of psychological testing in the air force, which eventually replaced the academic record and the subjective recruiting interview as the basis for trade selection. This new system was not yet in place when the ITS opened, and recruits were provisionally assigned trades at their first interview, taking into account their physical and educational background. Pilots had to have good reflexes and flying sense. The Link Trainer (a rudimentary flight simulator consisting of a plywood box, a shroud, and a control stick) served to weed out quickly those least likely to succeed. The bright students, especially those with ability in math, would presumably make the best navigators. Less promising students were more likely to be selected for wireless and gunnery training. Pupils were tested for their physical fitness for flying, particularly their reflexes, coordination, vision, and sensitivity to oxygen deprivation. But knowledge of the physiological dimensions of air medicine, and especially oxygen requirements for optimum performance at altitude, was at as early a stage as that of the psychological dimensions. Neither testing for trade selection nor for physical fitness could predict performance or leadership under the stress of combat.

Joe's medical board re-examination two weeks into the course confirmed him fit and healthy, but he seems to have rubbed the president of the medical board the wrong way:

> Athletic and educational qualification good. Rather off hand and sure of himself. These plus racial characteristics maybe a factor in his relation with associates. Good average – doubtful of his ability to handle men.[2]

Final selection came at the end of each four-week course, by a Board of Selection consisting of senior officers who relied on the second medical board report and instructors' recommendations. Joe wrote to the Pony Club the day the selections were announced:

> A great day in Canada's history is in the making. The future of the world itself will probably be affected by the tremendous events of the day – yes gents, to-day our fate was decided and we have been divided up for the duration of the war into gunners, observers and pilots. The ratio is as follows:

observers	18%	100
pilots	35%	200
gunners	46%	250

> Ace Jacobson is I am unhappy to announce an observer – my pal Jenson is a pilot and vows by all that's holy that I am going to be his observer. Be that as it may I am not as yet too excited about it all.

> First of all our rowdy flight has been decimated, most of them being gunners. We start from scratch again also we don't do too much flying. We learn navigation, photography, gunnery & piloting but our position is still that of the master minds – we don't get the real kick out of the thing that the pilots do. For once I was hoping to get a job where brains don't count.… However, a college grad. has no chance of becoming a pilot under present circumstances, but is compensated by being booked for the responsible jobs from the beginning. So that's the

> story – everything will probably work out for the best and we will all get there sooner or later.
>
> … Of the eight Jewish boys, only one is a gunner.[3] (JJL 21 August 1940)

There had been some concern in the Montreal Jewish community about how and indeed whether its sons might be accepted in the RCAF. The concern was not groundless, considering that Jews frequently encountered barriers to employment, housing and public accommodation, entry quotas in some universities and professions, and they were unwelcome in most corporations and clubs. But there were no such barriers in the air force, and over the course of the war, the RCAF was the branch of service for which the majority of Canadian Jews volunteered, and there was no evidence that Jewish flying crew experienced systemic discrimination with respect to promotions, commissions, or decorations.

Yet, at the crucial moment of trade selection during initial training, it appears that being Jewish could have consequences. Jews were vastly overrepresented as navigators and bomb-aimers in flying crews, and underrepresented as pilots, over the course of the war. Preconceptions of Jewish fitness for military service seem to have lingered in the armed forces. If Jews had not the sturdiness and grit required to prevail on the playing field and on the frontier, could they endure the suffering and hardship of war? Would they remain steadfast in adversity, and so be able to lead and inspire other men in battle? Would other men submit to Jewish leadership? A bomber aircraft was a combat unit, and its captain was the pilot. Joe Jacobson's medical board assessment, even if it was exceptional with respect both to other Jewish air force recruits, and to his own subsequent assessment by other examiners along the way, was an expression of those doubts about Jewish leadership capability and effectiveness in battle. A selection process that evidently directed Jews toward the air observer trade seems to have presumed a particular Jewish fitness for it based on mental skills, but perhaps also presumed a lack of fitness for leadership.

In any event, an air observer Joe would be, and when he wrote his parents he put a good face on it. Exaggerating, as he was sometimes prone to do, he made the job out to be the most important in the aircraft.

> The pilots are called the "chauffeurs," the observers "the brain trust" and the gunners are the real men. Naturally everybody wants to do the piloting but somebody has to do the other jobs, and when you get right down to it, we really don't give a hoot what we are as long as we get a chance to get overseas and do a little job all of our own. The spirit

> around here is really magnificent and there is a gang here that are going to be the backbone of the R.C.A.F. and what a backbone it will be and what a job we will do. (JJL 23 August 1940).

Joe remained at No. 1 ITS for another four weeks, as his course had been extended to include navigation, flight theory, signals, aero engines and airmanship. There was plenty of physical training, along with sports competitions with local Toronto teams. Joe's 79 percent average ranked him near the bottom of the air observer class, although he was characterized in his progress report as sound, keen, and capable. Among his classmates, Joe had acquired a reputation as a keen athlete, an engaging fellow, and always up for a good time. He was a good man to know because he seemed always to be well supplied with care packages from home and happy to share.

One hundred young men graduated as prospective air observers in mid-September. The class was split up and sent to three separate air observer schools across the country. The bonds of fellowship would remain, and they would meet again months later on their way overseas. Who were they, and what were their backgrounds? They were above all almost entirely of Anglo-Celtic origin. By name, only a handful betrayed a francophone or European background. And they were overwhelmingly of Protestant faith. Only a handful were Roman Catholic, perhaps reflecting the less than enthusiastic participation of French Quebecers, and the generally lower educational attainment of Catholics (and particularly francophone Catholics) at that time. Three were Jewish.

Joe's classmates ranged in age from nineteen to thirty-two, but most were in their early twenties, and almost all were single. His classmates were better educated than most Canadians. All had obtained at least their junior matriculation, and a dozen or so had university degrees. They were for the most part the sons of professionals, merchants, and office workers. Few came from working-class or farming backgrounds. Most of the boys had left white-collar jobs; some had been drivers and mechanics. Few, if any, were unemployed at the time of enlistment. All in all they were a middle-class lot, among the more fortunate young men in Canada at that time.

Joey had imagined the ideal woman to have a sense of humour, practical intelligence, and a strong mind. She would be a good sport, not spoiled, and not overly sentimental. He sometimes commented in his diary on the qualities of the girls he was dating but, speculating about the kind of person he would marry, or indeed whether he would marry, he wrote:

> When you fall in love (I haven't yet) I suppose it is impossible for either party to analyze each other's qualities. I guess you are carried away, as if in a dream and wake up in a couple of years to find you are either living with an angel or a demon. I shudder to think that I might someday fall in love and throw away my freedom for some empty headed, good looking fun loving babe, who possesses none of the qualities of women I admire in our society. (JJD 14 February 1937)

However much he enjoyed and sought female company, he was reluctant to commit himself and he had no steady attachment in high school or university.

Joe met Cecily Samuel in early August. The Samuels, who lived a few blocks from No. 1 ITS, were apparently acquainted with the Jacobsons. Joe wrote home in July that he had got in touch with them, but their daughter Cecily had been away at the time. They met shortly afterwards, and took up with each other quickly. Joe and Cecily were of similar background, coming from well-to-do families of Anglo-Jewish lineage, and members of their city's leading Reform congregations. Cecily, named for an uncle who had been killed in the British Army in the Great War, had been educated at one of Toronto's leading private girls' schools, and was studying for a degree in household science at the University of Toronto. She liked riding and skiing. She was the privileged one in her family; she had insisted on a horse and been given one. Cecily fit Joe's perception of what he wanted in a woman: good-looking, intelligent, athletic, adventurous, vivacious, well brought up, and presentable, summed up in his own words as "classy." And Joe – handsome, athletic, well-bred, and with a promising career ahead of him – was the kind of man Cecily was attracted to.

Joe wrote home in late August that he was spending more time with Cecily and less with his male friends. Seeing her on a regular basis was much more to Joe's taste than the competitive nightly skirt-chasing he had engaged in at Manning Depot. Whether Cecily entirely broke through Joe's reluctance to burden himself with a relationship is doubtful. But she was certainly on Joe's mind throughout his subsequent training in the west, and he was on hers.

⊙

Percy had followed Joe's progress through initial training:

> England is holding valiantly against terrific air raid by the Germans.... Canada is building thousands of planes and training thousands of

Cecily Samuel, graduation photograph, University of Toronto, 1942.
(Courtesy of Robert Willinsky)

> young men as pilots, observers, gunners. One of those men we are much interested in is our son Joe.... We expect him home late tonight on a forty eight hour leave. This is the first time we have seen him since he left just about two months ago. However, his letters have been intimate and interesting. His last letter shows evidence that he has become a fighting man. Today I am proud of the fact that he is single-hearted. Not so long ago I abhorred the idea. So we change. (PJD 30 August 1940)

> Joe has been home for forty eight hours. He has become a man, but he can still laugh and act like a boy. It has been a grand weekend. (PJD 1 September 1940)

> Joe home again for thirty six hour leave. He may be transferred to Edmonton the coming weekend. He looks fine and is seemingly very happy. He travelled from Toronto by motor car yesterday, arriving here at 9 PM stayed around the house talking to us until after eleven then went out with his friends, up this morning to play golf and then he will be on his way back to Toronto by motor at three o'clock. That is youth for you. (PJD 8 September 1940)

In Percy's eyes, the boy who had left home two months before was well on his way to becoming a man. Percy liked what he was seeing.

Five

Regina

Joe Jacobson awoke on Saturday morning, 14 September 1940, in the unbroken boreal forest landscape of northern Ontario. There was room enough there for 50 million people, he observed, "but what you could do with them beats me." He and forty air observer trainees were on a troop train to Saskatchewan. The boisterous throng of passengers also included thirty trainee pilots who would get off at Fort William that night, and two hundred wireless operators who would carry on to Calgary. All disembarked at Hornepayne to take a short route march through town for exercise, then continued westward. Each enjoyed his own sleeping berth and dining car service on white tablecloths, a luxury that would soon be done away with on transcontinental troop trains. The next morning would bring another brand-new landscape for a Montrealer: the open and endless prairie. The train pulled into Regina at five o'clock on Sunday afternoon. Classes at No. 3 Air Observer School at the city's airfield began the next morning.

Joe and his classmates would spend the next twelve weeks in Regina, followed by six weeks at bombing and gunnery school in Mossbank, Saskatchewan, and another four weeks of advanced navigation training at Rivers, Manitoba. They were among the first three hundred air observer trainees, the pioneers and the guinea pigs in the extraordinary undertaking of the British Commonwealth Air Training Program. The program was still being cobbled together at top speed in brand-new but as yet under-equipped facilities. Aircraft, navigation equipment, bombs, guns, and instructors were all in short supply.

Joe wrote home at the end of his first day at Air Observer School (AOS):

Joe, Regina, 1940. (Janet Jacobson Kwass)

> We are the first batch to set foot in this station and everything is as new as can be. Our barracks are really beautiful, roomy and as nice as any rooms at most of the college residences. We have individual sinks for washing, hot and cold water and all the modern facilities imaginable, including indirect lighting. We have two general duties men assigned to our squadron to keep our barracks clean for us.
>
> Then there is the dining hall. Separate tables, six to a table with waiters. In other words we get restaurant service and really tasty meals, fruit for breakfast etc.
>
> All this makes for very comfortable living. Added to that most of the boys here are from out east which makes for a pretty chummy bunch. I have my bunkmate and pal from the Hunt Club with me which makes it pretty swell. He is from the University of New Brunswick and is a good head if ever there was one.[1] … The course mapped out for us is difficult. We are supposed to work seven days a week … we get one 48 hour week-end per month and … thirty-six hours off every week.… Our instructors are all officers, all extremely young and they seem like pretty decent chaps and should know their stuff.
>
> The country out here is absolutely amazing. I can look out my window in the morning and see objects 5 to ten miles away. There is absolutely not a solitary tree in sight, the ground is flat as a billiard table and the earth as dry as can be. It will be extremely difficult to make head or tail of any landmarks from the air as they all look the same to me.
> (JJL 16 September 1940)

He told the Pony Club

> It is the old college grind over again only this time we have as much work to learn in three months as we had in 8 at McGill and it all has to be put in practice. It is a marvelous course they are giving us, real interesting, lots of fun, plenty of work. (JJL 4 October 1940)

"Observer" (or air observer) was originally a First World War designation for the person who observed, photographed, and reported back on enemy troop positions and movements on the ground, the function that had been the original purpose of deploying aircraft in war. When airplanes were later used to drop bombs, it was the observer's task to aim them. It was the pilot, however, who was the designated commander of the aircraft, and therefore a commissioned officer. After the war, the RAF discontinued observer training and gave the pilot pride of place. Up to the late 1930s, the RAF assumed that a pilot could both fly and navigate his aircraft. Far too late did it recognize that effective navigation in combat needed a member of crew specifically devoted to that task and properly trained for it. The pilot needed flying skills and quick reflexes; the observer needed intellect and mental agility. The requirements for one were no less exacting than for the other, the mistakes of one no less costly than those of the other, even if the observer's badge was a half wing, and the pilot's the full wing.

Marine navigation was an ancient science, and one the British were particularly good at. Navigating an aircraft involved some new wrinkles, however: moving in three dimensions instead of two, and at far greater speed, through a medium that is itself in constant, if not necessarily visible, motion. Yet the air training schemes in England in the late 1930s had given little attention and few resources to observer training. The standard text was the RAF's *Manual of Air Navigation*. The 1938 version covered maps and map reading, the compass and magnetism, basic meteorology, and radio direction finding. Air observer students were introduced to the basic concepts and methods of navigation and to the essential tools of the trade – compasses, sextants, computing instruments – and the principles of plotting track and position. "Dead" (deduced) reckoning was the foundation of the observer course, and counted for 30 percent of ground school marks. It consisted of calculating the "triangle of velocities": prediction of future position from one's current position, based on time, speed, and bearing from point of origin, taking into account the effect of wind direction and speed on an aircraft in flight. As error will compound quickly, frequent and precise recalculation of course and position is essential.

Once the students moved from the desk to the air, they were assigned a destination in preflight briefings, and expected to calculate the appropriate course. Other exercises included calculating wind velocity and maintaining a compass course. Pilots were instructed to fly the course the trainees gave them, even if in error, in which case pilots had to be able to find their way home. Usually two or three pupils were on board each training flight, one to lead the practice and the others to watch. It was helpful to all on board, in a pinch, that the landmark prairie grain elevators were clearly painted with the town's name.

The Air Observer School at Regina was staffed by civilian instructors under RCAF supervision. It was equipped with twin-engined Avro Ansons, transport aircraft of early 1930s design since adapted as trainers. Only a few were on hand at the start, but more arrived over the next two months to make up the requisite complement of twenty-four. Many of the pilots were Americans who had flown with commercial airlines, while most of the Canadians were experienced bush pilots. When observer training began in Canada, there were no non-pilot navigators. Some instructors were familiar with civil aviation navigation procedures, but most were university grads with math backgrounds, relying on Royal Air Force syllabi and equipment.

Joe couldn't wait to get airborne. The first week was taken up with ground school, but he was a student navigator on two flights the next week.

> We had a lot of fun on our first trip as we rode three fellows in a plane plus a pilot. We were only supposed to pinpoint ourselves on the map and learn to locate ourselves by land marks. However our pilot had not made the trip before and got away off the course, mostly because of a strong south wind, blowing at about 30 m.p.h. Since I started out as first navigator on the first leg, we had to get to work and plot out his course for him. Strangely enough we got him back on the track, heaven knows how, and I still don't know whether the pilot was more surprised than we were. We had a real nice trip though despite the rough weather. It was really bumpy at 4000 feet, which is the altitude at which we fly with the result that about two thirds of the boys were a little sick. I myself felt a little shaky at one stage of the trip but survived in rare style.
>
> From the look of things, that trip we took today is going to be about the only joy ride we will get. Our work is real tough. We have to crawl up in front of the plane, estimate the wind, give the pilot his course, estimate our times of arrival and report everything seen on the way. If you think you don't get a workout try it sometimes – you have to arrive at given places within one minute and one degree of your estimated figures, which is tough to arrive at even on paper....
>
> The country here from the air is absolutely flat. Most of the rivers have dried up and there are very few land marks to guide us by. You don't have to worry about forced landings here since you could land anywhere safely. We all have to wear parachutes up – they are worth $400 a piece and always work. We are all dying to get a chance to bail out but the pilots are too good so we don't need to figure on that type of job....
>
> The weather here is still lovely, clear, cooler but dry and fresh. I run two miles every morning at 6.30, play football for an hour or two in the evening and generally keep in good shape. (JJL 25 September 1940)

Every flight was a new adventure to write home about. He wrote his sisters about his next trip:

> The visibility was so poor that we could see very little with the result that we very nearly got lost permanently. However our pilot was an ace and dived over the main streets of every town we came to so that we could read the name of the town and get a thrill to boot, which we did. A few of the other planes turned back but our pilot had confidence in us and let us keep going. It sure is great flying. (JJL 27 September 1940)

He told Liliane, who had inquired how he had spent the holiest day of the Hebrew calendar:

> I was 6000' up working out courses like I never worked before[2] – and I was doing plenty of praying – praying that I had not lost the pilot and the plane – so I guess we were all pretty religious. (JJL 22 October 1940)

In October he wrote home that when flying with the chief pilot,

> he puts up the hood and flies blind. We do the entire navigation and when he pulls down the blinds we have been right over the destination on each occasion.... I struck up a little deal with the head pilot whereby he will let my flying partner and myself do the piloting as well as the navigating every time he takes us up. So if we are lucky enough to get him anymore, it won't be long before we will be ace flyers – which suits me. (JJL 16 October 1940)

Joe did not get lucky, because he was not assigned to fly with the chief pilot again. During his next months of training, he did occasionally get to handle the controls while airborne but was never taught to take off or land. Yet, as he wrote home, he was working so hard that he no longer had time for recreational reading, and probably he had less time to ruminate about not being selected for pilot training. He also, perhaps to console himself, wrote frequently of the observer's crucial role in aircrew, and of the exacting nature of his tasks. And although Joe seems to have recognized by this time that he would not rank high enough in the class to be commissioned on graduation, he remained enthusiastic, as he told the Pony Club:

> Despite commissions etc., I still think the air force tops everything. We learn aerial photography, meteorology, astronomy, navigation, wireless operation, and dozens of other things. It is real training, loads of fun and best of all you are either alive or dead – no in between processes – However, you boys have made up your minds, but I just thought I

> would let you know – that it's the R.C.A.F. for the *daredevils* and you beggars need such an outlet for your surplus energy. There are a lot of wild men around but I think we take as many chances as the best of them and can hold our own in the clinch – and you sure have to do that when flying. (JJL 27 October 1940)

⊙

Joe's time at Air Observer School was not all study and air exercises. He became president of the sports committee in his first week, and spent much of his recreation time playing basketball, touch football, Ping-Pong, and snooker. He was naturally gregarious and getting on with his classmates came easily. He also benefited from his family's generosity. The regular flow of food and cigarette packages from Montreal enhanced his popularity among his classmates, and as he told his family, resulted in his bunk becoming a regular gathering place for his pals:

> the effect of these various gifts and their unequalled quality and quantity has had the same effect on the boys here as similar gifts had on my acquaintances elsewhere – they have created the impression and maintained the Jacobsons' position as wealthy, influential citizens just bordering on the millionaire class. The boys in Preston swear by it, my camp friends … insist on it and my air force pals live by it. So whether you like it or not Pop, you are a millionaire from Montreal to Regina … (JJL 1 October 1940)

His boisterous camaraderie got him into trouble a few days later, however, as he explained to the Pony Club:

> We have duty watch a week at a time here during which time we have to stay on the station. The NCO [non-commissioned officer] allowed us to beat it as long as we got back in time for roll call at 10:30. The practice was to go to town. I did likewise on my duty watch trip and took along fourteen others – new officer didn't understand the practice here and called the roll call at the wrong time. The result that nobody was on hand – a big rumpus, search parties, etc. etc. and 7 days from the C.O. with a week's duty watch coming up. (JJL 4 October 1940)

This escapade involved some of Joe's half-dozen or so closest friends in the class who stuck together on base and off, a group that he later referred to as the Hell Hooters. Most were in the bottom half of the class standings all the way through, and most were a year or two younger than Joe. They all managed to graduate, but almost none was commissioned before going overseas. Joe at least had probably learned his lesson from being confined to barracks, as there were no further entries on his General Conduct Sheet for the remainder of his career.[3] Out West, Joe was well and truly away from the Pony Club and his Toronto friends. If the Hell Hooters lacked the intimacy and intellectual seriousness of the Pony Club, they shared purpose and circumstance and knew how to have a good time together.

Joe and the boys passed their spare evenings in downtown Regina drinking, bowling, playing snooker, and going to movies. On a thirty-six- or forty-eight-hour pass they would sometimes rent hotel rooms, buy booze, and search for female company. With luck, semen flowed and lust was sated. Regina was a rowdy place in the fall of 1940, with several hundred airmen in various stages of the Air Training Program. In addition to No. 3 AOS, there was a flying school ready to open at the airport, and an Initial Training School in the city. In town, Joe sometimes ran into fellows with whom he had played hockey and football at McGill. One notable event was a pre-season exhibition National Hockey League game between the New York Rangers and the New York Americans in late October. Joe related seeing the top players in the Hotel Saskatchewan after the game. On base and off-duty, there were rowdy alcohol-fuelled parties. Joe wrote to Monty, Gerald, and Herb about all these goings on with competitive relish, although he always added that whatever he was doing with his new pals in Regina could not replace the fellowship of the Pony Club.

Winter's chill set in sooner and more intensely than easterners like Joe were used to, and the winter days were shorter. Students were out of bed at five-fifteen, two hours before dawn's light appeared on the eastern horizon. Almost everything, including the students, worked less well in the cold, as Joe related to the Pony Club.

> The day is magnificent – fresh and springlike – after the bitter cold of the last few days – 20 below zero it is indeed a relief – talk about cold – this western cold beats anything I have ever experienced – and it is only November – it has been too cold to fly – the only time we went up it being around 25° F below zero and the windows cracked, the engines conked while we all leapt for our parachutes and the pilot made a miraculous landing – next week though the planes should be in shape to start again –

> … We have but three weeks to go here – big exams coming up next week – and then on to bombing and gunnery school – that is those of us who pass. Then a month at celestial navigation and on to coast patrol and over the ocean – maybe Egypt (I hope) maybe England – nobody knows.
>
> … We are in for a grueling battle, most of our gang won't be around to celebrate the victory – but by persistent work, lots of guts and determination the end should prove worthwhile and we should at least be able to decide how we want to live. The greatest kick in my life is going to be when I drop that stick of bombs over Germany or nail a sub while on patrol. Anyway we are all having a nifty time, and ought to be pretty well trained to do our job.
>
> … We have stiff exams to pass, to go to war – kind of funny when you think of it that way. But when guys have to take extra classes at night to pass stiff exams in order to keep from being flunked out – then it stands to reason if they are better than the next guy in our own country, they are going to be a hell of a lot better than the guy in the enemy's country, especially since their government doesn't have to worry about how much their crews know or what preferences they have –
>
> So all in all we are pretty well treated, well trained and well satisfied – and I would rather fight for a well-trained, gritty team any day of the week, win, lose or draw.… (JJL 15 November 1940)

Joe was quick to grasp the objectives, strategy, and tactics of the bombing campaign against Germany. He wrote home:

> I am fast being trained to carry out probably one of the most important tasks of the war – carry out the "master plan" for crippling Germany. That will probably be our big job – and to be able to carry it out efficiently requires the most highly trained, skilled and dependable men available. We have the men – we are capable of training them – so we will shortly give it to them real good. Our Reconnaissance Instructor – a young flight lieutenant from the R.C.A.F. who spent the first six months of the war on active service as a pilot, bombing, doing coastal patrol etc., told us that the Germans have but one skilled navigator in their mass raids over England. The remainder of the squadron don't even have instruments – they just follow along. The British just knock off the lead man and the rest can only drop their bombs at random and try and get back home. That means that the military effects of their

raids are slight as they are incapable of bombing military objectives. Besides that they are forced to fly at such heights that no matter how good they were they still could not hit many important objects – which all means that in the end the training and superior brain power will come out on top … (JJL 26 October 1940)

What Joe's reconnaissance instructor did not say, if indeed he was even aware of it, was that the deficiencies of German bombing methods he ascribed to the Luftwaffe were in fact the very ones already plaguing Bomber Command. It too was being forced to fly high and to spend as little time as possible over German targets, due to more effective anti-aircraft defences than Britain had. Three weeks later, the Luftwaffe would pinpoint the city of Coventry with deadly effect, the lead navigators using radio-directional aids that Bomber Command lacked, and targeting methods it had yet to develop. If Joe and his classmates thought the job awaiting them would be a walkover, they were wrong.

As final exams approached, Joe wrote home:

I am in the throes of a cramming period the likes of which I have never seen before – not even in the good old college days.… If we flunk in more than two subjects we get discharged. If we flunk in one subject we have to stay back a month, take the exams with the next class and lose our seniority which would be worse. (JJL 24 November 1940)

The tough work of exams [is] finally over, and for the first time in almost three months the only worry we have is whether or not we passed without having to take supplementals. Today we are being examined in drill and next week will be spent pleasantly, flying night and day and running around at every opportunity.

The orders for our departure are out and we are to leave next Saturday for the old reliable Mossbank – quite a bit further west and right into the very wilds as they have not yet got running water, the pipes having frozen, which should save us the trouble of washing more than once a week. A blessing says I.…

Nevertheless it is going to be a lot of fun as we fly in bombing planes and only have to learn to bomb and shoot, probably doing quite a bit of dive-bombing to boot.[4] Gather the planes are heated, something our planes here lack, which makes flying extremely uncomfortable here.…

The fellows in our gang are as nice a bunch of gents as I have met up with anywhere and since we move together from station to station, live,

> study and run around with one another, it makes it real pleasant and lots of fun. But probably the main asset of the air force lies in the leadership. Since all officers on active service are flyers you can feel fairly sure that they are brave and capable, as it takes an extremely capable fellow to handle these ships. If you have confidence that your leaders are top notch then you can really do a job – … (JJL 29 November 1940)

Flying weather was good during Joe's last week at the school. Pupils were filling in flying time right up to the very end, although Joe's total night flying amounted to only twenty minutes. Joe was graded average in his air training, and intelligent and industrious in ground training, coming twenty-ninth in a class of forty-four. He was judged unsuitable for a commission or as an instructor, but with the potential to be a good observer and NCO. He was greatly relieved to have passed.

Percy had all along followed Joe's progress:

> Received a nice letter from Joe … he has been up in the air and seems very keen about it … the lad is brave because I know that he knows fear.… (PJD 28 September 1940)

> Heard from Joe … he was confined to barracks for remaining out too late … learning discipline … there are quite a few accidents to fliers in training … we just hold our breath and do not think … we don't worry because we daren't … he is eager to get overseas and expects to be in the show by April. British and Canadian airmen are doing such miraculous things they make deeds of valour of the men famed in history child's play in comparison … I am proud that Joe is of the fraternity … (PJD 8 October 1940)

> Joe telephoned long distance from Regina, twenty four hundred miles. The charge was only about three dollars. It was comforting to hear Joe's voice. Things look bad for leave. The Telephone is the next best thing. Thank the Lord for it. (PJD 31 October 1940)

> Surprise. Joe's picture with two other airmen in the Star … heading Montreal's fighting airmen.[5] In reality he is still training as an observer in Regina but he does have to fight the elements. (PJD 17 November 1940)

Percy would return again to the matter of his son's fears and his courage in overcoming them. He did not explain what or how he knew of Joe's fears, but he placed great store in courage and bravery and was deeply gratified that Joe displayed those virtues. But as Percy had also observed before Joe left for the West, he still had the boy in him, as his prank that got him confined to barracks demonstrated.

Joe in flying gear, with Anson trainer, Regina, 1940. (Janet Jacobson Kwass)

Air observer pupils, No. 3 Air Observer School, Regina, 1940. Left to right: Joe, unidentified, Mac Keswick, and Les Jupp. (Janet Jacobson Kwass)

Air observer pupils and Anson trainer, No. 3 Air Observer School, Regina, 1940. Left to right: Mac Keswick, Joe, Cliff Chappell, Les Jupp. The photo was taken by the RCAF for publicity purposes. An outtake of Joe appeared in the *Montreal Star*. (Canadian Jewish Archives)

Six

Mossbank

On 9 December, Joe's class departed for No. 2 Bombing and Gunnery School at Mossbank, Saskatchewan. There, at the "hellhole" he had mentioned in an earlier letter, they would learn the bombing part of their job, as well as aerial gunnery in defence of the aircraft. The airfield, among the most isolated on the Prairies, was situated on a flat, treeless plain near a large saline lake that in drought years completely dried up. The little town of Mossbank, several miles away, provided no such opportunities for carousing as had Regina. More work, less play this time around.

Fortunately for Joe and his classmates, theirs was not the first group on the station, which had opened six weeks before. Construction had been completed, and the initial problems of too little indoor heat and too much outdoor mud had been largely rectified. But there were still shortages of bombsights, compasses, up-to-date flying kits, and helmets. The Fairey Battle airplanes they trained on – single-engine light bombers recently retired from active service – were often unserviceable and so flying was sometimes curtailed. Students used eleven-pound practice bombs, adequate for learning to hit a target from a moving aircraft, although miniscule compared to the five-hundred- and one-thousand-pound bombs then being dropped on German targets from much greater heights. The bombsights used in training were outdated, and as the training aircraft were without intercoms, bomb-aimers used their legs to signal the pilot to fly left, right, or steady.

Joe described his new situation in letters home:

> Altho only forty miles west of Moose Jaw, we are three hours by rail due to the poor tracks and slow trains. Mossbank is a town about half the size of Val Morin – with a barber shop, grocery store, tavern and

church. Our school is eight miles out of town and about ten times as big. It is really amazing the job they have done out here in about four months' time, building a tremendous place where six hundred are now living. Contrary to reports and rumours, this is as good [a] station probably better than any station I have been to yet. The food is good, we have a lovely gym, something we have been dying for since joining up, swell movies twice a week and comfortable quarters. And of course we have our same old gang trucking along together and we have our pal's place in Moose Jaw to go to over the weekend. He has a lovely family and the four of us who chum around together have a great time.

The rumours you have probably heard about Mossbank probably centred around the water problem. Up til now they had not been able to get the water supply going – even now we are not allowed to drink it.... aside from drinking water everything is fine – except for the rather secluded spot of course – we are more or less out of circulation.

As for the work – the first two weeks are hectic – eight hours of solid lectures per day in preparation for our flights. Then we have to cram forty hours full of excitement and bombing into four weeks – I will write more concerning bombing when we hit the airways.

From Mossbank we go to Rivers near Winnipeg for a month of night flying by the stars and moon etc. and then maybe we will get a chance to go home – but that is too far off to start worrying about now. The important thing is that a highly technical job has to be learned in a specified time to be of any use and since I happen to be too far from home to make use of weekend leaves – I am out of luck.
(JJL 10 December 1940)

... I am perfectly contented now because we got our hockey team started so I am back in old time shape again, and once more get a chance to travel around the country-side to more towns and meet new groups of people. Added to that our gym is almost ready for action and we start flying tomorrow, so nothing could be sweeter.

When we graduate from here we get our wings and get boosted to sergeants – the pay will be $3.75 per day – pretty snappy. When we get over in England we get R.A.F. pay and the balance is held for us by the Canadian govt. (JJL 15 December 1940)

Joe was again very enthusiastic about his bombing and gunnery training, as he wrote home.

We have an English bloke as our sergeant, instructor and mother and he is one of the first really popular chappies I have bumped into. He is only a young fellow, very bright, friendly, typically reserved but a bit of all right. Most of the English N.C.O.s here are hard-bitten old timers who don't understand the class of boys they are dealing with. None of the R.C.A.F. gang need very stern discipline. The better they are treated, the better they act as all are extremely anxious to really do a job.

Most of our gang would like to go down to Egypt.... the lads are sort of getting the bug to travel and would really like to get around to the other half of the world. But I don't think we are going to have any choice. (JJL 15 December 1940)

We have been having quite a time in the air. First of all bombing. I don't know why it is but you get a real kick out of letting the bomb (real bombs) drop and watching them explode. The same holds true when firing the machine gun, 1150 shots per minute – quite a gun. Incidentally we have an officer on our station who was with the Canadian fighter squadron in England. He brought back a much used German machine gun, and when you see the cheap affair that they have to use, you feel pretty confident in our own equipment. We have had many interesting chats and discussions with him – and he said that the Canadian boys over there do not have to take any backwater to anyone – they really hold their own and are the toast of England.

... Incidentally, don't worry about me flying – I am not the pilot – I can't do anything about the driving of the ship. Our pilots are all American aces – and how. I have been thru a loop, barrel roll, power dives and everything else imaginable with them and are they aces – and do I love it – what a thrill ... (JJL 2 January 1941)

You probably read of quite a few R.C.A.F. accidents from time to time. I advise you not to let the reports disturb you any more than reports of railway accidents, motor fatalities or every day accidents would.... We develop a fatalistic outlook. If it's in the cards you get it – if not you don't ... that has to be our strong point – remaining calm under pressure. (JJL 7 January 1941)

Joe also turned to a theme he would revisit frequently during the coming year:

There is one very noticeable difference we have observed between the English and American methods. All our planes and equipment are

> English made. Although they are durable they make no attempt to make use of modern gadgets or improvements. For example the Avro Anson training planes we used at 3 A.O.S. and which are still used in coastal patrol [have] a landing undercarriage that has to be wound by hand every time you take off and rewound by hand when landing. That has nothing to do with the quality of the plane but there is not a U.S. plane today that has not an automatic landing gear. Then the bombsight we use is really a joke. It has so many gadgets and devices to set and compute for and is so complicated that they have to train their best men (observers) to use them. The U.S. use general duty men as bomb aimers who require 10 minutes instruction before mastering the simple device – but the good old English plod along. But here's hoping they have the U.S. bombsight when we get over. (JJL 15 December 1940)

Joe was describing the course setting bombsight (CSBS), developed during the previous war and recently modified as the Mk IX, now standard equipment on all RAF bombers. It worked by combining the triangle of velocities, which air observers had already learned to determine, with the expected trajectory of a bomb of known characteristics falling from a known height. Because the CSBS could account for wind drift (assuming the observer could determine it), it enabled an aircraft to approach its target from any direction, not just directly along the wind line. It was challenging to use because the bomber had to preset the key values of altitude, air speed, wind speed, and wind direction before starting a bombing run, and the aircraft had to fly straight and level for several minutes before reaching the drop point. The U.S. Norden bombsight was an improvement in both simplicity of use and because it was gyroscopically stabilized. Days before the war started, Chamberlain made a desperate appeal to Roosevelt to obtain it, but Roosevelt denied the request on the grounds of American neutrality. It would be another year before Britain developed its own version.

Joe wrote his father at the end of the first week of January, full of Canadian pride:

> We have done amazing things, the Empire Air Training Scheme being the greatest.

> Americans of future generations will be ashamed and angry at the length of time it took their fathers to sum up enough courage to face the facts and a bully and then act accordingly.... Why our fellows are deliberately flunking so as to avoid being made instructors as we want to really give the Germans and Italians a double dose of their own med-

> icine. But the American youths are trying to figure out ways of avoiding conscription. Not much fight there. (JJL 7 January 1941)

Joe had discerned in his last summer in Vermont that while his American friends were in moral support of the democracies, they had no taste for volunteering to fight against Nazi Germany.

Poor weather had shut down the airfield in the second week of January, so there was still a lot of flying to complete. In the meantime, he had finished his exams and was playing hockey and basketball. Joe put in three successive days of bombing practice during his final days there. Before leaving for the hangar he wrote home:

> We are on bombing today, which means we will hit everything but the target. They say the safest place to be when we are bombing is on the target – the C.O. proved that by standing on the target during a bombing exercise. (JJL 16 January 1941).

Less modestly, he told the Pony Club:

> I practically led the class in bombing results which pleased me no end as I didn't use the bombsight, but trusted to my accurate, precise and sound judgement, and eagle eye for which I am aptly so famous. I was deadly with the machine gun and to top it all I swiped a real bomb and have it tucked safely away in my bag. If it doesn't blow up before I get home, I am going to make a lampshade out of it – it weighs 11½ lbs and is a humdinger, wait until you see it. (JJL 22 January 1941)

Joe was evidently exaggerating, as he left Mossbank graded only as an average bomb-aimer, perhaps because he really didn't use his bombsight. He received above-average marks in air gunnery, but overall he was graded unsuitable for commissioned rank, coming near the bottom of his class. But he had earned his Air Observer's badge and was promoted to the rank of sergeant on 19 January 1941.

◉

Joe had been scheming since October for a grand reunion with friends and family in Montreal over the Christmas holidays. As the train would take two days each way, flying was the only option, but a very expensive one. By mid-November Joe had persuaded his father to contribute $70 toward the cost. A month later he claimed he would pay for the entire ticket himself. But whether Mossbank's scheduled Christmas break would be long enough to enable him to get home even by air was always in doubt. When Joe had thought that they might get a sufficient break at Christmas, he concocted a story about his sister Edith getting married at that time so that he could get an extension. When that did not happen, his story was wasted, but as he noted philosophically, "such is the fate of the story tellers," and added "since joining the air force I have killed off an aunt, married my sister, shipped an uncle overseas and even got myself engaged – who is next on the list I wonder." However, he added, there was talk of an extended break over New Year's. So he asked his father to reserve a seat on Trans-Canada Air Lines on the 30th for a Pony Club New Year's Eve reunion in Montreal, a project he charged Gerald, in his capacity as club president, with organizing. In the meantime, Joe's entire bombing and gunnery class was invited to spend Christmas Eve and morning with families in nearby Assiniboia. As Joe wrote home with some astonishment,

> The various families took about two fellows each, put us up, had us for Christmas dinner, held open house for us, gave us parties, etc.... The spirit of these people out here is really something to rave about. We went from house to house, visiting, eating, dining and really felt at home. (JJL 2 January 1941)

With only four days leave over New Year's, Joe's fortunes depended on good flying conditions, but the weather did not co-operate on Monday night. So he found himself a hotel room in Regina, downed the rest of his "emergency" bottle of Johnnie Walker, and headed to what he characterized as a "sort of night club" to pick up some female company, which, after fast-talking his way out of a fight with some male competitors, he found. On the 31st he made his way back to Moose Jaw, where his classmate Les Jupp invited him to stay with his family for New Year. From there he wrote his parents about how he had inveigled his wing commander into granting him extra leave to no avail.

> Perhaps the most disappointed of all were the fellows in my class. My proposed trip was the talk of the station. Our gang went around bragging about their pal who was flying to Montreal for New Year's. Great discussions arose as to whether I was sane or crazy to spend a couple of hundred bucks to go home. Then I had letters to mail from Montreal, just to surprise the recipients, important phone calls to make, I was to keep a log of the flight, help the pilot navigate, etc. Well when the report of bad weather came thru the boys felt worse than I did. No matter where the fellows went for the holiday, Winnipeg, Fort William, Regina etc., they kept in touch with the T.C.A. offices to find out if the plane left or not. (JJL 2 January 1941)

Joe told the Pony Club how he saw the new year unfolding when he got back to Mossbank on Friday morning:

> Regardless of what happens I for one get a real thrill out of life to-day – customs, conventions gone to the dogs, old barriers uprooted – It's a day for swift action, cool thinking, daring performances. There is nothing beautiful or heroic about war. But there is something tremendous taking place from day to day as we battle with our backs to the wall to keep a few fragments of what is termed civilization – the worst elements in our society are rapidly disappearing – but make no bones about it we are locked in a real battle with real issues at stake and it gives a fellow a real kick to feel he is going to be an important cog in defending his own country and knocking the crap out of probably the foulest enemy any one could hope to have.... We either win or else, because there is not a man here who won't go down before giving up. And so the old year fades away and another one dawns, we should have nothing to worry about though, as we are young and healthy and smart and so should be able to do what is required of us. (JJL 3 January 1941)

Of his social life in Mossbank, Joe told his pals:

> The boys gamble here every night. I never play. I have not touched card playing since leaving school – I get more kick out of using the dough on liquor, women and various sensuous pleasures since they are the only ones available to us – no chance to see plays – or trips of interest for the time being. So don't gamble with cards boys – we always lose and always will.
>
> ... I am on the shelf – injured my leg in a R.C.A.F. hockey game – my record so far 4 games – 9 goals – 5 assists out of 24 goals scored. Coach, doctors trying to revive me for game to-morrow night but game leg won't heal before Tuesday's big game. Now have many girl friends in many towns – Boy how the Pony Club could function in this outfit –
>
> ... The next batch [of mail] should be addressed to me at No. 1 Advanced Navigation School, Rivers, Manitoba - the place where five RCAF acquaintances ran into tough luck – they were all killed.[1]
>
> ... We never figure on anything in advance now. We just take things as they come – already 10 buddies who went thru the Hunt Club with us, including a former bunk mate and Billie – a school chum whom I palled around with a bit in Toronto, have bit the dust in training acci-

> dents. If it's in the cards you get it if not nothing can touch you. (JJL 10 January 1941)

Joe had by then developed a larger sense of purpose for volunteering. He was not in the air force just for thrills or to conquer his own fears; there was an existential struggle at stake and a world to rebuild afterwards. The year 1940 had brought the dangers of his chosen course closer to home. As a warrior he adopted, or feigned to adopt, a fatalistic attitude. But nothing in the last year had blunted his determination to get the most out of every day of his life, or his brashness in doing so.

Saskatchewan seemed new and raw to Joe, and he liked that. Given to keen reportage, as he had been in Preston, he wrote home:

> The people out this way are becoming really air minded and air conscious as well they might be. Not only do they have a large representation in the air force, but there are dozens of flying schools all over the prairies, and there is hardly a spot in this territory that doesn't see half a dozen planes every day. (JJL 16 October 1940)
>
> I spent a fine weekend in Moose Jaw with a couple of the boys here who live there. It is a much nicer city than Regina with wide clean streets and a much nicer class of people.
>
> The family we stayed with were really delightful.... The Pop is a government railroad man and since we know all the country from air observation, we had an interesting time learning what took place in many of the towns in particular and the west in general.
>
> One thing noticeable about people and their thinking out here is the expansiveness and broadness of their thoughts. Since the communities out west are much smaller than in the east, and since they are also a lot more dependent upon one another's success, there is considerably more community spirit and mutual co-operation than in the east. You never get that helpless feeling that there is nothing you can do about it – they can and do things here. They have medical insurance, wheat pools, etc., and are always gunning for something better. It would not be a bad place to live – less chance of becoming really wealthy but more opportunity to get something for your work in the form [of] taking an active interest in what is going on. (JJL 22 October 1940)

You can't beat the western climate or the western people themselves. It will be a long time before you meet into people as easy to meet, as friendly and as hospitable as these westerners. I don't know why it is except probably it is new country and people out here have not had a chance to clique up – old families sticking together, etc. Also there is not the disparity in wealth amongst groups, no snobbery or high hatting and probably more than anything else there is comparatively little to do which permits people to take more interest in one another. But it is still barren country to live in, nothing to do outside of the show and dances which is why I would not relish living here. I like hopping up to the country, out for a ski trip, picnicking, swimming etc. and you can't do that here. (JJL 15 December 1940)

People in most towns out here absolutely accept people for what they are. There is no social or racial distinction amongst them. It's the person that counts and they can't do enough for you.... out here you have the real backbone of our country. The easterners are too wealthy, soft and spoiled. Out here they just can't be counted out, 10 years of drought, one good year and no chance to sell, and they are still optimistic, still happy – still not kicking. (JJL 2 January 1941)

Going to leave a lot of good friends around the nearby towns, Regina, Moose Jaw, Assiniboia whom I expect to keep in touch with.... these westerners are just down my alley ... – sure glad I got shipped out here – had some great talks on the wheat problem, railway question, population possibilities amongst other outstanding problems with top notch men – a real education.... need more interchange of young people between the East and West during holidays, just so as they will get to know something about each other. (JJL 13 January 1941)

Percy's diary entries and letters during Joe's stay at Mossbank were full of both pride and anxiety, along with high expectations for his son:

Joe writes that he is now settled in Mossbank Sask ... a small village ... there he will learn all about bombing operations for his work with the British Air Force when he goes across in the Spring ... he is now at the final stages ... the art of killing and all the work has led but to this objective. For six months the Government has given him the care that no loving mother could hope to give her child ... security, the best of foods, the best of medical care, fine warm apparel, surroundings of comfort, recreation, companionship, excellent mental training (better than he received at College so he claims). His horizons have been immeasurably widened … he has learned more about Canadian geography than all the years he spent in school. He has become aware of his country … and for the first time in his life knows the pride of being a Canadian. This our government … and other Governments throughout the world have been able to do for their young men for war … Good God you would think that they could have done as much for peace … it's a cockeyed world alright … (PJD 14 December 1940)

Swell letter from son Joe. He is quite mad over night bombing. After this war what civilian pursuits will satisfy these boys. I suppose some will go in for civil aviation. (PJD 5 January 1941)

Joe is getting a big kick out of his air experiences but naturally his mother and myself are undergoing a certain amount of nervous tension which we try and keep from each other. There was a sad accident yesterday. Five young trainees in a bomber at Rivers (the work Joe is now doing) were killed in an accident. Poor lads they didn't even have a chance to show what they could do in action … as for their families … five families with the joy of life knocked out of them. So futile. (PJD 8 January 1941)

He replied to Joe:

You will someday barring unpleasant accidents become one of the leaders of Canada. As you say we must all be fatalists. No use worrying about things beyond control. Civilian life has its dangers too – disease and accident and disaster.

You have given me a great deal of pleasure and the thrill of having a son I can be proud of without reservation and that is very important. Your mother, I do not need to tell you is a brick – she never lets on she worries, never complains about fate – or complains about how much she misses you – I know how much she does. If there were more Jewish mothers like her it would be better for our people. I read somewhere that a celebrated French statesman said that France lost the War because it had too many doting mothers who spoilt their sons and made them soft. I believe that is true. That is not the English way. Interested in what you say about Americans – in a way you are right – but keep tolerant. Don't go off half-cocked – which is what I meant by emotional (glandular) thinking.… (PJL 10 January 1941)

Joe in flying gear, No. 2 Bombing and Gunnery School, Mossbank, Saskatchewan, 1940. (Canadian Jewish Archives)

Joe in service uniform, with Fairey Battle trainer, Mossbank, Saskatchewan. (Canadian Jewish Archives)

Seven

Rivers

Joe and his class were posted to No. 1 Air Navigation School (ANS) for the final stage of their training in Canada. There, he wrote home "we will start on some real work – which will give us a chance to see who really has the superior race, among other things." The airfield was located on the open prairie in western Manitoba, seven miles from the small town of Rivers, on the transcontinental railway line. There seems to have been even less to do in Rivers in off-hours than there had been at Mossbank, and none of Joe's pals had friends or relatives nearby.

No. 1 ANS, which had opened less than two months earlier, provided air observers with training in astro-navigation, an additional technique for finding one's way in enemy territory where radio contact was forbidden and a forced landing highly undesirable. It consisted of taking successive readings on particular stars with a sextant, and using these to plot one's position with the aid of star tables. By this means, and under ideal conditions, a competent observer could locate himself to within five to ten miles. The RAF had adopted astro-navigation, or celestial navigation, as a standard technique by the end of 1937, but did not provide a course of instruction to observers until just before the war began.

Rivers, on account of its clear skies, was considered as good a place as any in Canada to learn astro-navigation. The school was supposed to open officially on Remembrance Day, but there was still no water, no heat in the hangars, and officers were still living off base. By February, there were ninety-one officers, 516 men (mainly ground crew) and fifty-seven civilians on the base. The standard course was four weeks and required, for the first time for Canadian trainees, much night flying. The course also included daytime flying for additional map-reading and navigation instruction. Flying was again, as it had been in Regina, on Avro Ansons. The chief instructor was already known to Joe: McGill math and astronomy professor, and now squadron leader, A. H. S. Gillson, who had previously been a navigation instructor for the British Admiralty.

Joe wrote home the day after he arrived at Rivers:

> As expected we bumped into the gang from Malton including Lionel and we had a hilarious get-together. It was quite a thrill bumping into all our old pals after not having seen them for four months. In two weeks' time the remainder of our bunch who went to Edmonton will be pulling in here which will complete the reunion of a hundred odd observers who were split up at the Hunt Club.
>
> Despite the considerable amount of work to be covered, we are not complaining for once as it is a really interesting course, including astronomy – navigation by the heavenly bodies. It is [a] rather interesting subject as you fix the position of your air[craft] by finding out its positioning in relation to some stars, a few billion miles away.… our instructors [are] all high ranking officers, either college professors or graduates in higher science.… One more month and we will start the bombs rolling, I hope. (JJL 21 January 1941)

Then he wrote the Pony Club, reminding them of his newly bestowed status as a non-commissioned officer and instructing them to address their mail to Sgt. Jacobson:

> The course here is the nuts – a complete study of astronomy – and how to plot position lines from shooting the stars. Imagine gents how I will be able to slay beautiful Egyptian babes by romantically giving the history of every star in the heavens. The possibilities are unlimited anywhere and everywhere.…
>
> Twelve of our forty will get commissions. I will assuredly *not* be one of them. The marks don't mean a great deal as long as you pass.… because of various adventures in other stations, I doubt that my recommendations are strong enough to get me under the wire. However, as sergeants with our wings we get $3.70 per day, okay for now – Then after 3 months service I can transfer to train for a pilot which I most definitely will do[1] – added to that we will get plenty of opportunity to do our stuff in actual service which is where most of us will probably pick up

boosts. For the present though we are all set. So you guys don't have to worry about saluting me for a while yet. (JJL 22 January 1941)

Late January was cold, with the temperature falling to –42°F on the morning of the 24th, although with clear weather on that date, flying continued all day and all night. Joe wrote the Pony Club about:

> a harrowing 36 hour flight where my cool head saved the lives of scores of men – ah what a hero and with but four hours sleep I am rushing this letter along before participating in a hockey game for the "observers" vs "fitters."
>
> Here's the story. Started out on a 300 mile flight Sunday morning. Ran into a terrific snowstorm – viz zero, turned back – weather closed in over Rivers, had to land at an emergency landing field 100 miles away – Ran plump into the storm again. Emergency field out in no man's land – missed it by 1/4 of a mile – couldn't see – pilot stuck his head out one window I stuck mine out the other – I navigated him by power lines from 200 ft – radio went on him – gas nearly out – pilot didn't know which way he was flying – for once I did – result happy landing after 3 hr 40 min in air.... Pilot was an R.M.C. boy who was pal of Chip Drury[2] ... Stuck at field two days as temperature dropped to 30° below – engines froze – had to fly mechanics out with equipment to start them. (JJL 25 January 1941)

He provided his family with more details on his work at Rivers. He had done only daytime flights during his first week there.

> It is 2 AM I am still in the class – so are the rest of the gang. The scene is an amazing one for any service. Forty men with sextants and clusters of books and tables, running in and out, shooting stars, working out positions from them and practically going crazy in the process. Next week we will have to do all this in the air which means we will be kept plenty busy....
>
> Will explain officer setup when I get home – ranks go – pilot officer, flying officer, flt lieutenant, squadron leader etc. An office clerk in R.C.A.F. gets the above named titles regardless of whether he flies or not – 10 pilot officers who have never been in air to every one that has – name deceptive but that's all.
>
> One third of our gang will get commissions, the remainder will have a chance to earn them in active service – I will be in that latter group. (JJL 28 January 1941)

Nearly half the flying time during January had been lost, but the weather improved in February, and Joe put in several long, late night flights. He commanded the Pony Club to be in Montreal for his arrival:

> New York trip out of the question – I have not been home for six months won't be home again for longer – so will stick around, outside of trip up north and a few dozen trips at nights to various hideouts – but remember gents – a sergeant with his wing must act like a gent at all times. (JJL 8 February 1941)

A few days later Joe wrote his pals about more delays. Bad flying weather was one reason. An outbreak of scarlet fever in the neighbouring barracks, with the possibility of a ten-day quarantine, was another.

> However, if all goes well we should have our first get together next week-end February 21st 22nd etc. I don't know how long I shall get but it might be a couple of weeks … *Note* – missed out on the commission business until I get overseas. My record for independence didn't go over so well even though I organized all athletics for our class in all stations. I won lots of dough by missing out because all the boys in the class took bets with me. They bet me that I would get a commission. Modest me, I bet that I wouldn't and won darn it. Seven of our gang received brass hats, six more are pending for around six months….
>
> Our instructor is Flt. Lieut. McClure of McGill – pal of Presty Robb's[3] – My pull here came too late – rowdy Joe had done the damage farther west. So you will have to put up with Sgt. Observer Joe for a while longer.
>
> … We had a humdinger the other night. This plane ran out of gas before reaching the emergency station when the weather closed in. The motors cut – & the plane dived down – and the pilot landed on his belly in the dark – no one hurt – pretty lucky and were their pants stained.
>
> Been playing hockey daily – in superb condition – raring to go – also roaring to go after six weeks of total abstention from women, from drink, from bullying, playing, pleasures, etc. – so here I come mates – gleamy eyed – roary old Joe – (JJL 14 February 1941)

Joe squeezed in his last flight that night. He had been on a dozen flights over three weeks, traversing the southern Prairies between Regina and Winnipeg, mostly at night. Only half of Joe's course was passed through on the

18th (three days after the scheduled date); the rest were quarantined due to an outbreak of scarlet fever and did not leave until the next week.

The top third of each air observer class was commissioned immediately upon graduation. The remainder of the top half would be eligible for commission within a few months based on distinguished service, devotion to duty, and display of ability while on operations. Joe knew very well that he would not be among them. He had improved his marks at Rivers, where he finished (barely) in the top half of the class. His former professor assessed him to be an average, dependable air navigator, and slow but retentive in ground school, in sum that he would "make a very good air observer." However, his overall mark for the entire training course was just under 68 percent, twenty-ninth in a class of thirty-four. Upon graduation, his commanding officer did not recommend him for a commission, but assessed him as "a good chap. Good educational background, very quiet and well mannered. Fine athlete. Will make a very good NCO, possible officer later."[4]

There is little doubt about why Joe was not commissioned upon graduation. The combination of his indifferent marks and the episode on his conduct sheet was enough for that, as he himself acknowledged. His irreverence, outspokenness and occasional cockiness, his insufficient deference to authority, and perhaps also his brazen persistence in pursuing leave requests undoubtedly rubbed some of his superiors the wrong way. He knew all that and was not surprised by it.

There was still the college boy and the camp counsellor in Joe. Military life away from home was like an extended summer camp for him: sports, adventures, activities, all regulated by institutional routine, with meals and laundry service provided. Free from the constraints of home and community, he could let loose in boisterous all-male company. He may have been somewhat intimidated by older men, or at least less at ease with them. Many of Joe's classmates were three, five, and even eight years older, but his closest friends were younger than he was, and perhaps it was only among them that he could be a leader. This too may have influenced his superiors' assessment of him as not yet suitable for commission.

Yet he was no longer the same young man who had gone west five months earlier, as Percy would immediately recognize upon his return. Death was no longer an abstraction, risk was ever present, and mistakes had consequences. Men he knew had already been killed, and Joe himself had survived some tight situations. He had adopted a calm and fatalistic outlook, which he found easier to do as a flyer because, as he told the Pony Club, "best of all you are either alive or dead – no in between processes." So he would live to the fullest while he could, and hope for the best.

Joe's classmates had now earned their wings as air observers, and would soon be on their way to Britain. How good was their training, and how well prepared were they to take the next step to engaging in battle? The Royal Canadian Air Force had undertaken to train an enormous number of airmen on short notice and in quick time. The Air Training Program was a stupendous achievement, even in those early days of 1941. But was it good enough? How did those first few hundred pupils stack up?

Many experienced being in the very first class in a brand-new school on an aerodrome still under construction. Buildings and facilities were incomplete, staff was short, and curricula were still being cobbled together. Sometimes there weren't enough aircraft, so pupils didn't get to fly as much as they should have. Essential equipment – bombsights and bombs, machine guns, radios – if it turned up at all, was sometimes better suited to a previous war. What Canada did not produce for itself had to come from Britain or the United States. By the summer of 1940, air combat equipment was so desperately needed in Britain that shipments to Canada had been suspended. And the United States was neutral and wasn't selling arms to combatants. In even greater shortage was time. Observer training, including bombing and gunnery school, was compressed to twenty-two weeks. The amount of flying time a trainee got during those weeks depended on aircraft availability, operability, and weather. For all that, however, the training schools had done the best they could with what they had.

Flying training for both pilots and air observers concentrated on daytime visual flight procedures and there was little instrument flying. Joe Jacobson got in twenty minutes of night flying at Air Observer School, and none at bombing and gunnery school. Air Navigation School provided him with twenty hours of night flying, and he ended his training in Canada with ninety-five hours in the air. Joe's experience was the norm, and the least that can be said is that the pupils of 1940 went forward with much more flying time than had their predecessors in the Great War. Yet the Royal Air Force was already committed to night bombing when the Air Training Program began in Canada, and it was already aware that both navigating to the target and bombing it in nighttime conditions over Europe was a significant problem. But the RAF needed men, fast. British officials acknowledged that the need for increased output had reduced the amount of training to the bare minimum. None of the early air observer graduates were retained as instructors in Canada. Not only were they desperately needed overseas, they were not yet good enough to instruct anyone else.

Those who were commissioned were not given any different or additional training to prepare them for their new role. They were simply informed of their new status by telegram before embarking. The British Commonwealth Air Training Plan was not intended to be an officer training school. Trade selection at Initial Training School focused on the recruit's aptitude for a trade and his ability to complete his training in the time allotted. Aptitude for a trade was not a predictor of courage and competence in the face of danger. Nor did achievement in ground school and air exercises necessarily provide adequate grounding in military practice and leadership beyond the confines of the aircraft itself. In the outcome, many operational aircrews in the early years of the war consisted largely or entirely of non-commissioned officers, and the basis for commissioning flying crew would be the subject of debate throughout the war, within and between senior personnel in the RCAF and the RAF, and in their respective air ministries.

Not everyone survived training unscathed. There were many crashes. Those who got their wings that winter were pressed into service as soon as possible. They were keen to go, and they were confident that if they applied their training in battle they would succeed. Those early graduates did not yet know that they were at the bottom of what would be a steep learning curve. The next test would come in England, where they would learn to operate real bomber aircraft, in flying conditions closer to those over Europe at night. They still had a long way to go to match their foes. While they were learning to fly by the stars, their counterparts in the Luftwaffe were learning to locate themselves far more precisely with radio navigation aids.

Eight

Montreal

On Tuesday, 18 February 1941, granted three weeks' embarkation leave, "a happy eastbound throng caught the train by the narrowest of margins." It was the day after Joey Jacobson's twenty-third birthday. Joe recorded the trip in his brand-new pocket diary emblazoned with the badge of the Royal Canadian Air Force on the front cover. He had received it as a birthday gift, inscribed "Lots of Luck, Love Cecily." He would chronicle the rest of his life in it.

> This diary is being officially started aboard the Montreal bound train and will aim at recording events as they occur while serving in the R.C.A.F. overseas. (JJD 18 February 1941)

> Slept tight after drinking rum & cokes with Hugh Miller, G. P. McLean & Mac Keswick, fellows you can't beat anywhere. Had a nip with a Group Captain & took pictures of ourselves in his hat when he wasn't around. (JJD 19 February 1941)

> Arrived in Toronto with Hugh & Roger set up headquarters at the Royal York – contacted Cecily – … to wow the lass had her brought down in a taxi took her out to supper and gave her an orchid – supper dance and really started to fall for good old Cecily – a swell kid – lots of fun & life and pretty smart looking. (JJD 20 February 1941)

> Arrived home for supper and it made a fellow feel good to see what a kick he got out of his family & vice versa … a memorable day as far as feeling at peace with the world & being happy was concerned. (JJD 21 February 1941)

Joe on eastbound train, 19 February 1941. "Had a nip with a Group Captain & took pictures of ourselves in his hat when he wasn't around." (Janet Jacobson Kwass)

The next weekend the Pony Club convened in Quebec City, where Monty had got work as a reporter with the *Chronicle-Telegraph*, the city's English-language daily. Joe and Gerald "set up headquarters at the Chateau Frontenac," skiing by day and drinking and carousing by night. Herb, now living in New York, did not attend, despite entreaties and scoldings by letter, cable, and phone. Nor, Herb advised the Club, would he be able to get back to Canada for the final reunion the next weekend.

During the week, Joey immersed himself with family and friends and their goings-on: Edith's still tentative relationship with her future husband, Janet's growing up (she turned eighteen that week), and his mother's intention to close her bookstore.

> down to the Peel Tavern to meet Clark, Smith, Solomon, Bernie after their C.O.T.C. Felt great to have my own gang around – Boys starting to get military bug – but weakly. (JJD 5 March 1941)

> Dropped in to school – saw all the old teachers, spoke to the class … family evening – the kind I enjoy – Janet & Edith were with me. Janet & I have become staunch pals – get a kick out of each other – she's a great kid. (JJD 6 March 1941)

The Pony Club's final weekend was supposed to have been spent with their girlfriends, topped by dinner and dancing Saturday evening at the Mount Royal Hotel's swank Normandie Roof. Cecily arrived by train on Saturday morning having broken out with German measles, and she had to spend the weekend in hospital. Joe was disappointed, but rather than mope, he immediately changed the plan. Monty, who had returned to Montreal for the weekend, had been stood up by his date, and Joe got Gerald to break his. After a few quick drinks at Monty's, the three musketeers proceeded to Westmount Station to catch the ski train for the Laurentians. In between runs, Joe called Cecily in hospital, and the three of them put in a thirty-minute collect call to Herb. On return to Montreal, Joe visited Cecily and then saw Monty off to Quebec City. The next day, Monday, was his final day at home. He took Cecily to lunch and then to the station. Their parting words, and what commitments they may have made to each other, are unrecorded.

Joe's last leave at home prompted much reflection by Percy.

> Friday, Joe came home for his last leave before leaving for overseas service. He is now Sergeant Observer. Naturally we think he is very

handsome in his smart airman's uniform of grey blue. Of course we are proud of him, awfully proud of him. What is most satisfying is the fact that he hasn't changed … he is still the same boyish lad … kind and good … and his face still has the good sweet look about it. He is sound in his opinions. God bless the boy and may he be spared not only to us but to Canada because I am assured that he will be of value to his country in time of peace. He has really become Canada conscious and now has friends from every section of the land. He tells me that all these lads discuss what will happen after the war and are determined to take part in a better world, a more just world. More power to those lads, may they be more successful than we were. God forgive us.
(PJD 23 February 1941)

Family news. Last night (Wednesday) a gathering of the Silver clan at the house to see Sergeant Joe … (there was another Sergeant here too, Lionel Silver who is also an airman same class as Joe). All of them very fond of our lad and he has been very thoughtful and nice to them. Like my Uncle Joe, dead now more than thirty years, his namesake is fond of family he really warms up to them. When he came home loaded with presents for all of us he also reminded me of this Uncle of mine who was the biggest hearted man that ever came into my life.…

Today Joe took Janet to the Laurentians for an all day ski. They're home now tanned tired but with a great day behind them. Tomorrow there will be explanations to be made at school as to why Janet should miss school for a day … Joe very lordly states that he will make it alright. He will personally call on Mr. Parker (his old schoolmaster and her present one) and explain the situation. Of course he rules the roost here while he is on leave.… can you blame his mother and me … Of course the little Englishers eat it all up … as for Joe's ma … is she proud of him? Oh no … (PJD 27 February 1941)

Perhaps it is because Joe is home on leave that all the family felt so close and warm toward each other. In the living room this evening were the whole family. Quiet and comfortable. Fear of the future for the moment forgotten. That future is very uncertain for all of us … not only our family but millions of families throughout the world. This night we are happy. (PJD 3 March 1941)

I said Joe looked the same as ever he did. I was not altogether right. He has a certain setness of expression at times which I have noted on many other airmens' faces. That expression makes for a peculiar uniformity. So much so that many of these boys look like Joe and pictures of airmen have a remarkable similarity. And there are times when he looks serious and thoughtful. He is better looking than he was before his training. Profile very good.... He and his two great friends have had a jolly time skiing and fooling around. We have had a regular round of family dinners and of course he is the white-haired boy with all the family.... We are never too serious in our talk with one another. Joe knows how I feel ... now and again in our correspondence we have dug a little below the skin ... but now it is too dangerous ... too much is at stake. All we can do is to keep our fingers crossed until the war is over ... perhaps now and then breathe a silent prayer with the forlorn hope that it may be answered and that there may be something in that sort of thing after all. Last night to Temple with Joe. Proud father and proud mother. Monday night he goes away to do his job ... the job that the Government has spent twenty five thousand dollars so that he may do it properly. I know he will give a good account of himself. He has been a good son. We have had good times together. And he has had a good life so far. Happy childhood. Well cared for. No worries like I had when I was a boy. Camp in the summer. He has had pretty much everything that a boy and youth needs. A fine mother, a happy home life, opportunities for expressing himself freely. Sports which he loves. Two or three very close friends. Mind and body well balanced and primed for full living. God grant that he may live through this war and come back to give a good account of himself and make good return for his good fortune. In the meanwhile he has put all his affairs in order. His fraternity pin, gold football etc. he is leaving with his mother. It isn't easy for her. But there is nothing to be done about it. Just take what comes in our stride. Millions of mothers and fathers are with us in the same boat ... and things happen in time of peace. We will never have to face a greater tragedy than the loss of Peter before he had a chance to fulfill himself. (PJD 8 March 1941)

Party for Joe and his friends tonight. You should see the huge turkey, the potato salad, the chocolate cake, ice cream.... May has been busy this afternoon ... she is never happier than when preparing a real dinner for her family. And she does it nicely without fuss. Expect Monty Berger, Gerald Smith and probably several other friends which he will bring back with him from the Laurentians.

This will be Joe's last Sunday for God knows how long ... when and if we all meet again ... lots will have happened ... it is well that we are not able to see into the future....

> Joe and nine of his friends and the champion skiier of Canada Dorothy Michaels[1] landed for supper. The house overflowed with youth. Life at his zenith. Nice lot of young men. Left them for a while to hear Paul Muni broadcast in Ibsen's play "Enemy of the People" a challenge to all men to fight for freedom of speech, freedom to fight against the tyranny of the mob. (PJD 9 March 1941)
>
> Joe left last night for the Maritimes. He was not alone. About a thousand airmen were with him. Youth spilled over. Bonaventure station was alive with lusty young lives. A fine lot. The cream of our youth. Handsome boisterous, and happy.... Theirs is rendezvous with death. Joe is amongst them.... We had seven of the air boys (all Joe's friends) for farewell dinner. Ah they were a nice bunch of lads. Clean cut, straight and alert. Two of them had several drinks and were a bit hilarious but they behaved themselves. We did not have to worry although the little Englishers and our own girls were here.
>
> May is a brick. Not a squeal out of her. When we were alone together last night I just felt her thinking. I knew what she was thinking. War is an accursed thing. No good comes out of it. It crucifies those who are left behind and kills or maims those who go to fight. But while men are as they are, while there is greed and corruption, while men disregard the ten commandments and are cruel to each other, there will always be wars. Hitler will go, Mussolini will go. But there will be other Hitlers, other Mussolinis to bring misery and death in the world of tomorrow unless a tidal wave, cleansing our diseased civilization, sweeps over us. Not a very good way of expressing myself.
>
> But it was heartbreaking last night to see those fine chaps being sacrificed because of our blindness. (PJD 11 March 1941)

To this day Joey's sister Janet recalls that night, the last time she saw him, in vivid detail. Joe's memory of his departure for Halifax was less vivid, as he related to the Pony Club:

> I vaguely remember Air Force, guests, visitors and friends streaming in and out the house to say goodbye whilst I vainly tried to pack. Mub's pop came up and gave me a miniature scroll with the ten commandments – the exact name has slipped my tongue – but it was really swell of him to come up and say goodbye ...
>
> What with the gang around – a couple well lit, and the rest of the excitement going on there was no time to fool around saying goodbye – and

we were off and gone before anyone had time to realize what it was all about.

> … My cousin Art Silver gave me a 26 oz bottle of Johnny Dewar & Son and with my … drinking cronies we had a beautiful glow on by the time Levis appeared. In fact we had such a fine glow on (that is the 6 of us – each with a bottle) we were all running up and down the station platform yelling for Monty. I had such faith in old Mub that I wanted to stay and wait, but the conductor plus the gang tossed me on the train and old Joe was forced to take to the bottle until well nigh morn to drown his disappointment. (JJL 13 March 1941)

Joe had told Monty to meet him for a final farewell at the CN station in Levis, where his train was scheduled to stop for twenty-five minutes in the wee hours of Tuesday morning. After three hours of COTC drill that snowy night, Monty caught the ferry to Levis and trudged to the station. After a long wait, he discovered that the Ocean Limited was running late, and if he stayed he would miss the last ferry back across the St. Lawrence that night. So Monty, who had to show up for work the next morning, headed back to Quebec City, defeated in his efforts.

Nine

Debert

The hundred air observers who had begun their training together in Toronto the previous summer, now reunited, continued their revelry through the night. A few of them had got married during their embarkation leave. Some would never see their brides again. Such a step would have been inconceivable for Joe, disinclined as he was to commit himself, even if he and Cecily had had more time to get to know each other. It was just not done in the uptown Jewish community, and neither family would have approved.

The journey ended the next day at the temporary embarkation depot at Debert, a military camp sixty miles short of Halifax. Over eight hundred Air Training Program graduates were already barracked there waiting to board, with more coming in each day than going out. German U-boats posed a growing threat to overseas convoys, whose routes and schedules were tightly guarded secrets and could change at short notice.

Accommodation was in such short supply that Joe and six of his best friends[1] were put up in a hotel in nearby Truro the first night, then bunked in two rooms across the hall from each other in the officers' quarters. The Hell Hooters, now reunited, would have a lot of time on their hands and little to do. They avoided work, skipped drills, and drank beer at the base canteen. Some nights they went into Truro, where the Army Third Division was quartered, and Joe encountered some boys he had met in Preston. They spent their weekend passes partying and hard drinking in dubious establishments in Halifax. Joe had money and he was free with it.

> Back to air force life, drinking, excitement, friends, complaining, free and easy happy go lucky times with a great gang of boys.
> (JJD 15 March 1941)

> Starting to go broke – had to wire home for $50 of my money – got a great letter from Pop back – warned against losing control during war time. However, he was in a thinking mood and felt like talking seriously & frankly – I obliged with the same type of letter in return and we both understand and appreciate one another. However, I feel he is rather banking a little too highly on my ability and future. I doubt that I could measure up to his expectations but I'll sure try. (JJD 19 March 1941)

Grateful for what he saw as his father's unshaken confidence in him, Joe explained his sudden financial jam. None of the boys had been paid recently, and they had little money to spend while waiting in Debert or, they feared, during their prospective debarkation leave in England.

> we needed some funds to keep the corporation going here, with all the free time we have at our disposal.... Last week we were called out on draft without any warning, of course. I had visions of arriving overseas flat broke. Fortunately the draft was cancelled later in the evening. I decided to wire for money while I could and at least be sure of seeing England for five days....
>
> As for your concern over my "binges" I consider it only natural that any family should speculate on how far off the handle their sons are going. But I don't think you have to worry too much on that score.
>
> My life has so far been more or less a series of adventures taken more or less in stride – camp, college, Preston and now the Air Force. I know the ropes pretty well. My feet are planted pretty firmly on the ground. I have done pretty well what I have wanted to do, gone where I pleased and said what I thought. Outside of flying, my experiences now are neither more and probably less than what they were before I joined up. I always had the chance to play cards and did until I discovered I couldn't win – so I quit when I started earning my own living. I always got keen enjoyment out of sports and activity of all sorts. I still do and am still the leader in the gang on that score – I could always get a kick out of a drink and still can. But I have never been really drunk and never expect to as I find I can hold whatever liquor I take extremely well and seldom require stimulants to keep me going. And finally I have always had a select display of female talent to choose from and probably was always much too choosy. I have not lost that choosy temperament despite the considerably lower class of females that often appear on the scene.
>
> And so I hope that you will continue to rest assured that I am quite capable of taking events in stride. Also as you have seen by the friends

> I associate with both in and out of the service, that there is none of that "short life and a merry one" amongst us. We are all very much interested in the aftermath of the war, and our part and that of our families in that period. (JJL 21 March 1941)

Percy described this letter as:

> one of the finest letters he has ever written to us … it made me feel that perhaps I have not lived altogether in vain if I have helped to make the lad what he is.… Oh yes I give fully seventy five percent credit to his mother … but I don't think any father has ever come closer to his son than I have to Joey and the other way around. That was the gist of his letter. He's a grand lad … I have said this so often … and as I think I said before a better man than his father which is as it should be.…
>
> Someone said recently that the most important quality, perhaps the one important quality for the time being is courage … if you haven't courage today the rest doesn't add up to anything. (PJD 24 March 1941)

⊙

It was at Debert that Joe encountered the first graduates from the other countries sharing the Air Training Program. He wrote home:

> There are now thousands of airmen all with wings from all parts of the Empire waiting to sail. During my training period I had a chance to bump into fellows from all parts of Canada. Now the scope is enlarging as we chum around with New Zealanders, Aussies, Blimeys and Canadians and Americans.[2] The New Zealanders get along best with us, and like us, they give the most trouble, kick up a terrific racket and have the officers tearing their hair out. The Aussies are not far behind although often inclined to be slightly harder to meet although just as rowdy as the rest. The blimeys are not far behind but they are more or less the conformists in this outfit, which is a good thing as somebody should show signs of behaving. But when you see the various flyers here – from small independent countries, all bright, smart, keen, independent and well trained you can feel assured that our end of the game will be well handled.
>
> The calling up of a draft here is an exciting event. The flight sergeant stands in the middle of a big hangar, the whole works gather round and listen breathlessly for their names to be called out and for those of their friends. Since often only a few hundred are called up at a time, many of

> the old gang are left out for the time being so we all eagerly wait to see how many will be together. Naturally when we are called up there will be no phoning or telegrams allowed as the whole secret would be given away – even letters are held.
>
> I spent another weekend in Halifax and despite its dirty squalidness and teeming multitudes, there is a real romance about the town. My pal and myself make a point of picking up as many seamen as possible and getting them to show us their ships and docks. As a result we have made friends with seamen from all parts of the world. Our newest pal is a young second mate on a merchant ship from the south sea islands who has been all over the world. Since we are also navigators we had a great time navigating ships and airplanes together. Both jobs are fundamentally the same – but ours requires much more rapid and accurate work. We also found time to sun ourselves on a quiet place at one end of the docks, watching the ships and sea gulls sail along – quite a life. So despite the lack of work, we have managed to get around, see a few new towns, meet a lot of people and learn something about this part of the country and its people.... (JJL 25 March 1941)
>
> As you see the ease with which young men drawn from all fields of work and different parts of the country can adapt themselves to a specific job requiring study, precision and daring, you can't help but figure that we are capable of producing men that can adapt themselves to any task or job which might be required and do as good and probably a whole lot better at it than any other young men in any other country. Not only that but without any pushing, prodding or pep talks there is not a man who has anything but the most ardent desire to set the Germans where they belong – the Italians don't rate – but the Germans certainly are not held in any awe around here – nobody is for that matter. We all feel we are as good as the next man and have not been brought up to bow to any man and don't expect anyone to do likewise – which is just one reason why a master race won't make much headway around here.... (JJL 27 March 1941)

As Debert became ever more crowded, Joe and his non-commissioned Hell Hooter pals were evicted from their rooms in officers' quarters and moved to a hangar. Their separate status was a taste of things to come. They saw less of their classmates who had privileges in the officers' mess. The NCOs stuck together even more closely, and had all the more incentive to get off the base at night and binge in Halifax, or get away to the countryside. One weekend they went to Pictou harbour to clamber around the boats and enjoy the sunshine, and then proceeded to a big dance in Stellarton. As Joe related to the Pony Club, his failure to get a commission was not without advantage, at least for the time being.

> Our gang of officers are not too happy. They have duties – and very boring ones on the station – have to put on the dog at all times and never really feel at home. We on the other hand can go where we please – do as we wish.
>
> … once in a while a woman is great – once in a while a real good drunk is swell – but nothing compares with a good outing with your pals when you all have the physical and mental equipment to be able to undertake any form of exercise or activity with ease – I suppose the ideal is the right mixture of each and I guess we have come as close to the ideal during our times together as it is possible to come. Unfortunately there are only women and drink for us here – I exercise strenuously in the morning. Outside of that there are absolutely no facilities or opportunities to do anything here but wait and binge – can't even get a place to read so the sooner we scram the better it will be for all concerned. (JJL 31 March 1941)

By early April, Joe told his family that the boys at Debert were getting "restless and crabby":

> This is army life in the raw. Absolutely no work, no facilities to keep us busy. Debert a sea of mud – quarters jammed – one thousand sleeping in hangars – no recreation rooms – barracks too stuffy to stay in – I do my exercises in morning, stand around on parade then get away to town. Then the fun begins. It cost 1 buck to get to Truro and back – you get hosed at every turn, meals, dances etc. (JJL 5 April 1941)

After two weeks of this stew of boredom and anxiety, Joe's thoughts turned to how he might engineer a final Pony Club reunion.

> If we are going to be here another couple of weeks, there is no reason why I should not get home for a couple of days, say next weekend – except that the C.O. stated that leaves will only be granted on compassionate grounds. In other words, Mub, I need a letter followed by a wire around next Tuesday telling me of a serious accident, sickness, death or tragedy and you must be ready to substantiate the story when the C.O. phones himself – might I suggest putting Janet in a Quebec hospital, having Edith get married, Smitty catch leprosy, Herb the clap or some such compassionate tear-jerking story. (JJL 26 March 1941)

A few days later he reconsidered:

> We are having a mass movement to another station, probably Halifax or Sydney, N.S. and I am liable to be stuck if I go home. Besides, after thinking it all over I decided that maybe it would not be a wise move to go home again. We did everything we should have done and did it as it can only be done by us during my three weeks at home. That phase is over and altho it would be nice to spin home it would probably be rather hard on my folks and I am liable to miss a draft. Further we are all decided on one thing our reunion shall be at Christmas – over the ocean. (JJL 31 March 1941)

There was much discussion that week about Herb's standing in the Pony Club. He had not returned to Canada during Joe's last leave, nor offered much explanation other than the demands of his work. Monty admonished him:

> Remember this: our boy is going overseas – the Lord knows when or if we'll ever see him again. Even allowing for his tales of wine & women, it still leaves him oodles of time to kill, to ponder, etc. He's gone thru periods – and still goes thru them – of wondering whether his pals have any qualities of courage or manhood in them. The least we can do is show him that we have qualities of loyalty – and buoy him up as much as we can.
>
> I know that five minutes means a lot to you, but think of what that five minutes of your effort means to him – especially when multiplied by three – it means – or should mean a letter a day from one of the three of us. I'm hitting at least three letters a week, Lord knows what I write but I write. I am in my office for 7:30 every morn, write all day, have just returned from 3 ½ hours of drill in zero weather, missed supper – my routine is something like that most every day. I certainly am rarely in a mood to write. But I still write.... Getting a letter out to Joe is more important to me than my job. That's my first duty. Once that is done the rest comes easy. (31 March 1941)

There would be no last-minute reunion of the four. Joe had not seen Herb for a year, and he would never see him or Gerald again. Only Joe and Monty would be reunited in England in the coming months. Joe was now by force of circumstance part of a new fellowship of shared situation and purpose. Yet, as he declared in his diary, the bonds of the Pony Club were closer than ever, and its circulating correspondence would carry on undiminished. Joe phoned home from Truro a few days later. Percy recorded:

> we knew what that meant … ready to embark for overseas … he is not permitted to say anything about it…. his voice sounded clear and happy … queer how much we wanted to say to each other and how little we could say … his mother was on a branch telephone upstairs and we passed the usual banalities and finally wound up with just the usual feeble "best of luck." What I wanted to say was … God Bless you my lad, do your job well and come back to us sound in mind and body. Well that is our prayer. There is the right stuff in Joe and as I said before I am proud to have fathered him. (PJD 5 April 1941)

That same day, however, a case of scarlet fever was detected, and all those waiting to leave had to be tested. Nearly nine hundred were posted for departure that day, but Joe and over a hundred others were left out of that draft, which prompted another drinking binge.

> Gang split up as G.P. & Mac were positive & left, Art & I negative and were left – all pretty gloomy especially as phoned home to folks & Monty for false alarm farewell. (JJD 5 April 1941)

> Most depressing day yet – boys left – about 200 sgts left on station. Place desolate. Pop Miller called Art and I over for a drink in evening….
> (JJD 6 April 1941)

> Hopes renewed – dick test again for those with previous inoculations.[3] Many of us tried to suck serum out, used hot towels, bottles, poultices and did everything imaginable to keep the red mark away.
> (JJD 7 April 1941)

> Art & I got past dick test – by using powder, noxema and squeezing arm to keep red mark down – we are supposed to be going on draft – whole thing a muddle – fellows all disgusted, thoroughly annoyed at being left behind & incompetence here. (JJD 8 April 1941)

The trick worked. Joe and his pals managed to pass negative the next day. Officially posted from Debert to "elsewhere," they were on their way. As the troop train emerged from the rock cut at the south end of Halifax, Joe could see the harbour lined with outbound ships. His whereabouts were now enshrouded in secrecy. He boarded the RMS *Laconia* on the 9th, although it did not weigh anchor until the morning of the 11th.

Canadians were a parochial lot in 1940, regardless of their social class or economic circumstances. No road connected east and west, and the newly established Trans-Canada Airlines route was prohibitively expensive for most. It took four days to cross Canada by train. English Canadians were tied together more by the Empire and the Union Jack than by personal bonds or mutual awareness. Most Canadians knew little of their country beyond their hometown. The war, and not least the Air Training Program, did much to change that. The Air Training Program quickly separated recruits by trade and assigned them to schools scattered across the country. Young men from all over Canada were thrown together in common cause and circumstance to spend months training in unfamiliar places far from home. Not only did they forge bonds of comradeship, they gained a larger sense of their country and what it meant to be Canadian.

The country Joey and his classmates left behind was still largely rural, and much of it impoverished by ten years of economic depression. It was provincial in outlook and socially conservative. Even Montreal, the nation's most cosmopolitan centre and largest port, was a commercial outpost of empire. The city's social and business elites looked across the sea to Britain as much as they did to the United States, fifty miles down the road. Britain represented sophistication and "class" in a way that the United States (except New York City) did not. But Canadians were also acutely aware that their American neighbours were richer and more technologically advanced, and Canadians were enthralled by American popular culture. The wonders of human achievement – technical, architectural, or intellectual – were to be found in Britain and the United States, not at home. So too was modernity – in surroundings and in attitudes – to be found elsewhere. Yet Joe, and surely the lads he had trained with, had also come to see Canada as a project under construction, a land of opportunity not just to benefit from but to shape.

And Canada had done something very big in 1940. It had become, as President Roosevelt would later say, the aerodrome of democracy. The Air Training Program would eventually send 130,000 aircrew to Britain. The boys on the boat were among the first three hundred air observers to go. They were the cream of the crop and they knew it. They went overseas with confidence and swagger, ready to take on the enemy. They had bonded as warriors, believing their cause just and themselves invincible.

Part Two

Discoveries

Existence is never so sweet as when it is at hazard.

— Winston Churchill, South Africa, 1900
(cited in Max Hastings, *Warriors*)

After the final destruction of the Nazi tyranny, [we] hope to see established a peace which will afford to all nations the means of dwelling in safety within their own boundaries, and which will afford assurance that all the men in all the lands may live out their lives in freedom from fear and want.

— Franklin Roosevelt and Winston Churchill,
The Atlantic Charter, August 1941

Ten

The North Atlantic

When the RMS *Laconia* left the confines of Halifax harbour for the open Atlantic on the morning of 11 April, Joe Jacobson entered a war zone. The Battle of the Atlantic, Germany's attempt to strangle Britain by naval blockade, was tilting in Germany's favour. The feared and effective U-boats preyed on the freighters and troop carriers that constituted Britain's lifeline from Halifax. Forward naval bases built in Brittany since France had capitulated the previous summer had enabled German submarines to operate far into the Atlantic. The U-boats had taken to operating in "wolf packs," a tactic that enabled them to detect and penetrate convoys with devastating effect. Over the winter, their success had been enhanced by the long hours of darkness when they could prowl on the surface undetected.

The best defence for merchant shipping was to travel in convoy. Halifax was the chief point of assembly for shipping to Britain, and several convoys departed each month. These typically consisted of three or four dozen freighters, escorted by naval vessels and armed merchant cruisers. Freighter convoys travelled at seven to nine knots, and might take two weeks to cross the ocean. The armed merchant cruisers were mostly ocean liners that had been requisitioned by the British Admiralty. Travelling at twice the speed of the freighters and fitted with batteries of six-inch naval guns, they had a better chance of outrunning U-boats and defending themselves. But not all convoys got through unscathed. Two that had left Halifax in February and early March lost ships before reaching Britain. In early April, U-boats sank ten ships travelling in a convoy that had left Halifax two weeks prior, with the loss of nearly one hundred merchant sailors.

Two troop ships and forty-two slow freighters carrying food, fuel, and steel had assembled into two convoys, TC10 and HX120, respectively. They left Halifax on 10 and 11 April, in fine weather, accompanied by eighteen escort vessels.[1] TC10 carried nearly four thousand men, among them over a thousand aircrew who had cleared out of Debert in the days before. Most were on board the MV *Georgic*, a converted Cunard passenger liner. The rest of the airmen departing Debert were allotted to armed escorts: the *Laconia*, and the *Montclare*, *Wolfe*, and *Rajputana*, which were accompanying convoys that had left a few days before. All had been assigned to patrol duty on the North Atlantic convoy route beyond Britain's western approaches. On this occasion, they were also carrying troops, but they would be dropping them off in Iceland before returning to Halifax.

HX120 steamed at seven knots for ten days. By the end of the second day, it was crossing the southern tip of the Grand Banks, well south of Newfoundland and the hazardous springtime parade of icebergs, growlers, and bergy bits. Then it turned sharply northeast into the Gulf Stream and the danger zone. From there on, gun crews were put on regular exercise. For the first few days, sun and fog alternated over calm seas. At night the convoy travelled under blackout orders, except in heavy fog, when running lights were needed to avoid collisions. Nonetheless two vessels collided in fog on the 15th, and the damaged oil tanker *Circe Shell* was forced to return to Halifax. Joe recorded the progress of the convoy in his diary:

> Hooray – left Debert – boarded the armed merchant cruiser *S.S. Laconia* – 124 airmen, 50 Norwegian seamen – slept on deck the first night, learnt that we carry six six-inch guns – two eight – we do the convoying – act as a suicide ship to draw enemy fire. (JJD 9 April 1941)

> Had a great time getting acquainted with the ship the crew and prospective trip while still in port. Men claim guns no good, not enough life boats, ship ready to be scuttled, captain goes looking for trouble – … but we should have some fun. (JJD 10 April 1941)

> Ship ahoy – anchors afloat at 0815 – beautiful day – battleship, subs, corvettes, cruisers and merchant ships all out – should be some real action – rumours – bound for Iceland they claim. Weather beautiful. Given hammocks to sleep in – real comfy. Food excellent. (JJD 11 April 1941)

> Fair weather – caught up to convoy by dinner time – started patrol for 39 ships in our convoy – Battleship left us on our own. Art [Hunter] & I started routine. Kept my big flask full of rum took it neat before every

meal & bed time – we walk the decks write our diaries, do exercises, read a bit, eat a lot, Art & I growing mustaches, smoking pipes. (JJD 12 April 1941)

Approaching danger area – trip full of suspense since we are protecting a large convoy and have neither the speed or armament to do it with. We go to stations at 5:30 AM. Art & I are on a spare gun crew – we do 7 knots on this convoy – our ship can do 16 – guns range but 5 miles – Battle of Atlantic raging so we expect trouble & don't expect to do much more than get sunk – this is a real adventure – sea still calm … (JJD 13 April 1941)

4th day at sea – calm, foggy – all's still well – weather warmer here in Gulf Stream. Reading Butler's *Way of All Flesh* – news reports British & Greeks holding out in Balkans, American ships allowed in Red Sea now – Battle of the Atlantic starting in earnest – that's us – boys getting lazy & no longer get up for action stations. (JJD 14 April 1941)

Beautiful sunny day – Art & I sunned ourselves half nude all morning – *Royal Sovereign*[2] back again with us – makes us feel much more comfortable – sea still calm. Sleeping in hammocks extremely cozy. We found a gym – Art & I can now work out … to supplement our walking – visited engine room today. Poor devils get locked in during action. No worse than us though. (JJD 15 April 1941)

Enjoying cruise immensely – visited helm – navigating a ship is a cinch – crew all English & Scotch – pretty good gang – we flatter them with questions they bullshoot us with rumours – keep in shape boxing, wrestling – skipping and walking with Art – We stick together at all times. (JJD 16 April 1941)

Rough weather but only a couple of boys sick – saw a grudge fight with two sailors last night – played bridge … down in ship's hold. Getting to know sailors pretty well – they all worry about subs are scared stiff of armed raiders & pocket battleships – they have had no leave in 18 months – are dissatisfied & scared – but a mighty fine crew just the same. (JJD 17 April 1941)

Played in a pingpong match – RCAF vs Navy – won both my matches – contest a draw. Finished *MacBeth* – reading *King Lear* – strong character & language appeals to me – weather rough – but Art & I eat better than ever – we good sailor boys – news broadcast seems to indicate Balkan war ended in favor of Germans – will probably see another

> issue & another front appear before long – mustache sprouting nicely. (JJD 18 April 1941)
>
> Started reading Galsworthy's *Forsyth Saga* – weather calm – picked up another convoy[3] – battleship keeps pretty close by. Played chess last nite – we have 16 at our mess table – all observers – we get along swell – have lots of fun at meal time – every man speaks for himself – don't do much during day but sleep eat, read, exercise a bit....
>
> Made slow time during first week – now in danger area – reinforced by submarine *Thunderbolt* – glad I joined Air Force rather than Navy – fun over – serious work begins. (JJD 19 April 1941)
>
> We had our second ship's concert last nite – impromptu – lots of fun – Norwegians sang some staunch songs – they are ... quiet & jolly but have little to look forward to but vengeance. They are all airmen of the Fleet Air Arm. Submarines rumoured around. Don't worry me. They would be lucky to find us & why spoil a pleasant cruise worrying – weather fine – heard we lost 3 of convoy thru collision in fog. (JJD 20 April 1941)

On the 21st, after ten days of plugging along at slow speed with the convoy, the *Laconia* was directed to proceed north to Iceland on its own. It doubled its speed and pursued a zigzag course, changing direction every few minutes, thus reducing the opportunity for a U-boat to line up a torpedo shot. The daylight hours lengthened rapidly as the *Laconia* proceeded north, providing added protection from U-boats, which required cover of darkness to attack.

> Left our convoy of 40 odd ships to 12 destroyers & corvettes – quite an impressive sight to see so many ships together in the vast Atlantic. We are now on our way to Iceland alone. Had a sports day didn't do much – played a good chess game ... quite a few chess enthusiasts. Reading P.G. Wodehouse ... he is real popular aboard. (JJD 21 April 1941)
>
> Saw empty barrels floating by today – ship sunk here yesterday[4] – we are zigzagging away from subs – play lots of chess now – lots of sun – weather rough but nice outdoors – sea gulls following along behind – could gaze at them for hours, floating – zooming – diving. (JJD 22 April 1941)
>
> Art, Pat Murphy & myself had a farewell rum swizzle party, around midnite & it was still daylight – uncanny but we are now in the land

> of the never setting sun – weather rough & foggy – we have to wear lifebelts at all times now – zig-zagging from mines & plenty of subs – thirteenth full day at sea – due Iceland tomorrow morning if all goes well – passed lots more wreckage today. (JJD 23 April 1941)

> Arrived in Reykjavik Iceland – people silent – pro-Nazi – women good looking – proponents of trial marriage – we are stationed 14 miles from Reyk – temporary barracks sleep on floor – little food or anything else – all C.B. [confined to barracks] met Harry Ryan, Les Smitten, Nick Durban[5] – awful hole they claim – mountains & lakes look good – Art & I will have a time despite the surroundings. Lots of soldiers all English – plenty complacent – C.O. a hard egg. (JJD 24 April 1941)

Iceland, a neutral country with no armed defences, had been summarily invaded by Britain in 1940. This quick and bloodless strike pre-empted Germany from gaining a stranglehold on the North Atlantic convoy route and potentially encircling Britain, and placed it at permanent disadvantage for the rest of the war with respect to weather forecasting. Iceland soon found itself hosting an occupation force of 25,000 British and Canadian troops, transferred there after the fall of France. Icelanders were not Nazi sympathizers as Joe believed, but neither were they especially grateful to their occupiers.

By the time Joe arrived, the British had established a naval base and nearly completed an airfield at Reykjavik. Most of the Canadians had been sent back to Britain the previous October, although the Cameron Highlanders of Ottawa remained due to a shortage of available machine-gun battalions. Now over four hundred Canadian airmen had come for a temporary stay, when the four escorts that had brought them returned to Halifax on patrol duty. They had no business in Iceland, and from Joe's account, it was not an enjoyable visit. They were confined to a military camp miles out of Reykjavik. Rumours of "loose morals" on the part of Icelandic women spread quickly among these young men, but they were given no opportunity to apply their excess time and energy to verifying them.

> What memories – driving rain, foul food off of greasy plates (tin) – C.B.'d in mud hovels – nothing to buy or do or see – attempts at secrecy futile – civilians can find out nearly everything – heard Germans occupied Ireland – Greece lost – so are we if they don't get us away from here – have to draw our water from the river – piss in tin cans – heat

> our own water – probably worried at home as I can't get in touch with them – maybe tomorrow will look brighter. (JJD 25 April 1941)
>
> Went for a long walk with Art this morning – climbed a mountain this evening – country barren – no trees – land rocky & barren good only for sheep grazing – English airmen respect a rank – honoured when we treat them as equals – most Blimey pilots unpopular – try to act superior – lower ranks seem better men – ships crew for example – we are stationed at Helgafel – all more cheery as we are due to pull out tomorrow – Art & I feast on canned apricots – biscuits & chocolate bars – met … a few other old friends here – all had dysentery last nite. Trip over Atlantic novel, pleasant & dangerous – Iceland a kick in the pants for us as we were herded treated like rabble & cooped up – just a bit of a test to show us we are not to get everything our own way – we learn to grumble, joke & take it – have to take the good with the bad. (JJD 26 April 1941)

The next day, all the Canadian airmen who had been dumped in Iceland over the previous two weeks, along with the Cameron Highlanders, the last of Canada's occupation force in Iceland, were herded on board the *Royal Ulsterman*. They were bound for Scotland without escort, on a vessel that in peacetime had served as a ferry between Glasgow and Belfast.

> Hallelulia – boarded the *Ulsterman* headed for England – now sailing up a deep fjord in smooth water between mountainous peaks past destroyer & tugs – the *Athol Empress* to refuel from a tanker – quarters cramped – food probably same but feeling cheery as our crew of shipwrecked sailors, soldiers, officers, entertainers & our sergeants make ready to leave – still have trusty flask of rum. (JJD 27 April 1941)
>
> Accommodation about same as that given cattle in ships hold & we would have no more chance of getting thru if ship torpedoed – food all canned – boat still docked in fiord – everyone grumpy again. The sooner this trip is over with the better – getting all the bad now – should pick up before the war's over – anchors up – sailed for England this afternoon – 2 troop transports – two destroyers saw the *Hood* anchored nearby with other battleships. No way out of hold in ship where we sleep – Art & I have steel pipes to force open gang plank entrance nearby – fast ship though should be safe. (JJD 28 April 1941)

> Plugged right along all day – smooth sea – weather better & Art, Grange & I had bull session … on war, future etc. started a rummy series with Art … cousin Lionel Silver aboard[6] – our main gripe – we are not treated according to our rank or like human beings – English can exasperate you at times – food all canned – margarine terrible – stomach surviving somehow. (JJD 29 April 1941)

> Dropped a couple of depth charges – no trouble so far – hit the coast of Scotland & sailed between it & the Hebrides – getting close – met by planes – weather warmer, feeling spry … getting spruced up for landing tomorrow but uniform really scruffy – hair long – mustache going to come off – days of peace about to end – a short leave & we are all set to get down to work – the usual over the rail bull session with Art. (JJD 30 April 1941)

Joe's diary provides rare detail about his experience of the Atlantic crossing. RCAF personnel had been warned on embarkation not to write anything about their trip that might reveal convoy routes, schedules, ports of call, armaments, aircraft, military engagements, or losses. Over a month later he managed to communicate to his family that:

> We did not arrive on that big convoy – we had a special trip of our own and arrived here after numerous interesting adventures on May 1st. I will write you about that trip via slow mail. I left [a] day by day account of the trip – one month all told and gave the letter to a sailor to mail to you privately. The boat arrived alright but he forgot to post the mail – it was a twenty page letter. (JJL 10 June 1941).[7]

Many of the arriving troops ignored their instructions and wrote home about their North Atlantic passage. But some of their letters got no further than the British Postal and Telegraph Censor's Office, which at that time was vetting about half of servicemen's letters bound for Canada. Most recounted the relatively uneventful passage of the liner *Georgic*, at least two spoke of their passage on the *Rajputana* (whose passengers were stuck in Iceland for two weeks en route to Scotland), but there are no accounts of the *Laconia*'s passage in the RCAF's censored letters file. In the circumstances, rumour and speculation abounded. Several letters contained exaggerated accounts of enemy encounters and ships sunk in previous convoys, and erroneous information on course and location.

In our home circle many things have happened. We had news that a young cousin Sergeant John Michaels of the Imperial forces had been killed in or around Egypt. He was only son. A boy with quite a history. Sensitive, artistic, lot of good in him.[8]

Although we have had no definite word we are pretty certain that Joe is on his way overseas. (PJD 19 April 1941)

No cable yet from Joe but then nobody else has received any word. We really are not worried because we know that this is war and the thousands of cables which no doubt have been sent home must overcrowd the service … but we would like to hear. Not that a cable will give us anything but the most momentarily assurance of his safety … from now on we can only hope and pray and keep our fingers crossed … we would disintegrate quickly if we allowed ourselves to worry. (PJD 2 May 1941)

We received a cable from Joe telling of his safe arrival in Britain. So he is Thank God safe for the time being. (PJD 7 May 1941)

Joe had been lucky. The *Rajputana* was sunk by a U-boat on 13 April, a day out of Reykjavik. The day before Joe arrived in Britain, the troopship *Nerissa* was torpedoed in the eastern Atlantic en route from Halifax, with over two hundred men lost. Hundreds of Air Training Program graduates had travelled to Britain on the *Nerissa* in January and March. This time, the only occasion during the entire war that Canadian troops were lost at sea, no airmen were on board.

Eleven

The Blitz

No sooner had the Canadian airmen disembarked at the Greenock docks than they were whisked away to a London-bound troop train. Joe saw little bomb damage on the way, but many balloon barrages and much pastoral countryside.[1] The next morning they were sent to RAF Uxbridge, just outside the city. Originally a recruiting centre, like Toronto's Manning Depot, it now housed No. 3 Personnel Reception Centre, a holding point for newly arrived Canadian airmen. There they were issued identity cards, battle dress, and clothing coupons. Within days, the new arrivals would be posted elsewhere for further training. Meanwhile they had enough time to see London on a forty-eight-hour pass, which Joe and his pals hastened to do.

> Piccadilly Circus, Leicester Sq – Lyons Corner House – good old London was taken in by the RCAF … drinks again in Wards – dance at the Astoria – took some nurses home got stuck in Hampstead – slept in cold air raid shelter without great coats – then on subway and really froze. (JJD 2 May 1941)

> Art & I took our farewell trip to London as Hell hooters … took a taxi tour of the Palace, Marble Arch, Hyde Park. Registered at the Beaver Club – met a few of the fellows – no word from G.P. or Mac – left messages – stopped over at the Regent Palace – drank at Wards – danced at the Astoria – turned in early … (JJD 3 May 1941)

London! The great capital of the mother country, the heart of the Empire, the cosmopolitan centre of the world. Even in the spring of 1941, with statues removed or hidden behind walls of sandbags, windows replaced by plywood, and the lights of Piccadilly turned off, it was glamorous and sophisticated, exotic and yet familiar. Even, or perhaps especially, for those from Canada's premier city of Montreal, arriving in London could not fail to be an exhilarating experience. The new arrivals set out to explore the city that every one of them had heard about but very few had seen. The hallowed monuments of Empire and Christendom they had learned about in school, and the landmarks, theatres, and shops they had read about in books and magazines – suddenly all were there to explore. And there was so much novel and different to experience: English accents, slang, customs, the penetrating damp and cold inside and out, women in uniform, four-o'clock tea, the tube, and crowds of people, many of them from unfamiliar parts of the world.

Not all of this was new to Joe, who had vacationed with his family in England and Belgium eleven years before. But now he was exploring London as a young man with his pals. The Beaver Club, conveniently located in Canada House on Trafalgar Square, was the first destination for Canadian servicemen on arrival and on leave in London. There one could get news, exchange messages, bump into friends from other units, and perhaps even broadcast a live message home on CBC radio. There was also the American Eagle Club, up Charing Cross Road, a social club for foreign nationals serving in the British Armed Forces, and the Union Jack Club on Waterloo Road, which provided short-term accommodation for service personnel. Newly arrived airmen soon gravitated to other hotels and canteens such as the Regent, the Strand, Chez Moi, and Crackers. Joe summed up his first few days in his diary:

> Got my first glance of war torn England – noticeable damage not great – no air raids for me as yet – plenty of drink & food for us – Canadians are well received – blackout novel – morals lax – women especially have gone hog wild – more so than in Canada – shoot the works now – there might be no to-morrow is attitude – war grave for us – Germans on march everywhere – outlook bleak but now is the test – stick it out for better times. (JJD 3 May 1941)

Joe was posted to an operational training unit in Yorkshire, and given a week's leave. He headed back to London for a final frenetic Canadian reunion with his pals who had been posted to other stations, which he related to the Pony Club:

> we all met at the "Beaver" Club in London – what followed was a week's solid binging – I was out on three all night sessions, I took in four plays – (we got free tickets) saw one movie – a few clubs – plenty of

> sights and women (if they may be termed as such). I saw plenty of London and no kidding things go along fairly normally – there has been plenty of damage by fire and H.E. bombs – but there is lots left and you get so used to seeing leveled buildings that it becomes part of the landscape – the people have the art of adapting themselves so admirably to the new conditions that it has become normal whilst our life would now be unnatural – they have two hours daylight saving so that it is light until 10:30 PM – nearly everything is over by 12 o'clock altho you can still find clubs, etc. to go to.... I doubt that you fellows would make out so well here owing to the fact that women over here have reached a status equal to that of men in all respects ... there are no innocent women to begin with – and they prey on you to end with ... Art and I had some difficult circumstances despite our intelligen[t] handling of our admirers – we were hosed on one occasion – left to spend the night in an air raid shelter on a cold night outside London upon another – and had numerous other more productive adventures which I will tell you about personally – too hot for this thin paper – still haven't met anything that comes close to Cecily, though. (JJL 14 May 1941)

Binging and partying could not hide the fact that London was, like the North Atlantic, a war zone. Blackouts, bomb shelters, plywood and sandbags for blast protection, dust and rubble in the streets from bombing, were the obvious features of a city under siege from the air. Food was rationed, and newspapers had been reduced to four pages. Joe observed that practically everyone was in some kind of uniform, including those who had escaped from the enslaved countries of Europe to fight another day. Of these, Joe told the Pony Club, "the Free French are disliked – the Poles are feared as bloodthirsty and are really out to get the Germans." The war was no longer new for England, and by that time the country had settled in for a long and gruelling test. But ordinary life went on, during the day if not quite so at night.

The first close-up experience of war for the newly arrived BCATP graduates was the Blitz, which had begun the previous September. Joe had arrived days before the heaviest and, as it turned out, final attack, in which over five hundred aircraft bombed London indiscriminately, killing or seriously injuring over three thousand people and leaving over twelve thousand homeless. The Luftwaffe's assault had damaged bridges, water mains, and gas mains, although few military or industrial targets. Churches, hospitals, halls and theatres, museums, libraries and many treasured landmarks – including the House of Commons, Westminster Abbey, and Lambeth Palace – were damaged or destroyed by blast and fire. As Joe described it in his diary:

> This is being written in the middle of a terrific blitz – bombs & fires roaring all around – we are all up in the YMCA – saw Women Aren't Angels – not bad – went tea dancing at O.C. Club – Out with boys early & back here for blitz.... Boy what a raid – plenty noisy – plenty shaky – ... never know a war is on until a blitz like tonight then you make allowances for lack of hilarity amongst people & give them credit for their remarkable courage. (JJD 10 May 1941)

> Emerged this morning feeling spry & alive & found the damage from the raid was very heavy – Rly Stations – King's Cross & others were out of commission – the Abbey & House of Lords was badly burnt – in fact the city was scarred – but people take it calmly & I am beginning to understand why – altho it is a rather terrifying experience to see buildings crumbling & burning & hear bombs & guns screaming – when it's all over you feel as if you have accomplished something & you have – you have survived a London blitz. (JJD 11 May 1941)

He elaborated to the Pony Club:

> everything looks dandy until you are unfortunate enough to be caught in a blitz – we got caught in the middle of one the last night of our leave – it was one of their worst – for 5 hours we would stand in the street – watch the tremendous fires burning all around us, listen for the motors of German planes – trying to dodge incendiaries and ducking for cover when the next wave of high explosives followed – we missed being leveled a dozen times by about 1/10th of a second – the town was rather bashed up the next day but with customary calmness and efficiency just another blitz was being efficiently defeated – added to that 33 German planes were brought down. The next morning a brilliant sun was practically obliterated by the smoke that overhung the city. Quite amazing when you figure how a blitz is taken in stride here – since no military damage is done on one of these reprisal raids – I would say that the expense incurred by the Germans is rather high considering the results. Well enough about the blitzes. After being in one though I might say that I am rather pleased that dropping bombs on Germans will be my job – I doubt that they have the guts to stand up to them – time will tell. (JJL 14 May 1941)

Then the Blitz suddenly ended. Hitler had concluded, correctly, that the Blitz was not having the desired effect on civilian morale in Britain. As the world would learn six weeks later, he was planning to use his aircraft to better effect elsewhere. The recently arrived Canadian airmen had found out what it was like to live through on the ground what they were being trained to inflict from the air. They were inspired by how London's people carried on during the Blitz, enduring blackouts, food rationing, sleepless nights in cramped and malodorous air raid shelters, bombed-out homes, and fires in the streets. The new arrivals bolstered the morale of Britons who had endured half a year of bombing. In every pub, restaurant, train, and theatre, civilians looked to the boys in air force blue to give the Germans hell. Airmen were quickly imbued with the rightness and urgency of their coming task. But it would be a long time before they were able to deliver the same devastating attacks on German cities that the Luftwaffe had brought to London that spring.

Britain had survived the threat of invasion, as well as what its people most feared when the war began: the bombing of the civilian population. Nonetheless it was still under threat of strangulation by blockade, and the shortages and rationing that would soon restrict every aspect of life were already beginning when the first BCATP graduates arrived.

After so many months of arduous training, the Canadian boys had hoped to maintain their brotherhood in arms into operational squadrons. Beneath the novelty and excitement of arriving in Britain, however, lay a hard fact whose implications would become more evident over the next few months. Upon leaving Canada, they had been attached to the Royal Air Force. Almost all of Joe's classmates were destined to fly in Bomber Command, but they soon learned that they would be split up and assigned to various RAF stations around Britain.

> Splitting from old Hell hooter pals … going to #25 O.T.U. [Operational Training Unit] with a couple of others from other classes – impossible to keep together from now on – can only hope for reunions – saw boys off & left soon after – arrived at FINNINGLEY near Doncaster – well received & treated in serg mess – looks like a good set up.
> (JJD 4 May 1941)

> Discovered Roger Rousseau & Stevie Stevenson on same station … station well organized – less red tape than in Canada – everybody knows their job – waaf[2] – (women) prominent around the station – and in most places – women playing a key part in war – filling in as equals all over & supplying the needed incentive & dash to keep the men on their toes … (JJD 5 May 1941)

Joe reported to the Pony Club:

> we have all been split up. The policy here seems to be to break up the "colonial" groups and more or less surround them with peaceful living blokes – you guessed it – Englishmen. We spent two nights in London binging before we were split up – Art and I were then sent to different parts of the country. (JJL 14 May 1941)
>
> we are taking a hosing financially – we pay 16s – 6d per week income tax – we have protested – beefed etc. We are still R.C.A.F. – never signed up for the RAF, but they are hosing us good and proper.[3] (JJL 25 May 1941)

Canadian airmen were effectively cut loose from the force they had originally joined. For all practical purposes, they had become members of another country's air force, even if it was that of the "mother country." The RAF would determine their postings, their discipline, their promotions and decorations, and their eventual repatriation. In 1941 the RCAF had no input in these matters as they affected its men at the unit level. It was unrepresented at RAF stations or even in Group commands, and indeed it was unable to tell Canadians at home where their sons had been posted. Those early arrivals had become the orphans of the RCAF.

Prime Minister King thought he had got what he wanted out of the negotiations that had established the British Commonwealth Air Training Plan in December 1939. Article 15 of the agreement called for Canadian graduates of the training plan to be organized in RCAF units and formations overseas. Canada understood this to mean that most, if not all, Canadians trained under the plan would be posted to RCAF squadrons in Britain. For politicians in Ottawa, the achievements of those squadrons would be recognized at home and abroad as Canada's glory and the nation's contribution to the war effort, beyond the skill and bravery of its individual airmen. In this war, Canada would not just say "ready, aye, ready" and offer its sons to the mother country. Canada would be an independent member nation of a wartime alliance.

But that is not how Britain's Air Ministry saw it. How and when would these squadrons be formed? How many were really required? Were they to be manned by Canadian airmen only, or also by Canadian ground crews? If the latter, how would these ground crews materialize, as they were already going flat out in Canada to operate the training program? And wouldn't all this entail unnecessary and unaffordable operational and administrative difficulties at that stage of the war? The situation in Europe in the summer of 1940, as training was ramping up in Canada, was definitely not as anticipated in the previous winter when the agreement had been signed. The Air Ministry had never been sympathetic to what it regarded as Canadian political posturing, and by 1941 was even less inclined to indulge it. It saw the training program in Canada as a vital feeder for the RAF, and that would be that. It would be nearly two years before Canadian bomber squadrons were established and unified as a separate operating group. Without them, the RAF saw no obligation and made no effort to keep the Canadian arrivals together. In the meantime, Canada's air force would be a colonial one from Britain's perspective.

Another hard fact that would become evident in the next few months was that many of the new arrivals would not long survive. A week after he arrived, Joe wrote in his diary: "learnt that only 12 of first 30 observers still alive – lot of good men gone…." What Joe heard about the first air observer class was not far from the truth. Thirty-seven of its graduates had disembarked in Britain in late November 1940. They were sent to squadron duty without delay, and many were on operations within days of arrival. Pilot Officer Lawrence Stanley Hill was a promising and highly recommended geology student from Saskatchewan, just graduated from McGill University, who had ranked second in his air observer course. He was posted to a Coastal Command squadron in northern Scotland within days, where he would be the observer in a four-man torpedo bomber crew. On 28 December he was briefed for his first operational assignment – to attack a German tanker off Trondheim, Norway. The Beaufort aircraft took off in the dim mid-winter light of the northern noon, and was last seen near the Shetlands. It never returned. Hill became the first Canadian-trained air observer to be killed in action. Over half of his class would meet the same fate before the end of 1941.

Twelve

England

The newly arrived graduates of the Air Training Program still had much to learn before going into battle. First, they would need to master operating the bombers they would fly over Germany, which were larger, faster, and more complex than the trainers they had flown in Canada. They would have to learn to act together as a crew – the basic unit of battle – while carrying out their individual tasks under duress. They would be drilled in the means of dealing with emergencies in the air and how to abandon their aircraft if need be. They would have to familiarize themselves with European weather and flying conditions, and with the hazards of battle they would encounter over Germany. Their first postings in Britain were to Operational Training Units (OTUs), which would provide the necessary instruction and ensure that what was new would become routine. OTUs served as finishing schools for those qualified to fly in bomber aircraft but not yet to take them into battle.

The Canadian airmen would undertake this next step in a new country, among unfamiliar people, far from the comforts and security of home, and now separated from most of the fellows with whom they had trained in Canada. The confidence, swagger, and sense of entitlement they carried overseas from Canada would be challenged and tested, but would see them through. There would be many grumbles about their new situation in England, but their enthusiasm and resilience would prevail.

Their leaders were neither surprised nor amused by the grumbling, which ranged from their training and treatment in the Royal Air Force, their disconnection from the RCAF, their reception by the civilian population, their living conditions in wartime England, and delays and thefts in overseas mail and parcel service. Both British and Canadian authorities relied on information provided by Britain's wartime postal censorship system to monitor the discipline, morale, and welfare of their fighting men. Shortly after the arrival of the April troop convoy from Halifax, British Air Intelligence began assembling a series of thematic summaries gleaned from the extracts it was receiving of Canadian airmen's mail. It routinely forwarded these summaries, along with individual letter extracts, to RCAF Headquarters in London, where they raised concerns well beyond those of "loose lips sink ships." Air Commodore L. F. Stevenson, air officer commanding the RCAF in Great Britain, told the censorship authorities that the main issue was "the effect on Canadian opinion irrespective of the justness or otherwise of the complaint so please do not hesitate to cut or stop letters wherever it appears to you advisable."

Such complaints, Stevenson added, could undermine both the willingness of Canadians to volunteer, in the absence of conscription, and the morale of servicemen's families at home. He recommended that "the Chief Censor be instructed to delete from the letters of all members of the R.C.A.F. serving overseas any passages which might disturb the minds of people in Canada."[1]

Joe Jacobson was posted to No. 25 Operational Training Unit at RAF Finningley in south Yorkshire, along with four other air observers with whom he had trained in Canada. Finningley, a recent addition to the training system, had taken in its first batch of trainees only two months before. The attendant pattern of cobbling things together and making do was familiar enough to the Canadian arrivals.

The week before, aircrew trainees had been moved out of barracks at the aerodrome to Rossington Hall, the mansion of an enormous estate that the RAF had requisitioned early in the war. The Hall itself, two miles from base, was a three-storey red brick Victorian building, with over twenty bedrooms now jammed full of airmen, several reception rooms, a billiards room, a conservatory, and a grand staircase leading down to the main entrance hall. The grounds included a circular stable, lawns, flower gardens, and several playing fields.

Joe's chief grumbles were about pay and mail. The most obvious consequence of being attached to the RAF occurred on the very first payday. To avoid friction among serving men, the two countries had agreed that Canadians serving in Britain would receive the British rate while there, but the RCAF would top up their salaries to Canadian rates. The difference would accrue in Canada, and could be assigned to a family member or kept in a Canadian bank account. Joe assigned what amounted to $23 each month to his mother. The combination of lower pay, higher taxes, and higher costs was an unpleasant surprise, as Joe complained to the Pony Club:

> we don't get enough money any more to move around as we please – we rake in 15 per week instead of $25 which the boys get back home and everything is expensive – especially liquor which is hard to get here. (JJL 25 May 1941)

Another shock was the weather. Many of the newly arrived Canadians were surprised by the cold and damp, inside and out, and May 1941 was unusually cold in Britain. Joe claimed to have been warmer in Iceland the month before.

Mail from Canada was crucial for the morale of those now far from home, but there were kinks in the delivery system. Airmail service, new that summer on a space-available basis, took at least two weeks. Even cables were subject to long delays. One sent from Montreal on 6 May arrived in Joe's hands on the 27th. Two weeks later he received twelve letters from Canada all at once (including letters sent to him at Debert), and then another bunch of nine. In Montreal, Percy speculated that Joe's letters had "gone down to Davey Jones Locker," while in England the newspapers reported the loss of overseas mail due to enemy action. It appears from Joe's surviving correspondence that most of the letters he wrote home during his first month in England – at least three letters to the Pony Club and another three to his family – never arrived in Canada.[2] Yet once the flow began, few, if any, letters went missing. The eagerly awaited parcels of food, cigarettes, clothing, and magazines from home for the most part arrived more regularly than personal letters.

Joe quickly took a liking to the other Dominion airmen he met, although less so to the English. He told the Pony Club that there were

> half a dozen Canucks on our station – half a dozen New Zealanders – someday we hope to get attached to Canadian & N.Z. bombing squadrons – we miss the old sing songs and rowdyism. The English blokes are okay when you get to know them personally. But English are English and they never go out of their way to get to know you and they are for the most part orderly and quiet – reserved and aloof … all Empire men are tops mentally & physically but take a while to get used to the restrictions and lower standard of living forced on them here … (JJL 25 May 1941).

> Canadians once over here have lots of pride but lack the community spirit of far off N.Z. & Australia. We are all alike though – independent – informal, fair – boisterous – frank. (JJD 29 May 1941)

Sports were the common currency of all those newly arrived young men, who were soon teaching each other their own brands of football, rugby, baseball, and cricket. Sports did much to take the edges off of national differences and build Empire solidarity. He wrote home that he had had

> a great game of football last night with our gang and we practically killed one another with NZ, Cdns, English, Irish and Scotch each trying to show the other how hard he could tackle – since I taught them our game I was at a distinct advantage – I am at least able to crawl around … give me a few good pals a bit of space to run around in – a few fellows to run around with and I don't kick too much.
> (JJL 10 June 1941)

Half an hour north of Finningley by bus lay Doncaster, a grim coal-mining and industrial city. Its blandishments – pubs, dance halls, music halls, cinemas, and dog tracks – held little appeal for Joe, and he found its inhabitants inhospitable, unfriendly, and tight-fisted. Nor was he attracted to its women who, he told the Pony Club, were a "poor calibre of babes," not classy enough for his tastes. Jack McIntyre, one of Joe's Canadian pals at Finningley, wrote home:

> I've been in England for eight weeks now, and as yet I've never been inside the door of an English house. I've been in hotels and stores, but never has anyone even asked me up for tea. They don't know what hospitality means.[3]

Yet Joe enjoyed the South Yorkshire countryside and villages. So in his usual way, he surrounded himself with an expanding circle of new friends and old, who explored the pubs of Doncaster and nearby rural villages on Saturday nights or when flying was washed out. The village pubs were novel venues for Canadians, the easy camaraderie, cozy atmosphere, and relaxed liquor laws quite unlike the beer parlours at home. Joe, Jack, and the other Canadians soon encountered intriguing characters, from ex-convicts to ex-prizefighters.

> Spent the night getting roary eyed with McIntyre – hit on the Smiths at the Greyhound Pub – gave us cigars – sandwiches – they had been to Canada & were as drunk as we were – good sing song in the Black

> Bull – had Tuffy – a DFM Gunner with us & we pulled down a few signs before leaving – (JJD 30 May 1941)

> Supping in the Mount Pleasant hotel – Gt. N. Road Doncaster – pleasant, peaceful, calm – air fresh – hard to realize we are besieged with our backs to the wall. Had a good meal in a quiet English roadside hotel – our Canada badges got us extra pie & a package of cigarettes which are scarce now – you can still get a fair meal here. (JJD 4 June 1941)

> Our station compared with others rates well – we get along fine with everybody … enjoy ourselves – lovely walking thru winding country lanes near here – (JJD 7 June 1941)

> Went for a long bike ride over peaceful English countryside with Roger Rousseau. It was quiet & we chatted long & pleasantly – decided to quit binges – to get back into 1st class shape – started by doing exercises at 12:30 AM. (JJD 16 June 1941)

> Had a sing song in Doncaster with Dave Davis – a Welsh pal who is a real good head – I seem to have lots of luck with my pals –
> (JJD 30 June 1941)

> Had a real good binge with Dick Davis my Welsh pal – we both like each other's company better than any of the fluzies around here – so we down a few pints & knock the town silly with our raucous singing – … – Dave is in my inner circle.[4] (JJD 9 July 1941)

◉

Life at Rossington Hall was turning out to be another summer camp experience for Joe, rather like Initial Training School the year before. He kept in touch by mail with many of his RCAF friends now elsewhere in Britain, and in June he and Jack McIntyre visited their friends at No. 16 OTU in Oxfordshire on a weekend leave.

> 3 AM – resting & eating in a roadhouse with Jack McIntyre & a couple of truck drivers. Arrived in London 5 AM – slept a couple of hours at the Union Jack Club – took the train to Oxford & hitched to Upper Heyford. G.P. was fine – had a jump from 200 [feet] in which the other jumper was killed – cracked up again yesterday and was nearly burnt alive – Hunter fine – got really stinko – the boys don't like their station – I guess we are well off. (JJD 7 June 1941)

After seeing them again in June, Joe wrote to his family:

> I have managed to see many of my old pals of late – we feel badly that the RCAF has been immersed into the RAF – for the time being we have lost our identity. I believe they are starting some squadrons in the near future – so you should have something to cheer about soon.
> (JJL 14 July 1941)[5]

In early June, Joe learned that Monty had enlisted to train as a radio mechanic. Joe immediately dashed off an impassioned riposte to him while eating egg and chips in a truckers' café in the wee hours of the morning, en route to Upper Heyford.

> It is urgent – essential and vital to you that you weigh my words carefully and act quickly.
>
> I congratulated you on joining up – but of all the goddamn silly things to get tied up in – the new radio mechanics course is the worst *for you* I have been thru the ropes to a certain extent – I know what I am talking about – Here's why you must immediately apply for air crew –
>
> *Firstly:* anybody who has not got a wing up is shat on from a great height in Canada – here – anywhere – you will rise no higher than the rank of LAC[6] – you will be treated as scruff – cattle – and nobodies – you just don't rate – your job is important sure – but it's a technical line – we came over in the boat with radio mechanics – we slept in cabins – they slept in the hole and peeled potatoes – we were the untouchables – they took a beating for the gang – many of them were skilled operators before the war.
>
> *Secondly* – advancement – very few of you will get commissions – you don't rise from the ranks in your line – LAC is your top – \$1.50 per day your max pay – as pilot or observer you will get \$3.70 per day within four months. Not only that – Mub you will definitely lead your class – I told you before, everything we did was down your alley – you will get a commission after six months – there is not the slightest doubt … I know how officers are selected – you are officer material – your marks will be tops – your work tops –
>
> *Thirdly – Prestige* – There is only one thing that rates here – a wing up – officers – captains – colonels take their hats off to us – we do as we please on a station – we get one week's leave every three months – plenty of weekends and thus ample opportunity to get around the

> country – see things – meet people – you will get one week per year – will be stepped on at every turn – be made to feel little better than a stooge – sucker etc.…
>
> *Fourthly – Adventure* – you won't get any as a radio mechanic – you will be stuck on a station – probably never see a raid … you will be cut off from most activity – as a writer you should experience raids from both sides – think of the advantage you will have over your contemporaries if you have flown over Germany – if you can explain how the airmen feel – everybody knows what a blitz feels like – few know what it is like to blitz and be blitzed in the air – I will guarantee you more story material in one trip over Berlin than you will get in a week on the ground – this is your big chance Mub – as a ground radio mechanic – you will not only be disillusioned – stepped on and feel out of it – you will be passing up the big chance of a life time –
>
> *Fifthly* – I'll bet your gang won't be over here before Christmas – you would be over next spring if you got into aircrew immediately – Don't let an extra few months influence you. By the time you can get here I will either have finished my operational flights or they will have finished me –
>
> I hope I have driven home my point Monty – you are too good a man to waste in a purely technical line – you have too much talent – ability – dash – take it from me – *ability* is rewarded in our line – a guy has to have his operational trips before we think anything of him – we are treated as highly intelligent – skilled and responsible men – it's fun – it's adventurous it's vital. You get results and personal satisfaction.…
>
> *Immediately* apply for pilot or observer – you would make a marvelous observer and would really love the work – pilot is the same – suit yourself – use all pull, connection available – don't let them stall you off – they will try – but get into aircrew at once –
>
> They need every pilot and observer they can get hold of and then some – *Don't* get stuck as a wireless air gunner. (JJL 6 June 1941)

Neither offended nor deterred, and already in radio training at the McGill detachment of the RCAF in Montreal, Monty resumed the old debate.

> About my course – it is terrific, it is hard & I am certain it offers all kinds of scope even though commissions may be scarce in the end. We learn in 13 weeks of radio physics more than several years of university

> work would give. Of course, our work is highly concentrated but when we're through we are supposedly masters of the latest knowledge in radio plus a key invention … which will definitely blast night raiders from the skies – and that is why our work is so vital, the speed is so fast and why I feel that there is possibly even more in it than in the air crew. After some practical experience at an air base in England, we will be highly skilled men of extreme value.
>
> But realize what it means to me. In 13 weeks, a thorough student of the liberal arts has opened for him a completely new world, the world of science – and science to the ultra-modern degree. Naturally, I can't go into any further details – nor does anybody know anything much about it[7] – but I can say I am tremendously hepped up about it for it is a far better course and much more interesting than I had ever expected….
>
> One of my prime motives for taking [the course] … was because we were fed up with the Army and this offered what every man wants when he finds himself going into service – speed and action…. I know radio mech lacks the glamour of air crew but the work is what counts – you have to have matriculation for this course while air crew is now down to ninth year – 2nd year High. But the chief thing is that this is something new and I'm in on the ground floor – with a few thousand others. (10 June 1941)

If Joe disagreed with Monty's course of action, he respected it. He didn't doubt Monty's courage or commitment, but he believed Monty could have done better for himself, at least in terms of status and prestige, so important to Joe. He was less sure about the rest of the Pony Club.

> Still reading mail from home – Pony Club not doing its part. Mub like me realizes the game that's up and is willing to make sacrifices although he is cautious enough to keep on the ground – Gerald tried – still hanging on – reluctant to leave what he thinks is life – Herby hopeless – disgusting the way our boys hang on to what they have longer than they should. (JJD 4 July 1941)
>
> Rec'd Pony Club mail – Monty is only alive member left – he made up his mind slowly – but he knows what he is doing & he is a real man – will be a prominent leader some day – Smitty lacks the necessary spark for accomplishment – Herby gets along alright – both fail to realize that there are more worthwhile things in life than just living.
> (JJD 23 July 1941)

Three months after leaving Canada, Joe's ties to the Pony Club were loosening. He continued to correspond with Monty personally, but otherwise wrote the Pony Club collectively and relied on Monty to circulate his letters to Gerald and Herb. What mattered more now were his comrades in arms, those with whom he had bonded in unity of purpose and action.

A month into his operational training, grumbles more or less forgotten, Joe was more than ever convinced of the rightness of his chosen course of action, and recorded that he had "no desire to return [to Canada] without finishing this job."

> Had a good bull session with a couple of operational gunners – the easy days are over, night fighters & ak ak are really bowling our planes over[8] – no more easy trip – I'll be pretty lucky to go thru 200 hrs. (JJD 18 June 1941)

> I wish Peter was still alive – he would be over here with me – there's a kid that was slated to be a top notcher. I will have to just be twice as good. (JJD 3 July 1941)

> Letters from home help keep my feet on the ground – life is pretty uncertain in the air force during war time and I feel that my life is but an average gesture to stand up for our principles, protect our families, our freedom. Naturally it is hard on them – but when I read those letters I feel it is worth it that I am lucky to be able to do what I am doing. (JJD 5 July 1941)

> Being left alone these past few days has allowed me to do some serious thinking about our world – destiny – life – future, etc. & my own position in it – firstly – the war – has made people realize that part of their labour – money – effort or brains has to be available to the nation for the common security of all – you can't be a pacifist – isolationist or anything else – we all have to pull together – all have to safeguard our rights & liberties. (JJD 19 July 1941)

> In letters from home Mom always says "don't change dear" – fortunately for me I am changing – I hope for the better – I still take a humorous outlook on life – but I now realize I have a responsibility to my country – people – family – because that responsibility involves danger – makes it all the more worth carrying out – a long life is no longer my objective – rather – a worthwhile one. (JJD 22 July 1941)

Thirteen

Operational Training

No. 25 Operational Training Unit had initially been charged with turning out twelve battle-ready crews every four weeks. Each course would provide additional ground schooling but most of all flying time, ideally about eighty hours, over a span of eight weeks. No. 25 OTU was one of two main units that provided training on Hampden bombers, the other being No. 16 OTU near Oxford, to which at least ten of Joe's classmates were posted.

By the spring of 1941, there were sixteen OTUs across Britain, training over a thousand men at any one time, and they were struggling to meet the demands on them. Completing a course in eight weeks required moderately co-operative weather conditions and enough serviceable aircraft on hand. Neither condition prevailed. Unusually heavy snowfalls during the late winter had closed down their grass airstrips for days at a time, and training was falling behind. Bomber Command, desperate to expand its striking force, was forming new squadrons for operations over Europe, even as some existing ones were being sent to the Middle East. The Command was increasing squadron size from sixteen to twenty-four aircraft, and supplying a select few squadrons with new four-engine bombers that required larger crews and more training. By the end of 1941, training on these new aircraft would be done at separately established Heavy Conversion Units, but in the meantime, it fell to squadrons and OTUs to undertake this task, alongside their regular operational and training responsibilities.

In addition to the needs of expansion, Bomber Command was pressing fresh crews into service to replace those killed in action. The arrival of thousands of newly trained airmen from Canada that spring, welcome as it was, further overstretched OTUs, which were by then gearing up to take in pupils every two weeks instead of four. Yet there were limits on how many aircraft Bomber Command could allocate to training units and still meet its own operational needs. The only way to increase output was to lower training standards, and that was the stark choice Bomber Command had to make. So, many courses were shortened that summer, with inevitable consequences.

Ideally, OTUs were supposed to turn out complete bomber crews that, having trained to the standard of a combat-ready unit, could be assigned as such to an operational squadron. That objective soon had to be scrapped for the time being. Having to muddle through bottlenecks and disruptions made it impossible to keep crews together for the full course, and even the shortened courses took longer to complete than intended.

With more and more aircraft flying about, the need for air traffic control and radio aids at each aerodrome became acute. Nearly fifteen hundred aircraft were written off or badly damaged due to airfield accidents and blind-approach training. Sneak attacks on aerodromes by German fighter aircraft occurred frequently that summer, causing damage and disruption, although few injuries or deaths. But these nuisance raids were overshadowed by what was feared to be a much greater danger. Germany's successful airborne assault on Crete in May gave rise to fears of a similar large-scale surprise attack on England's aerodromes. Bomber Command directed all station commanders to train and organize all staff for the defence of their stations, to ensure that every man had a weapon and be trained and prepared to use it, and to conduct regular drills for the purpose.

> The disastrous consequences of a German success in their initial onslaught must be clearly appreciated by every man in R.A.F. uniform, and he must understand that the attack can only be frustrated if he is determined to use every possible means of resisting it, and is prepared to die in the defence of his station.[1]

Although this threat never materialized, it placed an additional burden on both training and operational stations.

By war's outbreak, it had become clear that two crucial tasks could no longer be left to the pilot. One was navigation, the other was bomb-aiming. Solving this problem posed a particular problem for the Hampden bombers on which Joe Jacobson would train and fight. Unlike the larger five-man Wellingtons and Whitleys, the Hampden was configured for a crew of only four. Their stations consisted of a cockpit midway along the top of the narrow fuselage, a clear Perspex nose cone at the front, and two turrets above and below at the rear of the fuselage. So the problem of navigation and bomb-aiming in the Hampden was not only who should carry out these duties, but where in the aircraft he should do so. At the same time, Bomber Command was trying to figure out exactly what duties should be assigned to the newly revived trade of air observer, and how men should be trained for them. Several months into the war, Bomber Command was still sorting out how to crew a bomber that was now part of its main force.

When the war began, Hampden crews consisted of two pilots – a first pilot who was the captain of the aircraft, and a second pilot who was his understudy – and two wireless operators/air gunners (WO/AGs). The newly designated position of air observer was expected to be filled by someone already qualified as a wireless operator and air gunner, who would need some extra training in navigation and bomb-aiming. The pilot's cockpit provided no space to perform the paperwork involved in log-keeping and map-reading required for night navigation, even if he had the time for it along with his flying duties.

Several ideas were floated about who should sit where and do what in this configuration, some of which involved crew members changing places at various points in flight. The commander of the Hampden force (then Air Vice Marshal Arthur Harris, who would later become commander-in-chief of Bomber Command) put his foot down and insisted that two of the four crew positions were non-negotiable. The pilot, he said, must always be in the cockpit, and the WO/AG must always be in the upper rear turret, where the radio set was located. The lower rear turret was fit only for an air gunner who, facing backwards, could not possibly navigate, let alone aim bombs. So whoever was going to act as navigator and bomb-aimer had to sit in the nose cone, facing forward, where he could also man the front gun.

With only four positions in the aircraft, Bomber Command initially elected to dispense with air observers and assign responsibility for their duties to second pilots. The disadvantage of this solution was that, separated eight feet away by a narrow passageway down a ramp underneath the pilot's seat, the second pilot could do little else because it was a difficult and dangerous manoeuvre to crawl back and replace his captain in an emergency. Moreover, this separation meant that the first pilot was in no position to provide effective instruction to his second, who needed operational experience to eventually take on the duties of captain. It was an inelegant solution, "an attempt to make the best of a bad job," to a problem that Harris asserted had been foisted on him because Bomber Command had accepted the Hampden into service despite its manufacturer having ignored "almost every conceivable requirement ... in disregard of specifications."[2] The training problem was to be solved by providing second pilots with basic instruction in navigation and bombing.

Operational experience during 1940 made it evident that properly qualified air observers would be required to navigate each aircraft to its destination and to bomb the target, so it was decided to replace Hampden second pilots with air observers and to reinstate air observer training for Hampden service. This was an important reason why, during 1941, Hampden training units and squadrons came to rely so heavily on Canadian air observers, who were by then arriving in great numbers. The now displaced second pilots were taken on as first pilots as the force expanded and were given their own crews. But the newly installed observers were not given flying training, and so there was no one in the aircraft capable of taking control in an emergency even if, with great difficulty, he could manage to gain access to the pilot's seat. This decision would have important consequences for Hampden crews, as Joe and others would eventually discover.

The Canadian-trained air observers were better qualified in astro-navigation than those trained in Britain, but their map-reading skills soon proved deficient. The English landscape looked nothing like Canada's. In place of the vast landscapes marked by the regular grid pattern of farms, and the long, straight stretches of railways and roads that separated isolated prairie towns, England from the air appeared as a hodge-podge of tiny fields surrounding a multitude of towns and villages, connected by roads and railways winding everywhere. Canada had few aerodromes; Britain had many, none easily distinguished from another. The rivers and lakes so visible in the open prairie were largely absent in England. There, farmland was drained by roadside ditches running into small, tree-shaded streams and ponds that seldom revealed even a glint of reflected sunlight, let alone moonlight. Only fragments of England's landscape could be glimpsed through the clouds that frequently obscured it. At night, all signs of human habitation and activity were blacked out. Reading the countryside from the air was far more challenging than in Canada. Supplementary map-reading courses had to be laid on for Canadian-trained air observers.

For the Canadians, much of both air and ground training in the first four weeks amounted to little more than a brush-up on skills that had lapsed since graduating from Rivers, although they were flying in the much larger bombers that were in actual operational use, with their full array of up-to-date equipment. Flying training included the use of radio direction finding to determine bearings and to locate aerodromes, and the use of aerial cameras. In the second half of the course, pupils would learn to operate together as a functioning Hampden crew.

Joe was thrilled to be back in the air after nearly three months since leaving Rivers.

> Took my first flight in a Wellington today – felt good to get at it again – England looks wonderful from the air – like a quilt of lovely blended colours – all patches being trim & neat. (JJD 13 May 1941)

> The boys here from operations sure take things calmly – this is a marvelous training for thinking fast & accurately under fire – I need it … (JJD 16 May 1941)

He wrote to the Pony Club about life on a flying station:

> I have been flying on Wellingtons, later we go on to Hampdens and Manchesters – all tremendous machines and about the biggest bombers here. We fly with staff pilots for a while, all boys who have finished their 200 hours on operations and consequently all DFMs & DFCs[3] – we fly all over the place and keep on our toes – the obstacles – balloons – our AAK[4] – our fighters and at night – the odd Jerry. Next week we start flying with our own crews … have our own ship and own ground staff … best of all, I shall have a chance to get some piloting in myself[5] – but we still have another six weeks training before we go on operations if all goes well – but night training flights are about the same as operations – well almost – so there is lots of excitement when we fly –

> … we are pretty well occupied now either at lectures or flying – flying is definitely the nuts – navigating is definitely a headache at times, especially in dirty weather and at night – which is when we do all our work now … here at RAF Finningley active service conditions prevail and the thing I like about flying is that every plane is on its own – you get briefed and given all available data, etc. – climb aboard and shoulder the responsibility of getting to the target – bombing is the objective and getting home again … our new flying outfits are super … we are lucky to be given superior equipment to fight the b_____ds with. (JJL 25 May 1941)

In fact, Joe had not done as much flying as he'd hoped. He had managed to get six daytime flights for dead reckoning practice, but then flying was

106 Squadron Hampden at RAF Finningley, April 1940. (Metheringham Airfield Visitor Centre)

Crew exiting a Hampden bomber (83 Squadron, October 1940). The pilot is exiting the cockpit, the air observer, with his equipment satchel, is on the wing root, and the air gunner is coming up from under the wing, having left the lower turret. The wireless operator's twin guns point skyward from the upper turret. (Imperial War Museum, HU104657)

Hampden bombers in flight over the patchwork quilt of the English landscape. (Laurier Centre for Military Strategic and Disarmament Studies)

scrubbed six nights in a row in late May due to bad weather. In theory, he needed to get another sixty-five hours of flying time. He did two night-navigation flights before the end of May, and also started practising on a new bombsight. Not all of this went well, as he acknowledged that he was "blowing hot and cold" in his navigation. One night he had done "a sloppy job of navigation," but the next night had "a bang on flight."

By the end of May, Joe had completed the navigation portion of the course, and he had begun night flying on Hampdens. He was becoming attuned to a constant and substantial level of hazard both in the air and on the ground. German intruder aircraft had attacked Joe's base in early May while he was on leave, and there had been two flying accidents with the loss of seven men. None of this dampened his enthusiasm for the job.

> Got crewed up with Toby Jones a N.Z pilot who asked me to navigate for him – he is an athlete, a good head & we ought to get along fine – also picked a couple of likely looking gunners. (JJD 20 May 1941)

> I think my pilot is going to be an ace … our two English gunners and myself pal around together quite a bit – My pilot is a star athlete – a real cool head and so the new gang has sprouted. (JJL 10 June 1941)

Crewing up was essential to learning to work as a team on big bombers, but it was not proceeding smoothly at No. 25 OTU at that point. Joe did not actually get to fly with Jones until the beginning of June, and then only once. His new pilot had developed boils and been sent to hospital. Without him, and apparently with few pilots to spare at Finningley, there was little flying for the rest of his crew. A promising start had ground to a halt. Joe went eight days without flying in early June, and then he was assigned to another pilot to begin bombing practice.

Whether a crew was self-selected (as Joe's appears to have been) or assigned, how well they would actually function together was difficult to predict. They did not know each other's grades or standing in trades training, other than if they were good enough to merit a commission. But such clues were not necessarily a reliable guide to performance in the air under duress. Nor could they know much about each other's psychological makeup, or perhaps even their own – whether one could master one's fear and maintain calm would become evident only under the stress and chaos of actual operations. But how well a crew would bond, and so perform as an effective combat unit over time, was critical to success. Each man depended on the others. The distinctions between officers and men, strictly observed on the ground, vanished in the air. During the second week of June, Joe began bombing practice over the nearby Misson bombing range. This began with low-level target practice by day, with twenty-five-pound bombs, then high-level practice, including a night session. Each time up was with a different pilot, in Jones's absence.

Joe was enthralled by operational training, but it did not go as smoothly or quickly as he first hoped. Nearly two weeks passed with only one flight, which Joe described as a "wonderful day – bombed all morning trying to get ABS down pat."

The ABS was the automatic bombsight, an improvement on the course setting bombsight that Joe had trained on at Mossbank. The ABS, now the standard bombsight on the Hampden, simplified the bomb-aimer's work by enabling him to dial information on airspeed, altitude, wind, and bomb characteristics into an electro-mechanical computer on the run-up to the target, in order to maintain the correct track of the aircraft and determine the precise moment of release.

After seven weeks, Joe had put in six hours of nighttime navigation practice and one session of nighttime bombing practice. Joe found the inactivity demoralizing:

> Beautiful day spent sunning – this is an unproductive O.T.U. waste plenty of time – we now have the English grumbling about the slow-

ness. The mixing of different country's fighting forces in Eng. should put an end to English smugness – we all tell lovely stories about our homes & life there and the RAF boys want to see for themselves.

… I am worried at heart – the war effort is all out of gear. I am working with the finest men in the world – but too much of our effort is wasted by too many incompetents & too little drive – things are slack – easy going – as if we had shot our bolt – I hope we wake up. (JJD 21 June 1941)

Shooting the bull in the crew room with Toby Jones – Bill Fulton – Jack McIntyre, Knowles – Stn had quite a night & all kind of shaky[6] – most of our air[craft] are unserviceable – we do nothing most every day – take things leisurely still.… I will never get on ops if this keeps up – many fellows kind of get shaky about going on them – the sooner I can be of service the sooner I will be satisfied – one whole year in the air force & I have not earned my keep as yet. (JJD 28 June 1941)

Are we going to win the war – moan no 2 on this score – maybe. But boy am I fed up doing nothing – so is Bill Fulton & all the other boys – plenty of incompetence in the forces – no one willing to take the responsibility for any decisions. Put in the first honest day's work during the afternoon – went up three times – Toby should be a real good pilot – had a great time firing over Wash.[7] (JJD 29 June 1941)

Am watching course three pack out at the moment – six crews – there will be about three left in a couple of months' time – but we are fighting for something greater than ourselves – (JJD 30 June 1941)

Had our first cross country as a crew – Toby will be a good pilot – too independent & quick tempered at times but he knows what he is doing – Reg & Ron our gunners are not worth much – I am still too careless with my navigation – but I always seem to work & act better in the air. (JJD 1 July 1941)

A Spitfire's unexpected detour at Finningley in mid-June reminded Joe of his "one disappointment" – that he didn't get a crack at fighter piloting – but not for long. He was by now completely immersed in his role as navigator and bomber. By the end of the month his crew was back together again to complete their bombing and gunnery practice. Finally they were ready to begin the last part of their operational training: long-distance raid exercises over Britain and the North Sea. The weather was excellent in early July, and Joe was happy to have put in nineteen hours of flying time in eight days. In early July he recorded a "beautiful six hour cross country trip to the Bristol

Channel bombing – gun firing – picture snapping" in nice weather by day, a "marvellous life." The next day he wrote to the Pony Club:

> we have a six hour trip scheduled and I must get cracking – here's an example of what an observer does on a trip – 1. navigates, 2. handles the photography – takes pictures of all bomb bursts – and anything of importance on the way[8] – 3. does all the bombing 4. handles a gun in the plane I fly in – we do plenty of shooting – 5. Make up meteorological reports – reconnaissance reports, and keep a log – we really are kept hopping – and that takes place whilst [Messerschmitt] fighter planes are trying to shoot you down – anti-aircraft fire absolutely knocking the plane upside down or the weather so rough at times you can hardly write – yes sir we really are on our toes when flying. (JJL 7 July 1941)

To Joe's disappointment, after he was briefed, and the aircraft bombed up and ready for a long daylight cross-country training raid, one engine cut out on takeoff and the flight was cancelled. Then Toby Jones was hospitalized again, and Joe was grounded for ten days. In the meantime, most of his pals were completing their training and moving on.

> Jack McIntyre & myself had a farewell party of canned peaches & cigars – he is going on ops tomorrow[9] – we sat around & shot the bull on our crews – friends etc. (JJD 10 July 1941)

> Waiting to go on a long North Sea sweep with some conversion pilots on their last flight – I spoke to Sqd Ldr Beauchamp today – trying to get put on operations faster – I feel it is about time I started earning my pay & doing something – 13 months in uniform without striking a blow – about time I swung into action. (JJD 16 July 1941)

Joe expounded on these developments to a new female friend:

> If there is one thing I admire about the English it is their total mastery of the art of disorganization.
>
> I have been hanging around all week for my pilot who is still in the hospital. I need but one trip to complete the course. There are a half a dozen other observers here who, like me need but one or two trips. There are also over a dozen pilots hanging around with nothing to do. They are either staff pilots or waiting for reports on recent crackups of a minor nature. It seems to be too complicated to pair up odd observers and pilots. You start with a pilot here and come hell or high water

> you don't get another one if something happens to yours, despite the fact that a dozen young pilots are just about going crazy doing nothing.
>
> Well I now have another pilot which I got after numerous conferences. We will make a few trips together and then I hope we will get cracking on some worthwhile trips.
>
> But it really amazes me the way they do things. Honestly, at least ten out of every hundred get pushed around so much that when and if they do get on operations, they are so wild they get knocked off on the first trip. That is especially true with the Colonials who are anxious to get going – but it is a real feat to get thru the various courses, arrangements and round about schemes concocted here – intact.
>
> Fortunately, Roger is in the same boat as me. All my other pals have gone from this station. So we drown our sorrows together and hope for the day when somebody with a spot of dash – a nip of ginger – a sprinkling of intelligence and plenty of imagination gets hold of this country and starts things rolling. (JJL 18 July 1941)

And so the frustration continued. Flying was cancelled two nights in a row due to enemy action near the airfield.

> Weather cold – existence lonely unsatisfactory & uneconomical – still waiting to make two more trips – I feel as far away from ops as I did in Iceland – (JJD 20 July 1941)

Roger Rousseau was by this time Joe's only Canadian classmate still at Finningley. He too had been delayed in completing his training there by virtue of minor accidents. Joe and Roger, already good friends since training, would become even closer in the months ahead.

⊙

One in ten wartime deaths in Bomber Command occurred in training. England's skies were crowded and most hazards occurred in flight: malfunctioning aircraft, pilot and navigator error, and even "friendly fire" from RAF fighters and anti-aircraft gunners that failed to recognize their own aircraft, especially at night. During Joe's time at Finningley, there had been four fatal incidents with twelve men killed, six non-fatal accidents, and four intruder attacks. Joe was well aware that operational training was a dangerous business, but he confined the details to his diary.

> Met Mackenzie from [Leuchars] – on Beauforts – suicide jobs – they get really down at the mouth … Hampden crashed taking off yesterday – 3 killed. (JJD 17 May 1941)
>
> Lost our second kite in three days – 7 men gone. (JJD 19 May 1941)
>
> Got some figures on casualties – probably thirty per cent of aircrew get thru their 200 hrs ops – alive – they get the D.F.M. & deserve it. (JJD 20 May 1941)
>
> Sgt Cooper killed[10] … total 18 since arriving here – bad show – strange to see a pal go up – never come back – fellows in air force are what I consider cool skillful – brave men – nobody makes a fuss about the living or dead – & nobody worries about the category he is going to be in – we just do our best & enjoy doing it. (JJD 12 June 1941)
>
> Had a bull sesson with Morris, Tuffy & Bert White – they get "browned off" "cheesed" as they say on ops – O.T.U. flying as dangerous as ops – Jerries are held with respect amongst boys here – night bombing seems to be quite a strain & boys get nervy after a spell – the bloody Huns haven't scared me as yet. (JJD 13 June 1941)
>
> Rec'd letters from Jeep & Art – Jeep had his 4th crackup – Charlie Davis killed – Grange seriously hurt – 16 planes smashed at suicide Heyford – boys shaky there & for a good reason.[11] (JJD 26 June 1941)
>
> Went to Doncaster with Roger – met Milward who told me Mitchell "had it"[12] – strange how affected I used to be by the death of someone I knew – how remote & impossible it seemed from me – now the thought of dying neither scares nor worries me – I can now face anything without panicking. (JJD 18 July 1941)
>
> Pop Miller's had it.[13] (JJD 24 July 1941)

Of all this, Joe told the Pony Club:

> The intimacy amongst groups of friends is exactly trebled amongst aircrew friends. Every reunion is a last reunion. No one says so – no one worries about who it is going to be the last one for – but all make a night of it – it is the same on our station – no petty rules or regulations or worries. You can almost say we are pampered. When we get up – we get briefed for a flight that cost around $10,000 think nothing of the expense – climb aboard with provisions for when you get hungry – and

> you're off – it's a great life – thrilling – adventuresome and inconsistent – that's what makes it all the more exciting to me – you can't predict or plan – you must improvise and who does that better than your loyal Poneyite. (JJL 7 July 1941)

He said less of the hazards to his family:

> A recent check-up of my pals shows that all are still going strong and faring well – Roger Rousseau who is with me is running Jeep a close race to see who can walk away from the most crashes – Roger has now had three – one less than Jeep – but he completely wiped out a couple of his planes so it's a pretty close race. (JJL 22 July 1941)

But of his work he told them:

> flying renders more chance for quick thinking and acting, careful preparation and excitement than I have ever had before. But you soon assess the dangers, obstacles, and your own chances of meeting them and overcoming them. Once you get that clear in your head you can get a real kick out of it all.... I like action – I'm getting it. So I would not worry too much if I were you – I am having a lot of fun, leading a unique and thrilling life and getting more personal satisfaction out of my work than I ever got before – I am on heavy bombers going over Germany. Every bomb I drop is a bomb well placed. But best of all is being with the nation's finest men, young and old. Their ability, courage and personalities, absolutely make it impossible for me to get "browned off." As a group, I have met no finer men anywhere. I do not think there are many finer to meet. Their records tell the tale. Maybe someday I will be able to read you my special diary dealing with operational flights.[14] (JJL 17 June 1941)

> We are going on a long cross country raid by daylight today and I am flying again tonight … Since my second trip to Hale … I have been doing little besides flying. The weather has been marvelous of late and I have flown over most of England.

> … After getting briefed, bombed up and ready for the trip – one of our engines cut while taking off so the raid had to be cancelled for our crew.

> … I am really having the time of my young life. Imagine having a huge $200,000 plane at my disposal – filled with a camera – bombs, guns, radio – office for me, expensive and precise instruments – and best of

> all – nine hours fuel. We have our own crew, four of us, and have flown over every part of England and Wales. Next we tackle the continent. I know more about the different parts of this country than most Englishmen – the continent – France, Germany, Holland is also coming in for close scrutiny before long. Yes sir its loads of fun – keen satisfaction, plenty of excitement and activity. Of course night flying is a bit less comfortable – a little more strenuous and tiring. I find it hard to keep awake – however, there is usually a bit of noise and lighting effect to help – and so goes the flying. (JJL 7 July 1941)

Percy caught Joe's mood in his diary:

> He wrote his letter in one of the beautiful spots of English country … he mentions the peace and quiet and I think there is a certain wistful quality about the letter which I have not noticed before in any of letters. Most of his letters are quite boisterous bubbling over with life and fun. In this letter he [is] evidently eager to assure us how happy he is and has been and what a lot he has managed to get out of life. I felt that he was aware of the possible shortness of his life and wanted us to feel if anything God forbid should happen that he has nothing to regret. That is the impression I got … I don't know whether his mother had the same idea … but she was quiet all day … (PJD 1 July 1941)

Fourteen

A Canadian's Estimate of England

For the newly arrived Canadian airmen, the Blitz was but the most obvious sign of Britain's peril. Dismal war news headlined the papers nearly every day in May, as it had in April when the Wehrmacht overran Yugoslavia and Greece in a few weeks. Germany gained a foothold in Syria, courtesy of Vichy France, while Rommel's troops advanced toward Egypt, creating a pincer that threatened the Suez Canal and Britain's access to the East. HMS *Hood*, the Royal Navy's great battle cruiser that Joe had seen at anchor in Reykjavik only four weeks earlier, was sunk in an eight-minute naval battle, with virtually all hands lost. Meanwhile, U-boats were sinking merchant ships in the North Atlantic faster than they could be replaced. The most shocking news was Germany's airborne invasion of Crete, and the rout of the Empire troops defending it. That an island of such size could fall to enemy paratroopers while Britain still controlled its sea lanes reignited fears of a German invasion of the homeland.

Joe summarized how he saw the war's progress to the Pony Club.

> As things move rapidly in other parts of the world – a strange quiet has prevailed here in England – the result has been that you almost forget that there is anything going on – our complete mastery of the air during daylight makes it seem impossible that we are on a besieged island. During a blitz though your views change.

> Churchill … keeps them going. People feel he is fair, tolerant, honest, imaginative – when he speaks he gives them the news good or bad…. The British are not a mechanized race – the Americans are – this kind of war is right down the Americans' alley – *First* of all superior *production* – the Germans beat the British at it – the Americans beat the Germans. *Secondly* superior products – the British win hands down – U.S. – second – our planes top anything the U.S. produce – the boys don't like flying U.S. kites outside of the Lockheed Hudson – our planes often come back on one engine – completely shot up and stand up to terrific beatings – the new Spitfire is top fighter plane in the world today. *Thirdly* – organization – Germany has us both licked – *Fourthly* – imagination – that's where we bog down – it's a toss up between the U.S. & Germany – *Finally* stamina – you can't beat the British there – However, I still stick to the new world – too much formality – still too much class distinction here, and above all – the English are interested only in themselves – they know nothing about other people or countries and care less – they are truly amazing people. Half the time you curse them – the rest of the time you curse yourself for being so stupid – especially during a blitz or a crisis when everybody from the poorest up – takes everything in stride – most people from any other country would be in the bug house if the worries, problem, and tragedies that beset them here occurred to them.
>
> … it is tommy rot for the British to claim that the U.S. should fight to shorten the war – they haven't a chance here without practical U.S. aid and they know it – and the good old U.S. knows what they are in for if Germany wins – the sooner each ally gets straightened out on the score, the sooner their heads will come together and then things will start humming – (JJL 25 May 1941)

Penned little more than three weeks after his arrival, Joe's letter already identified some key themes he would return to many times in his correspondence over the next few months: the national characteristics of the combatants as these might affect the war's outcome, the need for the United States to throw its full weight behind Britain, and the dead weight of the class system in England. In early June, he wrote to his family about his confidence in Britain's eventual victory:

> based on what they have done and most important of all – what they are capable of doing. The defeat at Dunkirk cut about three fifths of the misfits, defeatists, boneheads, etc. from leading positions in the country, thus enabling the true ability of the country to burst forth and

> prove itself in many ways. The defeat at Crete, I believe, cut another fifth off the narrow-minded dead weight from responsible positions – and it is well that this has come about before it is too late – as it is a nip and tuck struggle for us to keep our heads above water for the time being. The main difficulty in England is to make room for some of the originality, daring, and dash that the Americans and Germans show. On the other hand there is a sturdiness and quality about Britishers that enables them to stand up to more than most people can. But quality alone is not enough. You have to think and act fast – change your methods and not only meet all novel attacks but conceive of new ones yourself – admittedly they are often a bit slow here – but they are sensible enough to thrash out weaknesses without getting panicky and in the light of constructive criticism and practical experience learn and act on the basis of it.
>
> … This is a real battle between free people and slaves. We absolutely have to prove that our system is superior to any shown so far. Those who want to can talk about their isms – I'll take my democracy and I'll fight for it – England is proving today that democracy is workable – I feel confident that the challenges of the future will eventually be dealt with with increasing success. At least we know and understand what we are up against – we feel the job can and will be done and *is* being done. (JJL 10 June 1941)

Yet as the bad news continued, Joe's confidence was tempered by frustration:

> Another evacuation completed – first Norway, then Dunkirk, Greece – now Crete – each one worse – always the identical story – unsurpassed bravery – superior odds & equipment – criticism is getting strong at last for the criminal & stupid way of fighting – for our slowness, complacency – the British absolutely don't think fast enough today – don't conceive of new ideas or changes – it's about time they started – before it's too late. (JJD 2 June 1941)
>
> People around here (Doncaster) have had no bombings at all & are not all out in war effort – there is still lots of profiteering – cheating, etc. The more regulations you have the more scope there is for evading laws & rules – war effort not at 100% – people lulled into false security again – waste, stupidity, red tape – short sightedness – still too prevalent. (JJD 19 June 1941)

> Will Britain win the war? – I do not know. *Against* – English complacency, stupidity, smugness – lack of drive & imagination. Weak points – 1. lack of coordination amongst services & amongst factories & administration – no plan – too much muddling & 50% effort – *For* – Adaptability – courage – complacency – can't scare – can't upset or worry English – their weakness is also their strength – it's a grave problem. (JJD 20 June 1941)

Germany's invasion of the Soviet Union on 22 June brought an entirely new dimension to the struggle. At first Joe treated it as a joke, commenting the day after "I like to see a couple of rascals kill each other." But he soon came around to support not only Churchill's declaration of alliance but to the need for Britain to act in full support, and not stand by and leave the dirty work to the Russians. In July the news improved. The United States took over the occupation of Iceland, relieving the British forces there, but more importantly sending a clear signal to Germany that it would not tolerate interference with the sea lanes of the North Atlantic. British and Free French forces occupied Syria and, so claimed the press, the Russians were beginning to hold firm against the German assault. Churchill announced that the bombing campaign against Germany would be stepped up, and that Britain was now much better prepared to rebuff Luftwaffe retaliation than it had been the previous September. The *Daily Express* began a weekly "bombing table" to tally the attacks on German cities. Three weeks after the Soviet Union had unexpectedly become an ally, Joe opined to the Pony Club:

> Despite Churchill's speeches and our alliance – a few of the old order still will have nothing to do with the Russians – that is – they can beat the Germans but that is all. There are quite a few of that English menace left who are responsible for many past evils – I don't think the real showdown will come until after the war. Then they will make a last dying attempt to keep control – to hang on to the old order – the Russians are winning everybody's admiration. Having Russia as our allies will probably result in one of two things happening in post war England. Either the ruling class and financial interests will have to make further concessions to the workers or the workers will be easy meat for communistic leaders. People are beginning to figure that maybe the Russians are not so bad if they can supply their men with adequate equipment, leadership etc. (JJL 15 July 1941)

Joe was a keen observer of these events, mainly through the daily press. He told the Pony Club:

> the newspapers here are cut down in size and content but there is absolute freedom of the press. Every battle, every campaign, every political, military or economic move is given a thorough going over – the tone is in most cases fair but critical – there is no fooling here – everybody is in the war and they want to see things done right.... The papers here ... give the govt a terrific going over for their soft gloved handling of Hess – they want a complete reorganization of the intelligence service – they want a lot more red tape in administration clipped – above all they want their leaders to get up to date in their military views – improve production & mechanization – and obtain air superiority – change bombing tactics, etc. etc. – in other words what's going on is understood thoroughly by everybody – as far as possible.... in Canada the papers try to tone down the failures, play up the victories. Here they try to get the whole situation in the proper perspective – that's where we are going to win out – we know the worst – we know what plugging lies ahead – no defeat can shock them here or make them lose heart. It makes them plug harder – as usual they are slow at catching on here. (JJL 25 May 1941)

Joe considered Beaverbrook's Express "the most interesting & colorful paper of the lot." Then the most widely read of the national papers, it had like the others been cut to four pages daily and six on Sunday due to paper shortages. Joe admired the British press for its lively criticism of the conduct of the war in the opinion columns: "as long as we are free to critic[ize] not too much fighting in vain." Whether Joe understood that war news, in contrast to opinion, was based largely on Ministry of Information communiqués, there being no independent investigative reporting from the front, is not obvious from his letters.

Joe was well aware that mail was subject to censorship, as RCAF personnel had been warned repeatedly. Letters must not contain any details of station locations, military activities, weapons, or aircraft. Offending words or passages were snipped out. Routine grumbling was generally allowed to pass, although derogatory comments about RAF discipline and living conditions, or about the attitudes of English civilians toward Canadian servicemen, judged likely to affect morale on the home front in Canada, might be drawn to the attention of the writer's commanding officer. Political disaffection attracted the censor's notice, but in practice it had to border on sedition to be cut. Straightforward political opinion, however trenchant, would generally pass. As Joe told his family,

> I should launch into a thorough politic article on conditions and prospects around here – recent alliances – attitudes, etc. – but I am afraid my old pal the scissor clipping stooge – locally called a censor would ruin a good letter (JJL 14 July 1941)

Nonetheless, a week later he expounded at length to his family on those very topics, even if he suspected that his views might be sailing close to the wind.

> Perhaps the Englishman's greatest weakness, vice, drawback or call it what you may is his lack of imagination – his lack of foresight – and his lack of drive – yet at the same time those very drawbacks are part and parcel of his strength – his power and his existence.
>
> They lack imagination – they don't conceive of many new ideas – changes – they fail to exploit their assets. Believe me there are more stirring tales – more thrilling episodes – taking place nightly and daily on the bombing raids and daylight sweeps than even the most imaginative writer could conceive. Every airman has trips to talk about that are really stirring – pulse tingling and bound to stir those who read and hear about them – few do. But on the other hand that lack of imagination keeps them from visualizing horrors – enables them to wait for anything – then regardless of what comes – take it in stride. If you go thru a real blitz you can better appreciate what I mean. The French imagined what a blitz on Paris would mean – they quit – gave up – Englishmen fail to let their imaginations run away with them – they took the blitz in stride – calmly – bravely – stupidly at times – but they took it – they won – and they are if anything better off for the experience. They lost their homes – their belongings – their families – but they gained a sense of comradeship – they learnt that there are more important things than money and wealth and property. They felt as a fighter pilot does when he shoots down a Jerry – as we do when we drop our bombs – that they had accomplished something – that they were worth their salt.
>
> The Englishman lacks imagination – fire and pep it is true – but he possess[es] other qualities that more than make up for it.
>
> Now for their lack of foresight – that is a more serious drawback – when the battle is on they show unexpected resources.... They work at breakneck speed to solve problems on the spur of the moment – they are capable of improvising under any set of circumstances, to meet any problem that confronts them while the battle is on. It is true that man

for man the British more than holds his own – civilian or soldier. But when the immediate danger is over they sink back to their old ways – and ideas. They seem to be incapable of preparing wholeheartedly for future exigencies.

The fall of France set them feverishly to prepare for the immediate attack on these islands. That danger passed for the time being – the people once more slipped back – everything is running smoothly now – there is no thought of a Russian collapse – of a German onslaught here. Many leaders see it – and trying to warn the people of it – but you just can't stir or excite an Englishman. If it comes – they will worry about it then. When they arrive they will figure out ways and means of handling the invaders. Feverish preparation now is out of the question – wait and see.

And so thousands of gallons of gas are used up by joy riders – and so the old red tape method of running and doing things – thus England rides along to her destiny – solid – slow-moving unimaginative England – fundamentally the same old England.

And so intelligent leaders, writers and thinkers worry – the papers without exception clamour for farsighted and vigorous action on the home front.... Britain, thanks to Churchill is once again the upholder of all the ideals that most countries expect of her – but he needs a vice-premier to look after the home front – to gear up all the branches of industry – to rout out the deadheads – to enable Britain to face the future with more than fortitude – with all the implements, materials, ideas and organization for any eventuality.

There is still another aspect about these Englishmen. Everybody know[s] of their patriotism and it is well justified and has been put to the acid test – but the majority of people here are small "towners." They have not travelled – many of them have never been out of their own constituency. They think everybody else is inferior to an Englishman. They know little about the education, culture, life or ways of other people. What is worse they don't try to learn anything about anyone else and what is still worse – they don't give two hoots in hell about anybody else – at least they didn't. But they are starting to think a little differently now.

Firstly the "colonials" a word they are frightened to use now are showing them a thing or two. We – that is Canadians, New Zealanders, Aussies etc – are bigger – smarter – more independent – original – than our equivalent ranks here. What is more we are used to a higher standard of living – we know more about people – have seen more countries – have done more than the people we mix with here. It is beginning to slowly seep thru that the English are not quite tops in this small world of ours. Then the crowning flaw has been their realization that America is now the big cheese – not England. Of course they still feel that good old England is still tops – but facts and figures don't lie – and American results are finally convincing them that there are a lot of fine fish in the sea.

Europeans are still looked down upon – they are definitely inferior according to the English. What they fail to realize is that lack of education and opportunity does not make a man inferior. They lack understanding and a certain amount of humaneness.

I never feel warmly attached to an Englishman – you might admire them – you often do – you might respect them but you certainly are not devoted to them.

Strange as it may seem most of the "colonists" here would like to take a good solid crack at many of these birds here – they just infuriate you at times with their shortsightedness – lack of understanding – stupidness. Then you watch them under fire – the real test – and you forget all your little grievances.

This fact seems obvious – they have the qualifications and the qualities – they need to travel a bit – learn a bit about others. That has not been necessary up to the present – but a new day is dawning. The world is now a small family – they will have to travel and mix and live with others – and they will.

Most of the first class leaders have been around – most of the deadheads have stayed put – their day is over – at least I hope it is because England is finished if they are not chucked out – and I don't think England is finished yet. They rise to the occasion – this is a vital moment – they have never failed yet – I feel sure they won't fail now. (JJL 22 July 1941)

Percy remarked:

Joe's letters are very interesting.... Of course we keep all his letters. Some of them deal quite exhaustively with the characteristics of the British ... the lad shows that he is not satisfied with surface values but digs for essentials. He writes with rare understanding of people. (PJD 30 August 1941)

Other readers also found Joe's letter worthy of attention. Two weeks after he dropped it in a letterbox in Doncaster, the Post Office sent it, along with other overseas mail collected that day, to the London branch of the Postal and Telegraph Censorship Department, which handled all airmail to Canada. Some days later, in the large hall where many thousands of letters were vetted each day, Joe's letter was delivered to the table of twenty or so "censorettes" charged with reading Canadian servicemen's letters. There it was assigned to Examiner 743.[1]

Joe's eight-page handwritten letter took a little extra time for her to read and consider. It contained no offending indiscretions that might reveal sensitive military information, or impair morale on the home front. It gave no suggestion of activities or infractions that should be brought to the attention of his commanding officers. There was nothing to which she was authorized to apply her scissors in defence of the realm. Nor even did Joe's letter provide any hint of a lovelorn or libidinous condition that might at least lighten her long day's work with a giggle. Nonetheless, after considering the letter in its entirety, she passed it up the table for the attention of the deputy assistant censor, who confirmed that the letter would indeed be of interest to the appropriate military authorities.

So it was that, on 7 August, nearly six pages of Joe's letter came to be typed onto the standard censor's report form, which, at the top of the first page, noted the origin, destination, date, language, and disposition of the letter, and provided with the subject heading "A Canadian's Estimate of England."[2] The original letter was then released uncut and sent on its way. The Jacobsons knew it had passed through the censor's office because, like many of Joe's letters home, the envelope had been reclosed with a censor's seal.

One copy of the examiner's extract was forwarded to the Directorate of Intelligence in Britain's Air Ministry, where it was received on 12 August. From there it was sent on to RCAF Headquarters in London where, two days later, at the direction of the Air Officer Commanding, the extract of Joe's letter was again typed out in full. He then dispatched this memo over his signature to the Department of National Defence for Air in Ottawa, with the advice that it was written by an RCAF sergeant and forwarded for information only.[3] The Jacobsons would have been quite unaware of the letter's readership in Ottawa, where the extract may have already been circulating by the time the original reached them in Montreal.

Why did Joe Jacobson's letter attract the attention not only of the British postal censor but also of senior Canadian air force staff in both London and Ottawa? Perhaps it was the concluding paragraphs about "colonials." Wartime relations between Britain and Canada were not without irritants, despite unity of purpose. Just as there were differences of culture, attitude, and outlook between British and Canadian airmen, so there were at the highest levels of their respective political and military leadership. Canada's Minister of National Defence for Air and his entourage were meeting with Air Ministry officials in London at that very time to resolve a host of concerns relating to both RCAF personnel in Britain and the implementation of the Air Training agreement. Some related to the status of Canadians in the Royal Air Force with respect to postings and discipline, pay and taxation, mail and accommodation, and promotions and commissions. Since the mass arrival of Canadian airmen in the spring, these issues could no longer be ignored. They were evident from postal censorship reports, and more importantly from numerous disciplinary incidents at RAF schools and stations, including a near-mutiny by Canadian wireless operators in April. Rightly or wrongly, many Canadian airmen expected better conditions and better treatment than what they actually encountered on arrival. Most of these problems that threatened to undermine morale were improved within months. Yet the two air forces would continue to hold fundamentally different views on the basis for commissioning NCOs for the remainder of the war.

Equally important was the future of the Air Training Program, soon due for renegotiation, with the question of forming all-Canadian squadrons at the forefront. Many Canadians, both serving airmen and senior politicians, believed that this measure would be an important means of resolving ongoing personnel issues. More importantly, perhaps, it would go some way to address the sense that Canadians were being taken for granted, as though it was entirely in the order of things that the right sort of men from the Dominions should ascend to the service of the mother country. "Ready, aye, ready" in this war as in the last. Joe's letter hints at something that was already troubling England about its Empire, that the tail might someday wag the dog. The RAF would only begin to take the problem seriously in 1942, first with its Dominion servicemen, and in later years with those from its Caribbean and African colonies.

Whether Joe's letter alerted British intelligence to trouble ahead, or provided Canadian authorities with an articulation of the national aspirations of their own troops, can only be a matter of speculation. But whatever the reason it attracted attention, it is by far the longest extract to be found in the entire censored letter file for 1941 and 1942, and the only one that reads like a considered essay.

That a young man so recently arrived in Britain could come to such assessments, and with such conviction, was unusual. Joe Jacobson had already taken an interest in current affairs before he left Canada. His letters home from Ontario and Saskatchewan revealed a young man of strong views, given to writing both humorous stories and serious jeremiads. Once in England, he was quick to engage people of all types in conversation, whether on base, in the pubs, on the trains, or in the street. As with many Canadians, rubbing shoulders with British and other Empire servicemen fired up his national pride. He was also quick to conclude that England needed to get rid of its deadwood and modernize its ways and attitudes if it were to win the war.

Joe was an avid reader of the popular press, especially Lord Beaverbrook's *Daily Express*. Beaverbrook worshipped Churchill and had recently served in his Cabinet as minister of aircraft production. John Gordon, the long-time editor of the *Sunday Express*, revered Beaverbrook. Gordon wrote both the Sunday editorial column and a weekly analysis of the war situation over his own byline. Gordon was a conservative and intensely patriotic Briton, and, moreover, viscerally anti-German. He was convinced of the need to wage absolute war until complete victory. To that end he advocated no less than total mobilization, unstinting preparation and vigilance, and Stakhanovite effort by civilians and servicemen alike. He also considered that new ideas and new men were needed, and frequently called for the removal of deadwood. In his mind, this included whichever bureaucrats and experts, along with the "Colonel Blimps" in the army, he regarded as obstacles to reorganization for greater effort and efficiency. Gordon was also an advocate of air power and unrestrained strategic bombing. With Russia now fighting on Germany's Eastern Front, Gordon asserted that Britain should redouble its efforts against Germany, and not fall for the idea that the fighting could now be left to the Russians. The *Daily Express* editorials were likewise filled with non-stop exhortation in support of greater production effort and efficiency, total mobilization of Britain's people and resources for war, and ousting those who stood in the way.

Joe, confident in Churchill's leadership and wholeheartedly committed to the war effort, readily took up these ideas. As a commerce graduate with practical experience on the factory floor, he took an interest in the organization and methods of industrial production. In that desperate summer of shortages in equipment and qualified instructors to deal with the flood of aircrew from Canada, Joe encountered plenty of bottlenecks, disorganization, and delays in his own daily experience of operational training. He took these frustrations as ample confirmation of England's insufficient determination to rid itself of the old guard.

The editorial line of the *Express* papers encapsulated a view that had gained traction on both the left and right of the political spectrum since the shock of the Dunkirk evacuation the year before. One of the most widely read books in England in 1940 was *Guilty Men* (anonymously authored by "Cato"), a charge sheet against the appeasers in Chamberlain's circle that called on Churchill to finish turning out the remaining old guard still clinging to positions of power. It was a call not simply for victory but for uprooting the old order. A year later the setbacks were continuing: a string of German successes in Greece, the Balkans, and North Africa, followed by British naval defeats and the rout of British forces in Crete. By 1941, the country had settled in for a long war, a "Peoples' War," a total mobilization for victory that would necessarily require a new order.

George Orwell provided one view of that new order in his long essay *The Lion and the Unicorn: Socialism and the English Genius*, published only a few months before Joe arrived in England.[4] Neither Orwell's nor Cato's names appear in Joe Jacobson's meticulous record of his reading material. Yet Joe's views on the English character and on England's prospects in wartime – the lack of imagination and foresight, yet the ability to act when needed; the English sleepwalking through the first eight months of war, suddenly waking up, then a "prompt relapse into sleep"; their insularity and stubborn adherence to old ways, the need for new blood – were as much echoes of *The Lion and the Unicorn* as they were of the editorial views of the *Express* papers. With his political ideas not yet fully formed, he seems to have been open to both the intense patriotism of the right and the class-consciousness of the left. And he was beginning to inform himself on political issues through books and film.

Fifteen

A Home Away from Home

Joe used his first weekend pass to visit his father's relatives in Manchester. Dan and Henriette Kostoris were enormously indebted to the Jacobsons for having taken their two young daughters into their home in Montreal, far from the dangers of wartime life in Britain. They were eager to have Joe visit them. As he recounted the visit to his parents:

> I doubt if I ever got more in such a short period of time as I did over the weekend. I found time to smoke some of [Dan's] best cigars … and had my share of the Laura Secords.… Then I worked my way thru the Scotch – and generally did a first class job of things.… Dan insisted I leave my shoes outside the door to be polished – since the maids had the night off when I arrived I didn't know who shined them and so … I thanked [Dan] and he nearly passed out – Evidently the maid did them but that made me feel bad because I would prefer taking her out to having her clean my shoes as she was fairly cute.
>
> … they speak of you two with reverence – you are God as far as they are concerned. Such voluntary hospitality more or less has bowled Dan over and the letters that the kids write have really made you appear Heaven sent.
>
> Everything that takes place has to be looked upon in this light. I myself am deeply obliged [to the] old boy.… He kind of looks upon me as a combination of son and a brother. I work with him in the garden, listen to confidences and appreciate his hospitality.…

> [Dan] is a likeable fellow who can be simply marvelous to you. On the other hand he is a hard working, hard headed … business man and plenty shrewd.… Henriette … has quite captivated me.… she is as kind as they come and what's more she has a keen business head and marvelous artistic ability as far as interior decorating and designing is concerned. I had some lovely chats with her … I think she would behave the same to me whether or not the present circumstances existed.
>
> Dan … is really too busy at work and in his garden to experience the loneliness that his wife feels. However, it is tough in a way on both of them, but they are pretty level headed and realize that as far as the kids are concerned – they are, if anything much better off than before.…
>
> Henriette wants me to bring my pal next time – Dan didn't think it such a hot idea – I guess he feels so far but no further.… They were delighted to see me whilst it was nice for me to be in a home again amongst friends.… (JJL 3 June 1941)

Their house, which Joe characterized as a mansion, was well stocked with the best of food and drink, and staffed by maids, a cook, and a gardener. As Joe later commented, "I believe they could go thru the 100 yrs war without being pinched or running short." But the house was also an empty nest: the children were in Canada and Dan's son was in the army. Dan, and especially Henriette, took an instant liking to Joe, and he would visit them many times in the coming months. On that very first weekend, Joe arranged to designate the Kostoris as his legal next-of-kin in England for official RAF purposes, listing them as his uncle and aunt. He used their address as a convenient mail drop. So began a relationship that would provide Joe with both material and personal support, and sustain his spirit and well-being over the coming months.

The family connection was through Henriette. She was one of a dozen children of the Freedman family of Antwerp, whose prosperity had been built on the diamond trade. Some of her siblings had for reasons of marriage or business settled in Montreal and Toronto, and until the war began continued to shuttle between Canada and Britain. Joe already knew some of them, especially Henriette's sister Rebecca, who had married Percy's favourite cousin in Montreal. Joe would meet many other members of the Freedman family in the coming months, and he would prove himself to be an astute judge of their character. He admired their warmth, intelligence, talent, and education, but came to regard them as neurotic (having "quaint problems") and impossible to live with.

On Monday morning, 23 June, Joe learned that his pilot was going on sick leave, and the crew had been granted forty-eight-hour passes. He left immediately for Manchester for a surprise visit. There he found he had just missed Hy Abrams, who had flown in from Canada the day before, and who had visited Joe's parents before leaving. Hy, with whom Joe had begun training at Manning Depot in Toronto the year before, was the first of several Montreal Jewish servicemen who would be welcomed by the Kostoris family over the next year or so.

More importantly on this visit, Joe met someone new on the scene: the Kostoris' niece, Janine Freedman. Janine and her mother Suzanne had moved in after her father was killed in the Blitz in London the month before. Joe would spend the rest of his weekend passes that summer in Janine's company at the Kostoris household. Joe described their first meeting to his parents:

> It was a hot day so I decided Janine and I should go swimming. The women started and practically swooned at my suggestion of encouraging her to skip her school classes in short hand and typewriting – the thought that frightened them most was Dan's reaction I think. After a little chat with Janine who doesn't look seventeen but talks and acts much older – incidentally, Janine is quite a girl – easy to get along with – a good sport and like most European girls I have met, surprisingly grown up mentally – But don't get excited after that big build up – she's just a pal of mine who is getting Canadianized ... (JJL 24 June 1941)

In short, Janine had class. Joe also told his parents about his increasingly complex and ambiguous relationship with Dan Kostoris:

> Janine and her mother have stuck it pretty well since their siege of tough luck – Henriette is marvelous to Suzanne – so is her daughter – ... Janine is pretty smart – she has Dan sized up about the same as Pop and me – we hit it off pretty well together and her case is exactly what would happen to anybody else whom Dan put up – thank God my sisters aren't in the same position as Liliane and Yvette because they would not make out nearly as well – ... He's a temperamental baby – his ambition is to be known as a "hale fellow well met" – he says so every time – he will do anything to impress you ... But when the visitors are gone – when the gloves are off – he is a tightfisted bully – He hasn't a friend – he is scared stiff of officers – policemen – bigger or richer men than himself. He takes it out on the women – It's tough on a family like Suzanne & Janine – they appreciate his kindness and generosity – But they have no say equal rights or independence – he bullies them as

> he does all his household – I am happy to report that here's a guy that puts and keeps him in his place while I am around. I kid him – I slap him heartily on the back – I make him feel a bit all right at *times* – But I decide what shall be done and he sputters a bit and takes it – What happens when I leave I don't know – Now don't get the idea that I am running the lad down – I like him – He can be a barrel of fun when he is in the right mood – which he is always in when I am around – He has to be because he wants me to write you what a marvelous fellow he is – He is a good enough egg. But I feel that you have to look at him in the proper perspective – I know him like a book – I have a great time with him – he really likes me – But I never want any of my family dependent on him ... I think any of our women folk would size him up – pop him in the eye – tell him off and scram – Janine probably would too if she didn't have to look after her mother. Henriette still has my unstinted admiration. She is marvelous – a real woman – which makes it all the more grating when I hear him behave badly to her. (JJL 26 June 1941)

The Kostoris became Joe's primary connection, such as it was, with Jewish circles in England. Although they did not attend synagogue on a regular basis, they kept a kosher house and Dan involved himself in Jewish community affairs in Manchester. Dan was a type familiar enough to Joe from his parents' generation in Montreal – more devoted to hard work and making money than to culture and manners. The Freedmans, in contrast, were transplanted continental bourgeoisie: gracious and cultured, and at ease in several languages, their first being French. They were European in outlook, and pleased to converse about art, music, culture, and politics. Their Judaism was more habit of mind than religious conviction and strict observance.

As Joe had recognized immediately, the Kostoris regarded their fine home more as a cocoon in which to shelter themselves from the outside world than as a venue for entertaining others or exhibiting their quality and taste. Although Henriette longed for company, Dan could do without. Playing on Henriette's desires, Joe visited again two weeks later, this time bringing several of his Canadian pals whom he had visited at their base in June.

Again he described the weekend's events in letters home.

> Good old Jeep MacLean – the short fellow from Timmins Ont, who sat at Mom's right – picked me up by accident in town Friday afternoon. I had just managed a 48 hour pass to visit my famous pals Art Hunter (hell hooter) and Ken Fraser in Manchester. They wired me to meet them at the Victoria Hotel, Manchester, Sat. night. I took Jeep along with me and we blew into Midfield as they were discussing plans about a nice

quiet weekend over a quiet Friday evening supper. We both got a warm reception – were duly fed and then Janine, Jeep and I grabbed some bikes and sped off for a swim.... Next day we played tennis and got Dan working on the phone to locate our pals – the hotel they planned staying at had been blitzed six months ago.... In the meantime the three of us again went swimming. This time Jeep and I had adequate toasting material. After all Jeep has survived four bad crackups and a parachute jump from an impossibly low height. He is still the same as ever so we had a delightful time at the pool – the problem soon developed though, how were we – that is Jeep and I going to get back – we attempted to ride the bikes – Jeep did alright so did I – despite the fact I found myself in the ditch on no less than three occasions – we staggered home and Jeep and I left for Manchester to search for the boys. Well a great gathering took place – and at exactly 12 o'clock, Sunday noon – an old cab with an ancient driver and four roary eyed airmen in the back pulled up outside of Midfield singing their heads off – to be met by Dan at his best. He was the regular country squire and he really set out to do us up in style. He was a treat – He drove us all out for a swim – a feat unparalleled by anyone else as gas is hard to get – then we all got into our shirt sleeves and stretched out on the floor of the living room with Dan and shot crap – yes my hearties – we rolled the bones – shook the dice – to top off a perfect story Dan won seven shillings and he was so tickled at trimming us that he really opened up – He is having the other boys send their mail through him – he drove us into Manchester to catch my train – in short – he put on an admirable display for us and when Dan wants to be nice – he knows how. When pals like mine who know how to conduct themselves appropriately and at the same time create an atmosphere of breezyness get hold of men like Dan – the fun really starts – Dan can hold his own at cracking jokes – telling us dirty stories – being more or less one of the boys – well a riotous time was had by all. Henriette of course gets the worst of it – Janine had a job on her hands but she more or less took Janet's place – you know – one snappy girl with four dashing airmen ...

Perhaps the funniest thing that happened was with Dan – he is a teetotaler and thought that Jeep and I were just hot from racing after him on his bike. We were both stretched out on the bed and telling Dan what a marvelous bike rider he was and praising his strength to the high heavens – well that really endeared us to him – and Dan spent the next hour telling us all about his adventures – prowess, etc – at the

> end of that time we were both sober enough to stand up and head for Manchester – of course you can't fool Henriette or Suzanne or Janine, but it was a pretty merry weekend all told and everybody left happy – I was particularly delighted with the reception my friends received. I was a little dubious as to what the reaction would be – but I guess my two quiet previous weekends paved the way for when the lid blew off because we were all treated, fed, and dined royally.
> (JJL 14 July 1941)

Two weekends later, Joe brought his pal Roger Rousseau along.

> Roger & I swung a 48 hr pass – set out for Midfield – surprised everyone as usual at 10 o'clock – rec'd usual warm – hearty & boisterous welcome – Yvon Freedman [Janine's younger brother] was around – he is a great youngster – absolutely wild about flying – he is 15 so won't get into this war I hope. (JJD 25 July 1941)

> Spent a delightful day – Roger & Janine & I went shopping in Altringham in the morning – then we took Yvon with us to … Manchester after dinner – we arrived early so Janine & I went to one movie – Roger & Yvon to another … – the whole family played cards (heck) when we got back. (JJD 26 July 1941)

> Spent the day playing tennis … Roger got along swell with the whole gang & has made the biggest hit of any of my pals – Roger is a great guy … (JJD 27 July 1941)

Joe wrote to the Pony Club about the Kostoris family and especially about Janine:

> You must look them up when you come over – they will treat you well – it's nice to have somewhere to go and above all – you could not do better anywhere with regards to feminine company than with my pal Janine – why I should discover really top notch girls for you I don't know – I think she might even have Cecily beat – of course I have only spent two weekends there with her and have only managed to have the odd word, swim, bike ride and tennis match with her.

> Then too I have never had a chance to settle down and discover what Cecily was really like – so I guess I am doomed to be one of these bachelor gents that will be welcomed in all the finest salons by his former lady friends. This much is certain – as a good judge of humans I say they are both top-notchers – I have not fallen for either – but I could

> do plenty worse and not much better. But I like to take a long term view on some things – one is – that it is easy enough to get carried away by all the excitement and glamour taking place to-day – but the majority come out and have to settle down when it's over. I would not relish swooping a young lassie off her feet and then have her stuck with me when the glamour wears off. I would rather start the other way round.... (JJL 15 July 1941)

> I could very easily fall like a tons of bricks [for Janine] even though I received a couple of letters and a smart picture from Cecily. Janine has first place now – but my position is difficult – when you don't know what is going to happen to you between visits – ... you are liable to kind of lose your sense of perspective and overstress your fondness. Something always becomes dearer and more precious when there is a very considerable chance of losing it – added to that Janine is rather lonely in a strange country – in a quiet, sedate community without any friends and recently bereaved of her father with whom she was on exceptionally good terms. So the set up was kind of a natural – we really get along exceptionally well and I have sort of fallen lightly – naturally the engagement or marriage stage has not entered our heads – mine anyway – I am not that serious. But I have a girl friend here of whom all Poneyites will definitely approve of – pictures will be forthcoming –

> ... on second thought better not make too much fuss about Janine back home – Cecily looked mighty good in her latest pictures – and it is possible that I might get back after the war – and bachelor Joe will still need classy girl friends in Canada's leading cities. (JJL 4 August 1941)

Joe's situation in England only confirmed his reluctance to commit to any long-term relationship. That would have to wait until his job was done.

The Hell Hooters. Left to right: Ken Fraser, "Jeep" McLean, Art Hunter, Joe. Midfield, Hale, July 1941. (Canadian Jewish Archives)

After a swim. Left to right: "Jeep" McLean, Ken Fraser, Art Hunter, Joe, Janine Freedman. Near Midfield, Hale, July 1941. (Canadian Jewish Archives)

Joe with Janine Freedman and Henriettte Kostoris. Midfield, Hale, July 1941. (Canadian Jewish Archives)

Tennis with Dan Kostoris. Midfield, Hale, July 1941. (Janet Jacobson Kwass)

Joe at Midfield, July 1941. Left to right, in background: Henriette Kostoris, Janine Freedman, Suzanne Freedman. (Janet Jacobson Kwass)

Roger Rousseau and Joe. Midfield, Hale, July 1941.
(Janet Jacobson Kwass)

Sixteen

Preparing for Battle

Completion of operational training required several long cross-country flights at night with searchlight, target finding, and bombing exercises. Joe's stint at Finningley wound up on 28 July after many delays, having taken twelve weeks instead of the projected eight. He would be posted to an operational squadron as an individual, not as a member of an established crew. His flying log records that he was graded much as he had been in Canada: an average navigator, bomber, and aerial gunner, not recommended for specialist navigation training.

> Made my last flight – I hope – here – my parachute broke open after taking off – but we got down alright – went swimming at Hatfield with Roger – took bikes – had a pleasant time – started doing Charles Atlas exercises – seriously – should put on plenty of muscle – I weigh 165 stripped – 5'10" – real exercise – makes me feel 100% better –
> (JJD 24 July 1941)

Joe was anxious by this time to get into battle after being in training for nearly a year.[1] He had more than once in his letters home exaggerated the similarity of his air training to actual operations over Germany. But there was more to this than Joe's self-admitted tendency to embroider the facts. There had been real dangers in training, and he was preparing himself psychologically for what he would be encountering soon enough on real bombing runs over Germany. Joe had already lost close friends before he left Finningley. He knew that at least six of the fellows he had trained with in Canada had been killed in flying accidents at other training units that summer. There had been fatal flying accidents at Finningley, and close calls in the air, and he was well aware of similar happenings at Upper Heyford. On the 30th, he noted in his diary: "heard Tyson & Williams also had it – the boys are starting to go … Ed Kennedy had it."[2]

After a weekend leave spent at Midfield, Joe and Roger returned to Finningley long enough to get news of their posting to 106 Squadron at Coningsby and be granted a three-day leave. Together they set off for London.

> Hard to imagine the change between flying & weekending at the Kostoris – all dangers & worries forgotten – peace & fun reign supreme – I like Janine more every time we meet. (JJD 27 July 1941)

> Arrived at the Park Lane Hotel at 5 AM – weather rainy – wrote Janine to meet me here – hope she does – doubt it though. (JJD 28 July 1941)

Signing off his letter with love, he asked Janine to come to London where, he suggested, she could stay with her cousin. Her mother did not approve of this arrangement, needless to say, and so Janine stayed at Midfield. Joe may have been disappointed but, as when Cecily had arrived in Montreal with measles, he quickly found other things to do.

The Park Lane, near Green Park, was one of London's newest hotels, adorned by an Art Deco lobby. There the two pals "looked after" Roger's brother Réal's suite for the weekend. Réal was then a senior Canadian official in London, and he had returned to Canada to get married. Recounting that weekend to his family, Joe told them

> I have been bumping into all kinds of old pals from College – school – and Canada.… It is great to see so many old time faces – it makes me feel quite at home … I believe I would feel at home anywhere now. (JJL 30 July 1941)

Among those he met was Adjutor Savard, who, he related, was a newspaper man,

> a pal of Roger's brother who is here to get publicity for the R.C.A.F. boys in England … a brother of Ernie Savard – a former director of the [Montreal] Canadians. He knows Harvey and Sandwell and everybody else so it was very enjoyable being with him – he gave us all the latest news about Canada [having] just arrived last week.… we drank champagne scotch – wine & liquor together – ate at la Cigale – set him back £3 – 6s (JJL 30 July 1941 and JJD 31 July 1941)[3]

Joe loved London and he couldn't get enough of it. Earlier that summer he recorded:

> Being in London gives me something the same feeling as NY – only more intimate – more friendly & more significant – they are proud here [to] have been thru hell & come out unchanged – perhaps bitterer – a bit shaken but still as independent as ever. (JJD 8 June 1941)

This time he wrote:

> there is a definite romance about London – its squares its cabbies – who roar thru the dark winding streets – night or day in their old fashioned reliable hacks. The city lacks culture at the moment – possesses a war time licentiousness – as do all cities now. (JJD 1 August 1941)

He told his family that London was

> quite different this trip – it is livelier – more bustling and spruce than last time. Previously people hated to read of raids on Berlin and other big towns because it meant retaliation raids on London and our big cities – now all is changed. There is no fear of German raids just now. The V sign is prominent – we are doing the shoving around and the people are definitely a lot happier because of it.... People are really making the most of the long days and raidless nights. (JJL 31 July 1941)

For Joe, New York and London were the two great cities of the world. New York was the capital of modernity and the twentieth century. But London had been the capital of the nineteenth century, and was still the capital of civilization. In 1941, London was New York with courage.

While in London at the end of July, Joe saw the film *Target for Tonight*, which he told his family about with great enthusiasm.

> You will no doubt see it soon. It is definitely authentic and has made a deep impression on everybody who sees it. The remarkable thing about it is that it is played down – there is no attempt to make it sensational – no exaggeration – in fact it is just the opposite. If all my trips were that easy – boy would I be happy – that was just a routine trip – and routine trips just don't seem to occur very often any more. (JJL 30 July 1941)

Target for Tonight, which had just opened in London earlier that week, was the Air Ministry's most successful film promotion of the bombing offensive against Germany. It depicted a night bombing operation by following the fortunes of a single Wellington crew, beginning with target selection at headquarters, through briefing and preparation on a bomber station, onboard scenes of the crew's sortie from beginning to end, and subsequent debriefing. Dramatic tension increases on the return trip, as the wireless operator is wounded by flak, the radio goes dead, the oil pressure is dropping, and the home aerodrome is enveloped by fog. Finally, through a gloom relieved only by the runway flare path, the lights of the aircraft appear and tensions ease. It was not quite the routine trip that Joe, exaggerating once again, had made it out to be.

Target for Tonight premiered when the public was eager to believe that Britain was striking back rather than just taking it, and both critics and audiences hailed it as an accurate and realistic depiction of the air war. The film critic for the *Express* asserted that it was the "greatest flying film of the war," and the paper editorialized that "the example of these young R.A.F. bomber pilots will inspire every citizen to heights of service and sacrifice for the state." The left-wing *New Statesman and Nation* called *Target for Tonight* the best propaganda film of the war, providing immeasurable thrills without sensationalism, and claimed it would do a world of good in America and the neutral countries.[4]

Target for Tonight, innovatively conceived as a docudrama rather than simply a narration of film sequences, became the propaganda success it was intended to be. Perhaps because it used actual RAF personnel rather than actors, and realistic settings, Joe would have seen it as an unsensationalized and reasonably accurate presentation of the planning and execution of a bombing operation, even if the return flight was by no means routine. The nonchalant banter in the crew room, and the phlegmatic but determined manner of the squadron leaders, must certainly have appealed to Joe. It showed the comradeship of the diverse national and regional origins of aircrews, while at the same time highlighting the distinctive upper-class speech mannerisms and demeanour of senior officers. Joe was close enough to operations to pass judgment on the film's authenticity on station and in the air. He must also have enjoyed the film's very English facade of nonchalance in the face of danger, something that did not come naturally to him but which he sought to cultivate. Yet even he (let alone a civilian audience) was in no position to question the veracity of film's depiction of the "destruction" of the oil storage facility. That he would discover through experience in the coming months.

Joe had had the summer of his lifetime. He liked England, and he admired the English, even if he found them hard to love. He was exhilarated by operational training, and especially by flying. The war was for him not only a struggle of good against evil, it was also a contest, not unlike a long, drawn-out hockey or football game. He engaged people easily, as he had in Preston and the West. He sounded opinion in the shops and the pubs, read the newspapers voraciously, and talked endlessly with his fellow servicemen about their training and equipment. He wanted to understand the public mood, how England was organizing for war, and the technical and strategic necessities for winning it. If he overestimated the English public's unity of purpose and commitment in "the people's war," it was more likely because it bolstered his own than because he had uncritically accepted the government and media line.

Writing letters was a way of organizing his thoughts on those issues of crucial importance to him. BCATP training had made a Canadian of him. Operational training gave him a Commonwealth perspective. He gained a sense of solidarity with the other Dominions, which seemed, like Canada and in contrast to Britain, more fortunately blessed by modernity and prosperity, and less burdened by class distinction.

It was Joe's good fortune to have family in England and a home to visit that was in complete contrast to life at his station. Most Canadians were not so lucky. For Joe, Midfield was a refuge. At Finningley, his work in the air was demanding and dangerous. Off duty he threw himself into rugged sports by day, and rowdy pub sessions at night. All the while he was forging a fellowship of airmen and a fraternity of air observers. Leave time in London was a non-stop round of searching out friends, going to plays, and wandering the streets. Joe loved London. To him it was the world's greatest city and he couldn't get enough of it. At Midfield he could reconnect with mannered and cultivated people (particularly the women), and through them indirectly with his own family in Montreal. He engaged in cultured conversation in the garden and at table, and he enjoyed the comforts of a good home well supplied with whisky and cigars.

Moreover, there was tennis, swimming, picnics, and dinners with Janine. She was a girl he could be proud to take for a nice dinner at the Midland Hotel in Manchester. She was classy, but their relationship remained platonic, whatever longings they had for each other. Janine was too close to being family, and too well supervised at Midfield. And Joe wanted no commitments, especially in wartime. Better Cecily from afar, perhaps, than Janine close by. Midfield gave Joe grounding and stability, kept him on the straight and level, and it would continue to do so. For three months in the spring and summer of 1941, Joe caromed between the intensity and dangers of training at Finningley, the delights of London, and the refuge and intimacy of Midfield.

What lay in store for Joe, and how well was he prepared for it? Much of his flying at Finningley had constituted a refresher course in navigation, bombing, and gunnery, although in larger aircraft. His night flying training had consisted of two navigation flights and one bombing practice. He had completed three practice raids averaging four hours each. Joe's operational training was typical of what the other trainees from Canada got.

Night flying had been limited at OTUs all summer due to the short period of night darkness, landing field limitations, and restrictions on non-operational flying. There were still many ground instructors with no operational experience who taught navigation and meteorology from a theoretical rather than practical perspective. Flying training was insufficiently realistic. Flying was not done at operational heights, there was little or no engagement with searchlight batteries, and even the final training flights were considerably shorter than operational flights would be. Air observers had no in-flight mentors because, unlike the situation with pilots and WO/AGs, there was only one per aircraft. Parachute practice was limited to jumping off a wall, there being enough ways of losing highly trained men without adding live jumps from the air. Not included at all in the curriculum was radio navigation because the RAF had not thought it necessary to develop the appropriate devices and systems for that until far too late, and in any event long after the Luftwaffe had done so.

Canadians would now make a significant contribution to Bomber Command's offensive. Close to two thousand Canadian graduates of the Air Training Program had arrived in Britain by May. Nearly a quarter of them were air observers, more than the British AO schools had graduated by that time. The roughly 275 Canadian air observers who had arrived in March and April passed out of operational training in June and July, just as Bomber Command's strategic air offensive was being ramped up. Those Canadian air observers were a major addition to Bomber Command's total strength of about five hundred aircrews, not only in numbers but also in their qualifications as navigators. If their map-reading skills needed improvement, they were thought to be strong in the other skills, especially astro-navigation. They had arrived in numbers none too soon, as there were already glimmerings within Bomber Command that too many bombs were falling far from their intended targets.

Their experience in operational training had made them more aware of themselves as Canadians, and perhaps reinforced their confidence and swagger. They were about to enter combat in a branch of service that seemed the freest of stale ideas and ancient traditions. They had become more aware of the dangers they would face, although still less aware of the technical challenges they would face as navigators over Germany.

Yet circumstances were changing fast. Could Bomber Command keep pace? Certainly the Air Training Program had not been. The gap between the content of air training in Canada and the realities of the bomber war in Europe had been getting wider. And operational training in Britain at that point was barely closing it, if at all. In the summer of 1941, there were high expectations of Bomber Command, and high public support for its announced offensive. Fighter Command had saved the country from invasion in 1940. Could Bomber Command win the war for Britain in 1941?

Target for Tonight recruiting poster. (Wikimedia Commons)

Part Three

Night Bombing

It is on the destruction of enemy industries and above all on the lowering of [enemy] morale caused by bombing that the ultimate victory rests.

— Air Chief Marshal Hugh Trenchard, Statement to the Parliamentary Committee for Imperial Defence, 1923

No power on earth can protect the man in the street from being bombed. Whatever people may tell him, the bomber will always get through.

— Stanley Baldwin, Lord President of the Council, House of Commons, 10 November 1932

Seventeen

Bomber Command

It all seemed simple enough. According to Lord Trenchard, marshal of the Royal Air Force, bombing would do the trick, and according to Britain's Acting Prime Minister Baldwin, nothing could stop it. Aerial bombing was touted by its proponents, and feared by the media and politicians, as the inevitable consequence and the decisive factor in any future war. In the late 1930s, German, Italian, and Japanese aircraft bombed defenceless towns in Spain, Ethiopia, and China. Photos and accounts of the destruction and panic aroused public horror in the Western democracies. England itself had suffered occasional aerial bombardment during the Great War. Being unprepared, there had been no defence, and considerable panic resulted among civilians, even if there was little material damage.

The RAF, a separate service, saw air power not simply as a tactical means of supporting army or naval operations, or even of attacking enemy forces directly. Air power would instead be the decisive factor in war because it provided the means of attacking the *source* of the enemy's armed strength: its factories, transport, communications, and cities. The objective was to defeat the enemy *nation*, not merely its armed forces, by means of a quick and decisive strategic offensive. The RAF needed a large fleet of heavy bombers to reach distant targets and deliver this "knockout blow," which, its proponents argued, would also avert the catastrophic slaughter in the trenches of the previous war.

Unlike more traditional forms of military engagement, strategic bombing doctrines remained at the level of theory. During the 1920s, the RAF was engaged mainly in containing insurgencies at the outposts of empire in Iraq and the Northwest Frontier. These attacks on camps and villages armed with rifles had made aerial bombardment seem like a piece of cake. They provided no useful operational experience of a full-fledged strategic bombing offensive against a technically advanced enemy nation. Nor was there yet any evidence that civilian morale would crack under a sustained bombing campaign, much less that Britain could count on this happening more quickly in the nations with whom it might be at war than among its own civilian population. Neither Britain's political leaders, nor the chiefs of staff, nor even the Air Ministry fully endorsed the RAF's strategic offence doctrine. The public largely opposed preparations for war, and money was short.

Nonetheless, the RAF prepared itself for a strategic bombing war. When, in 1932, international negotiations to limit aerial bombing ended in failure, the RAF promptly drew up specifications for modern bombers able to carry heavy loads to distant targets. In 1934 the RAF embarked on an expansion program to construct dozens of new airfields across the British island fortress. The next year, the RAF was reorganized, with Bomber Command established to conduct the strategic offensive (Fighter Command would be the RAF's defensive arm, and Coastal Command would be responsible for coastal defence and anti-shipping offensives). The third pillar of expansion was to recruit and train the great number of men needed to operate a sophisticated bomber force. New training schools were established in Britain, and many more were added in Canada under the British Commonwealth Air Training Plan. What aspiring aircrew would learn in their training, and what they would not learn, was rooted in the doctrines and practices of the Royal Air Force as these had developed for better or worse since the 1920s.

⊙

The RAF introduced three new bombers into service just before the war. These were the Wellingtons, Whitleys, and Hampdens, each incorporating the latest features of aircraft technology: all-metal, low-wing, twin-engine monoplanes, with complex electrical and hydraulic systems, equipped with variable-pitch propellers and retractable landing gear. These aircraft would finally and definitively replace the biplane bombers of First World War design.

The last and fastest of the three was the Hampden, which entered service in 1938. It seemed to promise much, but delivered somewhat less. It could carry a two-thousand-pound bomb load to a target as far as six hundred miles away, although it took four hours to do so. The Handley-Page Hampden quickly earned the nickname "flying suitcase" on account of its narrow, boxy, flat-sided fuselage. Its long, slim tail boom, and its manoeuvrability in flight lent it the appearance of a dragonfly. Three feet wide, the Hampden seemed more like a fighter-bomber than the larger Whitley and

Wellington bombers in the main force. Many pilots liked flying it, despite an alarming tendency for uncontrollable sideslip.

Yet none of these bombers fully loaded could reach much beyond the factories of northwestern Germany. Berlin was near the limit of range, but with little more than half the bomb load. The RAF had not addressed the problem of actually finding any of these targets after several hours' flying time from England in conditions other than cloudless daylight, despite being aware of it since the Great War. The new bombers were also thinly armoured and lightly armed: their machine guns fired bullets the calibre of a hunting rifle. Wellingtons and Whitleys had power-operated gun turrets, thought (wrongly) to provide a decisive defensive advantage. Hampdens did not.

At the outbreak of war, the RAF had established five to six squadrons of each type, amounting to less than three hundred aircraft in total. About 80 percent might have been available for action on any given day. This was the force that would put theory into practice. But how would these new airplanes fare in combat? The power and capabilities of military aircraft had progressed rapidly on both sides during the rearmament period of the late 1930s. The RAF's front-line bombers were already becoming outdated by the time they were brought into active service. They were nearly defenceless against by then faster and more heavily armed German fighter aircraft. Without long-range fighter escorts to support them, which the RAF did not have, the bombers were easy targets in daylight. The RAF had not installed radio navigation aids in its bombers, even though such aids were already in use in civil aviation in Europe. Radar, then only a ground-based defensive system, was just coming into use.

The view that "the bomber will always get through" still gripped the public and the media in 1939. The Air Ministry was less sure, and was hedging its bets for a long war, and even Bomber Command's commander-in-chief, Air Chief Marshall Sir Edgar Ludlow-Hewitt, had his doubts. Yet whether Bomber Command could actually deliver a "knockout blow," it was not authorized to do so. The Air Ministry's instructions governing both air and naval bombardment, issued the week before war was declared, specified that the intentional targeting of civilian populations was illegal. Thus, during the first seven months of the war, Bomber Command's offensive operations were limited to naval targets at sea. These became increasingly difficult to locate as weather conditions deteriorated and daylight hours diminished with the onset of winter. All that Bomber Command dropped on Germany itself that winter were propaganda leaflets.

In clear weather on the afternoon of 18 December 1939, twenty-four Wellington bombers set out in formation to attack the naval facilities at Wilhelmshaven on Germany's northwest coast. Luftwaffe fighters picked off most of them, and only seven returned to England unscathed. This was not Bomber Command's first catastrophic daylight raid, but it was the worst, and it put an end to the idea that a daylight formation could defend itself against modern German fighter aircraft. Evidently the bomber did not always get through, and indeed might have a less than even chance of doing so, at least in daylight. This inescapable conclusion prompted the most crucial tactical change of the long strategic air offensive: to conduct it by bombing at night.

Bomber Command was forced to resort to night bombing with aircraft unequipped for it, and crews untrained for it. Pre-war aircrews rarely flew in darkness or bad weather, both of which prevailed in Europe in winter. Flying was essentially visual, aided only by radio contact with ground stations. Cross-country exercises in Britain provided little guide to navigating long distances over blacked-out territory, except to confirm that it was quite possible for crews to get lost even over home territory. There was no long-distance flying training over the sea.

Then, in May and June 1940, the strategic situation was stunningly reversed as Germany attacked and defeated its western neighbours. Germany could project its air and naval power from anywhere on Europe's Atlantic coast between northern Norway and southern France. London was now an easy target for the Luftwaffe's new forward bases just across the Channel. Germany's military and industrial targets, on the other hand, were several hours' flying time from England, and Berlin considerably further distant. With the British Army chased off the Continent, only Bomber Command could carry the fight directly to Germany. Yet to do so effectively, it required newer, heavier bombers: aircraft that could carry a large bomb load for a long distance, equipped with the navigational and bomb-aiming technology to locate and hit a target accurately and with effect. Unfortunately, the heavy bomber program begun in 1936 would not even begin to provide combat-ready aircraft until 1941. Until then, the Wellingtons, Hampdens, and Whitleys would have to carry the attack.

Night bombing of Germany began in May 1940. Raids that summer were small and intermittent, and generally confined to the "moon period" of approximately nine nights around the full moon, especially when clear weather was forecast. Bomber Command was just then learning from its tactical support in the defence of France that its aircraft had difficulty targeting small objectives on moonless nights, even at low altitudes. At higher altitudes on such nights, crews could not map-read their way over the darkened landscape below, and neither could they rely confidently on dead reckoning or radio fixes to find their way because both became less accurate with distance from base. Crews fortunate enough to find the target area then had to "stooge" around for some time to get a visual fix on their specific target (such as an oil production or storage facility, an aircraft factory, or a railway hub), which might well be obscured by industrial haze. This could mean spending a half-hour or so in a blacked-out target area, perhaps aided by releasing a flare that might illuminate the target but also reveal their own presence. Crews unable to identify and confirm their target were instructed to bring their bombs back.

Bomber Command was still using 250- and 500-pound general-purpose (GP) bombs of First World War vintage. On account of their high proportion of metal casing to explosive, these bombs delivered a modest blast for their weight (if they actually detonated), and could not penetrate armour plate or hardened concrete. GP bombs could destroy a house, cause severe structural damage to a few more, and break windows over a city block or two. So a lot of them would be needed to do serious damage to a large factory or to naval yards. And they would have to be well placed, which was the exception, not the rule.

All through 1940 there was considerable discussion in Bomber Command of high-level tactics and objectives: optimum targets, levels of force or concentration required, and routing of attacks. Commanders knew the number of aircraft sent to various targets and the weight of bombs dropped, but very little about the effectiveness of these attacks. An initial assessment made in November, six months into the night bombing campaign, suggested that only 35 percent of the aircraft dispatched were actually reaching their primary target.

Doubters asked whether these findings were typical, and suggested that if navigation was the problem, it was most likely due to poor training or improperly maintained or utilized equipment. Senior air staff asked squadrons to submit systematic reports to headquarters on the numbers of aircraft failing to reach the target. The problem of wind-finding was singled out. Ascertaining wind direction and speed in the dark and cloud, without visible landmarks below, was difficult. Meteorological forecasting was still in its infancy. The longer the crews fly toward the target, and the higher they climb in the atmosphere, the less certain can they be that wind direction and speed continue to be as reported on takeoff, or as forecast to be en route. In short, crews become less likely to know where they are and where they are going. Astro-navigation can, over time, confirm the course of the aircraft independently of wind-finding, but not its exact location. Not all air observers had been fully trained in astro-navigation, and fewer still had enough experience to be good at it. Better sextants were promised, but they were in short supply.

Although crews reported difficulties in finding their targets, they believed they had bombed them successfully when they did. On return, crews described the bomb flashes and fires they saw below to the intelligence officers who interviewed them. Yet even on clear nights they could only speculate about exactly where these had occurred and what damage they might have done. And they could only hope that they had not been deceived by dummy installations and decoy fires. Bomber aircraft were not yet equipped with night cameras, but with disturbing frequency, subsequent daytime photos of target areas taken by fighter aircraft reconnaissance forays failed to verify crew reports.

Nearly every night of operations, a few aircraft did not return. Some were shot down over enemy territory, according to German reports via the International Red Cross in Geneva. Others were lost without trace – perhaps so badly damaged by enemy fire that they couldn't make it back across the North Sea, or perhaps unable to find their way across those dark waters. Navigation errors, whether the result of impossible weather conditions at night, or of simple blunders like reading a compass or radio direction signal in reverse, could be fatal. Both aircraft and crews were being lost faster than they could be replaced until the spring of 1941, when freshly trained Canadians began arriving in numbers. Nagging suspicions mounted at all levels of the Command – from crews to commanders – about the effectiveness of bombing raids, but there was little willingness to acknowledge them. Initial reactions were defensive, and excuses were found.

None of these problems was known to the British public. Every day the newspapers carried Air Ministry announcements of the ferocity of the previous night's attacks on German targets, the number of aircraft dispatched, and even the number lost in the effort. Readers were left to infer that much damage had been inflicted, but these reports said nothing about the actual effects of the bombing.

During the first year of the air war, the men charged with executing Bomber Command's offensive – the crews, the squadron leaders, the group commanders, and the staff specialists – were learning by experience about the difficulties and hazards they faced, and how to deal with them. They shared personal and anecdotal experiences informally in the sergeant's quarters and the officer's quarters. They also discussed lessons learned at periodic group and specialist conferences, many of these devoted to navigation and bomb-aiming. They applied themselves with ingenuity and resourcefulness to solve the problems they saw. As air force men, they had always put a premium on flying experience, especially for leadership, with little regard for engineering and even less for science, which they regarded as civilian concerns. They were practical men, consumed with the day-to-day problems of operations, and not much given to theory or theoreticians. Their work was not yet systematic.

In September 1940, a year into the war, a Bomber Development Unit was established for the purpose of investigating the causes of bombing errors, the problems of night bombing, navigation, and wind-finding, trials for new bombs and bombsights, and the development of new methods of attack. The Unit was expected to apply modern scientific methods, quantitative assessment and statistics, not to aeronautics, and not only to the development of new weapons and instruments but also to improving their deployment through combat tactics. Yet there were military men who doubted the utility of this approach and were wary of civilian encroachment. Some feared that the identification of "technical and scientific" personnel in the Unit's terms of reference would be "seized upon by our civilian brethren to stock the BDU with a mass of bowler hats, probably chuck-outs from other establishments."[1]

Those bowler hats would become known as the "boffins," the Air Ministry's civilian scientists who developed all kinds of ideas they thought worth testing. Some of these ideas were bizarre and cost the lives of aircrews, but others became lifesavers and war winners. The Unit's first report, issued in November, addressed methods of wind-finding. It challenged some current approaches and called for improvement of pilot and navigational skills. Many senior navigation officers decried its tone and questioned its findings, seeing them as impugning the work of those on the front line.

Over a year into the war, a very English ethos of amateurism continued to prevail at the unit level. The premium was on gallant effort, even if it led more often than not to heroic failure. The sure thread, from the charge of the Light Brigade through the Somme to Dunkirk, and from Scott's failed assault on the South Pole to Mallory's failed attempt on the summit of Everest, remained unbroken.[2] There was faith in Britain's indomitable spirit, and comfort in its people's seeming capacity to muddle through against heavy odds, but Bomber Command's task was not to avoid defeat but to find a way to win.

⊙

Unable to achieve precision bombing of its assigned targets, Bomber Command was soon directed to resort to the strategy it had always advocated:

the "continuous interruption and dislocation" of industry, although night bombing was not to be allowed to "degenerate into mere indiscriminate action."[3] The opportunity for a quick knockout blow had passed, if indeed it had ever existed. By midsummer, Bomber Command had to concentrate its attacks on the more immediate threat of invasion. Its primary targets were now the Channel ports in France and Belgium, although it mounted a few raids on German cities in retaliation for the bombing of London. One of the more desperate (and entirely unsuccessful) measures envisaged in the summer of 1940 was setting fire to Germany's crops and forests with incendiary bombs. Summing up the first year of war at the end of September, Bomber Command's senior air staff officer lamented that the diversion of its squadrons to defensive tasks prevented it from inflicting sufficient force to crack Germany's civilian morale and political will to fight. Yet if the offensive was so far without notable success, it was also without unbearable cost. Night bombing losses continued at less than 2 percent during the summer of 1940, grievous but within replacement capacity for both aircraft and crews.

As winter approached, the Air Ministry decided that:

> if bombing is to have its full moral effect it must on occasion produce heavy material destruction.... it is desired that regular concentrated attacks should be made on objectives in large towns and centres of industry, with the primary aim of causing very heavy material destruction which will demonstrate to the enemy the power and severity of air bombardment and the hardship and dislocation which will result from it.[4]

And so, step by step, and as much from necessity as conviction, precision bombing became area bombing, material effect became moral effect, and the by-product of attack became the end product. But even these alternatives required a large force that could overcome Germany's air defences and concentrate sufficient bomb tonnage in a target area. Yet the actual force rarely amounted to more than a hundred aircraft on any night, and these were often dispersed over several targets in the hope that the unpredictability and diversity of its attacks would sap German morale and reduce the vulnerability of the bombers to Germany's air defences. The cost of dispersal, however, was insufficient concentration of force over any one target to cause any significant damage, especially because the bomb load of each aircraft could destroy little more than a few houses. It would take a very long time to reduce Germany to rubble at that rate. That Bomber Command's nightly raids would even set off enough air raid alarms to disrupt the sleep of Germany's industrial workforce remained wishful thinking.

As winter set in, the weather deteriorated, and many crews turned back or failed to find the target. Bomber Command took risks, not so much to achieve specific vital war objectives, but to keep the offensive going. Yet its attacks were of little consequence except perhaps to spur Germany to retaliate (and in the winter of 1940–41 the Luftwaffe was by far the more accomplished bomber force), and to improve its air defences.

In January 1941, Bomber Command was charged with destroying Germany's synthetic oil production by means of concentrated attacks under ideal weather conditions. These conditions were rare, and successful operations rarer. Two months later, in the face of rising shipping losses in the North Atlantic, Bomber Command was redirected to attack Germany's naval docks, shipyards, and submarine bases. This new directive also called for something else: that priority "should be given to those [targets] in Germany which lie in congested areas where the greatest moral effect is likely to result."[5] In this way, bombs that missed the primary aiming point would not be wasted, as sometimes happened against more isolated military and industrial facilities. Conveniently for Bomber Command, the most heavily industrialized and populated areas of Germany were concentrated in the Ruhr, and thus within range of its aircraft. Crews were now authorized to bomb secondary targets such as city centres and built-up areas if they could not find the primary target, and so maximize the effectiveness of each raid. If Germany's factories, railways, and naval yards could not be destroyed by bombs, perhaps the morale of those who worked in them could be. The indifferent results of the previous winter's night operations would not be repeated, or so it was hoped.

Four months later, on 9 July, the Air Council provided new direction to Bomber Command, this time to unleash a wide-ranging attack on Germany's strategic war industries and transport systems. The objective was to inflict a crippling, if not fatal, blow to Germany's capacity to wage war, whether on the ground, in the air, or at sea. This was the green light that the most fervent proponents of strategic bombing had been waiting for. In fact, it was they themselves who flashed the green light. At a conference of Bomber Command's senior air ranks five weeks before, the retired Lord Trenchard had been invited to open the proceedings, where he reiterated his long-held view on the importance of cracking Germany's morale by bombing its cities. No German should regard himself safe from the reach of the Royal Air Force, he said. Precise targets should be secondary. All nodded in agreement and, after Trenchard left the meeting, they set about drafting what would become their new directive. They observed that they would have to draft the paper very carefully to secure the political support of the prime minister's Defence Committee, and if it were adopted, "the presentation of news concerning the results of the attacks would have to be carefully handled to ensure a favourable reception in this country and to avoid undue disclosure of our intentions to the enemy."[6]

Germany's strategic air offensive against Britain during the previous winter had already rendered the public mood more receptive.

On any given night in the summer of 1941, Bomber Command could theoretically draw on about 450 serviceable night bombers with crews, or about a 50 percent increase since the beginning of the war. In fact, accounting for crew leave, sickness, and detachments for training or ferrying, not more than 80 percent of that number was actually available on any given night, and the highest number of sorties on a single night to that point was 364. The average bomb weight per aircraft was just over two thousand pounds. This was not a large or effective enough force to do serious damage. Moreover, the old problems of navigation, target finding, bomb-aiming, and unforeseen bad weather remained unsolved, even as evidence mounted of Germany's improved air defences. Meanwhile, monthly loss rates had risen to 2 and even 3 percent. Could Britain's factories and the Empire's air training programs replace these losses and yet expand the offensive? Bomber Command and its allies in the Air Ministry continued to exaggerate the accuracy and power of the bomber force and its ability to inflict the necessary pain on Germany. Bomber Command continued to take insufficient account of the operational difficulties that confronted it, hoping the offensive would be saved by technical solutions that were months or years away. The Command continued to prefer misleading and over-interpreted intelligence from sources in Germany over what its own airborne reconnaissance photography was beginning to reveal.

This was the situation in which Britain would begin to attack Germany itself, in aid of its new Russian ally, until there could be a second front on the ground. These were the resources with which Lord Trenchard's doctrine would be put to the test. Thus began in earnest the strategic air offensive against Germany, a campaign of increasing ferocity and effectiveness over the next four years. What until then had been little more than a program of nuisance raids would become devastation, but it would take a while. In the meantime, Bomber Command would have to fix the many problems that had been either unforeseen or wishfully ignored up to the previous year. As the newly arrived Canadians would soon learn, wars are fought with the resources one has, not those one wishes for.

Eighteen

Initiation

Arrived on 106 sq with Roger & rec'd a warm reception from all the gang on 6 course at Finningley – Pop Miller & other Canadians – it was a grand feeling seeing the boys again – cool – confident, cheery.... I got all my old confidence & zip back again watching the fellows prepare for a raid on Kiel – 18 crews taking off – the boys all kid each other – take it easy & act as if there was nothing to it – that's the cool confident spirit that is the backbone of our victory spirit. (JJD 2 August 1941)

All planes returned from Kiel safely – it's thrilling to be on an operational station – everybody is informal – friendly – natural – you live from day to day – learn to accept & look at danger coolly, calmly & without fear – amazing what we are capable of doing when we get down to it – hard to believe that I once shivered at the word – death – (JJD 3 August 1941)

Was billeted with Roger at Woodhall Spa – an old widow with a nice home in a quiet village – Mrs. Lettice looks like a good scout ... (JJD 4 August 1941)

In his first letter home, Joe described Woodhall Spa as a charming and peaceful little English village. He immediately recognized in Clara Lettice the same good-hearted motherly qualities of Mrs. Graham, his landlady in Preston two years before. Mrs. Lettice had taken him and Roger in, he said,

because we were Canadians and wanted to stay together. We have a lovely room – a magnificent feather bed and are quite at home.

> Mrs. Lettice has taken us quite to heart. She stays awake worrying about us every night we fly. Then she has tea, or coffee – bread, butter & jam for us when we wearily plod in about 8 o'clock in the morning.
>
> … When we fly we get chocolate – an orange, raisins, biscuits, gum, tea and sweets to eat on the trip – we give her chocolate and cigarettes so we are all happy. When I get a package I take it downstairs and we pool our resources and have a real feed – the old lady is a real good scout and Roger & I have a lot of fun when we are around.
>
> The only difficulty here is that there is no running water. She fills up the basin for us – but it is hard to wash your feet. We discovered a bath in a special shed behind the house and after a week in this home we have decided that Roger will use the bath first – he needs it most – there are no toilets either which means it is rather awkward with only one under the bed bowl for two – if you get what I mean – but we manage….
> (JJL 10 August 1941)

Alone among the drab, austere agricultural villages of the Lincolnshire fens, Woodhall Spa was a charming, if modest, resort destination. The supposed curative powers of the local waters had led to the development of the spa, which in turn led to the redesign of the town centre by a London architect. By the turn of the century, several hotels and gift shops lined the newly laid out Broadway. Woodhall Spa, three miles north of RAF Coningsby, was one of several towns in which flying crew were billeted, dispersal being a key method of reducing the risk of aircrew coming under enemy air attack while on the ground.

⊙

About one-third of Bomber Command's night bombing force consisted of the Hampdens of 5 Group. 106 Squadron, which had been relocated to Coningsby in February, was one of seven Hampden-equipped squadrons in 5 Group. Squadrons were the smallest self-sustaining units of the air force for the purposes of aircraft maintenance and repair, administration, and provision of the necessaries for its members. Nominally they were twenty-four aircraft in strength, with a staff of perhaps thirty crews, led by a wing commander, and subdivided into three "flights" led by squadron leaders. Supporting them was a far greater number of mechanics, storekeepers, cooks, and drivers, so the total complement of a squadron amounted to several hundred people.

Stations consisted of a single aerodrome shared by two squadrons, under the charge of a group commander, with his own administrative and

Joe with Roger Rousseau in front of Mrs. Lettice's house, Woodhall Spa, Lincolnshire, late 1941. (Canadian Jewish Archives)

technical staff, including meteorologists, intelligence officers, and navigation specialists. 106 Squadron shared RAF Coningsby with 97 Squadron, also in 5 Group but recently converted to the new heavy Manchester bombers. In July these aircraft had been grounded due to recurring engine problems.

Until June 1941, Hampden squadrons were equipped with only sixteen aircraft, and on any particular night, 106 Squadron contributed six to a dozen crews to Bomber Command operations, mostly on naval and industrial targets in northwestern Germany. Between February and the end of July, the squadron lost fourteen crews on operations, but managed to come through the first three weeks of the new air offensive unscathed until another crew was lost the day Joe and Roger arrived. But things would soon get worse.

Until May, Hampden crews made their way to those targets using second pilots as navigators. The first specially trained air observers, mostly from Canada, began arriving that month, and within a few weeks they had entirely displaced second pilots from the "office."

The first two Canadian air observers arrived at 106 Squadron in May, and ten more were posted there in June and July. By August, three of the twelve had already become operational casualties, and three had been transferred to other squadrons. So Joe and Roger, along with Jack McIntyre, who had arrived the week prior, immediately became part of a Canadian fraternity of air observers who staffed a third of the squadron's regular crews. Only one Canadian pilot had been posted to 106, and no wireless operators. The Canadian observers were quick to make their mark, especially those who had arrived with a commission, which very few British-trained air observers had yet been awarded. Several were picked out for special training on daylight operations, including Jim Erly, who had graduated at the top of his class at Rivers in December, and was soon flying as his wing commander's observer. Erly was awarded the Distinguished Flying Cross for his part in pressing the attack on the battlecruiser *Gneisenau* at Brest without breaking formation under intense enemy fire during a rare daylight raid in late July. He and two other Canadian air observers would be selected for another daylight operation the next month. And some of the earlier arrivals were already well into their first tour of operations: Rae Dunn had completed eighteen sorties, Doug McIver ten.

The rivalry between the Dominion and British boys, now more friendly, continued. By moving on to an operational squadron, however, Joe had graduated from a world divided between instructors and pupils to one divided between officers and men. Even when they crewed together on a long and dangerous operation, after touchdown officers and NCOs made their way to separate messes and quarters to eat and sleep. But whether they were sergeants or junior officers, practically all aircrew were recent recruits fresh out of training.

They would soon enough figure out the established patterns of hierarchy and seniority. Despite the RAF's image as a meritocratic service unburdened by hoary traditions, the social distinctions between officers and NCOs, and between aircrew and ground crew, were deeply entrenched. The career pilots – upper-class men who had taken officer training at the air force academy at Cranwell before the war – were by then senior officers. Their place in the ranks was being taken by the influx of civilians to the RAF

Volunteer Reserve, the short-service volunteers in only for the duration of the war. Some of them had been attracted from England's public schools, but as the need grew, many others were drawn from the middle class, and supplemented by the newly arrived Canadians. Ground crew, many of them skilled tradesmen of long service but with no prospect of commission, were mainly of lower-middle-class origin. Not all of them took kindly to being leapfrogged by the new arrivals. To the extent that the RAF still regarded a public school background as an essential indicator of both leadership and flying skills, working-class lads were scarce on bomber stations, and even rarer in flying crews.

August 5 began with a gale warning, but turned fair. Late that morning, RAF Coningsby was directed by telex from 5 Group Headquarters to prepare for an attack that night on the main railway station at Ludwigshaven. Joe was crewed with pilot Gerry Roberts, who was on his second sortie as a first pilot, having served as a second pilot in the observer position on seven operations in the spring. The two WO/AGs had been on squadron for nearly a month. One of them, Duncan Hodgkinson, who had already begun operations in July, would fly with Joe and Gerry regularly for the next four months.

Ground crews brought out the bombs and loaded up each aircraft during the afternoon, while observers were briefed on the night's objectives and weather forecasts. Right after briefing, Joe charted his aircraft's course so as to arrive over Ludwigshaven between 0115 and 0200. It was still the practice in 1941 for each aircraft to make its separate way to the target area so as to arrive within a prescribed time period long enough for it to obtain a visual fix on the target and line up on the aiming point. If crews could not identify the primary aiming point, they were supposed to find some other likely target, or as a last resort, bomb flak concentrations visible through cloud, but they were not to return their bombs. It was, in effect, every crew for itself, do your best lads, and good luck.

Ludwigshaven lay deep in German territory, over a hundred miles further up the Rhine from the usual targets in the Ruhr. It was too far from Lincolnshire to be safely reached under cover of darkness in the short nights of midsummer, so this was Bomber Command's first big raid on the area since early May, amounting to ninety-eight aircraft. An entirely "freshman" crew would not have been assigned such a distant target, but Joe was the only new boy in this crew, and in good hands.

As the shadows of evening lengthened, the four men emptied their pockets of anything – bus or cinema tickets, letters, or photos – that might disclose their flight's origin. Then they donned their flying boots, sheepskins, helmets, goggles, and parachute harnesses, and gathered up their rations of coffee and chocolate. Then they were driven out to Hampden AE193, moored at the perimeter of the grass runway. Roberts as pilot climbed on to the port wing root and then into the cockpit. Joe, carrying his sack of navigation instruments, followed Roberts and sat behind him until airborne. The WO/AGs entered through a side door below the wing and took up their positions above and below at the rear of the aircraft. Jones, going first, took with him a wicker basket containing two pigeons, which he placed just forward of the upper turret. It would be his responsibility in an emergency to attach the tiny canisters to their legs, containing the location of the aircraft's distress the observer had written on rice paper, and release the pigeons through his open window, with the birds facing forward and downward to begin their flight home.

Hampden AE193 took off well after ten o'clock – just before sunset as the days were still long, and Double Summer Time was in effect. Joe crawled through the narrow passageway beneath the pilot's seat to the plotting table in his "office" in the Perspex nosecone, and spread out his maps and instruments. The wireless operator listened to his set in silence, as any transmission, even on the ground before takeoff, could reveal the timing and direction of attack. Nonetheless, soon after becoming airborne, they were detected by German radar stations along the Dutch coast. So they were already in danger, even if they no longer presented a visible silhouette against the fading twilight in the northwest. Joe checked his position as they crossed the Dutch coast at twelve thousand feet. From there he navigated by dead reckoning, periodically recording his track and altitude in his navigator's log and recalculating his course to the target on his chart. When openings in the cloud cover appeared, he tried to verify his dead reckoning by searching the moonlit but otherwise darkened landscape for visual fixes on landmarks that he could identify from his maps. Once deep into Germany, Joe tried to verify the direction and velocity of the wind through his drift sight so that he could adjust his bombsight accordingly.

A few minutes before he expected to reach Ludwigshaven, Joe stowed his divider, ruler, and protractor, folded up his table, and turned off his shaded lamp to let his eyes adjust to the darkness. The target area, a distinctive junction on the Rhine with Ludwigshaven on the left bank and Mannheim on the right, was not hard to find. But with mostly overcast skies, Joe couldn't see the railway station, so he decided to bomb the secondary target of Mannheim across the river. Kneeling over his bombsight, now swung into position over the Perspex oval at the front of the aircraft, Joe began lining up his target from about three miles away. Now pilot and observer needed the utmost coordination while trying to ignore the searchlights and anti-aircraft fire coming up from below. Joe needed Gerry to fly straight and level in order to stabilize his bombsight, while Gerry needed Joe to direct his course on the final run in. With the bomb bay doors now open, and at the moment Joe thought he had his target lined up, he pressed the bomb-release button. As the load of 500- and 250-pound high-explosive bombs, along with two cans of "deckers" (a form of incendiary bomb) fell away, the aircraft rose upward. Then Joe gave Gerry the course back to Coningsby, and settled in for the return trip. They arrived back at Coningsby safely, in low cloud, about two hours before sunrise, seven hours and ten minutes after taking off. Fourteen other 106 Squadron crews returned around the same time. Each was debriefed by intelligence officers about what they saw and did, over wartime coffee improved with rum. Joe's crew reported they had been unable to observe the results of their bombing.

By dawn, all crews were falling into bed, relieved to have survived, even if sleep did not come easily after the tension of the night's work. The operations room at Coningsby had notified the Air Ministry that one squadron aircraft had failed to return. Joe recorded this sortie in the operational diary he began the next day:

> Made my first trip at night over Mannheim – 450 miles – My pilot was Sgt Roberts – trip uneventful – weather bad – flew at 12000' most of way – did not bomb target – but target district – got caught in searchlights once – we had little aak aak trouble.[1] Arrived home after seven hours – safe and sound, tired but glad to hurdle the first trip successfully. We lost one plane – Jimmy MacIlraith, Les Knowles, Joe the Gen Man – saw lots of fires – we had about 200 planes around Frankfurt & Mannheim – only saw one fighter. The target was well plastered.
> (JJOD 5 August 1941)

More sorties followed in quick succession. On the 7th, the squadron was detailed to bomb the Krupp steel works at Essen. The weather was promising, but Joe's aircraft had to turn back as the intercom "packed up." The next night, the squadron visited Deutsche Werke's submarine yards at Kiel on the Baltic coast. Again the weather was good and the squadron record book claimed success. Joe set course mainly over the sea, avoiding landfall until close to Kiel. Helping him and Gerry Roberts along were two wireless operators who were decorated squadron veterans. They

> met little opposition – weaved in over the target – dropped the bombs & turned smartly back, leaving a terrific barrage of aak where we should have been it was mostly light aak aak and made a beautiful color display – the trip home was uneventful – we were chased around our drome by a JU88 & fired on by our own aak aak who were cockeyed – fortunately Mackenzie & Hammatt are a couple of veterans & lots of fun – there is no panic with them & they carry on a humorous running commentary at all times – Roberts is an excellent pilot.... Navigation on these trips is pretty well a matter of estimation & map reading around the target – the pilot has to be able to handle the plane & get out of the searchlight cones which are numerous & accurate. A lot of judgment has to be used when attacking the target. No sense barging in to a hail of fire – can often wait until they pick on somebody else, then nip in.
>
> Our squadron is getting real good – there are four top notch men who are responsible –
>
> 1. Wing Co. Allen D.S.O., D.F.C. He is young, leads the daylights himself
> 2. Sqdn Ldrs – Nelms, Boylan, Tudor – all go on raids – all top notch – Boylan & Tudor – the most popular – all young.
>
> (JJOD 7 August 1941)

Boylan and Hammatt had taken Roger Rousseau with them the night before, and Joe was deeply impressed by how the veterans helped initiate the "freshmen" on their first sorties.

> Amazing life on ops ... every day might be your last so a quiet stroll – a peaceful chat – a good book or a roary eyed binge is all the more significant – all the more appreciated. (JJD 7 August 1941)

> Lived thru one of the momentous weeks of my life – realized a cherished ambition – made two bombing trips over Germany – am well away – I can now realize just what stuff our type of civilization produces – we joke & kid around on trips as we do on a pleasure ride & we try for the target. (JJD 9 August 1941)

On the 12th, Joe was briefed to attack the railway yards at Hanover, deep in Germany, which he described in his operational diary the following day:

> The weather was bad and all our planes were not sent – only four got off – the weather over the sea was rough – 10/10 CU [cumulus]

at 10,000' – cleared over the Dutch coastline & again over the Zuider Sea – those were the only places I saw ground – we flew at 13,000' and often skirted around CB [cumulonimbus] clouds that towered to 15,000'. The black, powerful towering clouds were both beautiful and awe inspiring – we found Hanover by the searchlights – we dropped our bombs around the middle of the town – and were surrounded on all sides by searchlights and aak altho none put the bead on us. The trip back was the same as going out – 10/10 clouds – broken only at both coastlines and the added joy of good old English rain back at base – all our four craft returned safely.

After a few easy trips you get the feeling that the whole thing is a cinch – a piece of cake – but a nice few minutes in searchlights or flak – or with fighters on your tail or damaged engines, etc. I imagine that feeling of confidence is soon dispelled. But so far the trips have been grand. My ambition at present is to get thru 200 hours and get cracking as a pilot. (JJOD 13 August 1941)

The raid had been aborted shortly after takeoff, but four crews, including theirs, did not get the recall message and so proceeded on to Hanover. Nearly fifty years later, Joe's pilot had not forgotten the weather conditions en route. The reason the raid was cancelled, he recalled, was a very active cold front over Holland. With only a couple of hundred hours' flying time, he had had no experience flying in those conditions. It was a frightening affair, as they encountered thunderstorms over Holland, accompanied by both icing and St. Elmo's fire, "blue fire, around prop tips and cockpit glass, ice slinging off props," and the aircraft being "being flung up in the air several hundred feet and down again."[2]

Four days later the squadron sent twenty aircraft to bomb the railway marshalling yards at Dusseldorf. Joe's aircraft, carrying two 500-pound bombs, two 250-pound bombs, and canisters of incendiaries, was also equipped with a camera.

The weather – nothing to brag about – the trip plenty tough – there is a thirty to sixty mile long searchlight belt – and five to ten miles deep that has to be crossed – there is no flak in this belt but there are fighters which probably accounted for a good percentage of the thirteen planes lost. We lost two – Johnny Cook – and Acres – poor show – [nearly got it ourselves a couple of times].[3]

We could not identify the target but certainly got a pasting from the aak defences.

I have been blissfully ignorant of the fire we have drawn because most of it has been a little late and on and right beneath our tail – the rear gunner Hodgkinson and Robby the pilot have calm intimate discussions as to the proximity of the flak whilst Robby keeps on weaving and climbing or diving – it is all very calm and dispassionate.

We weaved thru the searchlight area in masterly style but about a dozen planes did not. They got shot down. It takes about 15 minutes to get thru. I lean over the navigator's table – eat my rations of chocolate and biscuits with coffee and wonder how soon they will pick us up. It entrances me to see powerful searchlights sweeping 15,000' high – sweep the skies trying to pick you up for their fighter & aak – we had a close shave at the airdrome when we missed one of our planes by 5 feet while circling the beacon waiting to land.

The whole trip was a test of nerves. Once the plane leaves the ground you become a different person until the wheels touch again. All the little problems and joys of life cease to be thought of your whole being is concentrated on flying – on the weather – [height] – air speed – navigation, map reading – Jerries, flak, searchlights and anything else of interest. You are wide awake, alert and active – you react clearly – most people are calm, level-headed – your nerves only trouble you on the ground when you think of the close shaves – near misses – real danger. (JJOD 16 August 1941)

106 Squadron's twenty Hampdens, the largest number yet detailed on a single raid by the squadron, constituted nearly one-third of Bomber Command's aircraft dispatched to Dusseldorf that night. Although the weather was generally good, the target was obscured by ground haze. Joe's crew reported to intelligence that they reached the city and bombed it, but had not observed any bomb bursts owing to flak.

Joe had been on five sorties in twelve days. He reported reaching and bombing the target area on each occasion (save the aborted sortie), but only once could he clearly see the target itself, and where his bombs actually landed. Twice the aiming point was obscured by cloud, and on the other occasion the anti-aircraft fire was so heavy he could neither see the target itself nor where his bombs dropped. Only the Kiel sortie seemed to have been an unqualified success.

Joe was exhilarated and amazed at having completed his first few sorties. He was now confident that he could do the job for which he had been trained, and inspired by the leadership qualities he saw in his squadron commanders. His senses heightened in the midst of action, Joe saw a terrible and awesome beauty in the dangerous cloud formations, the probing searchlights, and the rising curtain of exploding anti-aircraft shells. After his first few sorties, Joe summarized "life on an operational squadron":

> Briefing is exciting at first – routine later on – unless something special is up I guess – When the plane leaves the ground you are in a different world – the whole crew becomes suddenly intimate – your mind and body functions perfectly – you have to be ready and expect everything and anything – except getting pranged I guess –
>
> An operational trip is mysterious – hundreds of planes fly for the same target – yet none go together – only the occasional one is met over the target – then you anxiously inquire if everybody returned when you get back – often some are missing – mysterious & strange – all take off – some just disappear and are never heard of again.
>
> Casual comment goes on at all times – "that fellow is getting it" – laconically says the pilot about another plane caught in searchlights and aak aak – then you nonchalantly tell one another how you got caught in searchlights & flak & how you got out – you are still alive by a hairsbreadth – but that does not worry you any more –
>
> Standoffs & free nights are heaven sends – you feel light & free & no matter what you do – you do it well – it might well be your last nite – a week of flying is like a year or more of hectic living –
>
> But despite the unspoken tension – the dangers, strain & losses of fine & genuine pals you still keep your sense of humour & fun – you still get a kick out of doing things – anything – eating – sleeping – dancing and you still don't worry or fret – or above all – fear – it's a game of death – but its all a big joke – game & sport – at least I think so –
> (JJOD 20 August 1941)

Joe made light of his experience in his letters home:

> There is a great spirit on our squadron which is rapidly becoming one of the ace squadrons in the country. Our wing commander is under thirty – he has won the DSO and DFC – he leads the dangerous and toughest daylight raids himself.... our squadron leaders ... go on many raids themselves – they are absolutely tops with us – they are just one of the boys – we call them by their first names – they take almost as many

risks as we do – model leaders – great men – fine examples – that spirit spreads right down to us all.

… I look on our regular night excursions as a hockey game – sometimes we have a tough game (target) – sometimes an easy one – sometimes we are fooled – sometimes surprised.

We have loads of fun when flying – everybody is free and easy – no panic – no excitement – when the searchlights or AAK start shooting up at you there is a bit of suspense until you get out – then the jokes start flying fast and quick. Some fellows eat their lunch over the target – others fall asleep on long trips. But we all try pretty hard to locate the target – and hit it – we usually succeed – but the Jerries are smart – you can't be careless or they get you – you have to be on your toes and outfox them all the time – it's quite a game and I am getting a huge kick out of it – we blast them night after night and I don't imagine they are too happy about it – the Germans are not getting too much sleep these days.

It does not take long to learn the country and I can almost go around Germany – Belgium, Holland and France plus England – blindfolded – at least from the air – we use planes to visit pals at other airdromes and it is marvelous meeting some old pal from Canada in some Godforsaken spot in England. (JJL 10 August 1941)

I autograph all my bombs before every take off – the big ones are for Mom & Pop – the smaller ones for the girls and for requests – everywhere we are besieged by people to drop a bomb for them. I don't know what you have been eating of late Pop but you sure made some powerful explosions on the last couple of trips. One of our boys wrote Judy Garland and asked her if he could name his plane after her – she wired back and said yes.

… I don't like sending cables whilst I am in the midst of heavy work – it is bad luck – I just write my steady weekly letter and leave it go at that….

It is difficult though after an epic making and thrilling raid to try and start giving you the local chatter – just doesn't seem to make sense but they won't let us talk about our trips in our letters home.

… I joined the local lending library and am catching up with my reading. Since I have a nice home with a fireside and radio and food I am very comfortable. (JJL 21 August 1941)

In his exuberance, Joe characteristically exaggerated his familiarity with German territory in his letters home. He would soon enough be disabused of this conceit. Perhaps this was Joe's way of dealing with his fears, but there is also a note of fascination with what he was seeing in the air, and the forces he was engaged against. He was in a constant state of elation and anticipation. He could have been on call for operations on any night. On his free nights Joe went drinking in nearby Lincoln, Horncastle, or Boston with his newfound comrades. In his spare time during the day, he played pool, went on bicycle rides with his pals, and wrote letters and read books. He was also learning how easy it was to get killed. Three 106 Squadron crews – people who were no longer strangers to him – failed to return in those two weeks, and news continued to arrive of the loss of his Canadian pals at other stations. He added a "grim note" in a letter home:

> I am addressing two letters care of our home – one to Mrs. Abrams – the other to Mrs. Kennedy who lives on Grosvenor Ave – since Ed Kennedy was one of my best pals and Hy a good friend I thought their folks would like to hear from me – both ran into a bit of tough luck and were killed. (JJL 21 August 1941)

⊙

Joe was given a week's leave, which he began in London with Roger Rousseau and Jack McIntyre (who was also billeted in Woodhall Spa) on the 18th. They shared a room at the Central Hotel, and spent much of their time at the Beaver Club, where they found dates for a dance at Covent Gardens, and where Joe ran into several of his McGill buddies now in the air force. He saw some plays, and enclosed two theatre programs in a letter home. Percy characterized these, in his own diary, as historic documents on account of "a paragraph in black type advising the use of [a] certain air raid shelter nearby the theatre in case of air attack but stating that in any case the show would continue and those in the audience who wish to remain seated could do so …" (PJD 23 September 1941).

> Left London after 2 days of merriment with Roger & Jack – we were all aware one or all [of] us might not be together again – we enjoyed ourselves without going haywire – now as happy as a lark.
> (JJD 21 August 1941)

Joe proceeded on to Midfield where, as he told his family, in Dan's absence:

> Everybody is in high spirits and Suzanne and Henriette have been laughing like they have not laughed in a long time – we have all been

> having a lovely time … talking, laughing and joking for the past five hours about family – travel, countries, politics, music and every other conceivable subject. They are all well-educated, informed, traveled and able to talk and laugh with real continental charm and intelligence – we had a delightfully evening together and Suzanne and Henriette especially were really lively and thoroughly enjoyed themselves – we certainly have some lovely times together when we are alone …
>
> … I am going back to my squadron tomorrow night. This has certainly been one of the nicest weeks I have spent anywhere. I feel thoroughly at home here and they all feel thoroughly at home with me. Their charm and kindness is overwhelming and I hope I shall be able to do something for them some day – I think that if you could get a very nice cigarette case with an air force crest on it for Henriette that she would like it – plus a nice lighter for her if you can find them – give them to Monty to bring over with the stockings and other items.
>
> I swanked it last night – took Janine to the Midland Hotel in Manchester for supper – she's about the best find over here – (JJL 24 August 1941)

He confided more than that to his diary:

> the more I see & go around with Janine – the better I like her…. yes I am falling – for Janine. (JJD 24 August 1941)
>
> Being in the company of intelligent people has put me on my mettle. I can still handle my end of it but not as adequately as I would like to. I intend on improving my English vocabulary & speaking which has become shabbier than ever. (JJD 25 August 1941)
>
> Have been thinking of Janine & my position all day – definitely fond of her – but still a lot of obstacles to a real love match – different countries being one & my slipshod character another – I have slipped badly of late will have to buck up as she is too good to lose – not many Janines around. (JJD 26 August 1941)

Nineteen

Confidence Affirmed

Joe returned from crew leave brimming with confidence, ready for another crack at German industry.

> Back to the station & home again with old pals … flying talk & tension – Jim Erly killed whilst away.[1] (JJD 26 August 1941)

> Went for a delightful bike ride with Roger & Dave – we rode to Horncastle – had a few beers, rode back in the dark, singing and watching the searchlights … Jack, Roger & I have decided we want commissions when we finish our 200 hrs – the three of us planned the same things – I wonder which of us will live to see our plans realized.
> (JJD 27 August 1941)

Jack, of Scots origin from Toronto, Roger, a French-Canadian from Trois Pistoles, Quebec, and Joe, a Jew from Westmount, might have been an unlikely threesome in civilian life back home: a Canadian fable of sorts. On operations in the same squadron in England, they shared a natural bond of citizenship and danger.

> Spent the day sleeping & getting briefed for our trip to Duisberg – it should be hot – and heavy … funny how you put everything in order before a trip over Germany – feel in another world whilst flying – then think nothing of it … (JJD 28 August 1941)

> It is hard to believe but I am sitting quietly in Mrs. Lettice's kitchen with Roger enjoying a quiet supper. Last night we had a shaky do & just about had it – can't understand how or why they did not hit us –

> vitally – yet when we reeled back we talked & joked about our adventures like I always do about all events of all kinds. (JJD 29 August 1941)

The operation on Duisberg's railway yards, from which one of the squadron's crews failed to return, had indeed proved hot and heavy.

> We really had our problems this trip. We made a landfall over Borum & the Zuider Sea – from there to the target was one mass & maze of incendiaries. We were picked up in earnest on the Rhine just west of the city & they held us for fifteen minutes. Once the searchlights caught us the aak aak started to pot at us & were we ever pounded. They were so close they hit our wings with bits of shell and there was a steady crunching & booming as the gunfire got closer & closer. We turned and dived and dropped from 12,000' to 2,000' before escaping – only to be picked up again and fired at from the low levels. I honestly thought that we were done for. It was uncanny with the dozens of searchlights from all angles holding you in their vice whilst the accurate guns came in for the kill. We dropped our bombs over the city. We escaped uninjured and without damage for some unknown reason – fate played a hand – we were lucky even then we had to fly straight back over Jerry Land thru searchlights – fighter patrols & aak. It certainly felt great to have the wheels touch the ground again. But you still joke and talk about your trips as you do about a hockey game – a trip in the country or any other pleasant adventure – the fact that you come within a foot or two of being hit and killed does not worry you in the least. It is a lot of fun while it lasts – at least you can make it seem like fun if you do not have too many narrow escapes – also once you lay off your imagination & reasoning powers take command and you realize the danger and start to worry. (JJOD 28 August 1941)

The Duisberg sortie seems to have been the closest run affair of all of Joe's operations. Decades later his pilot recalled that, coned by searchlights, the cockpit was lit brighter than daylight, while shells were bursting all around them. In the blinding light they could see neither the target nor the ground, and had to find their way out of the target area by reference to the pole star.

The next day Joe wrote to his father, who on account of the news he had been hearing in Canada, was less optimistic than Joe about the progress of the war. Joe told him that he was encouraged by the fight the Russians were

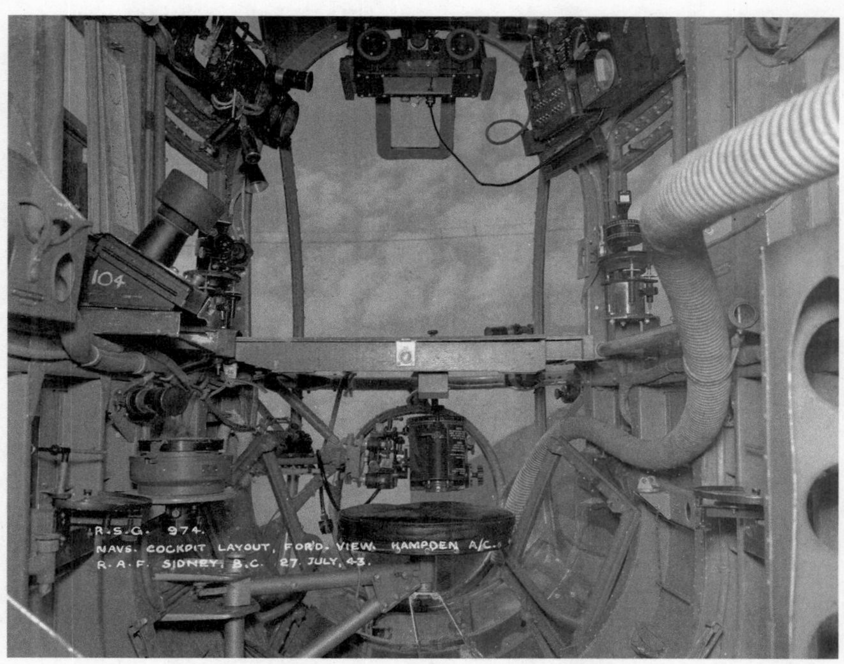

Above: Internal view of the air observer's cockpit, looking forward. The table is in the working position and can be slid back along the bar on the starbord side and stowed in raised position. The bombsight is shown in lowered position beneath it. The bomb-aimer's switches are on the starboard side (top right of the photo), and the drift sight on the port side (labelled "104" in this photo). Patricia Bay, BC, 1943. (Library and Archives Canada, PA-178902)

Right: External view of the air observer's cockpit. Canadian Jim Erly, DFC, is demonstrating the use of the electrically driven Mk. II automatic bombsight. 106 Squadron, RAF Coningsby, summer 1941. (Metheringham Airfield Visitor Centre)

putting up, and the Americans' inching progress toward war, but most of all by the bombing campaign:

> we are really keeping the hopes of peoples alive for today – that is especially true of the more unfortunate ones. Thru special informed sources, which we have access to – various facts emerge.[2] Our nightly raids – those steady sorties made practically every night of the week with anything up to four hundred planes, some of which you read about – some of which you do not, are the main hope and inspiration to our friends and allies, whilst at the same time they rock and devastate the morale as well as the possessions of our enemies. We drop leaflets still on every raid – we sometimes drop tea for Holland – those leaflets are devoured by all – by French, Belgians, Dutch – yes and by the Germans. The steady drone of our airplanes is active proof to the sufferers of our fighting strength and determination. And they are also a true proof to the Germans of our fighting strength and determination.
>
> So although isolated news items might look gloomy and depressing from where you are, I feel that the great, gradual, mighty forces are slowly hemming the Germans in, tracking them down, crushing them. It might take a longer time than we can yet foresee – it will bring many more localized set-backs – but slowly and surely the power of those who refuse to be dominated by the German race is becoming effective. Since that power is practically the power of the peoples of whole world outside of Germany itself – I see nothing but hope, encouragement and victory if we stick to it and fight with brains, might and courage until the end.... (JJL 29 August 1941)

Joe then turned to

> a more personal matter which I have never yet discussed with anybody so far – I have only vaguely thought about it in my own head at times. I feel as you probably do that we all have some reason for living – we do not decide upon our coming into or going out of the world as we know it. That is at least one weight off our shoulders which probably explains why I have not the slightest qualms about any of the more perilous jobs I am on. When your turn is due you "get it" and that is that.
>
> But there are certain events which we can control thru our own character, personalities, knowledge, intelligence, training etc. Now here is the whole point which I have come up against. Where can I fit in? Not

now particularly, but after the war if I am still around. The question is what is my capacity and what are my abilities in particular. I don't particularly feel like spending all my time and energy upon a purely selfish, petty life. I would like to do something that has more scope that would perhaps start making others conscious of others. It is definitely hard to explain but the point is – could I be of the best service in business exerting as good an influence as possible thru the various formal channels and societies or is there not something a little more imaginative I might do? I mean there should definitely be a new spirit developed after the war and somebody has got to help develop it. But here is the biggest problem of all. What would my abilities and capabilities enable me to do? Frankly and honestly I would say – at the moment not very much. Most people I know would probably be optimistic but I know myself better and I would say I have a long tough battle ahead to fit myself for anything big or small.

I know this will all seem a little puzzling and muddleheaded – but I seem to have reached the belated stage where I have to find myself. It might seem foolish thinking about these problems when engaged in the type of job that I am, but I feel that now is the time to try to formulate a plan – more or less get my ideas straightened out in order not to go to pieces once the war is over. For if the war was to end tomorrow I should find myself a very perplexed young man [not] knowing either what I wanted to do or what I was capable of doing, though the latter question does not really faze me – I now feel I could tackle anything – in fact I have – almost.

… In the meantime do not worry about me. I am having the chance of a lifetime and I certainly enjoy it. (JJL 29 August 1941)

Two days later Joe's crew was dispatched on a mine-laying sortie off Kiel Harbour, which he thought was a complete success, having "planted the vegetable" in the allotted position from a height of seven hundred feet. He saw the parachute open and the mine strike the water. It was a long trip, eight and a half hours, but Joe considered it:

A most enjoyable trip – a long 340 mile sea trip during which time it is possible to relax – use the available lights to check up on your progress – eat – talk & enjoy yourself.

> We hit the German coast north of Sylt – pinpointed myself in Denmark – cruised down the Baltic – found our exact spot and dropped our mine. We saw some ships in Kiel Bay – one fired at us but we had no difficulty. The weather was perfect – the whole operation was a complete success. Upon our return we were diverted to North Luffenham because of the weather. We stooged around the beacon there for over an hour amongst dozens of our own planes, Jerries, OTU planes, etc. Naturally you cannot see any other planes – but it was uncomfortable so we went to Waddington & landed there. It was extremely enjoyable, satisfactory and a tonic for rattled nerves. (JJOD 31 August 1941)

Mine-laying was a very different type of operation from those over industrial targets on land. On arriving near the target, the crew had to pinpoint on a designated point on the coast, and then at the end of a timed run out to a point a mile or so from shore, release the mine from a few hundred feet above the sea. The mine was a long cylindrical affair weighing nearly a ton, with a parachute attached so that it would drift down and descend to the shallow seabed intact. There it would wait to be triggered by the magnetic field of a passing enemy ship. The Hampden bomb bay was uniquely suited to the purpose and during the early years of the war, mining operations were generally assigned to Hampden squadrons.

Routed to the target over the north coast of Holland and Germany, crews avoided the Kammhuber line and the night-fighter threat on mining operations. On the other hand, when flying at such low altitudes, they were highly vulnerable to shore-based and ship-borne anti-aircraft batteries guarding the waters the Germans expected the British to mine. And crews were instructed to be absolutely certain to find the right location to deposit the mine, or bring it back, and it was not uncommon for them to fly around for up to an hour to pinpoint the location, all the while exposed to anti-aircraft fire from close quarters. On release, crews would see only a splash, if cloud and fog permitted, never an explosion.

RAF jargon for mine-laying was "gardening." Crews were instructed to plant their vegetable, and enemy coastal waters were divided into areas with code-names such as "forget-me-not" (Kiel Canal), "nectarine" (Frisian Islands), "onions" (Oslo), or "artichoke" (Lorient). Hampden crews on mine-laying sorties were also equipped with 250-pound wing bombs, and were expected to use these and their machine guns to attack enemy ships as the opportunity arose, after dropping their vegetables.

In an ebullient mood, he decided to buy a bicycle, or, as he told Janine,

> Roger decided I should buy a bike since he had to drive me everywhere on his handlebars. Our other pal, Dave Davies, our honest Welsh pal rides his landlady's 1890 model about so I took the plunge and bought one from the local dealer – a second hand one to be sure – but a magnificent machine we all agreed.
>
> By way of celebrating we drove to the nearby village of Horncastle and whilst polishing off the odd half dozen in a pub my lamp was stolen. We were exceedingly annoyed – yes they were all in a condition to take my loss to heart. Suddenly a copper – known as a bobby in these parts, stopped me and hauled me out for not having a lamp. Despite the fact that I always have had an extreme distaste – in fact wholesome dislike for the so called enforcers of law and order – I politely tried to explain why I was riding in their lovely town by the light of a full moon, with three hundred yards visibility, in a village devoid of life and traffic without a lamp. He was bone and bull-headed enough to remain unconvinced. By this time the three of us had four constables, one sergeant police and the chief to deal with – we put up with as much as our exuberant spirits would allow and then gave them a solid telling off. But when I told them to get some Ruhr hours in over Germany – they really blew up and tried to bring up their war record – then the fun began – a wordy battle ensued and the flying Canucks left their names in the police records and their words of wisdom firmly implanted in their desolate heads.
>
> But now for the bike. The tires on my magnificent bike were flat and after putting three patches in the back tire it was still leaking like a sieve – well we struggled home. Next day I bought a new tube. Roger insisted on putting it on quickly – he did but it still would not blow up – he ripped it putting it on so we had to patch a brand new tube up. I at last rode my magnificent bike for the first time to-day. It took me so long to get in that I missed dinner to-day but it is a lovely looking bike, and should be very handy once it gets used to me – so the moral of this long winded story is – beware of bikes – mine cost me four pounds – a police record – a lost meal and I am still frightened to breathe hard for fear of putting too much stress on it. (JJL 4 September 1941)

Joe kept his notice of fine in the amount of ten shillings, issued by the Petty Sessional Division of Horncastle, as a souvenir of his encounter with the authorities.

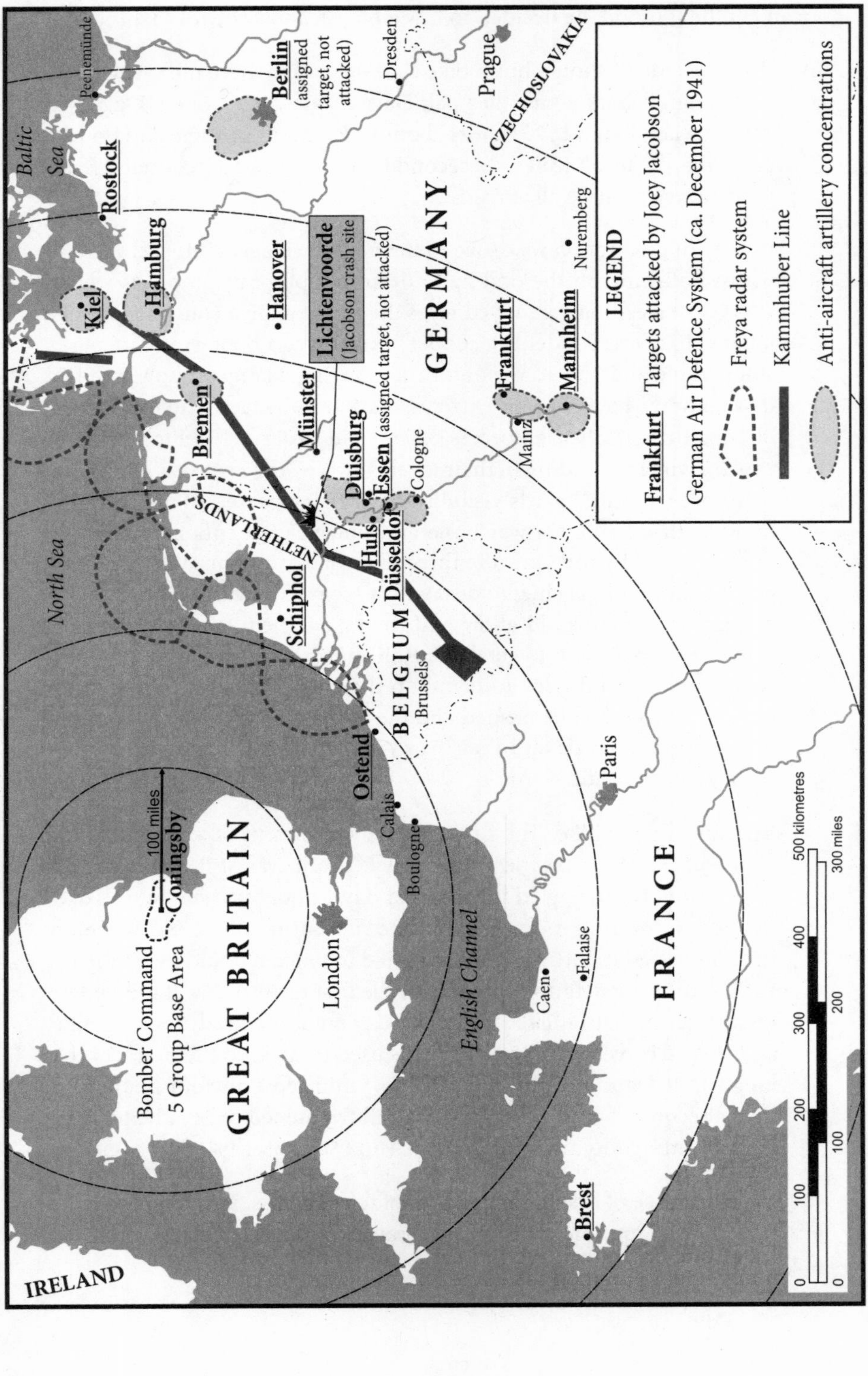

Joe's objectives, showing distance from RAF Coningsby, and the location of the Kammhuber Line. (Map created by Mike Bechthold)

Twenty

The Four Horsemen

Sooner or later, every aircrew would be confronted by the four horsemen of their apocalypse: unpredicted weather, icing, anti-aircraft artillery, and night-fighters. Any one or more of them could be encountered on any sortie over Germany, and any of them could be fatal. Joe Jacobson gained experience of all four during his first month on operations.

The ideal conditions for finding the target were clear skies and a full moon, but these were also the ideal conditions for the German defences to find the bombers. Partial cloud cover, especially low cumulus cloud, provided bombers intermittent cover from anti-aircraft gunners and night-fighters, but also made their targets more difficult to find.

Exceptionally low temperatures at altitude could impair aircraft function and subject crews to mind-numbing cold and even frostbite. Unpredicted changes in wind direction and speed could send an aircraft off-course or delay its return to base to the point of running out of fuel. On cold mornings, fog creeping in from the Lincolnshire fens could completely obscure aerodromes when returning aircraft were running low on fuel and their crews fatigued by the stress of battle.

It was the heavy cumulonimbus clouds associated with advancing weather fronts, however, that signalled the worst hazards: turbulence, violent updrafts or downdrafts, electrical discharge, and icing. And in those days, the normal operating heights of bomber aircraft corresponded to the layers of those storm clouds at which those hazards were at their worst. Those conditions were common over the North Sea in winter with cold air above the sea, and in summer over the Continent with warm air rising into cold. Crews encountering these situations early but unable to overcome them could abort their sortie, but on return, they could only hold tight and hope for the best.

Meteorology in those days could not reliably forecast weather conditions over Europe twelve hours ahead of a bombing operation, or even over England eighteen hours ahead when the bombers would be returning. Meteorological readings were no longer shared among nations in wartime; weather forecasts became military secrets, no longer released to the public. Britain had the advantage of access to weather data from Iceland, Greenland, and ships in the Atlantic. But with no direct observations from Europe, weather maps of the Continent could only be projected based on known meteorological principles. Regular meteorological reconnaissance flights over Germany were yet to come. It was difficult to predict how quickly fronts would move in from the west, or whether fog would form the next morning. Forecasting cloud cover and height, and wind speed and direction at various altitudes, that might be encountered along specific routes and in target areas was especially problematic. So each morning, Bomber Command planned its nightly operations on a best guess about the weather, and navigators soon learned to take the information they were given in afternoon briefings with a grain of salt.

Of all the natural hazards crews encountered in the air, the worst was the second horseman: icing. Icing occurs when an aircraft enters dense cloud at subfreezing temperatures, and most dangerously when it encounters a temperature inversion in which rain falls through freezing air. This rain accretes on the surface of the aircraft as hard, clear ice, weighing it down and impairing the lift capability of its wings and the responsiveness of its controls. Ice accumulation can plug up the external airspeed indicator, damage the wireless mast, and obscure visibility through windscreens. Even engine performance is at risk if ice forms in the carburetors. An extremely hazardous and uncontrollable situation can develop within in minutes, to the point of unrecoverable stall or spin, forcing an aircraft down.

Preflight meteorological forecasts of air temperatures aloft, and visible signs of potential icing conditions – storm clouds associated with cold fronts – warn of dangerous conditions ahead. Civilian pilots are instructed to avoid them, but bomber pilots heading to a target on schedule must press on as best they can. The summer icing associated with cumulonimbus storm clouds that Joe encountered on the Hanover operation is normally sporadic, and may be easier to avoid by going around the worst concentrations, or to escape by rapid ascent or descent. With luck, the ice sloughs off without damage and nothing is lost except a little extra fuel supply. In more severe and pervasive conditions, most likely to be encountered in winter as warm, wet air associated with an incoming warm front rises over cold air below, there may be no safe altitude except above the cloud formation altogether, and reaching that was beyond the capability of most aircraft and most crews. But descending into colder, dryer air will not necessarily solve the problem if the ice is too dense to shake off.

The problem of icing was well known, and more than a few Hampden crews had been forced to deal with it in previous months. Inflight de-icing mechanisms, notably movable de-icing boots installed on the wing's leading edge, had been developed in the United States many years before, but this was yet another technology not applied to bomber aircraft in Britain, most likely because the additional weight would have reduced performance and payload. There had been experience with applying de-icing compound to the wings before takeoff, but the benefits were short-lived. Of all the hazardous weather conditions that might confront a bomber crew, forecasting ice conditions in cloud was especially problematic. Crews were instructed in tactics to deal with icing, but few gained sufficient operational experience to get good at them. Pilots had to be lucky to survive their first encounters.

The other two horsemen of the apocalypse were of human creation. They were the enemy's defences: anti-aircraft artillery and night-fighters. Germany defended itself against night bombing with radar, searchlights, and anti-aircraft guns on the ground, and night-fighters in the air. None of these was new, but by early 1941 the Luftwaffe had not only increased the quantity and capabilities of each, it had figured out how to combine them into an integrated barrier stretching all the way from Denmark to France.

The first line of defence was the chain of radar stations along the North Sea coast that warned of approaching aircraft. About a hundred miles inland, through eastern Holland and Belgium, there ran a line of night-fighter bases and searchlight arrays from Denmark to the Rhine through eastern Holland and Belgium, along with a second line of radar, the so-called Kammhuber Line. The Luftwaffe divided this line into sectors or boxes about twenty kilometres deep, and assigned one night-fighter to each. As soon as an incoming bomber entered the box (which took several minutes to cross), the main searchlight sought it out, the rest of the battery coned it, and the ground controller guided the night-fighter to it from a central beacon known as Kleine Schraube (Little Screw), within each box. The RAF was still trying to figure out how the system worked. But what crews did know for sure was that searchlights without flak meant you were being hunted by a night-fighter. And Germany's night-fighters, much faster than the RAF's lumbering bombers, were now better equipped to hone in on those bombers, except in conditions of heavy cloud. By midsummer of 1941, the night-fighters had the advantage of better weather, clearer skies, and shorter nights with longer periods of twilight against which to spot incoming aircraft. On nights with thick cloud, the night-fighters were grounded, but the anti-aircraft guns could still operate, even if with reduced effectiveness. When Joe Jacobson began operations, there were over a hundred of these night-fighters based in Holland, and they were accounting for over half of Bomber Command's aircraft shot down.

The third, inner line of defence consisted of searchlights and anti-aircraft artillery batteries placed around the major cities, industries, and military facilities of northwestern Germany, and around Berlin. The searchlights could capture a bomber in an intense, dazzling cone of light, even at three miles up, disorienting its crew and setting it up as a target for anti-aircraft artillery. These guns fired 88 mm shells that rose to that height in ten seconds and exploded into a spray of shrapnel, or flak. A direct hit could take down an aircraft, while an explosion within ten metres or so could cause serious damage and personal injury. Most anti-aircraft shells exploded without effect, but a bomber aircraft's thin aluminum skin offered little protection to its crew or such vital components as fuel lines, hydraulics, and oil systems. It was common enough for aircraft to return to base with small holes in the fuselage. Once coned, a bomber pilot had to dive and twist to try to escape it and avoid being shot down. By mid-1941, the ability of anti-aircraft batteries to locate their targets was enhanced by on-site radar capable of detecting the speed and track of approaching aircraft. What they lacked in accuracy they more than made up in quantity of fire.

At bomber height, the shell bursts from intense anti-aircraft fire, with dozens of guns firing twenty or more rounds a minute, appeared to oncoming aircraft, and especially to the bomb-aimer surrounded by clear Perspex in the nose, as a curtain of smoke from explosions and light trails from tracer fire. For novice crews, it was an awesome and fearsome gauntlet to have to run on approach to their target. More experienced crews could better judge the hazard and try not to let it distract them from the task at hand.

In combination, the searchlights, anti-aircraft guns, and night-fighters had become a formidable, although not impenetrable barrier, especially in clear weather. It didn't have to be impenetrable to do its work; it had only to be ruinous enough to deter. In 1940, Bomber Command's operational losses, running at about 2 percent, had been thought mostly due to bad weather or faulty navigation. Losses to enemy action were attributed very largely to anti-aircraft fire. By August 1941 the operational loss rate was approaching 4 percent, over half of which was attributed to night-fighters.

In 1940, the bombers had been able to operate in the target area for up to an hour to identify their aiming points, and then attack from a few thousand feet up. This was no longer safe practice. Better to fly high, drop one's bombs as quickly as possible, and get away. Nor could pilots safely maintain straight and level flight on their final approach in the face of such intense opposition from below, so bomb-aiming became less accurate. It took a strong stomach to resist the temptation to bomb short and get the hell out of the zone of most intense danger. So not only was Germany's air defence system now inflicting punishing losses on bomber crews, it was making accurate bombing nearly impossible.

Bomber Command developed several countermeasures. Flying higher over flak batteries was one, taking indirect routes to skirt the Kammhuber Line was another, penetrating that line at lower heights and greater speed yet another. But whether the existing tactic of each aircraft making its separate way to the target should continue, or instead fly together in a concentrated stream, was a matter of continuing debate. The first was thought to confuse the defences; the second, it was hoped, would overwhelm them. But Bomber Command had neither sufficient numbers of aircraft, nor the techniques to keep them safely separated over the target, to carry out the second tactic successfully. So the first continued.

The old problems of navigation and bomb-aiming at night were compounded in 1941 by Germany's increasingly effective air defence system. And Bomber Command's main force still consisted of undersized and underpowered aircraft, in insufficient numbers. So the necessity of area bombing deepened. Crews were told to attack any town or built-up area so as not to waste bombs. And to make those attacks more effective, Bomber Command was developing the means of fire-raising with incendiary bombs.

A month into operations, Joe had satisfied his curiosity about the course he had embarked on and the hazards he might face. Imagination would not help. Raw courage would be needed to confront the four horsemen each night.

Twenty-One

Confidence Tested

Not long after Joe had penned his confident assessment of the bombing campaign to his father, he would have read the August edition of the *Navigation Bulletin*. Bomber Command issued this mimeographed document of several pages to all its stations for the benefit of air observers. This month's edition featured a synopsis of a study of fifty recent air photos taken by crews during their bombing raids. Only three of the fifty photographed explosions, it turned out, were within a ten-mile circle around the target. "10 mile errors," the article concluded, "come into the sphere of navigation and cannot be rectified by the bombing specialists."[1]

These were only the barest details of a study – the "Butt Report" – that Bomber Command had received two weeks after Joe had begun operations.[2] Night cameras had recently been developed for use on bomber aircraft, but only a few as yet carried them. Yet, enough photographs – over six hundred – had been taken of the purported target areas in June and July to make the study possible. During that time Bomber Command had dispatched over six thousand sorties, and about two-thirds of their crews had claimed to reach the target area. So these photos amounted to a 15 percent sample of crews supposedly over target. The study method was simple enough. The photos taken of the locations identified by the crews were compared with the known target areas as they appeared in daytime photographs. Less than one-third matched, meaning that the rest of the photos were taken of areas that had been misidentified by the crews.

Target areas, defined generously as a radius of five miles around the aiming point (an area of about seventy-five square miles), reached far beyond the built-up extent of most cities. So even the minority of crews who bombed within the target area did not necessarily do much damage, as their bombs were very likely falling on open countryside. The situation was even worse over the industrial targets of the Ruhr, commonly obscured by ground-level haze and heavily defended by anti-aircraft batteries, and it was especially problematic on moonless nights. The report estimated that in conditions of thick haze and no moon, only one in fifty aircraft had correctly identified the target area.

Very simply, although the great majority of aircrews believed they had succeeded most of the time, they were not seeing what they thought they were seeing, and their bombs were not falling where they believed they had. And as dismal as the report's findings were, they spoke only to problems of navigation and target-finding. The study was not designed to determine the actual damage caused on the ground by the relatively small proportion of bombs finding their way to the aiming point. That required daytime photo reconnaissance by fighter aircraft.

Concern at senior levels that bombers were sometimes not on target was not new, even if the difficulties were thought to be occasional or temporary. The Butt Report initially set senior air staff scrambling for explanations and excuses, but the scale of the problem was completely unanticipated, and its implications were devastating. Once Churchill himself had been apprised of its content, the need for correctives became urgent. The Chief of the Air Staff, Sir Charles Portal, undertook to improve astro-navigation in aid of reaching the target area, to mark the target area with flares for bomb-aimers to see it, and reassured the prime minister that radio navigation aids would soon come into regular service. But in the view of Bomber Command's Air Officer in Chief Sir Richard Peirse, the problem lay squarely with his navigators, who needed to pull up their socks. Improvement, he asserted, would come if air observers "take a personal grip on the situation and kill any tendency to complacency which may have grown up because of the known difficulties of night navigation."[3] Only eighteen months prior, the RAF had dismissed the importance of navigation and the need for trained air observers. Things were turning around far too late.

In fact, it was nearly impossible to find a target by dead reckoning over a darkened landscape. Astro-navigation could confirm proximity to a target within a few miles, but only when the upper atmosphere was cloud-free, a condition that would rarely prevail through the coming autumn and winter. And once close to the target, the crew had to find it, accurately aim a bomb at it, and hope the bomb would do the damage intended. Portal acknowledged to the prime minister that the accuracy of night bombing was the greatest operational problem facing Bomber Command. But there was no prospect for an immediate fix.

The findings of the Butt Report, even if not fully disclosed to aircrews, must have been as disturbing to them as it was to their commanders. Joe knew that he had not always been able to find or hit the exact aiming points he had been assigned on his first sorties, but believed he had bombed the target cities with attendant destruction on at least three out of four of them. Other crews were providing similar reports to intelligence officers on debriefing. "Large flashes followed by explosions," "bursts observed in target area," "fires seen to break out," were phrases commonly recorded in squadron diaries. Another common one was "results not observed." This last meant more than intended: fires, flashes, and bomb bursts did not necessarily mean destruction, as was now becoming evident, but looking at the ground at night, crews could not know that. Joe's pilot recalled that while interrogators and crews did their best to reconstruct what happened, the debriefing process was not noted for its rigour.

Six months earlier, when these problems were first suspected, the Command's senior navigation staff had called for the investigation and analysis of inaccurate navigation (deemed to be where an aircraft had failed to follow its prescribed track, or where there was an appreciable difference between actual and calculated ground speed), based on the flight log and chart from each sortie. A new questionnaire was devised for debriefing officers, designed to root out what went wrong regarding proper procedures, to detect and correct error, and better understand the effects of adverse weather conditions.

What came of all this data collection was less than hoped for, mainly because station staff had little time to assess it. Nonetheless, the monthly *Navigation Bulletin* began drawing attention to individual cases of careless or lax dead reckoning and radio fixes, failures of communication between navigators and pilots, and insufficient attention to astro-navigation. Concerns about how intelligence officers conducted and recorded their debriefing sessions continued into the summer, as did the nagging question of bombing accuracy. Everyone knew that the key problem was navigation, and that radio-navigation aids were desperately needed. But everyone also knew that none would be available until 1942. In the meantime, air observers would be under fire to improve their performance by honing the dead reckoning, astro-navigation, map-reading, and radio-fixing skills they had already learned, and making better use of the compasses, sextants, radio direction finders, and wind-finding aids already available to them.

The more immediate effect of the Butt Report was that cameras became standard equipment on all bomber aircraft. When the observer released his bombs, a flare was also dropped that was timed to light up the target area before the bombs landed. The observer opened the camera shutter just after impact, so a good photo required the pilot to fly straight and level for the additional thirty seconds or so that it took the bombs to fall. Subsequent interpretation would normally provide confirmation of the location of the aircraft and pinpoint bomb bursts, although searchlights and decoy fires could obscure the results. Night photography documented the occurrence of navigation failures, but it couldn't fix them.

On 4 September, Joe was dispatched on a raid of 140 bombers on German battleships in the port of Brest, this time with a new gunner, Sid Harding, and Duncan Hodgkinson, now first WO/AG. This would be Gerry Roberts's regular crew for the next three months.

> We reached the French coast near Moraix – but the weather was closing in fast near our base and all over England so there was a general recall of all ships on the operation. We were supposed to bomb the Gneisenau, the Scharnhorst and the Prince Eugen. One or two kites evidently were over because we could see terrific flak going up – the coloured tracer is definitely a sight – when it is on somebody else. (JJOD 4 September 1941)

The raid was unproductive. Two-thirds of the aircraft were recalled, the remainder bombed the estimated position of the battleships through a smoke-screen the German defences had generated before the bombers arrived.

Two days later Joe was briefed for an operation on the Chemische Werke synthetic rubber plant at Huls, in the Ruhr, which produced half of Germany's synthetic rubber for the tires that kept the Wehrmacht moving. This would be the first of several trips Joe would make to this factory.

> We were first over the target and received enough attention for the whole effort – we were ringed and blinded by searchlights and accurately pasted by aak aak so we had no chance to stooge quietly over and bomb accurately – Jack McIntyre did and I imagine others did whilst the defences were busy with others.
>
> We were attacked by 3 ME109s over Amsterdam but shook them off – The searchlight belts were not as concentrated as usual – but we saw two planes shot down – The moon was almost full and you have an extremely exposed and vulnerable feeling when flying during these light periods.
>
> You get rather used to these more or less shaky do's. I had a game of billiards after I got down past midnite with Curtis Gunners – they shot

> down a ME109 – we nearly had it from 3 of them – yet it worries us little now – of course if we think about it too often or long you get nervous but by leading a normal, active life you manage to take it all in stride – just part of the game. (JJOD 6 September 1941)

The crew reported that they had located the target visually by reference to adjacent water features and bombed it from eleven thousand feet, although they did not observe the bomb bursts. They had carried three high-explosive bombs intended to blast the factory open. The squadron record states that four of the aircraft dispatched could not locate the target, but the other fourteen bombed

> with good effect on what they presumed to be the target, despite surprisingly heavy opposition returned safely to base. All crews emphatic [said] they had successfully bombed required objective, but photos taken in daylight revealed the works to be almost unscathed. It would appear that despite brilliant moonlight the raid was not a success.[4]

Subsequent analysis of night photos taken by bomber crews themselves produced an even more dismal result. Of thirteen photos successfully taken, six reported as Huls were plotted at a location forty miles east, and the others were eight to twelve miles from the target.

The Huls raid was among the first to be analyzed by Bomber Command's newly established Operational Research Section, charged with improving operational efficiency as measured by bombs on target per aircraft loss. The report suggested that interrogation officers should pay closer attention to verifying target identification by crews, and that navigators be provided with a photo as well as a map of the target.

The next night Joe was assigned his first crack at Berlin. Berlin was a well-defended target, and so distant as to be at the limit of range for a Hampden carrying a two-thousand-pound bomb load. There was no room for mistakes or misjudgment. It was the ultimate prize for aircrews even if it inspired dread when announced in the squadron briefing room as the target for the night. Joe was thrilled by the opportunity.

> 7 AM – just got back from the big show – 13 planes from our sqdr – 7 Canadian navigators – all keen on their look at Berlin – the others all shaken rigid at the thought – my pilot & gunner complained of the cold – refused to go so we pasted Kiel instead – very hot … it was a hectic night with everybody getting pasted from all places along the line – going to bed for the day when Rouse & Dave get back from intelligence. (JJD 8 September 1941)

He added in his operational diary:

> A most exciting night for our squadron. Last night we were the only 5 Group station on ops – to-nite we supplied most of our group's effort – there were 200 planes on Berlin all told.
>
> Since the Hampden can fly only for ten hours – most of our pilots viewed the trip with misgiving – but half the navigators on our squadron are Canadians and we all wanted to bomb Berlin – and so a pilot-navigator feud developed –
>
> Our heating system did not function and the cold which was considerable allowed Robby & Hodge a fine excuse despite my energetic protests, cajoling – disgust, etc. – I just couldn't make them go & Robby is captain of the aircraft.
>
> McIver was North of his target & bombed Kiel – Rousseau got within 50 miles and got back with 20 min. reserve petrol – McIntyre got there – was wounded slightly in the foot – had their plane shot to hell when forced down to 200 ft and came back with bullet holes everywhere – but likely winners of the DFM.
>
> Good old Pop Miller got there & back somehow – Dunn got there – Matkin is missing[5] – and so it is with a sense of failing to carry out a stated and desired objective that we bombed Kiel – a real hot spot.
>
> I was so disgusted that we tracked onto the docks despite aak all around – we stooged around – took pictures – got pasted a bit and came home – ordinarily Kiel itself is a shaky do – but evidently it seemed easy compared to Berlin – but I will get a crack there yet –
>
> It was an extremely exciting evening and made the trip of the night before fade into the past and appear to have taken place ages ago.
>
> This much is certain – the biggest mistake the govts made was training so many Canadian observers – we are the keenest men on the station – but the most initiative lies with the pilot – that is what we should be – if and when I finish my 200 hrs I am going to train as a pilot – I want the authority to make and carry out the decisions when flying. 20 planes lost this trip. (JJOD 7 September 1941)

By his own account, at least, Joe wanted two things above all out of his wartime flying career. One was the thrill of being in complete control of his own airplane, which was why he wanted to become a fighter pilot. But the other was to be in a position to lead his men into battle with courage and determination. For that he would have to be a bomber pilot, or at the least, the captain of his airplane.

◉

Failing to reach Berlin had been a huge disappointment to Joe, and it prompted him to write home a couple of days afterwards:

> I hope that … your connections still hold good at Ottawa, Pop. I am in pretty well here and should be able to swing what I am aiming at. I have another twenty trips over Germany to make before going on my rest. That will take at least three or four months as the weather slows us up shortly. Instead of going on the usual three months instructors job I want to go back to Canada and train as a pilot which will take me next to no time. Then I would like to take things easy and come back here as a fighter pilot.
>
> However, twenty more trips is still a rather classy feat these days so there is still a considerable period before we need to start panicking. However, if you know the right men who can get my application thru when it comes along it might help.… I don't want to get stuck in the regular routine over here. But for the present my hands are full. We have a real job to handle and I probably get more kick out of it than anybody else, though truth to tell, the Canadians here are mostly full of enthusiasm – yes – we are doing our end of it very nicely and efficiently.…
>
> Roger and I and some of the other Canadians were wondering why we did not feel homesick in England – the answer for me was not hard to find. Outside of missing my family – my friends are all over here or will be shortly. I have more pals – real ones now than I ever had before. We fly to see each other when making our night flying tests. We go on leave together – some of us live together – we write and generally never get that lost feeling of knowing no one – having nowhere to go. Added to that I have a home to go to and a very nice one at that – a girl friend and a lovely one at that plus a nice billet and an adventuresome life. This is one of the greatest shows I will ever attend and I would not have missed it for the life of me. Also I would not be in it in any other capacity. The fellows we meet – the things we do and the trips we have are vital experiences.

> I think most of us have a thorough and solid appreciation for many things in life that we once took for granted – also we have learnt that it is not until you are ready to take the very considerable chance of losing your life that you can begin to know what living means and should mean. Oh yes I have become quite the old philosopher and between my trips over Germany and those with the boys after our trips – with the odd peaceful quiet evening by Mrs. Lettice's fireside – with our bikes and holidays and undisturbed rest – excellent feeds ... I can safely assure you that no one ought to have any qualms about Joe Jacobson taking care of himself over here and making the most of his time in England. Roger and I stick together of course – fly on the same trips – have the same number of hours fly time and what is more important he is teaching me French – and don't get alarmed by any rumours that probably will start floating around about my romancing. I can still see straight and have both feet on the ground – at times so I shall arrive home, sane sound and still a bachelor. (JJL 10 September 1941)

He added, in the next week's letter home:

> events that occurred last week seem now to have taken place in the far past – things I did in Canada seem to be closer at hand than things I did a couple of nights ago. Everything now moves on such a rapid scale with us – the panorama of a lifetime takes place within a few hours, that after I write a letter I can no longer become a part of that letter in a few days time than I can remember what I did when I was six months old.
>
> However, despite the rapidity and transience of events and people with whom we are associated I do not think that I have in any way lost the graceful art of living which I have been brought up to appreciate. That has been mainly due to my good fortune in being billeted in a private home. Altho there is no particular brilliance or vitality about the home or its owner – there is a quiet dignity – a restfulness and comfortableness about the surroundings which is of more value to us at the moment than anything else could be.... (JJL 18 September 1941)

Joe had no complaints other than not being top dog in the aircraft, but even in the immediacy of battle, he was making plans for his life. Percy marvelled that he could do so. "In the midst of his bombing operations, operations that are full of peril, thank God he can still think of his future."

Joe went on two more operations shortly after the Berlin fiasco: one on the distant Neptun submarine factory at Rostock on the Baltic coast on the 11th, the second another attempt to bomb the German battleships at Brest two nights later. Of the first, Joe wrote:

> We were all pretty keen on this job – it was the first time an attack had been made on this target and the defences were not too strong. Dunn is missing.... That is about two-thirds of the plane losses on our squadron have been from our flight. Roger and I will have to break that jinx.
> (JJOD 11 September 1941)[6]

His crew reported bombing the town in the vicinity of the target, but observed no bursts due to almost complete cloud cover.

Of the second, he recorded:

> An uneventful trip to bomb the Gneisenau & Scharnhorst. The weather was 10/10 cloud at 3000' so we could not see our objectives. The flak was not as heavy as Kiel – we were over the target at 0400 – I guess the battle ships are still safe and sound since it was impossible to see them. All our planes returned safely.
>
> All in all a most uneventful and unsatisfactory trip – I don't mind taking chances or risks but I like to get a show for my money. Of course the only risk this trip was the fear of hitting English balloons or meeting English fighter planes, but still I like to feel I did a good job.
> (JJOD 13 September 1941)

On debriefing, Joe's crew reported bombing flak guns estimated to be in position of the cruisers from twelve thousand feet.

The bombing of German battleships at Brest was an Admiralty priority, which in Bomber Command's view had been foisted on it at great cost to its own resources and with the effect of diverting effort away from the attack on German industry. Over a thousand bombs had been directed on the battleships that summer and fall, but only four were believed to have caused significant damage. The Air Officer Commanding of 5 Group, Air Vice-Marshal John Slessor, opposed further attacks, especially because it had become obvious that by the time his force arrived, the ships and docks were obscured by a smokescreen. Over eight hundred tons of bombs had been dropped on Brest, but only four of those bombs were considered to have inflicted damage. It was useless, in Slessor's view, to make up for lack of bombing accuracy by multiplying the attacking force, and he asserted that his crews were unhappy about being sent on useless operations.

Both of Joe's final two targets that week had been blanketed in cloud and were identifiable only by flak concentrations, and thus the cameras they carried were rendered useless.

Percy had followed Joe's work closely:

> Read tonight that our RAF are stepping up their bombing operations over Germany. Read with mixed feelings that there have been heavy casualties amongst the civilian population. Berlin had its share of this long promised offensive. I know that it is only human to want to give the Germans back some of their own medicine, I know that the Germans have bombed London and other cities of England in a most cold-blooded callous bestial way, I hate certain Germans but I cannot help feeling that there is something in what George Bernard Shaw recently said and that is that this sort of retaliation gets us nowhere; it just means that thousands of innocent civilians are punished for the crimes of a group of wicked men.... (PJD 3 September 1941)

> Find myself telling people about Joe marking the bombs he drops over Germany with our names ... large ones for Ma and myself and small ones for Janet and Edith. These bombs kill ... am getting callous. (PJD 17 September 1941)

Every letter home from Joe was a reassurance, but life on Grosvenor Avenue had been on a knife-edge during the fall campaign.

> tough on us to have our only son (left [to] us) in constant danger: like being on the edge of a precipice, any moment we may be pushed over. (PJD 30 August 1941)

> Joe heard from by cable last night. Always a relief. He is right in the midst of the bombing of German towns and we feel quite powerless: prayers may be helpful to some folk but I cannot but remember that the parents of those boys whose names appear on the daily casualty lists also prayed that their loved ones should be saved. All we can do is to keep our fingers crossed which is perhaps much the same thing and no doubt just as useless. (PJD 3 September 1941)

Top: 106 Squadron flying crew, September 1941. Above: A detail showing Gerry Roberts' crew. From left to right are Duncan Hodgkinson, Gerry Roberts, Joe, and Sid Harding. (Metheringham Airfield Visitor Centre)

Twenty-Two

A Brotherhood Lost

The Brest raid was followed by nearly two weeks of inactivity due to poor flying weather. Joe needed the break. Four operations over enemy territory in one week had exhausted him:

> I am tired – no sleep for 26 hours – Dunn missing – also another crew – all just about finished – makes a fellow wonder how he can ever get thru 30 odd trips – keep plugging – trust to luck (JJD 11 September 1941)

But after sleeping all day, he awoke well rested, his mood improved.

> The most unusual and perhaps amazing feature about the air force and particularly with regards operational sqdr is the easy manner in which firm, close, lasting friendships are made and kept and then suddenly lost – and you hardly bat an eye. (JJL 13 September 1941)

Joe was hard-pressed to maintain this phlegmatic front as bad news continued to follow. Later that day, as he recorded in his diary, the letter he had written to Mac Keswick at RAF Mildenhall was returned to him.[1]

> looks as if my old air force pal has had it – Mac was a real man – the first of my real pals to get hooked. (JJD 13 September 1941)

> Jack McIntyre & crew missing from last night's trip to Hamburg.[2] Another pal finished … feel very let down because of the loss of two fine pals & bunkmates & two first class men – went to Bardney with Dave & Roger & after 5 pints we managed to forget our little miseries which can get you down if you are not careful – (JJD 16 September 1941)

Losing Matkin and Dunn the week before had been a blow, losing Jack McIntyre with whom Joe had trained at Finningley was an even bigger one. Six weeks into Joe's operational tour, 106 Squadron had lost ten crews or about a third of its men. The Canadian air observer contingent at 106 Squadron had peaked by mid-September. There had been eleven during the month of August, although not all at the same time and never more than five on any one operation. In the first two weeks of September, over a third of the crews dispatched to Huls, Berlin, and Rostock had been manned by Canadian observers. That short period was as close as Joe ever got to his imagined "regiment of chums." Now most of them were gone. Miller and McIver were still there, but being officers, they messed in separate quarters. Joe's immediate circle was now down to Roger Rousseau and Dave Davies. They seldom visited the pubs in Woodhall Spa, preferring to binge in nearby towns away from the watchful eyes of Mrs. Lettice and her neighbours. Fond as they were of her, he told his family that he didn't think she knew "too much about our spare time activities even though she is all ears."

He let his guard down in a letter to Janine, which he immediately regretted. He replied:

> I received your thoroughly sound and chastising letter to-day and it made me feel about the same as it did five minutes after I put the letter in the box – to wit – I needed a good swift kick in the pants for allowing myself to go batty – remind me to bend over as soon as I see you and you can do the honours with gusto –
>
> I sure got caught off guard that day.... make sure you rip that letter into minute pieces and deposit in the deepest rubbish bin you can find – I will leave at least four days of my leave for you to thoroughly castigate a guy that allowed a few minor details get the better of him for a day.... for once I offer no excuses – do no blustering – and accept the fact that for a short time I started to feel a wee bit sorry for myself – But God Blimey I soon beat that out of myself and my complexion now turns a crimson red as I think of "*you*" of all people being able to tell me to buck up – you live and learn I guess but boy oh boy it shakes me rigid when I think of me allowing myself to get like that after only getting about halfway thru the job – be it only for a little while.
>
> (JJL 25 September 1941)

The squadron was stood down during the new moon period in late September, mainly on account of fog. Joe had time to himself, for the first time since he'd arrived at Coningsby.

> Dave and Roger are both going on a week's leave over the weekend so I will be left on my own to recover from the fast pace we have set of late – I have allowed myself to narrow down my scope too much and am not using my old bean in the way it should be – should get back into reading style again – and thinking form. (JJD 18 September 1941)
>
> The sqdr has almost a complete change of personnel since my arrival – only a few of the old familiar faces left – I really miss my pals – we don't make many new friends here and lose many old ones so we hang together at all times. (JJD 20 September 1941)
>
> Flew near Manchester today – nearly hit the balloons at Crewe – I sure like flying & am really anxious to finish my 200 hrs and get cracking as a pilot – fighter pilot preferably. Lot of new crews in. They soon get experienced and become aces like the rest of us … you just naturally become an expert – or you have had it. (JJD 21 September 1941)
>
> One thing about bombing the Germans. Everybody has a wholesome respect for the German defences – but nobody is scared of them – not a bit of it. Weather bad so a new friend Doug Carmichael and I took things easy – he remembered me from a football game – Lennoxville vs McGill Frosh. He is level headed – thinks little of the [English] as do most of the boys from the Dominion. (JJD 22 September 1941)
>
> No ops – have the old homestead to myself – just listened to Haw Haw[3] – says he Russia has lost (Kiev) we are getting hooked by the U.S. – should give up the ghost now – trying to split U.S. & Britain up now – but we will show him – Went to Horncastle with Doug again – ate at "The Bull" run by Canadians – what a difference – really friendly – (JJD 23 September 1941)
>
> An important day – received a profound & inspirational letter from Pop in reply to a personal one of mine concerning future prospects & hopes of mine. Pop has sturdy faith & hope in me – perhaps too much & feels that public service is my niche – Pop is extremely sensitive & idealistic – as am I and he hopes to see me accomplish what he always wanted to. (JJD 24 September 1941)

> Have been writing, thinking & receiving highly idealistic letters from Pop. Was brought down to earth with a thud by Donahue – a hard bitten American who has done everything from sailing the seas – teaching – being groomed for the priesthood etc. – a good way of getting the problems & existing conditions lined up and what to do about them.[4] (JJD 26 September 1941)

> Went to Lincoln with Doug, but left him [to] get tight with his pals & came home early. I didn't like his pals & didn't feel like ruining my hard won battle to get back in shape by downing hard liquor with them – finally getting some sense in my old bean & self control.

> One day the past week might turn out to be the most important one of my life – I wrote Pop a while back – told him my uncertainty concerning civvy life & my hopes to do something worthwhile – it really inspired him – gave him higher hope for me than he ever had – I am now on the spot. I can't fail him & I can't fail my friends who have been killed so I might be driven to wonders yet – (JJD 27 September 1941)

The conversation between father and son had taken a deeper turn.

> One point in particular has been fairly obvious to me since arriving in England – most people do a better job of facing "the battle of death" than they do the battle of life. Perhaps it is because the possibilities and issues are more easily seen in the former case. I think a good many people are more worried and afraid of the uncertainties of life than death. A good subject for a play – don't you think? I think the hardest battle is the latter one.

> Now I don't want you to think for a moment … that young Joe is going to arrive home a worried wreck, whose nerves are all shot to pieces as a result of his experiences. They might be yet, mind, but at the present moment I am an extremely healthy, well fed, rested and cared for young fellow, who is having the time of his life. Despite the odd adventure which I still look forward to, I have managed to retain my customary composure and domestic ways….

> Monty should be over soon. I shall never welcome seeing anyone more than I shall him. I think he probably feels pretty much as we do Pop….

> One thing though for which I shall always be grateful is not only the understanding you [and mother] have shown "most" of the time but

> the quiet way you go about it. I don't think any of us can put [up] with emotionalism or a show of feelings which is a mighty good thing.
> (JJL 26 September 1941)

After a two-week hiatus in operational flying, Joe went on his twelfth sortie, this time to the railway yards at Frankfurt. It was another dispiriting effort.

> Weather was so poor that we could not see the ground for the entire trip. We searched for the target for an hour. We had incendiaries and were supposed to light up the target. We finally stooged towards the heaviest searchlights and flak we could find. We made a beautiful glide despite numerous searchlights to obtain a good picture but the photo flash did not go off so we cannot be sure we were over Frankfurt.
>
> On returning, Belgium seemed to be poorly blacked out. We were diverted to Linton near York because of poor weather at base. Since we were going on leave and wanted to get paid we came back anyway and managed to wangle permission to land.
>
> The heavy clouds gave us a secure feeling, from searchlights and fighters but it was hard to be sure exactly where we were.
> (JJOD 29 September 1941)

According to the squadron record book, none the eleven crews saw the target area, which was blanketed by fog, rain, and intense darkness, and they could make only a rough estimate of the position of the town. All dropped their bombs, but guided only by flak and searchlights, the raid "was not entirely a success." Joe's crew, like the others, observed no results.

⊙

The novelty and amazement of Joe's first few bombing operations had by now worn off, giving way to both a more realistic view of their effectiveness and a more sober assessment of his own chances. In a pattern typical of what later research on flying stress would reveal, Joe's sorties in September had made him fully aware of the magnitude of the task he had undertaken, his vulnerability in carrying it out, and of the dangers he would confront before completing it, but he remained resolute and confident. And he would put up a good front to everyone as the losses mounted. That too was part of flying stress. Repression did not come easily to him, although it was part of his family's fabric, but it would keep him sane and capable now. Like his father, Joe channelled his anxieties into his writing.

Joe now assumed the mantle of duty borne by his lost pals, determined to do a good job on their behalf. He expected a lot from himself, and he continued to expect his Pony Club pals to show their mettle in wartime, not least as an example to the Jewish community back home. When Joe received word that Gerald Smith had joined the Air Force as a radio-locator, he commented:

> I feel that my fellow poneyites have slipped away from me a bit by their conduct – as ground crew they have not & will not experience what I am in aircrew – neither the dangers nor the thrills – too bad but they are still my best pals. (JJD 5 September 1941)

Joe commented on this development to his family, once again raising his dim view of what he saw as risk-aversion among his old crowd.

> I heard Gerald finally took the plunge – being an exacting young fellow of late, I would like to see a few more of our boys take the plunge – only I would like to see them plunge into a little more dangerous work – a radio-locator is about as safe over here as I would be at the North Pole. I am afraid too many of our family like that element when taking their belated decisions if you get what I mean – or am I getting too subtle or hard bitten – it is just that I feel we are being a little too cagey – picking out the soft spots per usual, let the other boys do the risky jobs. If I ever get back to Canada I will be very much inclined to give a thorough shaking to a number of people – but that's another ambition that can wait for a while. (JJL 10 September 1941)

Joe returned to this theme two months later in a letter to the Pony Club:

> I see the same old names keep appearing in most letters … are they intending to do anything or are they going to sit the whole affair out – needless to say neither my pals or myself are here for our health. I have seen a lot of good men bite the dust and shall have no compunction about sending lesser men to that fate in less honourable fashion when this is over if I am still around and the lads that hang around home get the least bit troublesome.… (JJL 9 November 1941)

Joe was by this time reconsidering, or perhaps only beginning to consider, what his religion actually meant to him beyond perfunctory attachment. He seems to have lost all interest in religious observance, and had found no occasion or inclination to attend synagogue or avail himself of chaplain services. If there were any other Jews in 106 Squadron's flying crew, Joe made no mention of it. It has been said of the RAF at that time that few men wore their religious faith on their sleeves. Joe's modest religious devotion seems to have been further diminished by his recent experiences. In response to one of his father's letters, he wrote:

> You mentioned our religious training and upbringing. I believe your views were logical sensible and correct. There is not much faith to be discovered in our religious institutions at the moment. I have so far been rather disappointed in both the leadership and the inspiration supplied by our religious institutions. The matter of faith which you have and I have is something that has been gained and held on to quite outside the sphere of formal religious teachings and worship. At least mine has. Mine has come from the little I have seen and learnt in the world so far, the people I have met, the things felt. (JJL 29 August 1941)

The day before the Jewish High Holidays began (21 September), Joe wrote home to say that he had not sent out any greetings "because I did not have the foggiest idea when the New Year was until it was too late." His explanation seems ingenuous. Two days prior he had written home, saying that he had received an invitation to supper at the start of Rosh Hashanah, but implied he would not be accepting it because "events and incidents have taken on a peculiar tone of late." He did not elaborate directly, although he must certainly have meant the news of Keswick and McIntyre. Other than accepting an invitation to break the Yom Kippur fast with one of his father's relatives while on leave in London, Joe had again given little thought to the holiest days of the Jewish calendar.

But Joe's attitude to the High Holidays that year was grounded elsewhere than in his spiritual and religious reflections. Two months before, Joe had commented in his diary:

> Judaism – how that word has degenerated thru our own actions – we are held in universal disrespect with a few exceptions – every group, gang or crowd I am in – unconsciously looks on the Jew with *no* admiration – little respect – why? – because we have forsaken our fighting traditions – our fighting history and have become a grabbing – materialistic selfish people – I intend trying to inject a little fight & self-sacrifice into my race. (JJD 19 July 1941)

It's easy enough to guess what prompted this entry, which he seems not to have shared but kept to himself. Joe surely encountered casual contempt for "the Jew," popping up like mushrooms after a rain in everyday conversation on air bases and pubs in Britain, as he had in Montreal, Preston, and Regina. Unexamined but often repeated, generally by people who had never met a Jew and perhaps even bore no malice toward any individual Jew, they had become habits of mind among many Britons. The sources and specifics varied: lingering ecclesiastical views; the long canon of English literature from Shakespeare and Marlowe to Eliot and Buchan; notions about race and biology still prevalent among sectors of the intelligentsia; and a widespread popular suspicion of foreigners and of anything that smacked of "un-British" appearance and behaviour. Jews had long been subjects of music hall jokes for most Britons, and objects of disdain among the upper classes. Nazism had gained very few dedicated converts in Britain, but in the climate of the times, it had raised public "Jew-consciousness" and nourished latent but widespread negative views about Jews. Joe would have heard such comments and jibes from people who might have had no idea that he was Jewish, or if they did, might not have attributed these characteristics to him personally.

Joe did not attempt to conceal his religion or his reaction to Jewish jibes, however offhand. His response to popular anti-Semitism continued to be to assiduously distance his own behaviour from the stereotype, and to demonstrate that he as a Jew embodied the very opposite characteristics. Fond as he was of the Kostoris family (his main contact with English Jews), and as much as he appreciated the good life at Midfield, he was also embarrassed by Dan's ready access to goods in short supply, and to servants when people were being mobilized into factory and farm labour, as well as by how little the war seemed to have diminished his daily comforts. And perhaps he had seen the prominent item in the *Daily Express* about the supposed Jewish ancestry of Marshal Timoshenko, commander in chief of the Soviet Army, and wondered why his was not a more common example.[5]

Under the duress of operations, and gradually drawing in on himself, Joe seems to have given less and less attention to what Jews in general were doing or not doing. But he remained keenly disappointed by some of his closest friends.

Twenty-Three

Action and Inaction

Joe began a seven-day crew leave in London at the end of September. Roger and Dave had left on their own crew leaves the week prior, and as Joe wrote his family, "the only other two pals I could have gone with had to bail out over Germany."

> Back in London – feels great to be alive and whole and in good spirits – met Roger in the Regent Palace bar ... also Ken Jackson & other acquaintances who revive old memories of our lost pals – I feel lonely at being alone but happy to do something I like doing – exploring – wandering – doing as I please – (JJD 29 September 1941)
>
> Sitting in the Haymarket Theatre alone – No Time for Comedy – excellent – ... – walked thru Hyde Park & Kensington Gardens – having the time of my life going where I please & meeting people like Sandwell etc. – However, I don't like travelling alone but can make the best of it at times. (JJD 30 September 1941)
>
> Strolled around Covent Garden market all morning – met Bill Fulton & lunched with him – saw Up & Doing at the Saville – met Littlefield at the Beaver Club & since it was the first old pal either of us had met since arriving in London we spent the night in favorite pubs thoroughly enjoying the reunion.[1] (JJD 1 October 1941)
>
> Sunny day feels great to be alive – I bounded thru St. James Park & all around Whitehall feeling like a kid – I love London – it is vast limitless – human and exciting – beats any city I have ever been in. (JJD 2 October 1941)

> Dropped into the air ministry and saw Savard – he is the big shot who is on a special mission here … he then called up B. K. Sandwell and L. S. B. Shapiro for me.[2] Both were out but I went over to the Savoy later – snared B. K. had a pleasant chat with him. (JJL 2 October 1941)

> Another marvelous day – I met Ev Littlefield & we explored London together – including the pubs – visited Blackfriars – the Brown Bear etc. also Fleet St. – St. Pauls – & down to the east end – Ev & I both think alike – both think London the finest city in the world – we absolutely got pie eyed & I had to go to Mrs. Jacobs for supper – luckily I was able to walk & talk – nice people too.[3] (JJD 3 October 1941)

> A personally important week for me as the time spent alone allowed me to straighten out many of my ideas & ideals & I sized myself, my friends & the world we live in & the war we die in … I felt definitely buoyed up & have renewed confidence in my ability to look after myself & my future destiny. (JJD 4 October 1941)

From London he went on to Midfield for the weekend.

> An unwise moment to write a diary as I am stretched out on my bed in Midfield reflecting upon my delightful evening with Janine … it's getting bad I fall a little more for Janine each time – she's really first class. (JJD 4 October 1941)

> Janine is the best rounded girl I have met – she has everything that I like a woman to have – we are both level headed & neither imagines itself to be in love so we have a marvelous time together & thoroughly enjoy each other's company … (JJD 6 October 1941)

The more he enjoyed Janine's company, however, the bigger the problem he had at Midfield, as he revealed to his parents.

> Dan … is rather jealous of the attention I show Janine – that is whisking her out in the evenings whilst only devoting the day to him.… Dan can't stand any discussion or intelligent talking. He is the most boring and self-centred, petty man you could meet. Yet he has great determination – a one track mind and has the power and ability to make a success of any practical project he undertakes. So I ration my time. I kid around with him in the morning and at the table. Then I put him thoroughly in his place – firmly but pleasantly and get the women started on subjects I am interested in. They all have the education, upbringing,

> intelligence and charm to intrigue you and me or any sensible human being … I have to mother Dan away from fits, moods, quarrels and bad temper, then overcome the women's fear of annoying Dan with subjects he is not interested in and get them talking, laughing, reminiscing and enjoy an opportunity to talk about people, ideas – adventures and thoughts as they please; then finally I have to find ways and means of smuggling Janine from Dan (a hard job) and from Suzanne and Henriette (comparatively simple) and take her out and show her a snappy time…. (JJL 7 October 1941)

On returning from leave, he wrote Janine:

> I zipped into the squadron to-day and zoomed down to the operations room and found everybody alive and in fine fettle. They have not made a trip since I left a week ago[4] – Everybody was quite amazed to see me looking so well and dapper and cocky. Roger and Dave took me up to the mess and trimmed the pants off me in a game of snooker and so cooled me off….
>
> There is great excitement here – our squadron – at least half a dozen ace crews have been selected to do a low level job (200–300 feet) on an important target. The boys have been practicing all week but we are going to get on – they could not get along without "suicide Joe" and his trusty mates – so if you think of it – better cross your fingers again but don't breathe a word about it to anybody. (JJL 7 October 1941)

In the outcome this did not happen, or at least not right away. After being weather-bound since the beginning of October, the squadron participated in a raid on Essen on the 10th, Joe's crew not among them. But a few Hampdens from other 5 Group squadrons were sent out for searchlight suppression along the Kammhuber Line in support. It was a new tactic, and Joe would soon enough take his turn at it.

Joe was now one of the veterans of 106 Squadron. Only eight air observers had served longer than he, and a dozen new ones had arrived in October. But they had little to do as England was fogged in for a week and all bombing operations ceased. Joe and Roger spent their free time boxing and working out in the gym with Dave Davies, who often came back to eat with them at Mrs. Lettice's house before going out on a spree.

> We have a miniature Pony Club without the ties – bond, interests or understanding – excellent for the occasion – … – but I am anxious to do some work – some real bombing. (JJD 9 October 1941)

Joe had been on only one sortie in the previous four weeks, and he was getting restless. The latest *Navigation Bulletin*, which he would have read on his return, doubtless added to his sense of frustration. Resorting to the analogy of boxers wasting strength by wild hitting, the *Bulletin* reminded its readers:

> The effective striking power of this Command largely depends on the efficiency of its navigators.… every bomb that falls on an open field is wasted strength; every bomb that is dropped on the wrong target merely scores a point. Only those bombs which hit the actual target are knockout blows.
>
> YOU, the navigators, are responsible for seeing that the bomb is dropped on the right target at the right time. Yours is a great responsibility whether your work lies in the aircraft, in the lecture room, or even in the offices.[5]

Shortly afterwards, Joe

> went to Huls in a do or die attempt to blast the rubber plant – because of bad weather & sloppy navigation landed up somewhere in the Ruhr – only one or two found it – I hate doing a sloppy job & failing in a task. I did both last night which made it a poor day for me – especially since [McIver &] I was entrusted with incendiaries to light up the place – a responsible job. (JJD 12 October 1941)
>
> A big flop … the weather contrary to expectations was 10/10 cloud at 6,000' – we could not find a break in the clouds and stooged around for 40 min. looking for the joint – landed up around Duisburg, judging by the heavy flaak so we dropped our stuff there – a great disappointment & personal failure from my standpoint – one or two were lucky enough to find a cloud break & stooged in low. (JJOD 12 October 1941)

The Squadron's record acknowledged that the raid was not an "outstanding success," but claimed that better results were achieved than in September. Five of the twelve crews dispatched definitely claimed to have scored hits, while the seven unable to locate the primary target bombed various alternatives in the Ruhr. Joe's crew reported they had started a large fire with their incendiaries. Roger Rousseau had been unable to pinpoint the target and bombed a nearby aerodrome, but McIver's crew descended below cloud and claimed to have bombed the factory from a low level.[6] Once again, however, daylight reconnaissance photos taken a few days later showed no change to the rubber factory itself, although they revealed a dummy factory located over five miles to the southwest, also undamaged.

> Going to Kiel to-nite to lay a vegetable – action makes me feel fit … wire from Mub today – it will be a memorable day when we meet. (JJD 13 October 1941)

> Tired after 2 nites on – sore after turning back last nite – our wireless packed up – I argued for 50 miles but failed to make the boys disobey orders – once I start on a job I like to see it thru – risks or no risks … (JJD 14 October 1941)

> Had the misfortune to have our wireless pack up around 100 miles out. Group orders are to return. I did not want to and argued, ranted and delivered a superb speech for the best part of 10 minutes trying to convince my crew to continue without success. I nearly swung them around but not quite … anyhow we had a lively argument and I am more convinced than ever that my job is as captain of the aircraft. This was really my 15th trip as we turned back from Essen a long time ago due to intercom failure.[7] (JJOD 13 October 1941)

So began another week of inaction, mainly due to bad weather, during which he boxed and binged with his pals.

> I heartily dislike this inaction & would like to fly more often regardless of the type of jobs or weather – I like to feel I am doing something during these crucial days – but life is indeed pleasant & happy – obviously I like action & usefulness better at the moment. (JJD 15 October 1941)

> Gigantic battles & decisions are taking place in the world whilst we cool our heels & do nothing in particular of importance – blasted lack of drive & imagination in all places practically floors me – we all want to play our part, stop & beat the Huns – but we do nothing – or next to nothing. (JJD 17 October 1941)

⊙

> Went to Bremen which is about the best defended place I have been to – really confusing & smartly done – we managed to get thru – but it was twice as hard getting out – many fellows – especially as they come

> within reach of finishing their time lose a good deal of zip since 20 out of original class of 40 navig at Regina are now missing I would say that our strategic bombing policy is costly in men, morale & material.[8] (JJD 20 October 1941)

> Convincing proof that a good proportion of strategic bombing trips are not worth the cost in crew, planes, fuel, etc.

> The weather [was] … hazy which made it difficult to pick up landmarks. We picked up the river Weser and went as far into Bremen as possible.

> Defence – the defences were cagey – searchlights were everywhere in numbers & usually capable of tossing up light flaak – there were magnificent displays of light flaak at Wenermunde, Cuxhaven – and many other nearby hot spots. Thru careful & cagey flying & with unusual good luck we escaped getting picked up by the searchlights for any length of time & when they did get us the flak was not as accurately close as usual – but it was a grind getting in and nip and tuck getting out again – My navigation was right on which got us home as usual – safe, sound and relieved. (JJOD 20 October 1941)

Joe's crew reported that owing to haze and searchlights, they did not locate the target (the railway junction), but they dropped their bombs on the flak concentration over Bremen. Seventeen squadron aircraft had gone out; most claimed to have reached and bombed the target area, but only two claimed the actual target. Bomber Command noted that very few aircraft had identified and attacked the specific aiming point, although about half the attacking force of over 150 aircraft attacked various industrial targets in the city, and others attacked anti-aircraft and searchlight installations. Five aircraft were lost, including two from 106 Squadron. However, the Bremen records characterized this raid as "small."

> Staged a reunion in Lincoln with G. P. [McLean] & Art after a phone call from Art – Dave Roger & I met them & had a typical, warm-hearted drinking bull session – our ranks are thinning rapidly & such gatherings enable you to feel the power of friends even our pals who have been killed – we include them in our thoughts and conversations without being maudlin & do them the honour & speak of them as if they were present. (JJD 21 October 1941)

> Going to Kiel to-nite in bad weather to bomb diesel factory & other points of interest – loafed the day thru – don't feel much like writing or reading – feel in the mood to do some neat bombing jobs – the more

> work I get the better I like it because I have only one reason for being here – one thought in mind – to do my part. (JJD 23 October 1941)

> Drifted way up north of Sylt – browsed around Denmark and the Baltic and map read down to Kiel. It was not as hot as usual, plenty of heavy flak there though, which was well predicted. A couple of kites were picked up while we browsed around the outside of the cone. Nothing exciting happened, we did not really get shot up or picked up by searchlights – mostly a question of navigation and sleeping during the 800 odd miles of sea. (JJOD 23 October 1941)

The attack occurred in two waves. The first, consisting of Wellingtons and Whitleys, arrived to find their target (the Germania and Deutsche works) completely cloud covered, and could not observe the results of their attack. 106 Squadron aircraft, arriving later when the clouds had drifted away, had greater success. Joe's crew reported that they had attacked from eleven thousand feet and saw their bombs burst within one mile of the primary target. The squadron report stated that all but two of the eighteen aircraft detailed to Kiel successfully located and bombed the target area, and the raid was later verified to have inflicted damage on the U-boat yards and naval base.

> Got back after finding the joint and slept, ate & saw a movie – not too satisfied with the spirit of my crew and from now on the private understanding is that I shall take charge – the boys are losing their nerve and are not too keen on seeing the job thru – I shall put an end to that we have to blast the target – or else. (JJD 24 October 1941)

> No ops went to Boston with Roger – get a real delight spending the odd evening in a real [English] pub chatting & drinking with the various characters. The corner pub, especially in rural districts is almost the home of the Englishman – at any rate an institution where he can meet his cronies & talk & act in perfect peace & freedom.

> I have a sacred trust to carry out the mission of ours and other struggling & oppressed people if we fail – we are lost – altho I don't always agree with our policy I must carry out tasks assigned to me – regardless of the consequences to me – that shall be done. (JJD 25 October 1941)

The Bremen and Kiel operations had gone well: the weather co-operated, there were no close calls, and Joe believed he had bombed his targets. He was briefed for his third operation that week on the 26th, this time against the Blohm und Voss shipyards in Germany's heavily defended second city, Hamburg.

> Had a swell trip. Went in north of Kiel – straight down across the centre of town and pranged it. There were a couple of nice fires, hundreds of searchlights. We were lucky – we sneaked in between a couple of cones that caught somebody else, dropped our bombs and nipped out without having a shot fired at us – or a searchlight pick us up, and Hamburg is a hot spot.
>
> The weather was terrific going out and the cracking of ice forming on the wings sounded worse than aak aak – the weather was really foul until the other side was reached.
>
> Coming back over the 360 mile stretch of sea was restful – I put up my back rest, parked my feet on the bomb sight, spread my rations out on my table – munched my eats, drank my hot Bovril and then philosophically smoked my pipe as we raced a few hundred feet off the sea to get below the dirty weather. It was a grand, satisfactory trip.
>
> We had Popeye[9] with us – he has done 65 trips. (JJOD 26 October 1941)

The squadron record states that eighteen aircraft were dispatched to Hamburg. Thirteen located and bombed the target and area, causing explosions and starting several fires. Three aircraft returned early due to technical failures, and two aircraft were lost.[10] Joe's crew reported bombing from eleven thousand feet, but the results were not observed owing to searchlights. The city recorded more damage and casualties than in average raids, although work disruption was short-lived.

Joe recorded in his daily diary that he had "passed the halfway mark now – thundering down the home stretch," and he was satisfied with his performance in his last three operations.

There was more action the following week as the full moon approached.

> Going on a low level to attack Jerry planes going to raid us – boy just what I have been waiting for – a real honest to goodness crack at these birds who think such a lot of themselves and so little of everybody else. (JJD 29 October 1941)

It was a low-level raid on Schiphol airfield near Amsterdam, mounted in response to a large force of enemy aircraft detected there. The weather was most unfavourable, however, and only three aircraft located and bombed the target. The rest abandoned the task after a long search, and one aircraft failed to return.

> There were supposed to be a number of Jerry planes ready to bomb one of our towns – we were sent to bomb them before taking off – they never took off but not because of us – but the weather. We stooged over roof tops in Holland for one whole hour looking for the joint. Every now & then we would get fired at but nothing hit us. We had to bring our bombs back the Dutch have enough worries without our bombs. (JJOD 29 October 1941)

Two nights later, the Squadron dispatched fifteen aircraft on Hamburg, of which twelve found and bombed the target and adjoining area. The others bombed alternative targets at Kiel and Eckernforde. Opposition was intense and accurate. Of the total Bomber Command force of 123 aircraft on this raid, only fifty-six crews claimed to have bombed, in conditions of poor visibility. Hamburg reported that one person was killed, eight were injured, and 175 were bombed out.

> Back to [Blohm und Voss] sub works at Hamburg to-nite – have reached the stage where I appreciate this job – [I] like flying with Roberts because he is old for his years, skillful modest & cautious to make up for my reckless careless tendency – we get along well together and have confidence in one another. (JJD 31 October 1941)

> The same type of trip as a few nights ago – the same objective – submarine factory – weather was too cloudy over target to pick out the factory so we dropped our bombs on the town – Again we got thru luckily without getting molested – the place is dynamite but we are still lucky at Hamburg. (JJOD 31 October 1941)

In the midst of all this, Joe reunited with Monty

> Swung a 48 hr pass – caught a train & whizzed down to Bournemouth – after the usual telegrams & near [misses] I found Monty – good old Monty & we proceeded to make up for lost time – we drank, smoked cigars & talked until 4 AM – a really historic meeting for the two of us. (JJD 27 October 1941)

> Back in stride with Mub, snooker – ping pong – cigars – talk – jokes companionship – he is a great fellow who will work & live with me and think & inspire me as long as I live. (JJD 28 October 1941)

After three months hemorrhaging of his close circle at 106 Squadron, Joe had suddenly, miraculously, been reunited with the friend who mattered the most to him. Joe's bonds with Roger and Dave, now those most close to him in the squadron, had been formed by the immediate daily reality of shared purpose, circumstance, and danger, and their emerging interest in politics. His Pony Club pals were far away – he had not seen Herb for over a year. Gerald had brought to the Pony Club his sense of humour and fun, he was sharp and adventuresome, always a good source of news and gossip of the Montreal crowd. The bond between Joe and Monty was deeper, based on shared experience, outlook, and views. It was not conditional on being in the same combat unit and its intensity would not fade if that ended. They did not need to explain themselves to each other or put up a good front. For the next three months, they would be inseparable on their leave times, which they made every effort to coordinate. As time went on, Joe's friendship with Janine would become secondary to his bond with Monty.

Joe returned to Coningsby invigorated, with renewed enthusiasm for action. It also reignited his correspondence with Gerald and Herb:

> Last Sunday I was flying. I arrived back from Hamburg at dawn, hopped a train and was making a square search of the town for Monty by 6 PM after travelling all day. In traditional style Mub and I bumped into each other. Why I do not know – how I cannot explain – we merely did the logical thing and bumped into one another in England – amazing but true.
>
> It is hard to depict my reactions at seeing Mub again. Imagine yourself away from home for seven months. Then imagine yourself in a strange country. Then try to imagine the insecurity of flying over Germany week after week and you will realize what a reunion it was. The impossible occurred. Nothing seemed more fantastic to me than that I should see Mub again – even up until after Sunday night. Yet nothing seemed more natural than to be calmly smoking Mub's cigars, consuming his liquor and spending the night until 4 AM chatting, talking, planning and mulling over the past seven months with Monty and listening to stories of my family, Poneyites – Monty's and your families and adventures.
>
> … Women for a change did not enter into our activities. I only had a day and a night and we had too much to talk about to bother about females.… It was a great occasion for both of us and ended with a hectic taxi ride thru town to catch the last train for me which was gathering up steam to pull out. (JJL 2 November 1941)

Inevitably he took the occasion to exhort them to train as aircrew:

> If you want safety join air force ground crew since you will be safer than you are on civvy street. If you really want to live – join aircrew. If you get fooled and get knocked off you still have nothing to worry about because you will never know … what hit you.
>
> … We never thought a great deal of Hy Abrams. But he showed he had guts and stuff in the pinch. He took the hardest and most dangerous course. He got what fifty percent of my pals got. But you have to admire and respect men like that –
>
> But don't fool yourself with regards your job – the dangers are non-existent – therefore you can't expect much in return – at least not the life I consider worthwhile.… But if you want to be a flyer don't think that you are one when you start repairing radio sets – you are a plain ordinary electrician, and doing a nice, safe, uninteresting, routine job. If you are a man with plenty of guts and spirit and determination you fly – yes you get killed too but you can't live forever and if you can show your stuff early and clear out you justify your presence. Just hanging around for three score and ten years doesn't suit me – …
> (JJL 2 November 1941)

Relating all this to his family, he wrote:

> The four continuous days and nights of constant, exciting and varied activity, far from wearying me, made me feel better than usual – the more activity and work and excitement the better I like it, the better I feel and look and the happier I am. (JJL 1 November 1941).

All the while, Joe was considering his next moves. He told his father

> I am really getting intrigued with possibilities here. Don't bother with Ottawa Pop – I can handle everything that requires handling for the time being. I am over half thru on this job but I am going to stick around for a while. I could not stand it in Canada while the war is on. I get exasperated when I go to places like Bournemouth over here or other resorts full of evacuees. This is the chance of a life time to live with real men – who don't talk about what they are doing or have done but what they do is hard to do justice to in black and white or mere words – I have lived with men before but I like this gang on operations if not always for their personalities – at least for what they do and the way they do it.… (JJL 1 November 1941)

Whether Joe was referring to their personalities or their views is unclear. His own views on class, creed, and government, as they had evolved by this time, were probably not widely shared on his squadron. But all that would have been secondary to the job at hand, and the qualities that enabled his comrades to do it.

The month ended on a satisfactory note for Joe. In the last three weeks, 106 Squadron had been operational on eight nights, and Joe had been dispatched on seven of them to a mix of industrial, naval, and airfield targets. On most nights he had found the target and believed he had been more successful than in September. Perhaps this was because only one of them was in the Ruhr with its heavy haze and smoke, the rest being targets on Germany's north coast. By the end of the month he had completed eighteen sorties amounting to about 120 hours of operational flying time, or about 60 percent through his first tour. He had also been briefed and taken off on two sorties that had to be aborted. Joe was no longer under any illusions about the dangers he faced, but the end was close enough that he could begin to count down.

For flying crews operating out of English aerodromes, bouts of danger and terror in the air were separated by intervals of comfort and safety on the ground, with ready access to the pleasures of civilian life. Their experience of war was very different from the infantryman's. Aircrew did not eat and sleep rough, they were not filthy and lice-ridden for days on end, they were not directly exposed to the brutality of deadly man-to-man fighting, and very rarely did they see the men next to them suddenly dismembered, disembowelled, or disintegrated. Flying crews on active duty received a week's crew leave every five or six weeks. Yet the alternation of danger and tranquillity within hours of each other – the sudden and mostly unpredictable shifts between terror and relief – placed its own physical and psychological stresses on bomber crews.

Flying stress was not well understood in the early years of the war. The physical stress of long flights confined in cramped, noisy, and unpressurized aircraft that had most certainly not been built for comfort, was obvious enough. Flying for up to eight hours at high altitudes in those conditions brought risks of oxygen deficiency, and especially in winter, extreme cold and even frostbite, but young flyers were hardy enough and sufficiently well equipped to endure these conditions, even if not at peak efficiency.

The psychological stresses were less tangible but more cumulative. A man might laugh off a sortie as a piece of cake, yet the prospect of coming to grief from flak or night-fighters, from adverse weather conditions or running short of fuel, was always present. In the darkness of enemy skies, crews were hunted by invisible but omnipresent lethal forces that could strike without warning. They pressed on for hours with no control over these dangers and little defence against them. As they approached their target and the German defences, their anxiety and adrenalin rose. Crew cohesion, faith in each other's competence, and mutual dependence helped, but each man was on his own in his duties and at his station in the aircraft.

Psychological stress was not restricted to the air. The tension began at briefing time, especially if the announced target was known to be a difficult one, and it continued to build during flight preparation. Yet being told at the last minute to stand down as operations were cancelled brought little comfort and no less stress. Extended periods of inactivity meant only frustration, and they lowered morale. With loss rates running at 4 or 5 percent on every operation, the likelihood of surviving a tour of thirty sorties was very low. Every man knew the odds. Yet at the same time, experience built confidence. Most wanted to complete their tour as soon as possible rather than spin it out.

Fear and anxiety were ever-present, and over prolonged periods became physically exhausting and psychologically draining. Flying stress wore down even the strongest over time. Aircrew kept such fears to themselves as they could not let themselves or their comrades down. The premium was on repression and self-control. Joe was strong on the latter; for the former, he channelled his letters and diaries for release. The penalty for not being able to carry on was not only loss of face, but being labelled LMF (lack of moral fibre) resulting in dismissal and disgrace. That happened to very few men in Bomber Command, but many more came to carry the scars of what would be characterized, many decades later, as post-traumatic stress disorder.

Percy, from the other side of the ocean, observed Joe's progress:

> Monty and Gerald here for dinner tonight.... Monty's farewell visit he expects to leave for overseas service the end of the week. Fine lad, brains, sensibility and humour.... Gerald too a nice kind lad, sensitive and fine ... I think Janet rather likes Gerald ... understatement perhaps. Pleasant evening. Will miss Monty. Know May thinks of Joe a lot. Her sleep is sometimes disturbed. Hard for her. She never complains. (PJD 23 September 1941)

Letters from Joe are always so lively and sound so happy that the dream I had about him the other night seemed so vivid by contrast. He had come home unexpectedly from the front. He looked straight and strong but his eyes looked so tired and strained and there was something that seemed to be bothering him, something he could not express. He looked so unhappy. Possibly due to a headache which persisted while I slept. Still it was disturbing and rather unnerved me.
(PJD 8 October 1941)

[Joe] is more concerned about facing life after the war than facing death now. He feels that it is harder to lead the fine life than it is to face daily danger. I guess the lad is right. He is eager for his life to be as valuable in peacetime as it is in wartime. We keep all Joe's letters. I wish I was not his father so I can say all the things I want to say about him. Anyway he is a grand lad and I cannot help but recording that I am as proud of him as his mother is … if he is only spared. His letters are racy but every now and again they strike the bullseye with an eternal truth.
(PJD 15 October 1941)

Letters from Joe again today. It is difficult at this time to discuss this lad of ours with restraint. His letters will tell why. He has so much understanding of people he is so kind and wise beyond his years and has such gay humour. One of the letters was to his mother. It was so understanding so tender without being maudlin.

My partner says he wakes up in cold sweat every night thinking about his son's danger (he is in the navy) and asked me this morning how I managed to keep my nerve. I did not tell him that there are times when I too get panicky. I am darned if I am going to let anybody know about it. Not even May. (PJD 20 October 1941)

Twenty-Four

Questions and Doubts

The problems of the autumn bombing campaign preyed on Joe's mind when he was not flying. In October he started filling a notebook with his thoughts, which he characterized as:

> merely personal views obtained from limited experience, observation & discussion with my friends. They represent fairly accurately our views. Probably most of them can be shown to be feasible. But I do not imply that the present morale is low – it is not – there is a fine and dashing & enthusiastic spirit. But then we are getting well paid and treated and very little flying in during the winter months – the fact remains we are taking everything nonchalantly, philosophically and in stride but we are in a fast moving, ruthless war – we have to move faster and more accurately and more deadly to crush the enemy. (JJN 3 October 1941)

He began by commenting on Bomber Command's aircraft.

> Halifaxes – Stirlings & Manchesters looked upon with dread and fear by crews because they don't go high enough or fast enough and are too big and easy a target for the expert German defences. The British should be [building] light fast planes with a high ceiling and a big bomb load per square foot of wing space. I would like to see searchlights pick up a machine travelling 300 mph – It's duck soup when we go at 150 or so – for them. (JJN 3 October 1941)

Joe's views of the new heavy bombers, and most especially of the Manchesters to which 5 Group squadrons were converting, were widely shared among aircrews. Perhaps they looked forward to an early conversion to the Lancaster bombers – Manchesters equipped with four engines instead of two – that would soon be coming into service in 5 Group. What Joe was really looking for turned out to be the de Havilland Mosquito, then still in development, and top secret. Perhaps already rumoured among flying crew, it really would travel at over three hundred miles per hour, and much higher than any existing bomber.

Joe also wondered why the offensive was still so hampered by bad weather:

> Too many trips or raids are cancelled because of ground fogs over England for the return – the blind landing or Lorenz or an improvement should be available by now. The flat Lincolnshire County with no hills and few obstructions should at least offer good scope for blind landings – civil air schedules are no longer cancelled because of poor weather. Why should a raid? Just as we had the Germans on the run they were saved or spared by the weather. (JJN 3 October 1941)

106 Squadron crews had been practising with Lorenz since Joe's arrival, but only for blind approach. It was not yet utilized as a landing aid. So morning fog over the Lincolnshire fens was still a hazard for returning crews. More importantly, the events of the previous month had persuaded him that

> Night bombing is no longer accurate – too many valuable trained crews are wasted on unimportant raids – they might be of better use in the Fleet Air Arm or Army Co-op or some specialized task on a special target. Half-hearted raids are not worthwhile. They have to be on a big scale to be effective. (JJN 3 October 1941)

He would have more to say on this topic a couple of weeks later, after the disappointments of his second sortie on Huls and the aborted gardening sortie near Kiel.

> The Command seem obsessed with … the affecting of German morale. We disperse our bombing strength by sending out scattered forces on various targets for general effect. Statistics prove few planes reach the target or achieve positive results – proof … lies in the number of visits the RAF keep making to the same target.
>
> Two examples – knapsack[1] which provides all or most of the power for the Ruhr & Huls which provides ½ of Germany's synthetic rubber needs – we continuously bomb these targets with small forces and

> achieve no results. I have been twice to Huls – it has not been damaged as yet. The same goes for most other targets – we usually drop our bombs in heavy flak or when we do find the target – there is not sufficient bombing strength to bring about decisive results – we have the strength because we sometimes send out 200 & 300 planes but scatter them on different targets – here is what should be done – Knapsack for example should be destroyed – in a suitable period start first with the daylight Blenheims in early evening when target cannot be mistaken. Set the place ablaze with incendiaries – then get low level Hampdens, Wellingtons & Whitleys pasting it in waves and finally have the Stirlings, Manchesters & Halifaxes drop their 4000 pound bombs – simple – effective & quite within our range – losses would be high but no higher than we lose night after night on senseless, indecisive but dangerous and costly operations – (JJN undated [October] 1941)

Joe was not troubled by the objective of lowering the morale of Germany's workforce by night bombing. The argument in favour of dispersal of effort was to keep as much of Germany's civilian workforce sleepless, if not actually homeless, as possible, by setting off air raid alarms in many different locations, with no predictable pattern. It was an argument that made a virtue out of necessity, so long as there were neither sufficient aircraft to launch a concentrated attack, nor the technical means to ensure their concentration in time and space at the desired location. The bomber stream – dozens or hundreds of aircraft travelling together in overwhelming force and arriving in precise sequence and time – was a tactic not yet developed.

In the meantime, the problem that had become apparent to crews from their own experience in the autumn of 1941 was that, whether or not they were successfully disrupting civilian life, they were not doing sufficient damage to industrial or military objectives. The problem, Joe continued, was that

> the indecisive bombing policy has caused further effects. The trips are merely sorties and it matters little whether you drop your bombs smack on the railway station or some quiet country home – the results are about the same and since the German defences are good you are glad to get rid of your bombs regardless of where they fall & you often have to since the majority of fellows are sensible, intelligent & practical that is what is done. (JJN undated [October] 1941)

In short, the revelations of the Butt Report, and the absence of any immediate prospect of improving navigation and bomb-aiming techniques by more than a margin, seem to have persuaded flying crews that since they were not capable of precision bombing of key military and industrial targets, then dropping their bombs on any built-up area was good enough, and indeed as good as could be expected. Under the circumstances, only heavy concentrations of aircraft sent in sequence – first to mark the target, then raise fires with incendiaries, and then blast it with heavy explosives – could inflict serious physical damage on key targets, as opposed to morale. These tactics had been under active consideration at senior levels in Bomber Command for some time, but Joe's notebook suggests that the issue was also well understood by those on the front line.

Engaging in what amounted to no more than nuisance raids was detrimental to aircrew morale, Joe asserted, and he set out the tactics and incentives he believed would correct the situation:

> Individual squadrons and planes must be given definite tasks so that they will be willing to take greater risks to accomplish a definite task and responsibility and see definite results – there is too much haphazard bombing going on – too many senseless trips being made which breaks down the spirit and fight of even the best men.
>
> No sense taking foolhardy risks when nothing is achieved or gained worth taking risks for. Now the majority of fellows are cool, brave, courageous, daring & ingenious. We all have fighting spirit and a burning desire to achieve concrete results, to sell our lives dearly – to put the Germans where they belong. The way to utilize the qualities of our airmen is to give them something to aim at. A definite important target with our full powers used would achieve miracles. If each group – each squadron, each individual was made to feel that their collective & personal reputations were at stake – then results would follow – if the whole available air force co-operated on one target at one time – then the bombing results would prove positive....
>
> ... squadrons should be run like football teams. Each man competes against the other to prove their superiority – yet all co-operate together to show their collective superiority – with individuals, squadrons & groups competing against one another for the best results yet working together to obtain them must be the keystone for successful and decisive results with the type of fellow in our air force ...
> (JJN undated [October] 1941)

He singled out the tour system, "the stupid rule that you do 200 hours or 35 trips on operations," as a perverse incentive because "after a certain number of trips – that objective – that aim – that hope is prevalent during your operational trips." Everyone, he claimed,

> is obsessed with (1) Finishing 200 operational hr. (2) Winning a DFM or DFC (3) Getting a commission. The first point dominates – instead of concentrating on blasting the target – of socking the Germans – of winning the war by these means – we continuously count our hours and trips and forget why we are making them. This attitude is encouraged by our strategic policy – since many raids are half hearted, conducted in bad weather and on fiercely defended targets, some fellows feel as long as they drop their bombs they are doing their stuff – our whole plan must be more definite and better executed.
>
> We must get away from our 200 hrs and get a policy based on achievement and give definite responsibilities to those who succeed – sending everyone to O.T.U. on a rest cure is stupid – it is also criminal – everyone dreads going to those wasteful death traps – give the men who show their capabilities something worthwhile instead of a dangerous, depressing so called rest. We are young we can stand work and danger and responsibilities. (JJN undated [October] 1941)

Of decorations and commissions, Joe observed:

> Most fellows want some badge of recognition to show they have done their 200 hours which feat is well worth being proud of. Sensible distribution & awarding of awards greatly improves the morale of the squadron.
>
> … no more commissions should be awarded until a minimum number of operational trips have been made – say ten. New classes of men are being given responsibilities before they have proved themselves, whilst true, tried, dependable and brave men remain NCOs – thus the greatest use is not being made of their ability as leaders – a fairer and more sensible system also improves the spirit of the men.
> (JJN undated [October] 1941)

The existing system was, for Joe, one more example of the hidebound nature of the upper echelons of command, and was in urgent need of correction.

> It is this senseless organization – this stupid adherence to a so called plan or policy that is our undoing – wake up lads and take advantage of the materials at hand – make use of our great young youths –

I have seen many a good enthusiastic fellow ruined and unnerved by our system – also many a capable man rot in liquor & women –

… We are not worried for the most part about our lives – the Dominion boys especially – but the English fellows are not far behind – arrive in England chock full of enthusiasm – they want to do heroic deeds and justify the confidence & responsibility placed in them – but what happens over here. By the time they have finished being tossed around, kept inactive and stepped on their enthusiasm has been dampened, their initiative submerged, their talent left unutilized.
(JJN undated [October] 1941)

Joe cannot have been alone in his views. These matters would have been the regular topic of discussion among flying crews based on their recent experience. His notebook provides substantial evidence that, three months into Bomber Command's all-out strategic offensive against Germany, its flyers were well aware of its limitations and the reasons for them, even if they were not privy to the 9 July directive itself, or to the full details of the Butt Report. Bomber Command crews knew perfectly well that they were engaged in area bombing, and why. They were also aware that it was directed more against Germany's "morale" than its actual military and industrial capacities. And they knew that precision bombing would not and could not be achieved by more attentive dead reckoning and astro-navigation, more meticulous paperwork, and more intensive intelligence debriefings.

Even the most confident aircrews had begun to realize that they could not prevail on fighting spirit alone. That was a lesson that airmen of all the combatant countries would learn the hard way in the coming years. Allied victory would rely on technical superiority and the application of modern management techniques, as Joe had already perceived. And Joe was coming around to the view that achieving those ends was not simply a military issue but a political one.

The most consistent concern in discussion of both Dave & myself is the rut we are in and the absolute inability of the present leaders in Engl. to cope with the ideas & problems – economic, social, military etc. today – we *cannot* win the war until courageous, imaginative efficient men cast aside old prejudices & fifth columnists and take steps to win this war. (JJD 19 October 1941)

Looking thru "The Aeroplane" list of awards & casualties today one of our basic injustices was clearly demonstrated – most of the awards for bravery were to officers – especially the high ranking ones who fly

> seldom & whose bravery is often open to question – an odd sergeant is condescendingly given an award – but the casualty lists are mostly sergeants with comparatively few officers – right thru our whole system is found that striking inequality – that injustice – the ones who do the work – take the risks – suffer the most – receive the least credit – return or consideration. (JJD 1 November 1941)

None of these concerns deterred Joe from the job at hand, and a good sortie reinvigorated him.

> Did a mine laying job in Kiel Harbour again, bombed & machine gunned a ship – had a pleasant time.... (JJD 4 November 1941)

> We had a lot of fun flying at 2000' all the way. The weather was mucky all over but after persistent searching around the Baltic we found a pin point on the desired island – dodged a few flak ships and made a perfect run over the desired spot from 700' and dropped the mine. We then bombed a schooner which I missed and made four attacks firing our machine guns at it from about 50' – the bloody ship ignored our aggressiveness entirely – I guess they were all asleep.

> I fell asleep coming home and was too lazy to take any loop bearings or star shots – subsequently we landed around London with warships flashing challenges at us. We were a mere 150 miles off track and proceeded home. Upon arrival we were given a warm reception. Firstly because we had been given up as lost – secondly because we were one of the few crews to actually drop the vegetable in the required spot.

> We have a pleasant time on trips. Robby and I usually have an argument about where we are – Hodge chides me good naturedly and all congratulate Robby vociferously when he smartly fools the searchlight and aak battery. I really enjoy our little jaunts with my crew. Robby is a top notch pilot. (JJOD 4 November 1941)

Joe added, in a note to Monty, "We have the only crew in captivity that smokes cigars as they machine gun the Hun."

Joe's performance on the return trip from the Baltic did not gain him a place on the list of outstanding navigation errors in the monthly *Navigation Bulletin*, although similar lapses by other navigators often did. Joe's squadron leader would later characterize him as a brilliant navigator, who conducted his duties with skill and courage. He may not always have been a meticulous one, or consistently used his tools and training to best advantage, as he occasionally criticized himself for in his diary. The *Navigation Bulletin* repeatedly exhorted navigators to be alert on the return journey, and navigate home as carefully as they had to the target. Perhaps on this occasion Joe thought that having completed his primary task successfully, he could provide his captain with a homeward course, and relax. Joe was not alone in succumbing to cold, noise, oxygen deficiency, and fatigue on long trips, drained of adrenalin after completing the attack. Star shots involved disconnecting his oxygen supply, crawling up from underneath the cockpit to the dome behind the pilot each time.

Perhaps Joe and many others had absorbed the lesson that regardless of how many star shots they took, or how neatly they kept their logs, finding the aiming point was the exception, not the rule, and that any destruction in a built-up area would suffice if they could not. Perhaps all that many airmen, like Joe it would appear, wanted at this point was to get through this difficult period and live to see the day when they would be better equipped for the task. The higher-ups could nag them about their performance, but not much would or could change until the promised radio-navigation aids arrived.

Joe summed up his situation in his operational diary.

> After three months on operations … I can better review life on a bomber squadron.
>
> *Firstly:* I have definitely settled down. I know the dangers, the chances we take, the chance we have of getting thru the first batch – having accepted the situation calmly and logically I have settled down to an orderly life.
>
> *Secondly:* I still get a kick out of my operational trips because
>
> 1. I am with an experienced crew. We all know the score – that cancels off plenty of the risk.
>
> 2. I love action. Unfortunately, this is all negative destruction action. Nevertheless it is activity that calls for skill, cooperation, courage amongst other qualities.
>
> 3. most important – it is concrete, tangible and effective way of fighting the Germans. Since their ideas and actions should and are being fought, I as a fighter willing to stand by mine and my coun-

try's form of living against Germany's get satisfaction while others & me get the benefit out of my small part as an individual.

Thirdly: I am making use of some of my spare time by

1. keeping physically fit
2. keeping mentally fit

To enable me to fight the next battle – the battle for a better life with the required assets (which I have) and the required ammunition which I have not as yet.

Physical fitness – Dave, Roger & I ride about 15 miles per day on our bikes and manage to do the odd bit of boxing and gymnastics in our gym. I also do setting up exercises.

Mental fitness. I have been delving into social problems, our society, problems and solutions – I have read "Let My People Go" by Cedric Belfrage – mostly concerned with religion how it does and does not function in the U.S. in particular. Also "The Socialist Sixth of the World" by the Dean of Canterbury concerning Russia & comparing their life, problems & solutions to ours – we have come out poorly in both books and I intend reading the Bible, Marx, Lenin, etc. I also have a book on public speaking to study.

At this stage the operational trips serve a useful purpose outside of the military effects. Before and during every trip, unimportant petty worries and difficulties fade away – you soon get out of the habit of letting them enter your life – you are concerned with only two big problems – destroying Germans and preserving yourself. (JJOD 6 November 1941)

Twenty-Five

Winding Down

On 7 November, while most 106 Squadron crews were engaged in sea-mining operations in Oslo Fiord, two were sent to the Ruhr, and in support, two others, including Joe's, were sent as "intruders" to the Kammhuber line. Carrying eight 250-pound bombs, their purpose was to disrupt searchlight operations in the Bocholt section by low-level bombing and machine gunning, which they did for an hour from between five hundred and two thousand feet.

> Had to bomb and shoot out searchlights in the searchlight belt so that the boys could get thru to Essen more easily. Stooged back and forth for an hour, dropping bombs, shooting them up and generally scaring the ground crews. We had a singing contest over the intercom – every time we sang a song Robby did not like he would stick the nose of the plane down and stand us on our heads. (JJOD 8 November 1941)

The main action of the air offensive that night had been elsewhere. Bomber Command dispatched nearly four hundred aircraft, virtually all of its serviceable force, and nearly half of them to Berlin, despite adverse weather forecasts. It was one of the largest raids on Berlin so far in the war, and it was a disaster.[1]

> 37 planes missing last night 20 in the sea – including McIver – I guess they will start worrying back home – Roger back after a rough trip to Norway from Scotland ...[2] (JJD 8 November 1941)

The Berlin raid was big news, and it did cause worry at home. Percy recorded, the next day:

> The worst air disaster of this war last night over Berlin. Thirty five of our airships lost. Main reason not anti aircraft guns but poor visibility. Airmen started out in the moonlight but ran into terrible weather conditions. Joe almost sure to have taken part in the raid. He has been in every major raid so far. After this war is over we will well wonder how we lived through these times. We cannot imagine anything happening to Joe, this is the feeling that all parents have so we carry on as normally as possible. I have just finished a letter to Joe. My sense tells me that it is just as likely as not that he may have been one of the unfortunate ones but my instinct refuses to accept such a possibility. In other words we refuse to accept any idea of disaster until disaster is upon us. And so tonight we go to see *Target for Tonight* a movie recommended by Joe. A movie by the way which is a document of what happens when a bomber goes over Germany. Not fiction. We don't want to get away from the war, we want to keep as close as possible to it, we want to talk the same language as Joe when he returns to us. So we read Tally Ho and Bomber Command and everything else about aerial warfare that we can get hold of. (PJD 8 November 1941)

The Berlin disaster broke the War Cabinet's patience with Bomber Command. Churchill demanded an explanation from its Commander-in-Chief, Air Marshal Sir Richard Peirse. Peirse blamed the unreliability of weather forecasting for the unanticipated extreme icing conditions and high winds encountered on the return trip from Germany. That so many crews ran out of fuel in these conditions, he claimed, was due to their insufficient knowledge of long-range flying. The fault lay, he implied, with his men. The Cabinet and the Air Ministry were less than satisfied. Peirse's days at Bomber Command were now numbered. Aloof and never popular with flying crew, he was removed to the Pacific theatre less than two months later.

Bomber Command was ordered forthwith to reduce its strategic air offensive to a bare minimum over the winter, and conserve its resources in order to build a strong force by the following spring. The directive acknowledged that while heavy losses must be faced in vital operations, it was

> undesirable in present circumstances and in the course of normal operations that attacks should be pressed unduly especially if weather conditions were unfavourable or if aircraft were to be exposed to extreme hazard.[3]

Sorties and bomb tonnage fell to about half the daily rate of the fall campaign. There were many nights with no operations, due largely to adverse weather. Operations were restricted mainly to naval targets on the French and German coasts, with only a few raids on the Ruhr and Hamburg. Bomber Command would not revisit Berlin until 1943. Over the next two months, there were only thirteen nights when over a hundred aircraft were dispatched, and only seven on which over a hundred were directed to the same target. Wellingtons, Whitleys, and Hampdens still constituted the main striking force, and the men flying them still relied on the same old inadequate methods and instruments for navigation and bombing. The old policy of dispersal to multiple targets continued, as did the practice of each aircraft finding its own way there. Yet even if sorties were fewer, loss rates continued to run at about 4 percent. The available night bombing force on any given night had declined by over a tenth since Joe Jacobson had begun operations in August, and the Hampden force by even more. The number of new heavy bombers coming into service could not yet compensate. It would not be possible to maintain the morale of flying crews indefinitely in the circumstances. The situation, as measured in both losses and results, was unsustainable. In the short term, the prospects for the bombing campaign were dismal, but as the authors of its official history observed:

> it was not possible to withdraw the force from the line. The war in the air was necessarily continuous and through the dreary winter of 1941–42 Bomber Command continued to engage the enemy as best it could.[4]

The failure of the Berlin operation marked the end of the fall campaign, although Joe did not know that right away. He thought he would have to fly again on Monday the 10th before going on leave the following day. But as he told Monty, getting through the remainder of his tour of operations would be difficult:

> Since this station started on operations about six months ago twelve Canadians have been here – no one has ever finished – three are left – Roger, myself, and old Pop Miller who is not flying any more – He is station adjutant. Roger and I are defying the fates – Gods and Germans – I need ten more trips to finish but it is a long ten trips as my pilot needs but one more so that I shall have to fly with a new inexperienced pilot – No new pilot has lasted more than a dozen trips since July – Boy I sure have to do some red hot navigating to pull thru. But those are figures and facts – not fictions – I merely employ them to urge upon you the necessity of taking advantage of every chance we get

> to see one another. The trip today was out of the question otherwise I should have been there – but make sure you click next weekend – Incidentally Roger is still asleep from his Norway trip – they flew through everything that the heavens could produce. (JJL 9 November 1941)

On a somewhat more optimistic note he wrote the Pony Club about his situation:

> when and if you finish your 35 trips – approx 200 hours you go on what is called a "rest" – that is you are posted as an instructor at a training centre. Since I can't do too much damage to the Germans to suit me and also since I hate inactivity which is what an instructor's job is, I am pulling every string I know to keep on operations.… I am trying the impossible – to get on a pilot's course and learn something new and go back as either a fighter or bomber pilot – preferably the former but depending on what I am best suited for. It might be trying to stretch your luck too far but both Roger and I are doing that if we get thru alright. If that is impossible we shall apply to go on Coastal Command, the Middle East or Russia. When I get started on a job I like seeing it thru and from the driver's front seat – but any thought of remustering is purely to keep in the thick of it – not because of any dissatisfaction with being an observer – that is the best job in the crew – the key man on a squadron – you probably still hear only about pilots but speak to bomber pilots and you will hear only about observers – so you see the old maestro is still very much in the thick of everything and intends to remain in the thick until the end. (JJL 9 November 1941)

On that same day after the Berlin raid, Joe reflected in his diary:

> One tragedy of the war – the young vigorous fellows of top notch calibre like Keswick, McIntyre, McIver, Erly, Carmichael, Dunn etc. who would be the leaders have been killed – since I am one of them my task must be twofold – *first* to take over their share of responsibility – *second* – to try & find others to do as they would have done – that is work & struggle to give equal opportunity to as many as possible because there are more of that calibre & they must be found & given a chance. (JJD 9 November 1941)

> Spent a lot of time reading about & thinking of the big problems of the day – social – economic, religious – they all hinge around capitalism – which has definitely outlived its usefulness – it is going to be a tough battle to convince the winners of that fact but it will be done. (JJD 8 November 1941)

Joe had survived the autumn campaign, beating the odds by completing twenty operations in three months. At that rate, he might have finished his first tour by the end of the year. Now he and many others would have to wait. During the coming winter, Bomber Command would bring the new generation of heavy bombers, and new radio navigation aids, into service, and adopt new bombing tactics. This would augur well for the future. But the airmen who had come through the intensity of the autumn campaign would have little operational flying to do in the meantime. The coming winter lull would be hard on morale.

Joe then left for London on his third week-long crew leave. He was relieved to go, but the next day, Armistice Day, provided a sombre reminder of all those who had failed to return during the previous three months.

> Hopped down to London with Hodge & Harding[5] – had a few drinks in the Cavalier club before retiring. Feel free & pleasant & relaxed & secure for one whole week – which is the whole value of the leave. (JJD 10 November 1941)

> Armistice day – thoughts are with McIntyre, Keswick, McIver, Davis & all the other boys I know & do not know who have "had it" …
> (JJD 11 November 1941)

> Met good old Everett Littlefield and started another binge … –
> I strolled back to the hideout rather mellow.
> (JJD 12 November 1941)

> Spent the day with Ev – a good sound head – thinks like me – smart boy – went to all our clubs – felt bang on all day – poor weather kept us indoors with no chance to scout around – brought Ev home to sleep with me – I sure make my place my pals home – met Jim Whelan who has 3 planes shot down – Massey Beveridge[6] amongst others around town. (JJD 13 November 1941)

That morning he wrote his family:

> I saw "Jupiter Laughs" by A. J. Cronin. It was one of the finest plays I have seen anywhere and staged superbly. I could almost see it again – it is significant that serious drama plays concerning faith and God and other such phenomena of life are starting to creep back into peoples' consciousness.

> I meet more people that I know in London than I would in Montreal – army – air force – civvies – a lot of fellows talk about wanting to go back to Canada – few would until after the war – what's good enough for your pals is good enough for you....
>
> Roger, Dave and I not one of the *37* – and going like a million.[7] (JJL 13 November 1941)

Joe left London on Friday for Midfield, where he spent the remainder of his leave.

> Janine and I went to the "Yeoman of the Guard" & met Monty at the Midland Hotel ... Great to see dependable – good old Mub again – nice to be with Janine whom I have stopped falling for and settled down to a solid friendship based on mutual likes – Mub of course fitted right in per usual and the old duo talked far into the wee hours of morn.
>
> A hectic – binging rather dissipated few days in London with old pals, liquor & women – then a magnificent homecoming at Midfield with Dan & Henriette and Janine & Susanne & finally Monty & Sammy [Janine's cousin] which warmed the heart, stirred the soul and stimulated the mind as a spirit of family comradeship and warmth developed – (JJD 15 November 1941)
>
> A truly marvelous day – an enlightened fireside discussion on Zionism about which Dan & Henriette are thoroughly immersed and then the four boys went out to the pub for a few and came back high to find the three women putting on a better act with an empty whisky bottle to everyone's thorough enjoyment. (JJD 16 November 1941)
>
> The real Dan – under the annoying traits that show up when living with Dan is an honest, kind, generous, good natured, sporty, loyal man – next to Pop – Dan is my closest friend – I look upon him as a father in many ways – I am really fond of him despite what I have seen & said & felt at times. (JJD 18 November 1941)

Joe wrote to Monty a couple of days later that Dan regarded him

> as the "Jewish White Hope" – Dan is a real Jew at heart – your Jewish feeling struck deep and true with him – He is developing another ambition – to launch you in Palestine.
>
> He knows every big shot and important person worth knowing – your own family are probably pretty well connected on that score – but more

> important – Dan has or wants to take you under his wing he will do everything and anything to help you with regards [to] your desires in Palestine – That is important – it should be a comforting feeling to know that you will at least have a first class launching when setting out – They all think that you are first rate – I had to boost at least one of my friends up after all the other drunks.... Until the moon period we fly on a regular schedule – every third night weather permitting – so I would like to see you a bit more often which should be feasible with intelligent handling, even though we are supposed to start lectures again at 915 every morning.... (JJL 18 November 1941)

He wrote to Dan the same day to express his gratitude.

> Next to my father you are the one man to whom I can look upon as a father and feel that in return I am considered and treated and made to feel as a son.... I say this because not knowing me as well as my father [does] you might take my breezy ways and frequent sorties as a sign of disrespect or ingratitude which they are not.
>
> ... Without a home to go to about once a month I shudder to think what would become of me. To say that I should have already "gone to the dogs" and have been digested by them is a model of understatement. That I expect and desire to see you whenever possible goes without saying it again. (JJL 18 November 1941)

Joe was indeed fortunate to have two homes away from home, even if of very different sorts. He and Roger were by now calling Mrs. Lettice "Maw." As he described the scene to his parents, he was

> cosily seated before the fireplace ... Maw ... is sitting opposite me reading one of my books ... and telling me odd bits of the day's gossip. My pipe ... is filling the room with its delightful if slightly musty smoke and soot. (JJL 21 November 1941)

Of other news, he added:

> The King visited our station – and had a chat with Roger – I was on leave – so I will have to drop in on the palace and pay my respects.
>
> ... Whoever told you I was coming back to Canada soon was cockeyed – I would not go back if I had the chance – I have gone this far and would not miss the rest of it from the driver's seat for the world ... (JJL 21 November 1941)

106 Squadron had, as Joe told Monty,

> been on ops every night last week. Every trip has in turn been scrubbed because of bad weather. Since the moon is in full fettle for the next couple of weeks I will be on call every second night at least – possibly more. (JJL 28 November 1941)

Bomber Command carried out its first major operation since Berlin on Sunday night, 30 November, and 106 Squadron took part.

> Going to Hamburg – on a good sized blitz. Should be interesting for all concerned … (JJD 30 November 1941)

> This was Robby's last trip so we were pretty careful – the weather was lovely for a change and the searchlights around and in Hamburg virtually lit up the sky – we met no fighters and did not get caught – except coming back over Lubeck. We were floating calmly along when a couple of close woomphs indicated the beggars had the range – we wasted no time hurrying along, nineteen planes were lost – around 10% but the moon was bright enough to make it easy picking for any fighters – and so I look for a new pilot to finish off with. (JJOD 30 November 1941)

They arrived back safely a half-hour after midnight, after an eight-hour trip. They reported that they had bombed the Blohm und Voss yards from twelve thousand feet, but could not observe results owing to haze. They were among the lucky ones. 106 Squadron had dispatched fourteen aircraft, of which ten reached and bombed Hamburg. Two aircraft returned early and two were lost without trace. Hamburg recorded significant damage and casualties. But Bomber Command also suffered significant losses: thirteen of 181 crews dispatched, roughly matching the sixty-five Germans killed on the ground.

Gerry Roberts, having flown as second pilot on seven sorties before getting his own crew, had now completed his first tour of operations, for which he would soon be awarded a Distinguished Flying Medal. He left 106 Squadron to become a flying instructor. He later received a commission, survived a second tour of operations in 1943, and after the war became a career officer in the Royal Air Force.

Part Four

Holding the Line

Tyranny, like Hell, is not easily conquered; yet we have this consolation with us, that the harder the conflict, the more glorious the triumph. What we obtain too cheap, we esteem too lightly: it is dearness only that gives every thing its value.

— Thomas Paine, *The American Crisis*, 1776

Imagination … when allowed to run riot … becomes a menace to the soldier, but when controlled by character it blossoms …

— Lord Moran, *The Anatomy of Courage*, 1945

Twenty-Six

New Ideas

The immediate effect of the November directive on Bomber Command was a sharp drop in nightly sorties. Operations occurred on average every second night during the next three months, but amounted to only a small proportion of the force, mostly for the purpose of coastal attacks, warships, or nuisance raids. The industrial heartland of the Ruhr was attacked on only six nights. Bomber Command was not idle, however. Attention now turned to experimentation in tactics and accelerated conversion to heavy bombers. Both of these involved significant hazards to crews.

For Joe Jacobson, there would be a change of crew, a change of aircraft, and a change of regime at the squadron. All of these would test his resolve in new ways. Without the distraction of frequent operational flying, and without the company of most of the men he had begun with three months before. Joe's imagination now had time to work. Imagination could be the warrior's enemy; the lurking dangers and the stress of an operational tour could more easily come to the fore, and the prospect of death could not be submerged and avoided. Joe, fired by new ideas, was well armed to imagine life, to imagine the world of the future and his own place in it. His band of brothers much diminished, he became more solitary, relying on Roger and Dave for company on his station, and on Monty, who was for the time being stationed at nearby Cranwell, for companionship on leave or short passes. Reading became his main refuge, the study of civilization and politics a means confirming what mattered to him and why he was fighting.

> Reading "The Socialist One Sixth of the World" by the Dean of Canterbury – the reading I am doing is 1. stimulating me to delve deeper into social problems and possible solutions 2. make me feel my colossal ignorance & the tremendous task ahead to make up for lost time or I should say partially wasted time – 3. I am unsettled – neither risky trips, liquor or women can rid me of it – I feel something stirring & pushing me to do something – I have not discovered what yet.
> (JJD 2 November 1941)

> Sitting alone in Letwood plutocratically smoking a cigar, listening to the radio & musing after a day's reading … my entire outlook on our social system is undergoing rapid changes in the light of my studies altho not my outlook on life or people. (JJD 6 November 1941)

Joe began writing home about his emerging political views. Feeling out of touch with Canadian and American thinking, he asked his family to send Canadian news magazines, especially *Saturday Night*, while again praising how the British papers bolstered his confidence because they attack all problems "frankly, honestly, and constructively." He returned to the views he had propounded in the summer about the urgent need for change, and then turned his guns on the United States.

> When you see the tasks that confront us you realize what has to be done – we have the resources we have the capacity and ability and above all the cause – but by gum a colossal shake-up in organization and leadership must take place. We can win this war but it is going to take more imagination and intelligence on our part and the active – and I mean active aid of the U.S. I wish I could say a few things about U.S. aid – the censors would probably not let it pass – but they should because this is the United States' battle as much as ours and they have [to] make the same sacrifices and effort as the British and Russians and other nations are making – or else.

> It is amazing – absolutely astounding that a nation such as the U.S. which prides herself on her practicalness should be so unpractical and wishful as they are.

> They vote funds for war aid and think that is all that is needed to stop and beat the Germans – but dollar bills never will beat Hitler and since the money god reigns supreme the necessary tools and men are lacking – Canada is in the amazing position of really playing a vital part in this war in every conceivable way and not knowing it. Canadians can

well be proud of what they are doing in the front and back lines – yet they are not particularly.

Americans imagine they are doing great deeds in this war. They have no front line men with but a few individual exceptions and their behind the lines workers – factories etc are so much bull – yes I repeat – but a drop in the bucket.

For my money the US has gone down so many pegs that it is not even funny – talk yes – action – no and their stock is dropping everywhere in the world. The Americans that fought and died for ideals – that toiled and laboured to overcome difficulties is a long way away. Let the world burn we will make hay boys and they still imagine that they are the arsenals of democracy – we want men with guts the kind that are gathered here – not talkers and bullshooters or dodgers or cowards – they have all those kind everywhere – but every country in the world including Germany has shown some men that at least are not afraid to die – wake up America or be blown up. (JJL 1 November 1941)

A week later he wrote home:

The past month has been really tremendous for me. Firstly because I flew more often and on more first class jobs than I did during August and September. But despite my flying duties I did something else which is still more important and which indirectly is the real reason for my flying – I started prying into some fundamental problems which beset our society.

I felt that I had a pretty good idea of how and why the world runs or doesn't run from the top-side – which was my side – based on what I saw, learnt, and heard from college, camp, wealthy and influen[tial] friends as well as nobodies and working people.

Having a pal who is a socialist or shall we now use the previously improper word "communist" we did considerable talking and arguing. The trouble was that we both had identical views on most subjects. The only hitch was I did not have any solution – he did – that was not good enough for me – I started reading. First I read "Let My People Go" as I told you – Now I am on "The Socialist Sixth of the World" by the Dean of Canterbury. The effects of those books are rather startling or what might be considered startling. I consider it natural. For they have set me going and trying to get a complete picture of why things are as they are and what changes are desirable and practical as well as possible. It's a stupendous task and requires time, study and work – the only real time I get is when Dave and Roger go on leave.

Now the reason I write about this is as follows. I cannot possibly write down the thoughts, views and ideas that I have in letters. I can though tell you some of the things I do and let you draw your own conclusions. In order to keep pace with my development I drop you a little personal "letter" more in the nature of a bombshell – labeled "I am changing" – watch out.

I don't mean changing fundamentally or even superficially. But when you start delving into social problems with an open mind, some practical experience, reasonable intelligence, and plenty of guts – a change is bound to occur – both ways – so I start wading thru the Bible and Lenin and Marx and that gang as well as the Toronto Sat Nite, New York Tribune, London Times, etc. as well as by continuing to pay close attention to all whom I meet, I might come out of the mad jumble with some fairly sound ideas and understanding of what can be done in general to set things right and what I in particular am qualified and able to do in particular.

But I have not changed into a flaming red hot fanatic or idealist – nor a discouraged cynic. I change yes but you have to change or sink and get moldy. I get the same kick out of going into this as I do out of anything else – but it is only fair for me to let you know what is going on in my bean so that when I come home – rush down to the office – tell Hayman that the profit system is morally and scientifically cockeyed and to make Miss Paton etc. full partners at once or be strung on the nearest desk – you will not say "My God – the boy [has] gone bugs." Rather you either say "get the hell out until you get some brains" or perhaps "well maybe this guy knows what he is talking about – let's hear what he has to say."

Anyway I am not marking time anymore which was what was worrying me at the time I started writing you. I still don't know where I am going but I realize what I have to have to go anywhere at all. Our letters have more or less transcended the immediate jobs at hand as we more or less took stock to see what assets were on hand and how far they would go – at present I am trying to accumulate some valuable stock – "knowledge".... (JJL 6 November 1941)

While on leave in London, Joe recorded that he "went into a seemingly conservative bookshop asked for a book on Lenin and got a ½ hour lecture on communism from the red hot kid who ran the joint." He expanded on the incident to his family:

> I was in the booksellers area yesterday whilst buying some theatre tickets. I wanted … Paine's "Rights of Man" and perhaps dig up something by Marx or Engels and see what they had to say. The books in the window were all innocuous looking affairs – so I asked the owner – an accented lad of twenty-one if he perhaps had something in connection with Russia – that's the last word I spoke – his eyes lit up – into the shop he sailed and within five minutes he had enough communistic literature before me to keep me reading day and night for a life time. Not only that – half of the stuff was banned as treasonable stuff about six months ago – Russia's entry into the war sure boomed these babies trade – but I didn't just run into a left wing bookshop – this guy told me that he was so radical that the Communist Party in Britain wanted to kick him out for being a radical sort of Red – … if you can picture anything like that – I was starting to have a bit of fun with him but like most socially minded party men he started handing down his stump speeches – in a loud voice for all in the neighbourhood to hear. Needless to say I beat a hasty retreat after giving him a thorough going over for not being in the army – of course he was practically blind in both eyes but I figured that we could do with a little more action and a lot less talking for the present. (JJL 13 November 1941)

He went on to assert that

> The whirlwind days of the early part of the war seem almost over – the need for "escape and entertainment" is temporarily past. The people have had a respite and have been able to get their bearings – the war has been pretty accurately figured out by most people – they now know exactly where they stand – what they have been able to do – what they still have to do.
>
> There is absolutely no diversion of opinion where they stand, what and why they are fighting for. Every Englishman knows only too well from actual experience or at least from actual facts what they are fighting. Then everyone knows where they stand – they stood up to the Germans, they took the Jerries' measure – they found they were wanting only in equipment and they know they have the resources to supply their needs – So good common sense has resulted in most people kick-

ing up a stink about the quality of their leaders – they have more than enough resources to defeat the Germans that is with the U.S. and Russia on our side – well says the old hard-headed coal digger – we got the coal, you got me to dig it – why am not I digging it – I don't know whether or not they have been suppressing in your papers the criticism that has been going on over here – if they have they should not because it is not a sign of weakness but of extraordinary strength – the people want to give their all – they are only able to give their three-quarters – they want to know why and are trying to find out who is slipping up so they can give their all – It is as simple as that – I have never yet heard anybody ever even mention the word "*defeat*" – Few mention the end of the war – But when anybody consciously or unconsciously – in the services or out of the services thinks or talks about their position or hopes or chances after the war – it is always assuming England to be the victor – that is a crucial point upon which we have it over the Germans – a calm, quiet, tenacious confidence and faith that have, shall and always will win the war.

But all that does not enable us to sit back and merely let things unfold – that is a tendency that always has to be checked especially in the English. Nor does it mean that the best men for the purpose are running the show and making the most of what they have – which is what they have to do to win – I think that if about three-quarters of the higher ups in every conceivable branch were taken for a nice quiet ride – whilst their places were taken by alert, bright hard-hitting young Canucks, or Aussies etc. – things would really happen for the good – and seeing that anything for the good means saving the lives of young fellows don't let yourself get soft about making the ride a first class one. Of course this sounds seditious and radical but it is plain horse sense – Canada is probably doing more in this war in proportion to her population than England – But Canada just ain't got no say about what should be done – if about 2/3 of the RAF are Dominion men – it's about time a few young Canucks and Aussies and New Zealanders etc. got right up on top in the Air Ministry and started running the show – Mr. Censor I am just a hefty young Canuck that thinks Canadians possess a lot of qualities that died in Britain with the Battle of Trafalgar – nothing like putting the Mother Country on her mettle and the so-called "colonies" are the ones to do it. (JJL 13 November 1941)

Flying was frequently cancelled in November due to rain. 106 Squadron conducted only one small raid during the rest of the month. Joe had plenty of time on his hands to indulge his reading program, and for combing newspaper reports on industrial and military production in the United States for whatever salvation this might provide to Britain's war effort. After the intensity of his previous week's leave, Joe looked inward.

> Reading political economy can see where I missed the boat at school & wasted my time – never really got the main point – have plenty of work ahead to get to the fundamentals of present evils …
> (JJD 19 November 1941)

> Starting to realize … how much studying I have to do to make up for what I didn't do if I want to fit myself for any useful task after the war – my war or athletic record will not be of any use if I do not have the ability & knowledge to go with it – neither will my personality without character & knowledge. (JJD 20 November 1941)

> Spent the evening quietly reading – the tide has started to turn as I can stop home, read, think & take notes & start to learn again – of course my thinking now is more honest & thorough which makes me realize how thoroughly I wasted my time at school – it goes further than that – 90% waste their time at school – partly due to the poor teaching curriculum & attitude & understanding of education. (JJD 21 November 1941)

Three weeks earlier, after his reunion with Monty, he had begun to fill a notebook with reflections on his reading material. He started with *Let My People Go* by Cedric Belfrage, and proceeded the next week to *The Socialist Sixth of the World* by Hewlett Johnson. Two weeks later he began to read Stephen Swingler's *Outline of Political Thought since the French Revolution*. The first was a "mighty book" in Joe's view, and while the other two informed him, *Let My People Go* inspired him. Each was published by the Left Book Club in its familiar red hardcover edition, the authors being either socialists or communists (although Joe ended his November reading with *The Rubaiyat of Omar Khayyam*).

Let My People Go was a political tract in the form of a novel. Its protagonists, one a rural preacher, the other a Marxist organizer, came to unite in the fight against poverty, racism, and the oppression of labour in the coal-mining towns of rural Kentucky. Their struggle unfolds as a debate between the Christian social gospel and communism, but the idiom of the debate is particularly American – progressive and populist rather than strictly Marxist. Both were committed to challenging corporate power, from the standpoint of republican virtue, the ideals of Abraham Lincoln and the example of Jesus, and a sturdy faith in family, community, and craft, in an era when the pursuit of happiness rested more on solidarity than consumption. The underlying premise is that if only people can be given the right message, they will be enlightened and emboldened to act. They would come to see that science and the machine age had brought untold possibilities of universal well-being, but the profit system was holding back production and creating inequality.

Hewlett Johnson, the Dean of Canterbury and one of Britain's senior clerics, was an unabashed admirer of Soviet communism, and his book was a plea for Anglo-Russian friendship. Joe seems to have been most interested in Johnson's self-described path from his bourgeois background to his evolving critique of the socio-economic order in Britain, and his melding of science and Christianity into a program for achieving full human development through brotherhood, internationalism, material advance, and collective security under communism. Much of the book describes the economic and social achievements of the Soviet Union, but if Joe read those chapters he did not take notes on them.

Swingler's book was a Marxist introduction to political philosophy, illustrated by the evolution of politics from its eighteenth-century bourgeois traditions through the development of working-class and social-democratic politics to "scientific socialism" and the Russian Revolution. Both the language and the argument would have been familiar to any theoretical Marxist in the late 1930s. Joe took copious notes.

Joe's point-form notes consisted for the most part of short extracts, rather than commentaries, as one might expect to find in the notebook of a first-year student rather than a candidate for an advanced degree. This was fitting enough, for Joe had just embarked on a self-taught course in philosophy, politics, and economics. His notes give the impression of one eager to understand the bible, religion, science, Marxism, political economy, the American Constitution, and the shape of the world to come. He was trying to focus the idealism he had been expressing in his diaries ever since he arrived at Manning Depot in Toronto the previous summer. No one had ever characterized Joe as an intellectual, but he was trying diligently to make sense of the events unfolding around him. He was, under the circumstances, an autodidact without formal instruction. In July he had believed that Britain needed to rid itself of the wrong people in high places to achieve victory and democracy. Now he was coming to the view that the economic system itself must be changed. Perhaps the idea that socialism was not simply a utopian vision but a scientific project appealed to him.

What prompted the left turn in Joe's politics? He seems always to have been motivated by a sense of fairness and egalitarianism, notwithstanding his privileged background and his personal ambitions. He had absorbed these values from his family, and they were honed by his experience in Britain. His friendship with Davies, a Welsh coal miner's son with communist views, and his exploration of the Charing Cross Road bookshops, channelled his indignation. The Soviet Union's recovery and ferocious resistance in the battle against Germany had sparked widespread sympathy and admiration in Britain. Joe knew he had made his way through university as an athlete and fraternity brother, not as a student. He had not really started to think about the wider world until he was in Preston. Now, two years later, and perhaps because he knew his own existence was at risk, his outlook on life took a more serious turn. Although he had begun some notes on politics – both world and Canadian – in September or October, those tentative thoughts had not yet been informed by his new reading program.

There was, intriguingly, one thread of public debate that Joe never mentioned. Pacifism still had its advocates, and although their views were certainly marginalized, they were not entirely suppressed. The Anglican Bishop of Chichester, George Bell, had provoked a debate about night bombing in the *Times* in April 1941, and a similar debate was played out in the pages of the *Telegraph* the next month. By October, a small group of church leaders, members of Parliament, and public intellectuals had organized the Campaign Against Night Bombing, which presented a petition to Parliament at the end of October. Ironically, the campaign rested on the implicit assumption that Bomber Command's nightly attacks were successful, and that great numbers of German civilians were actually dying as a result of them.

It seems unlikely that Joe would have been unaware of the campaign, or at least its announced aims, given his interest in public affairs. Nothing in his background would have disposed him toward its particular strain of Christian pacifism, and nothing in his experience since arriving in England had generated any sympathy for its position. He had dismissed pacifism months before, in the current circumstances "we all have to pull together – all have to safeguard our rights & liberties." However much Joe was concerned about the effectiveness of the night bombing offensive, and even its priorities, he had no doubt whatever about the legitimacy of its objectives or of the need for night bombing to achieve them.

In early December, Joe got a forty-eight-hour pass to visit Monty. He returned to find several packages and letters in the mail, including what he characterized as a "great effort" of his father's. He responded immediately:

It is remarkable how much alike Monty and I feel, act and think, how much influence one has upon the other. We both feel the same thrill and zest for life and people, for ideas and action for romance and adventure. We feel that your ideas, ideals and zest is pretty much the same as ours. You might yet find yourself an honorary member of the famous Pony Club and an active participant in at least some of its adventures and battles one of these days.

At present we are at the cross roads – we know that the armistice will only end the first battle – the second one is a good deal tougher, complicated, involved and everything else. We have both phases fairly well in perspective – at least we feel we have. We realize the main issues that will be fought out during the next battle – the class struggle – the social war – the fight to reconstruct physically, mentally and morally. We know some of the qualifications necessary. We are trying to analyze ourselves to see where we measure up – where we fall down – where we must develop. We have confidence in our minds, our bodies, in our balance and in our hearts – we might be called cocky – we are in a quiet modest way at times – we are not know it alls – quite the reverse – we feel how little we do know in relation to what there is to know and learn and do – our abilities are different but we both aim at the same end – something better – we both have at least some conception of what a job it is to lead people, what obstacles have to be faced what equipment is required.

… Here are some possibilities under serious consideration – we want to head East – Palestine and Zionism is one of Monty's guiding stars – to a lesser extent it is mine also – Monty might be shifted out east – voluntarily of course – in which case I should immediately follow – I am anxious to head that way – I might land out there – voluntarily in which case Monty would follow – the point is we are getting the world tracked down – we aim to follow some of the tracks – like you we refuse to get narrowed down, squashed in and buried – risks don't matter – the bigger the risks – the bigger the stakes – …

Japan and America are at war to-day. This is not a political letter so I shall let you get your facts and opinions from the papers – England though was thrilled and excited at the possibilities and also at the issues becoming that much clearer – America is probably amazed, stunned, angry and relieved as well as unprepared.…

Don't start counting the hours I have left – I am only beginning – this life agrees with me – I am trying to swing a deal – I want some real action – that is on fighters – not bombers – that is when I finish on bombers which will take at least the winter – that is if the weather clears long enough for me to make my few remaining trips....

Don't start building any castles about the two prodigies or even one of them over here – we are just a couple of ordinary guys who are looking facts as honestly in the eye as they can and hope to shake a few people up whilst on their journey thru life – (JJL 8 December 1941)

Joe with Monty Berger, England, late 1941. (Janet Jacobson Kwass)

Twenty-Seven

December Doldrums

The winter sun skimmed along the southern horizon for a few hours each day, ascending barely more than a hand's width by noon. Bomber Command was at its nadir, station life was in a funk. Boredom and anxiety reigned in equal measure, occasionally punctuated by a noteworthy event. The first, upon Joe's return from leave, was his wing commander's wedding. Both he and Roger, now senior NCO aircrew, were invited.[1] He told Janine the following day that it was:

> a colossal affair to use a conservative term.
>
> The babe he married was wealthy. Her old man spent in the neighbourhood of 500 pounds to get rid of her – the swanky hotel in Woodhall Spa was the scene of the starting celebrations. In a pleasant atmosphere, with soft music from the instruments of a well-known orchestra in the presence of a few chosen officers and sergeants of our famous squadron, the distinguished gathering imbibed wine, cocktails and champagne to their hearts content. The more robust of the men smoked choice cigars, made mellow speeches, danced daintily and ate the finest hors d'oeuvres and salads.
>
> Yours truly and Roger did justice to the occasion. After two bottles of champagne and a fine cigar, plus wine and cocktails Roger passed out. I continued and drank another bottle before proceeding to the sergeants mess where the whole shindig – officers, guests, group captains, etc. were our guests – the orchestra came along and strengthened by some

> of our better musicians played pieces no one has ever heard before – the bar was open – drinks were on the house – to provide femininity to the mighty occasion we carted in a couple of truck loads of WAAFs – (see what you missed not joining up in the WAAFs – lucky girl). The party went ahead full blast until our bar was cleaned out – whence the whole gathering proceeded to the officers mess. There dancing took place in one room whilst an amazingly vociferous sing song bellowed forth in another. Roger's Allouette was one of the evening's highlights.
>
> Of course the whole affair was lavish and mellow – rowdy but pleasant and above all friendly. I feel that I emerged a better and wiser man – never again shall I touch champagne – at least not three quarts – it hits you after the damage is done – two hours after the last quart you feel like a million bucks. Four hours after your head feels swollen and splitting – your stomach upset – your body weak – six hours after you pass out groaning – next day you vow never again – of course I am not subject to any of those common weaknesses. I merely record how Roger and some of the other boys made out.... (JJL 10 December 1941)

America's entry into the war consumed Joe's attention for the next few days.

> Initial success in Pacific all with the Japs – Prince of Wales & Repulse sunk off Malaya. U.S. caught napping & not too well prepared – Britain lacks the req'd strength at the moment – but after the original onslaught we shall get our resources – men & brains going & slowly but decisively & surely we shall win. (JJD 10 December 1941)
>
> The Pacific battle taking on the old familiar phase – lack of air support – unpreparedness on our part resulting in alarming setbacks – we are sure taking a pasting in the Pacific for the same reasons as in France & Crete – boneheadedness. (JJD 12 December 1941)

Joe provided the Pony Club a "brief discourse" about these new developments:

> No doubt you are much more excited, influenced – captivated and over-awed than we are – war – real war is still a novelty for you – we have been right in the front line for a couple of years now – our one reaction is one of cheerfulness – about the same as you would feel if you were a hockey manager who secured the services of a new star during the homestretch race – especially if he had some injured player and the opposition were tough – the Stanley Cup has yet to be played for –

For us it is like the relief of Tobruk – we held the fort while the U.S. made up her mind what she was going to do – we all know what she can do – therefore we are glad – but not too elated – you don't get elated easily in war –

It is all old time stuff for us – we are still in the front line and the present position is if anything worsened – it is only the ultimate results that are vitally affected – so we struggled and continue to make our sacrifices and put up with additional hardships and inconveniences but with fortified determination – don't forget we had never lost hope – we never gave up even before Russia became our allies – and the victory picture was blotched. Now, the way to victory can be clearly seen – it requires only courage and skill – intelligence and hardware to translate that vision to a reality – we can do it – and will do it in the end –

Where Herby stands we want to know – no doubt he will be swept like everyone else to action realizing as we did that personal considerations, future possibilities, comforts, safety, money and jobs don't count for the time being. Everybody has to take the country's interest and security into consideration first or there will be no personal interests.

For my part I don't expect too much for a long time to come – you need bitter and cruel experience to teach you – even in this grave hour in Britain itself there are selfish interests and selfish people – as well as ignorant ones, etc. – obstructing the war effort to various degrees. It is too much to expect that the people of the U.S. probably the most self-interested in the world putting self ahead of everything else – will change overnight as the danger seems to decrease – as tension eases – so will the war effort – it is a long, hard pull and it will need some good bombing raids on New York, Pittsburgh etc. to shake the people out of themselves – to put them in a position where they as individuals feel their tiny insignificance in the swirl of humanity –

However it is all very thrilling and exciting to me – this vast, tremendous world conflict is also cruel but no more so than more insidious peacetime cruelties like – slums, poverty – disease, etc. – The potentialities and possibilities and scope of a world battle are tremendous. Living at the crossroads of history is thrilling.

Realizing that the possibilities for winning and going ahead against losing and sinking back in world evolution can't help but stir you profoundly.

> For once in a lifetime we have an opportunity of being lifted right above the struggle whilst at the same time being right in the midst of it all. You face the realities of life and death – the colossal issues at stake from both a human and material standpoint and take an active if minute part in the entire issue. Yet you are freed of the imagined luxuries of civilized life – of an often sordid struggle for existence – it is still a struggle for existence now but on a much loftier and pleasanter scale – the only difference is you stand to lose quicker in war – that is lose the struggle for existence via extermination. (JJL 15 December 1941)[2]

Joe wrote home with news of his friends.

> Don't know what happened to Les Jupp – lost contact with him – don't know whether his mother is dead or alive – lost touch with all the old gang for various reasons – have a complete new gang including two Scotsmen – two Irishmen, two Welshmen (Dave is one), the odd New Zealander and Rhodesian and South African – also the odd Englishman – plus Roger and Pop Miller the only two other Canadians left here – … all vitally interested in politics and social progress – some fairly bright – all about as conservative as Tim Buck.[3]
> (JJL 10 December 1941)

During a visit to Midfield, Monty updated the Pony Club:

> Joe has begun to think about the world of tomorrow and is out for better things. He also means to get them. It has not been new stuff to me, but it has reawakened me after a lapse of some years and with Joe's starting spark, it has been rekindled and promises to stay lit and nurtured along.… we all have chums in our respective spheres and we like them and are happy with them, but … there is a richness and depth of feeling between Poneyites that is something extra and beyond every friendship I have ever experienced.
>
> … [Janine] is obviously a strong-willed person and Joe says her heart is in Belgium still. While Joe is fond of her, I think he is far from sunk and think that he can do much better for himself. The original "hitting it off" must have come from the natural set-up – girl and boy in same house, airman in love, girl lonesome and homesick – it would have been cruel had the two not got together.… (15 December 1941)

Monty saw immediately that Joe's relationship with Janine was mostly an infatuation fed by circumstances. Joe would soon come to see Janine as a good friend, but certainly not a prospective life partner. Only a few days before, Joe had mentioned to his parents that he had received a box of Laura Secord chocolates from Cecily: "yes I guess I must be fond of her – just don't realize it until the candies come through … "

Cecily had not forgotten about Joe, but she too sensed the distance between them. On the 8th she sent an airgraph[4]:

> This is something new – do let me know how long it takes to receive it. I am terribly sorry I have neglected you for so long. I haven't any good excuse and in reply to your questions in that respect I am not engaged or married or anything silly like that. By the way I would like to know if you received the candies I sent. You know I haven't had a letter from you since your last one of September 22nd – gone down I suppose.
>
> They seem intent on working me very hard at school this year, between seminars, demonstrations and tests every week, my life is not my own. I have almost become a slave to my work. However, I do manage to enjoy myself at odd times. How are activities for you – social and otherwise? I hope you have a very merry Christmas. Take care of yourself and don't get shipped to Hong Kong.
>
> Love
> Cecily

Their relationship in Canada had been so brief that it was by now sustained by imagination. What they had expected or planned or committed to when Cecily left Montreal nine months before, Joe never said. Since then, Joe's life as a warrior far from home had created a chasm difficult to bridge with civilians back in Canada, even or perhaps especially with Cecily. Now, as 1941 was coming to a close, they had no prospect of seeing each other any time soon. Joe's inclination to keep romantic entanglements at a distance, and keep some latitude for himself, was now reinforced by circumstance. He was prepared to devote himself to duty until something else happened, either war's end or his own. The one person in England with whom Joe had an intense emotional bond, forged by more than force of circumstance, was Monty. They would spend more and more of their free time in each other's company.

> Hodgkinson, Harding & I have a new sprogue pilot – supposed to fly to-nite – it will take all our experience & plenty of luck to pull the guy thru the opening stages – he looks capable – needs experience – ah well – somebody trained me – guess I have to do likewise –
> (JJD 14 December 1941)

Thus did the consequences of the previous winter's muddling about how to crew a four-seater bomber play out. Hampden pilots who managed to survive their first two hundred hours of operations were sent on to Operational Training Units as instructors, which deprived their crews of their captains. There being no experienced pilots to spare, Joe, Duncan, and Sid would now fly with a freshman, as much as they wished otherwise. By this time the three were among the most experienced men on 106 Squadron, a picked crew that could be assigned the most demanding tasks, but also best qualified to coach a novice pilot on his first sortie. So now they would revert to freshman assignments, on which they would be the instructors, and Joe as the air observer would be the captain, even though none of them had been taught to fly. The choice was to deprive the squadron of the capabilities of one of its most experienced crews and putting it, for the time being at least, at greater risk.[5]

Selfe and crew's first assignment was to the Belgian port of Ostende. It was a target commonly reserved for freshman crews because it did not require flying over German territory. The return trip took less than four hours. They reported that they had bombed in conditions of good weather and visibility, and had observed their bomb bursts in the outer harbour.

> Took our first trip with our new pilot Robin Selfe – and got back – it was like riding a horse – teaching & training our pilot the tricks of the trade – if we can get thru two or three trips without getting caught – it will be plain sailing – but it takes plenty of luck & training before you get the hang of the Germans. (JJD 15 December 1941)

> Did a beginners trip with our new pilot – a sprogue and as green as the leaves in spring – he is a conscientious capable Englishman about 28 years old – however, he is inexperienced and not too good a flyer – we are trying to teach Robin Selfe everything we have learnt to bring him up to scratch – I felt as if I was on my last ride tonite – [he] had never weaved before so we taught him weaving on the way out – he had never seen searchlights or flak so we stooged up and down the French coast for half an hour viewing the display of fireworks before going in – on the way back we did a few mild power dives – he has a lot to learn – our petrol consumption was 106 gals per hr – it should be 70 – next time

> he will know to how to climb more economically – he will take a long time before he can handle a plane like Robby – which is the way you have to handle one to stand a reasonable chance of getting thru – with luck and skill by me we should manage – but it is hard for the pilot to get enough flying in to keep up – we all heaved a hearty sigh when we landed completing our first operational trip as a crew.
> (JJOD 15 December 1941)

Joe told Janine about his new situation:

> I am not due to go on leave until around the New Year … indefinite as yet. But leave is the least of my problems. My Flight Commander graciously apologized to me because of what he had to do – give me a sprogue – yes novice pilot. True I am the Captain of our plane and I have my old gunner and wireless operator – but still the pilot is as green as the fields.
>
> Fortunately we know just about everything the pilot should know – altho a P/O he is capable and willing to learn – Thus we instruct him in all the ins and outs of operational flying. We have taken him up nearly every day and on one beginners night trip to Ostende. He is improving rapidly and if we don't get sent to the hot spots for a few trips we might have a reasonable chance of pulling him thru – It's quite an experience – this instructing. But am I getting out of this observers racket in a hurry when I am thru – It's a pilot or else – of course when you have an experienced pilot everything is fine but when you pilot the pilot from the navigator's pew it is slightly different – Nevertheless the boys on the squadron all think it is quite a joke – as a matter of fact it is not too bad watching your pupil improve before your eyes to your mutual safety – but he has a long way to go yet to attain par for the course.…
> (JJL 18 December 1941)

There were exceptions to the rule that captains must be pilots, and Joe's situation was one of them. He was an experienced NCO observer paired with a commissioned but brand-new pilot, not uncommon among Hampden crews at that time. The status of the observer was under review at the highest levels of Bomber Command. John Slessor, the Commander of 5 Group (consisting mainly of Hampdens), observed that modern heavy bombers relied largely on the observer to reach and hit the target, and without him the efforts of all the others in the air and on the ground were wasted. He argued that observers, who in his experience were often more intelligent and better educated than pilots, should have equal standing with pilots for promotion, commissions, and opportunities for command, not only in the aircraft itself but in squadrons and stations. Peirse, of the old school, and still commander in chief of Bomber Command, was unmoved by such arguments, and at that very time advised the Air Ministry that observers should not be captains. Nonetheless, it did occasionally happen, and perhaps more often in 5 Group squadrons where Slessor's views would have been known, if not necessarily shared, among his senior staff.

Then a shocking accident occurred at Coningsby.

> Witnessed a tragic crash as a Manchester – tail fin shot up from Brest raid tried to land – visibility poor – he overshot – tried to take off again – lost control – plane rose vertically like a wounded monster – stood in midair and plunged into the ground & exploded …
> (JJD 18 December 1941)

He added a postscript to his letter to the Pony Club:

> We just had a bad show on our drome – a Manchester back from a daylight raid on Brest – badly shot up crashed on the drome as we were all standing around and wiped the whole gang off – seven – three of whom were real good friends including a Canadian.[6] Tough break all around – amazing the way you get hardened to tragedy and remain unshaken at such scenes. (JJL 18 December 1941)

By this time Joe had learned of the death of many of his fellow airmen, either by their failure to return from a raid or by reading the casualty lists. Actually witnessing the event, however, was uncommon. Even if one saw an aircraft shot down over target, illuminated by a cone of searchlights, it was at a distance and there was no way of knowing which crew was involved. The flyers never saw their comrades' charred and mangled bodies on the ground, as did the German soldiers who inspected the crash sites the next morning. In this respect, the airman's experience of war was very different from that of the infantryman's. To watch an airplane crash and its crew burn to death before one's eyes was horrifying and deeply unsettling, despite Joe's proclaimed equanimity.

In the midst of all this, Joe continued his program of self-education. He told Janine:

> I am in the middle of an excellent essay "civilization" by Clive Bell. Since we are supposed to be fighting for civilization my father thought I ought to make sure I know or realize exactly what civilization was and

> is and so sent me this book. It is a remarkably reasoned essay that can stand much studying and pondering upon. (JJL 18 December 1941)

Bell, an art critic and aesthete associated with the Bloomsbury Group, had posed himself the question of what constituted civilization, since Britain claimed to have fought for it in the previous war. His analysis was grounded in the values of the Enlightenment, as understood by England's classically educated cultural elite. A civilized society, Bell claimed, was marked by a sense of values expressed in appreciation of beauty, aesthetics, and truth, and the application of reason. The essay was a forthright apologetic for elitism that asserted the necessity of a leisured class to develop and disseminate civilization and its values. Joe appreciated the book, saying that he "[didn't] agree with all points" but "sympathized with most." Clive Bell could hardly be confused with Tim Buck, but given Joe's newly absorbed political perspective and his own background, he could easily have elided elitism with vanguardism.

> Weary all day after last night's [mess party] & yesterday's soccer game – the squadron is starting to bind again insisting on gas masks – P.T. – discipline – training, schedule, etc. – this bull always occurs when ops fall off – I would not mind training & learning if they taught us something new & original – we should be experimenting with new tactics – new ways & methods of doing things – after 150 hours operation flying over Germany I don't need elementary training. (JJD 20 December 1941)

> Another moan – we lost another plane on daylights today – on sneakers[7] – another example of our stupid air brass hats use of skilled airmen – a single Hampden as outdated as the hills is sent alone by daylight on a 1000 mile trip over Germany to bomb an objective & shake up the people relying for protection on low cloud & an ardent prayer – sneakers my eye – suicide & for a stupid objective not worth the waste in lives. (JJD 21 December 1941)

Daylight sneakers, also known as "cloud cover attacks" or "mole operations," were among Bomber Command's more desperate experiments that winter. 5 Group had initiated them on 10 December, using Hampdens, and 106 Squadron had sent four Hampdens out in daylight on the 12th, losing one. The idea was to make surprise low-level attacks using cloud cover for concealment. These were thought to be "comparatively safe and provide excellent training in navigation, blind flying, and low bombing."[8] Preferred targets were railway lines that could be easily followed and that offered the possibility of derailing trains on open track or of leading to a factory. Crews were instructed to abort such operations if cloud cover broke up; nonetheless, losses on such raids approached 5 percent.

> In the middle of another brassed off period – the result of inaction – without the stimulus of danger & the prospect of death & excitement I get lazy, dissatisfied – for a while I can read seriously – but reading & binging become monotonous – I steer clear of women so I had better have a trip in a hurry – or perhaps it is the underlying suspense when not flying that tends to get you down. (JJD 22 December 1941)

Christmas 1941 was a subdued affair for Joe, compared to the festivities in Moose Jaw the year before.

> Xmas is a time for family gatherings – I miss those warm friendly gatherings circulating around my family – especially Pop & Mom – during war there is too much grabbing & grasping for pleasure – people wanting the pleasures of a lifetime in one evening – the result is usually a drunk & sexual intercourse up a back alley – neither pleasure under such circumstances being really satisfactory. (JJD 23 December 1941)

> Food – liquor & luxury to spare – we served the airmen before settling in to our own mighty feed reminiscent of former mighty feeds – everybody happy but I miss some of the old gang – now killed or scattered – however many are still intact & still able to celebrate merrily & freely which we did. (JJD 25 December 1941)

> Had a sumptuous dinner with Mrs. Lettice & her crew – all well meaning but intellectually – socially & morally binding & stifling – and anything but stimulating – Churchill made a great speech in the American Senate which will inspire America & Britain to work in closer contact – (JJD 26 December 1941)

> Personal outlook – lack of action – increase in festivity – renewed regulations & binding training schedule on squadron stumped my reading & thinking during the past week – made no headway – probably lost ground – … all we now do is crab – complain & beef we don't know how lucky we are to be let off so easily around here.
> (JJD 27 December 1941)

Before departing on a week's crew leave, Joe wrote home about Christmas on his station:

> Considerable fog blanketed country for entire period, making flying impossible –
>
> … sergeants and officers on our squadron mingle with one another at all times – the officers to the extent of having their pants hauled down and the hose turned on them by us during a rambunctious celebration in our mess. We fly together – we go out together and stand for no monkey business in the way of formality.
>
> … [his gang] two Welshmen, two Irishmen, two Scotsmen, one American and two Canadians.… had a wizard time listening to a vivid description on the radio of a job our squadron (we were all on) did blowing up a big factory in Germany – quite a contrast blasting a factory one night – then mauling a turkey and a liquor cabinet on the next …
>
> Despite … shortages of most Xmas necessities, people in and out of the services in England can still manage to let loose with friendship and generosity and relax and enjoy a festive occasion whilst still striving against destruction, and existing in the most tumultuous, stirring and uncertain period of their collective lives. Whilst many people have much to be sad about and more to be worried about they still have a good sense of perspective and can laugh and sing on occasion and appreciate their position in relation to others and also in relation to what it could be – I think that it is with renewed confidence if with increased responsibilities that they start back on the old grind with a feeling of determination perhaps a touch of exhilaration because of recent trends and certainly still with a sense of humour.…
>
> You ask who Dave is … his pop is a coal miner – they are thru force of circumstances socially conscious – here called communistic – he has given me most of the literature I can read fairly varied and including all topics but I don't get time to get down to it thoroughly …
>
> About life on operational squadron I cannot say much … we have a first rate group of men especially the older ones in point of service – the newer men don't have the background, education and general outlook of the more experienced men who were in from the first – I can't tell

> you anything about operational trips and probably never shall – I am used to them being the oldest navigator but one or two on the squadron – we don't bother about talking about what we do – we get a kick out of the whole show and leave it go – when not on operations there are too many other things to occupy us – (JJL 30 December 1941)

Bomber Command operations had been much reduced in December, even during the moon period in the first week. Selfe and his crew did not fly again until the end of the month when the squadron returned, for a third time, to bomb the synthetic rubber plant at Huls.

> 3 AM – just arrived back from a raid on Huls – dropped my 2000 lb parachute bomb square in the middle and blew it sky high – my explosion & fire was seen 60 miles away – Selfe still ropey – swung us around the aerodrome on takeoff bounced us landing – but he's learning – had a nice singsong on way home – in high fettle now. (JJD 28 December 1941)

> Guided my pupil safely thru – we started badly swinging to starboard on the take off – nearly crashing with our bomb load – we pulled up in time and started over again – this time successfully.
>
> We weaved thru the searchlight belt without getting picked up – I map read in the bright moonlight to Dorstend – managed to avoid the hot spots until someone dropped a load of incendiaries lighting up the entire area –
>
> We flashed in dropped our 2000 lb parachute bomb nipped out without getting picked up and watched our bomb rock, shake and shatter the area – then the fun began as everyone nipped in and bombed our large explosion and fire –
>
> We sang Allouette coming home by way of celebration –
>
> But the trip is not over until the wheels stop moving and you walk away – with Robin Selfe as Pilot – we hit the deck – bounced, bounded, swerved and finally pulled up as we merrily clamoured out.
> (JJOD 28 December 1941)

They reported that their bombs and incendiaries fell across the target and started a fire. Roger Rousseau's crew had been detailed as a fire raiser, but

Robin Selfe, 1941. (Courtesy Marilyn Farias)

had been unable to reach the target on time so returned with their bombs as instructed.

The target, assigned exclusively to 5 Group, had not been much damaged in two previous raids. Picked crews were assigned to mark the target with incendiaries within a ten-minute period starting at 2030, with the remainder to concentrate their attacks over the next forty minutes. Although this was Joe's third operation on Huls, with a new pilot his would not be one of the picked crews that would carry incendiaries for target marking. But he knew the target and he knew how to place parachute bombs. According to the squadron record, the target was easily located in moonlight, "and judging by the huge fires and numerous explosions there is little doubt that the raid was a complete success." The fires were confirmed by the camera photos. No aircraft were lost, although flak was reported as intense and accurate. One aircraft was attacked and damaged by a night-fighter, but returned safely. Reconnaissance photos taken ten weeks later suggested that the plant was still only partially operative. This third raid had finally inflicted substantial damage that had not yet been fully repaired.

Bringing Joe up to date on the home front, Percy commented on recent press reports:

> Don't get led away by some of [the] things that are said about the French Canadians. They are alright with exceptions. These exceptions are a few leaders of the Hitler type who want to make political capital out of sowing seeds of discord between French and English. There are a number of this kind in Ontario amongst the English Protestants. I hope you will take a broad view of this whole situation. Study it well from all angles and avoid being led astray by what you hear and read. This is your province. It will be your job to try and maintain amity between the French and the English. (PJL 21 December 1941)

As the new year approached, Percy wrote to Joe of his high hopes and expectations for him:

> I never thought it possible I could be able to write to my own son this way. Your letters have made it possible. I certainly do not think that if our lives had not been churned up by catastrophe that we could have written to each other the way we have done.

… With these letters [family and Pony Club] and your letters and your private log and the personal war diary I am keeping … certainly a pretty complete history of the past three years has been written. A very interesting one too I think … interesting perhaps beyond our own family circle.…

About your plans going to the Far East or training as fighter pilot … Neither your Ma or myself have a word to say except do what your inner self compels you to do … then you cannot do wrong. However, there is an old fable of mice and men or Man proposes and God disposes that will have something to do with your life. Churchill himself will tell you that … destiny shaped him for this moment … God be praised for that because he is now accepted by Americans, I should say the whole English speaking world as the leader for victory and peace.… Roosevelt equals him almost to a close second. Did you hear him speak to Congress. Everything you are doing, everything you [and Monty] are thinking today … is shaping you for your hour of destiny. Whether that destiny is with your own people or whether it is even in the larger sphere that is hidden.…

Last week's letters I kept mostly to the facts of our living, this time I have been inspired by your letters to let myself go a bit in letting you know something that is in my heart and thoughts. I mean it about your destiny, some firecrackers sputter and go off prematurely pure waste, even if a bit spectacular at the time, the real stuff goes off with a magnificent bang, the timing is perfect, the result magnificent.… I think I have been mostly sputtering but it is hard to say, I might have made a direct hit somewhere … time only will tell. So Joe I am going to end this letter on that note. (PJL 29 December 1941)

Twenty-Eight

New Directions

Joe's crew leave began on the last day of the year. He immediately headed to London to meet Monty, with whom he spent most of the next seven frenetic days. First, they took the train to Salisbury to meet an American friend from their summer camp days.

> Spent a magnificent New Years Eve with the doctors & nurses & officers at the A.R.C. [American Red Cross] – the finest New Years Eve of our lives – went right thru the night … ideal women – gents & clean cut fun – jauntily left the Red Cross without sleeping a wink – took the bus to Bournemouth washed & shaved & found Dan & Henriette.
> (JJD 1 January 1942)

The next day, Joe and Monty returned to London, and the day after that Joe went on his own to visit Janine and her family. As much as he enjoyed the day, he commented that he and Monty had a more intelligent & livelier time together. He returned to London the next day, where he bumped into his cousin Leonard Silver, who was serving in the Canadian Army and, as he told his parents, was looking

> dapper, tough and fit – I told him I heard he had been stepping out with Betty who up and married another Canuck. He told me he heard I was trotting around with Janine which explains my hasty declaration of independence … to thoroughly dispel any doubts as to my Spartan leanings. (JJL 9 January 1942)

> Met Monty … had a few beers – got our tickets & were in the Savoy by 6 PM The Man Who Came to Dinner was excellent … we went back stage after – met some of the cast – took a couple out for drinks – talked theatre – went to the café – looked around town & turned in tired. (JJD 5 January 1942)
>
> Mub & I decided Janine too fond of me situation getting too involved – for a Poneyite. (JJD 6 January 1942)
>
> Met Janine – had dinner – went to see old acquaintance – left early so Mub could catch train to Glasgow – missed it – binged around town finished off with 2 hour walk around Hyde Park discussing philosophy etc. – had a feed back at hotel & turned in at 3 AM to sleep for 3 hrs – end of a magnificent leave … (JJD 7 January 1942)
>
> Back on sqdr reflecting on leave *Janine* not the girl for me a great kid but continental upbringing & outlook entirely diff[erent] from mine – besides I don't want to get tied down to her – Mub a magnificent man – level head – bright intellect – balanced outlook sporting spirit – we had an epic week together – should accomplish something in life together or alone … we know or are learning how to live as well as act – Monty will be a prominent vital man some day – so will I. (JJD 8 January 1942)

Joe wrote Monty that he had got back from his leave at 1:30 PM and "got away with it," but found a few things had changed:

1. I am on a daylight schedule every second day – the bastards – sneakers at that.

2. We are being converted to Lancasters in a month or so.

3. We have to train on Manchesters by night and day around England

4. Besides all that we are on regular operations

5. The bloody squadron is going to be moved in a month or so to Syerston

6. I think that all 48 hour passes have been cancelled

7. It looks like work and binding schedules and training – my only hope is to pray for nice weather and get the hell out and on a pilot's course before the squadron moves and is converted. I don't want to do my last few trips on a blinking experimental machine before it is perfected.

8. All the boys safe and sound – all except a flt sgt friend – DFM – lost on his 63rd trip.[1] …

11. Bought Thomas Paine's "Rights of Man" on the way up….

13. Rec'd Janine's New Year letter – alas she is too fond of me – alas a withdrawal will have to take place – alas I shall probably be cussed up and down by all parties concerned – alas I shall extract myself only to find that she wanted to do likewise and that I really liked her all along – alas you bugger you are responsible for ruining an innocent romance with all your bloody logic and reasoning …
(JJL 8 January 1942)

Joe told the Pony Club that he would be "starting to train on what will probably be the biggest bomber in operational use in the air force."

The information (or rumours) Joe picked up on his return was not entirely correct. The sneaker raids that had begun in mid-December had ceased by the time he got back from leave. None had been carried out with much effect, although two aircraft were lost. Flying training on Manchesters would not begin for another month, conversion to Lancasters would take two or three months longer than Joe had been led to believe, and 106 Squadron would not move to Syerston until October. But his anxiety about operating on Manchesters was widely shared among Bomber Command's aircrews. Adding it all up, his prospects in the near future did not seem good. In the meantime, he faced another week of inactivity. And it was exactly at such times when the pointless exercise of authority was most likely to occur.

> Supposed to bomb the Scharnhorst & Gneisy but I was scrubbed at the last moment – squadron getting binding with rigid training program – read Rubaiyat of Omar Khayyam again – great stuff but I can't resign myself entirely to "a loaf of bread beneath the bough a flask of wine a book of verse & thou" – I need the excitement of making that possible.
> (JJD 9 January 1942)

> Had our regular sat nite bull session in Boston with most of the old gang – Russians really pushing the Germans back – the only power today capable of handling the Germans – Singapore in grave straits bec[ause] of incompetent so-called colonial leaders believing whites superior to coloured people and acting accord[ingly].
> (JJD 10 January 1942)

> The whole gang went to a show in Boston – did a little too much rough house – rec'd a nice letter from Mom – Pop's play a real success – both are sensible, reasonable, warm-hearted people – I shall have my work cut out after the war trying to live up to their hopes & my reputation – I should be able to give a good account of myself though.
> (JJD 12 January 1942)
>
> Loafing by day by day getting lazier – inactive & listless – a few trips will wake me up – had a visit from some Canadian officers attempting to clear up grievances – see that we get promoted properly with our commissions, etc. might shake up the RAF stooges – Eng[land] certainly expects plenty from [the] men without giving much in return – time the hereditary geniuses were kicked out.[2] (JJD 13 January 1942)
>
> Some old pals from Waddington landed here last nite – had a bull session about our pals at O.T.U. about three quarters are missing – yet you accept the fact calmly – in fact you become conditioned to the prospects of death and watch others go & nearly go yourself without too much fuss. (JJD 14 January 1942)

Always pleased to provide the Pony Club with a lecture, Joe sized up the war situation and America's place in it:

> Herb is spreeing around giving his all to the old firm – I would not be surprised to see the reserved occupations become more unreserved shortly – besides you will probably experience a psychological change with regard to your desire to be a civilian or a soldier once the uniforms become obvious in the streets …
>
> Britain by sheer courage, will power, luck and a little brains stood up to the Germans – partly took their measure and held on long enough to marshal her resources and rally the world –
>
> Russia by sheer hard work, foresight, good hard common sense, unselfishness and courage prepared for the evil day – took the measure of the Germans and did more than that – she showed herself prepared and able to hand back to the Germans what she received.…
>
> The United States thru sheer greed, selfishness, downright stupidity and fantastic lack of foresight failed and partly refused to prepare for the evil day as did the Russians – they escaped the fate of France purely because of an ocean instead of a river – now they are awake – too cocky and far behind in the race for munitions of war having little equipment

and what she has is hopelessly outdated – don't get too cocky when you read all you are going to do – don't forget that is only going to be possible because of the Russians – the British and others – Americans will probably crow again about winning the war – actually they nearly lost it.... Since U.S. power won't be really felt for another year we stand a good chance of still being in uniform next New Years – maybe together – maybe separated – maybe not at all.

Naturally there are hundreds of other guiding, influencing and controlling factors – I can't begin to consider them – I only sketched the broadest of outlines mainly to keep Herby in his place. The letter you sent showed little appreciation for any factor in this war outside the U.S. It was too narrow-minded, shallow and uninformed for a Poneyite. The war is not in the bag simply because the U.S. is in – the U.S. has done little so far to affect the outcome and what it is doing won't be effective until the outcome has been decided – you are only a reserve my boy – a substitute – so don't act as if you are the star – American products and people are held in none too high esteem over here – of course I would not let that worry you but I am trying to impress upon you yankee doodles that you are only little bits of piss in the ocean as are everybody else – so let's remember that – do our best together and let it go at that –

Now this diatribe is not directed against our loyal Poneyite – a former Canadian and future American – it is to be read to the public around Times Square, Delancy's Lane (don't give those slugs my address) and everywhere that people gather – I won't let a bloody Englishman breathe a sentence of reproach against my American confreres – but I thought I ought to tell you privately just for the hell of it – but don't tear up your U.S. citizenship papers because Mub and I might settle down in New York some day – but tuck some of the baloney away in the corner of your head to act as an inspiration to you to right past mistakes – to correct wrong impressions – and above all – to do something concrete to plaster the haughty Germans and the crafty Japs. (JJL 8 January 1942)

On the morning of 15 January, Coningsby was instructed to prepare eleven Hampdens from 106 Squadron, and six Manchesters from 97 Squadron, to participate in a raid on Hamburg as the main Bomber Command target for the night. It was Bomber Command's first raid on Hamburg since Joe had been there on Roberts's last sortie at the end of November. This time the tactics would be different. The wing commander outlined the forecast and strategy:

> a certain amount of mist in Hamburg, also some frost, 15°. All public services suspended. 5 Group to take advantage of these conditions. Crews are to be told that the intention is to burn the town of Hamburg. If Hamburg cannot be identified – bombs are to be brought back. No incendiaries to be dropped on Germany tonight – except Hamburg. Success depends on our concentration in time and space. The route is approx: base to a pt. 54°30N, 4°E. This is to take advantage of the prevailing wind and for best visibility. Picked crews to go in first and act as a guide for the others. Leading crews may attack from low level – even 1,000 ft. if Captain of aircraft desires – … – all incendiaries in centre of town – aiming point 'C'.[3]

Joe recorded in his diary that day that he been detailed to Hamburg that night "to burn the city." These were not his own words. They had come directly from Bomber Command Headquarters at High Wycombe. Aiming point C was not a military target. The objective was to inflict maximum destruction and demoralization on the city's inhabitants by burning it down, using tactics recently conceived but not yet implemented. Comparative assessment of the results of the previous winter's Blitz versus the RAF's recent area bombing campaign showed that the Luftwaffe's success had relied primarily on the deployment of large quantities of small incendiaries rather than high-explosive bombs. Fire rather than blast was apparently the most effective way to destroy a city. To succeed, however, several tens of thousands of two-pound incendiaries had to be dropped within a small area over a short time, and then followed by high-explosive bombs, in order to overwhelm the ability of the city's firefighters to respond. If the results proved satisfactory, the Air Ministry opined, "it may well be that we shall find ourselves able to undertake the systematic destruction of German towns at a much earlier date than we have been able so far to hope for."[4] But although such an attack had been planned since October, the necessary conditions for success – clear weather and a large enough stock of incendiaries – had not come together until now. Hamburg, and especially its old centre with its timbered buildings and narrow streets, was thought a good place to experiment. So it was that all aircraft participating in the attack on Hamburg on 15 January carried incendiaries, not for target marking but for fire-raising. That was the purpose of concentrating the attack on the centre of the city in as short a time as possible.

The weather was fair early in the day although snow was forecast from the west. Joe's aircraft was one of two that did not take off, due to what he described as a "taxiing crackup." The crew was uninjured, but their flying was done before it started that night. The raid was unsuccessful in any event – besides the two aircraft that did not even start, one crashed on takeoff, two returned early with engine trouble, and one failed to reach the target because of engine trouble and jettisoned its bombs in the sea. Only four claimed to have reached the target; however, because the target was obscured by cloud, they released their bomb loads, but not their incendiaries, on what they assumed was at least approximately the target area. So the experiment still awaited ideal test conditions, and in the meantime, incendiaries would not be carried as part of a normal bomb load until further notice in order to conserve them until sufficient stocks could be amassed. But that night's raid on Hamburg was a practice run for many more such operations in the years to come, and would culminate in the destruction of Hamburg by firestorm eighteen months later.

Joe's immediate concern, however, was that by twenty minutes after midnight, one aircraft had not yet returned. It was declared missing a couple of hours later.

> Roger is not back yet and I am goddam well worried – … it is essential that I get a trip in soon before I lose my taste for flying.
> (JJD 15 January 1942)

> Roger Rousseau missing – with crew Dashwood & Horseman from last night's operation – the second of the McIntyre – Rousseau – Jacobson trio to go – I feel a bit empty at heart with the Rouse missing – another true pal whose bombs I will have to drop with Keswick, McIntyre & Kennedy – with Pop posted I remain the sole surviving Canadian here from the original fourteen – I wonder how long for?[5]
> (JJD 16 January 1942)

Joe wrote to Monty immediately.

> Roger is missing from a low level on [words cut out by censor]. I see a good many men lost week in and week out but very few really mean much to me personally – few losses really strike home – the loss of Roger really does as we have been together for 15 months thru thick and thin and had one another sized up pretty well … – in fact altho I am more conditioned to seeing or hearing about fellow friends killed or lost – Roger's bad luck makes me feel about the same as when I lost my own brother seven years ago as we had lived and flown together for longer than most people ever have –

> There is still a minute possibility [words cut out by censor] but so slim that it is not worth hoping for – I have not heard of navigators of [word cut out by censor – presumably "Hampdens"] ever bailing out or not very often – that is something to remember should I hit the same bad luck – the observer chances of escaping are *nil.*
>
> I am going out with Hodge and my crew to drink a few toasts to Roger and his crew – all our closest pals and thus usher still another band of friends into a select corner of our memories. (16 January 1942)

Joe told Janine that he was

> still plugging along but Roger is missing after a low-level on Hamburg a few nights ago. The station is not quite … the same and most everyone feels badly – my old landlady was really broken up – the town feels sad whilst his close pals and myself in particular feel really a bit lost – thus another fine friend disappears … I guess I have to finish for the rest of the gang. (18 January 1942)

No loss struck Joe deeper than this one. Joe and Roger had gone through their training in Canada and at Finningley together, they had been posted to 106 Squadron together, and they had roomed together. And each was an outsider in his own way, as both knew and recognized. If Joe had an extra hurdle to jump, as a Jew, so also and perhaps more so did Roger, as a French Canadian. It was no accident that so few French Canadians had entered the RCAF in 1940. There was no provision for training in French, so anyone not fluent in English was going to have a hard time. Several French Canadians were flunked out of air observer training that year and re-mustered as air gunners. Roger was one of the very few who had made it. Joe knew that and admired him for it.

Already at the stage of his operational tour where he just wanted to survive it to completion and move on, Joe's confidence was now badly shaken. The combination of cancelled operations and the gathering sense of doom sent him into a malaise and for the next few days he seems to have lost his sense of the future. He was in a state of simply going on, drowning his sorrows with his pals until something happened to him. On the 17th he had "an amazing adventure," which he described to Janine.

> I have been laid up slightly with a bit of a cold but that has not impaired my faculty for getting into scrapes. Dave and I and another friend Robby missed the 7 PM bus from Woodhall where we are billeted to Boston where we planned to meet the boys in the pub and talk over

past adventures & friends – Dave made us miss the bus despite my stalling tactics with the bus conductor which delayed it 5 minutes – well we had to get there so we canvassed the town for a taxi with no luck. The distance is seventeen miles – but we heard of a well to do farmer who had two cars – with unequaled gall we got hold of him – gave him our story which for a change was true and he offered us one of his cars – a big one – gas and all – Incidentally he knew my landlady well which helped – so off we went – but Robby insisted on driving against my better judgement and what a ride – the lights went out at one stage – most of the time we were on the wrong side of the road and when we did go on the right side we smashed into a post – 12 miles from Boston completely demolishing the fine car. No one was hurt but we had to push the car a couple of miles up the road to a farm house and walk a couple more before getting a hitch back to Woodhall – so we got nowhere – wrecked a car and somehow or other we have to get the car fixed – None of us have driving licences but that is the least of our worries – I hate to put a kind heart and good car out of commission.

… I have been briefed and ready to fly practically every night since returning from leave – yet I have not taken off the deck due to failures of all kinds – including a taxiing crack up – But we will get off yet – …
(JJL 18 January 1942)

Another magnificent evening at Rysdale with Hodge, Stevenson, Steve, Dave – Tome, Paddy, Max & Robby – they put up a feed that does justice to my mom – plus scotch & beer in unlimited proportion.
(JJD 18 January 1942)

Loafed around camp playing snooker per usual with Hodge and Dave – saw Smithson with Robby and told him about his car – went to bed early – pleasant fire – smoked a cigar and read – life easy & lazy again plus tricky as I avoid signing books – attending lectures cagily.
(JJD 19 January 1942)

Joe advised Monty that he was

revising slightly my instructions in the event of my disappearance – Mrs. Lettice will have your address and all my personal belongings such as diaries, pocket books – money etc. will go to you instead of Dan.[6]

You can have Savard or one of the officials from Canada House send what you think should be sent home censor free – some of the things I have written might be interesting.

> I am sending all Roger's stuff to Savard – to send home for him but his family is a bit different than mine as they have never showed any real interest in him –
>
> This is not a particularly cheering topic but it has to be attended to so from now on my boy – you inherit my rubbage.

He added that without Roger, and badly needing company, he had decided to move to barracks at Coningsby.

> Still hanging on with Mrs. Lettice but I might either get Dave to move in with me or move into Camp with the boys as it is rather dull without Roger – but the old lady is badly shaken so I shall stay on alone a while yet – (JJL 19 January 1942)
>
> Had my last supper with Mrs. Lettice. Moving to the mess – had a wonderful time here with Roger – but that stage has past – the good food can't compensate for the loneliness and my desire to have a pal at hand – it's Dave [Davies] now. (JJD 20 January 1942)

Joe advised Monty that as he was going to Cardington on the 21st for his medical board, he would see what he could do to get to London for a few hours.

> I won't be flying before then because I have a cold and am off flying until I get back. My pilot is crapping his pants for fear he should be on without me whilst Hodge is hanging on to his cold for dear life.
>
> Roger was certainly well thought of as many officers and men of all ranks plus civvies have been coming up to me and speaking about him – unusual around here – with Mac and Roger gone my folks will really start getting worried – I think I will send more telegrams – will return your letters tomorrow. (JJL 19 January 1942)

He also visited Janine, as she was staying with Freedman relatives in London.

> Definitely cooled off on Janine. Too many others things to do – people to see – the old bugaboo of refusing to get tied down or hooked up. (JJD 22 January 1942)
>
> Talked & planned with Monty all night in clubs, lines & on street – starting to get concrete plans. (JJD 23 January 1942)

Not long after Joe and Roger had reunited with Jack McIntyre at 106 Squadron, they determined they should apply for commissions. Joe had wondered then which of them would live to realize it. Jack had been killed in September. Roger and Joe had applied in October, and they seem to have progressed at a similar rate. Roger was recommended by his squadron leader and wing commander in October, he passed his medical exam in November, and was finally recommended by his group captain. No doubt both Roger and Joe had pursued the matter with the RCAF officers who visited Coningsby the day before Roger went missing. Joe, by his own account, had been interviewed by his group captain on 3 January, and had passed his medical exam three weeks later. All having gone well, he wrote to Dan that

> The Commission will be through in about two to four weeks depending on how long they take to mail my notification. Can't rush these boys you know. Don't say anything to anybody until I actually receive it.
>
> As soon as it comes through I will hop up to your place and buy a uniform if you think I can get a better buy from your tailor than a strange one in London. I would just as well get a ready-made uniform if possible as it would be quicker. However, we will discuss those details when it comes through whence we will get together and surprise one and all. I think though that your man is probably the best bet, but I only get a week off to get fitted out so he will have to step on it....
>
> (JJL 23 January 1942)

RAF commissions could not be put into effect without the final approval of Britain's Air Ministry, where delays were often encountered. Somewhere between Coningsby and the Air Ministry, the process seems to have got stuck, and nothing more was heard by Joe, his family, or by Roger's family.[7] Was it simply the wartime press of other duties on overworked staff, or a reluctance at higher levels to commission air observers? Joe's former pilot also applied for commission while at Coningsby, but was later told the papers had disappeared, and he had to reapply at his next station. However, the record also shows that of the approximately eighty sergeant air observers taken on by 106 Squadron since May, no more than one or two were commissioned by the following February.

Joe returned to his squadron on the 23rd to find that he had been promoted to flight sergeant, with a raise in pay.[8] He also learned that his previous pilot, Gerry Roberts,

> who has finished his time on ops and who did most of my trips with me has been awarded the Distinguished Flying Medal – so I thump myself

> heartily on the back as do one and all for there is only one key man in the crew who holds the fate of the successful operation in his claw – yep the good old observer.... (JJL 23 January 1942)

The prospect of a commission, but above all his visit with Monty, restored Joe's confidence and sense of balance. Surrounded by his remaining close pals on base, he could more easily put the events of the last week out of mind.

> Returned – 2 crews missing.[9] 11 letters for me – Monk & Don Henderson missing[10] – Dave & I living together – very satisfactory with books – victrola – food – convenience – thought of an idea for a play – Monty & my reactions, exper. & development since war – also future hopes. (JJD 24 January 1942)

He wrote his family:

> You probably know by now that Roger is missing from a trip last week. I gave Savard a good story on Roger and I believe it will be printed in the French papers back home. Mrs. Lettice of course feels badly and is now quite lonely since we were all moved from our billets back to camp yesterday. Dave and I now bunk together and have a room resplendent with good books and good music – cigars, cigarettes, tobacco and food. He has an anthology of Shaw's plays – we have stuff by Darwin, Paine, Stalin, Marx – Vici Baum, Sinclair Lewis, Streit, Belfrage, etc. etc. so I have high hopes of getting some reading done if I can ever catch up with my mail.
>
> Don Henderson who was at our place – a Winnipeg boy is also missing so a few of the old gang have run into some tough luck – heard nothing about Moe yet but it is still a little early to know definitely – the same goes for Roger – since Roger was on a low level attack his chances are considerably diminished.[11]
>
> ... We saw Dave Legett who is a captain – looks well – sends his regards along – also Bob Forester – Rod McGinnen – all officers in the newspaper field from back home – Monty and I are really well connected with the big shots around Air Ministry – we have also met H. W. Smart the representative of Howard Smith Paper Mills in England. He is a big shot over here – he came up to Monty and myself in Blackfriars famous pub and started chatting with us – he is a pal of Crabtree's – we know Roy the son real well from College. We spent three hours in the pub – got Smart as merry as a lark – made a valuable and important friend –

> saw his offices – talked politics, business and everything else with him and learnt a lot of valuable facts and figures and picked up some good information. (JJL 23 January 1942)

Percy, for his part, sent news from the home front:

> We are preparing here for a long war and the whole population will be mobilized for war within two months. No more autos to be built after March … manufacture of steel products (including quite a few of our own lines) drastically cut. Price ceiling on all commodities. Canada is awake. (PJL 3 January 1942)

He also began responding to Joe's newfound political convictions:

> Never lose sight of the fact that the object of living is to live fully … you do not live for an institution, a form. For the moment you are fighting for the things that make life worth living when the fight is over you must be sure that you make that life which you are risking well worth the living. If you don't live fully from the inside out … you will not be much use to others.… (PJL 3 January 1942)

> The problem will be how to destroy the rotten portions without bringing down the whole structure. There is a whole lot of good in democracy a lot worth preserving. Well that is the problem for you youngsters to tackle … even if it cannot be completely solved. But tackled it must be and with the head and, if the errors of the Russian revolution are to be avoided, with the heart as well. Whatever the system it must be remembered that we are fighting for people's rights and not to glorify and worship an institution. Please keep this in mind Joe that institutions or governments if you like to call them are made for the people and not the people for the institution. It must be a human system and not a mechanical one. No robots. After all that is what we are fighting for. I am willing to go with you a long way as long as you bear these facts in mind … the little man must have his day whether he belongs to a party or not … I don't think the little man has had his day yet … certainly not in communistic Russia … and no one denies there are good things … many good things there but one of the bad ones is the glorifying of the party … no more aristocracy please whether communistic or fascist. Some day when you have marshaled your facts let us hear from you … (PJL 18 January 1942)

Twenty-Nine

28 January 1942

The weather in Lincolnshire was terrible the last week of January, and the squadron had been unable to fly since the 22nd. After several days of snow, Coningsby aerodrome's grass runways were waterlogged and unserviceable. Joe lamented to Mrs. Lettice that he had done no flying for a month, and was anxious to get off the ground. In the meantime, he had plenty of time to write. He started work on a play in three acts about squadron life, getting the outline and some bits of dialogue down in one of his notebooks.

> Received a superb letter from Pop – discussing destiny – we have now reached a firm, solid understanding & appreciation of one another – developed from the narrow scope of father to that of friend – went to the Leagate – with Dick Bird, Hodge – Sid – Popeye – Hammatt – talk on cynicism with embittered proprietess –[1] (JJD 26 January 1942)

He replied to Percy that day, deeply appreciative of his letter. Depth of feeling and understanding, Joe remarked, seemed to grow with distance. He then elaborated on his discussions with Monty about what he characterized as "Destiny," and two factors he saw affecting their future efforts:

> One is the effect upon me of those friends I have lost – about three quarters – the other of those I have. In the first case the result has not been what might have been expected – I have not been disillusioned embittered – angered or frightened – Naturally I have been saddened but that does not last long as there are too many exciting, pulsating and thrilling occurrences plus too many new friends to step in to allow for more than a fleeting sense of loss at odd times. But it has made

me *determined* – determined to do what I can to do what my missing friends wanted to do – could do and would have done – that is a tall order but knowing them as I do and what they were worth – anything I do with that trust as an inspiration should at least be something in the right direction.

Now for the living. Amongst practically all my friends without exception – even the most capable – there is that one dominating all important and vital thought "what am I going to do after the war." With some it is purely a question of not wanting to give up the zestful joy of life in the air force for one of routine and aimlessness. For others like Monty and Dave and myself it is that and more – it is an instinctive feeling that we have all the elements in the world to make life worth living – not only for ourselves alone but for others as well – knowing and appreciating many of the difficulties to even starting in the right direction without getting bogged down – we are trying to puzzle out where and how to begin. The materials are there amongst most of us – to get it directed into the right channels is the problem – despite the uncertainty of everything I still have a profound optimism, hope and confidence – thus the second result.

Now for the third – whilst puzzling all these things out an idea sprouted. These thoughts affect nearly everyone to a greater or lesser degree – they are human – they are fundamental – when reviewing my past activities experiences and development it suddenly dawned upon me that what has been happening to me would make a bloody good play. There are a dozen angles that could be expanded to strike home to everyone – for example

1. Father and son relationship with our lives as background

2. Monty and I would certainly be typical of two young men facing the realities of life together and preparing and wondering about the future.

3. Mother – a magnificent story could be based around the way she handles every situation – a son overseas, evacuees – two grown daughters – her husband etc. etc.

4. Youth and war

5. Youth and peace –

> The latter two based on the Pony Club's reaction and activities plus many of my pals, [the last] would be based on the present and looking to the future.
>
> … what is happening to us is so engrossing as well as indicative of the time and age we are living in that I feel it should be expressed in writing.…

He suggested to Percy that he, as an accomplished playwright, would be best suited to putting their ideas down effectively.

> My wireless operator and air gunner have applied to go to Canada and have a good chance of landing up there. Both are capable men – Sid Harding is one Hodgkinson is the other – Hodge is a capable lad – something like Monty – make sure you have plenty of beer etc at home. If you don't have the time of your life getting Hodge to tell you about some of our humorous trips together (after the appropriate number of drinks of course) I miss my bet – he will keep you young all night with some of our finer efforts as he has been on nearly all my trips with me and he will also tell you about Dave, Pop, Robby, Roger and the gang – they are really looking forward to going and no doubt you will see that they are toasted and feted long and pleasantly and put up, accommodated, pampered and spoilt as they well deserve to be – pump Hodge and you can find out a good bit as we go around together quite a bit and know and like one another well – in fact he is on a par with Dave and Roger which puts him well up. But remember that a few judicious drinks will really do the trick.…
>
> Also my future plans have been changed as I am going on a conversion course to fly in our biggest bombers so I guess the fighter pilot stuff is shelved for the time being – unfortunately.… (JJL 26 January 1942)

He wrote Monty that day, scolding him for not addressing him in his new status as flight sergeant, and commending him on the idea of the play. He hoped he would get another pass to visit on 7 or 8 February, after which he was to start flying in Manchesters.

> Going on to [two words cut out by censor] after my next leave – so I guess I will get a taste of flying in the [words cut out by censor] before I am thru. (JJL 27 January 1942)

On the 28th, he wrote a letter to Roger's brother Réal in Montreal:

Your one dominant thought is naturally what chance had Roger of getting out of the plane. Without trying to dash all hopes I say not much but there still is that possibility. Anything can happen in this game – even a long shot like that. We keep in constant touch with the German news via our wireless and will be the first to receive any good news that may come thru.

Roger and I did all our training in Canada together – all our time in England together – living together here and doing about the same number of operational trips. I think I am about the closest friend that Roger ever had so it is with a great deal of pride altho a good deal of sadness that I write this letter to you as we both agreed to do should one of us be missing.

Firstly, Roger had just been promoted to the rank of F/Sgt as have I backdated to Oct., 1941.

Secondly he had been recommended for a commission by the squadron – it had been passed and was due thru by the middle of February when I will get mine. He particularly wanted you to know this because it had been done entirely on his own merits and his own record on this squadron, where he was looked upon and considered by officers and men as an astounding navigator competent, daring and resolute. He rejected the idea of using either your influence or that of your father to get him his commission. He got it the hard way – he might never wear his new uniform but he earned and won it which is the most satisfying part.

After all he was perfectly happy and satisfied as a F/Sgt – his main object in desiring a commission was that it would cause you – the one he was fondest of and his father no little pride.

Since flying is rather hazardous at best and we get accustomed to seeing one another come and go – most fellows are so absorbed and involved that few take the trouble to tell the family of one of their missing pals exactly what their pal and the families dear one was like while they knew him.

Roger was about the best liked man on the squadron – also the best known because of his ready smile – outspoken manner, clean cut appearance and general good humour and high spirits.

> Our pals all over the country have expressed their regret concerning Roger's bad luck – unusual over here – all members of the squadron and myself in particular feel a genuine loss.
>
> As a Montrealer in close association with French Canadians I can honestly say that Roger during his eighteen months in the Air Force has done more to bring about an understanding between French Canadians and all other English speaking countries, including Canada, New Zealand – England, America etc. – than ninety per cent of the French Canadian writers, politicians, etc, have so far. That might sound exaggerated but we come in contact with so many people and so many born prejudices that a personality such as Roger's was able, unconsciously perhaps, to shatter then conquer all he came in contact with.
>
> You happen to be Roger's brother – I feel and look upon him as one too, so I can only say whilst there is still a scrap of hope – all is not yet lost …[2] (JJL 28 January 1942)

Joe then summarized his thoughts on recent discussions in one of his notebooks, first with Monty during their leave, and then:

> Discussion at the Leagate [26 Jan.] with Dickie Bird – Hodge and the proprietors –
>
> *Cynicism and hypocrisy*
>
> Dicky a corporal actually runs this squadron – he is in the orderly room – personally handles everything for dim sqdn ldrs and dimmer G.C. He has done much for individual aircrew – rec'd no thanks from them – People are nice to him only until they get what they want then they ignore him – he puts thru all commissions, awards, postings transfers, etc. – He is quiet, intelligent pleasant, young and inexperienced – he has been hurt altho he doesn't show it – is getting cynical because of human ingratitude, stupidity
>
> I should say he has been disillusioned more than anything else –
>
> The woman encouraged him was a real cynic – had probably being stepped on having lived in Malaya for years. My outlook and point brought out was –
>
> 1. You don't get what you deserve – you don't get what you don't fight for as a rule – So shout – or talk people into things or see that you

> get what you think you deserve and there is no need for cynicism – accept the fact that humans aren't perfect and rewards seldom chase after you and your whole outlook changes – you get a kick of seeing that what you think you deserve takes place – perhaps subtly perhaps not so subtly – you also get the odd thrill of the advantages of the reward.

One of the first keys to happiness is an understanding of human virtues and weaknesses. Thus you rationalize away the wrongs done to you or determine to fight or counteract them – but you are not embittered or disillusioned as a result – only angry and sore which is a lot healthier –

Thus the great philosopher retires until further topics pop up.
(JJN 28 January 1942)

106 Squadron had seen little activity since the Hamburg raid in the middle of January. Six aircraft had been sent to Bremen on the 21st, while Joe was on leave. It was another inauspicious raid. Three crews returned early because of heating system failures. One was Selfe's, with Joe replaced by one of the most experienced observers still remaining in the squadron. Joe would thus not have had another operation to his credit even if he had been on board. Only two crews found the target; one failed to return. Overall, only half of the aircraft Bomber Command dispatched that night claimed to have bombed Bremen.

The next night, Bomber Command sent forty-seven aircraft to Münster, a railway centre northeast of the Ruhr. This was the first raid of the year on an inland target, and it achieved modest success. 106 squadron did not take part. Operations were scrubbed for the next few days on account of weather, but on the 26th, a larger raid was mounted on Hanover, another inland target. Again the weather was less than ideal and fewer than half of the crews bombed the target.

Just before ten o'clock on the morning of the 28th, the Operations Room at Coningsby was advised of a major effort by 5 Group for the night. It would be the largest attack on an inland target since the Huls raid at the end of December. The target was initially specified as Hanover again, but in late afternoon was changed to Münster.

Ultimately, twenty-nine Hampdens were detailed for the operation, along with fifty-five Wellingtons from 1 and 3 Groups. The primary target was the main railway station, but if crews could not identify it, they were instructed to bomb the town. Each aircraft was loaded with one one-thousand-pound bomb and two five-hundred-pound bombs. The Münster operation was not intended as a fire-raising raid and no crews carried incendiaries. Time over target was specified as 2000 to 2030. Ten 106 Squadron crews, including Joe's, were detailed for operations that night.

Observers went to briefing at 1400. Within the hour Bomber Command asked all crews going over Holland to take particular note of weather conditions, snow, and ice, and to send in a report as soon as they landed.[3] The ten aircraft took off in fading light and into the clouds, a minute or so apart, starting at 1754. Their track would take them directly over the North Sea to the northwest tip of Holland, then with a slight turn southeastward, to Münster, with a prescribed time over target of just over two hours later. Selfe, Jacobson, Hodgkinson, and Harding, flying AT122, were fourth up at 1757.

Two of the ten aircraft returned to base within the hour, one with wireless failure and the other with engine problems. Another returned early, having encountered severe icing en route and jettisoned its bombs at sea. At the same time, Coningsby received a message from AT121 over the Dutch coast that it was returning at half-speed owing failure of its port engine. Half an hour later, a fourth aircraft returned, having been unable to locate the target in ten-tenths cloud. Its crew bombed Ostende on the Belgian coast as a last resort target before returning. Two aircraft returned before midnight, having bombed from eighteen thousand feet on estimated time of arrival. The target was not visible, but both aircraft encountered heavy flak over what they believed to be Münster. Four aircraft failed to return, and were reported as missing at 0230 on the 29th.

X3058 ditched off the East Anglia coast on its return. All four crew managed to get into the dinghy, but when rescue came late the next afternoon, all but the pilot had succumbed to cold. The air observer was another Canadian, Sgt. Alexander Granton Patrick, who had been posted to 106 Squadron ten days before.[4] Joe had barely met him. AT121, which was last heard from over Holland, suffered engine failure and crashed into a house in the Langestraat at Den Helder. Two of the crew were killed and two taken prisoner. Nothing was heard of P4398 and AT122. The squadron diary recorded of the Münster raid:

> so far as the squadron was concerned, the raid had disastrous results, no fewer than four aircraft failing to return. Never before have so many aircraft been lost in one raid. The weather was almost certainly the cause of these losses, as it was intensely cold with snow storms and severe icing.[5]

Of the approximately eighty-four aircraft dispatched to Münster, fewer than half reached the target. None actually saw it, and so they bombed flak concentrations through cloud on estimated time of arrival. Northwest Europe was blanketed in cloud that night – not ordinary winter cloud but towering cumulonimbus with severe turbulence and icing conditions, which no aircraft was capable of surmounting. Most of the aircraft that turned back did so because of those conditions, and most of those that did get to Münster encountered icing. 106 Squadron had indeed borne the brunt of the losses that night, although one Wellington aircraft from 214 Squadron was also lost without trace.

The night of January 28 turned out to be yet another in a string of futile raids on German targets since the Berlin raid in November. If ever the weather conditions were unfavourable and aircraft exposed to extreme hazard – the very conditions under which the Air Council had in November advised against operations – it was on the night of 28 January. The loss rate of 6 percent cannot have been entirely unforeseen.

Was the Münster operation an attack unduly pressed in the circumstances? Where is the line between aggressive action and unnecessary risk? How important was that operation in the scheme of things at the time? The November directive had cautioned against taking excessive risks in bad weather, although it did not preclude experimenting with new tactics or techniques while regrouping for a more effective offensive the next spring. Yet there does not seem to be any evidence that Münster that night presented a target worth incurring heavy casualties. Was there some other objective or experiment in mind on the 28th, as headquarters' specific instructions about observing weather and ground conditions might suggest?

Bomber Command could not cease operations altogether; at the very least, it had to demonstrate its determination to strike regardless of adversity. The Command pushed the operational limits in its desperation that winter – the daylight attacks on Brest, the daylight sneakers, and night operations in terrible conditions – in order to engage the enemy as best it could. Over two hundred crews were lost in the offensive between mid-November and the end of January. Perhaps the best that may be said of those months is that, although little damage was inflicted on Germany at the time, the Command was learning how to do so in the future.

Something had gone very wrong on board AT122 between the Dutch coast and Münster on the evening of the 28th. Certainly the aircraft passed through a weather front over the Netherlands an hour or so after takeoff. It must have experienced severe icing en route, as did so many other aircraft on the Münster raid that night. The weight of ice would have slowed the aircraft and made it more difficult to control, and increased its rate of fuel consumption. Critical aircraft instruments, including the airspeed indicator, may also have been impaired. It was a difficult situation for even an experienced pilot, and Selfe did not yet have that experience. These conditions likely delayed the aircraft's progress enough that it would have arrived late over the target. Still, AT122 was aloft at eight o'clock, so it had managed to pass through the initial zone of freezing conditions. But these likely recurred en route.

By then AT122 was approaching the Kammhuber line at the eastern tip of Holland, about fifteen minutes' flying time from Münster. The Luftwaffe's night-fighters were grounded because of the weather, but the anti-aircraft guns to the east had free rein, and flak was reported by other crews to be heavy and accurate despite the cloud cover. A direct hit by flak that could have punctured a fuel line or tank, perhaps even damaged an engine, would certainly have compounded the situation AT122 was already experiencing. But the aircraft almost certainly never got as far as Münster's anti-aircraft batteries. With the prospect of severe headwinds on the return journey, the crew was already confronted with a fuel problem that reduced their remaining available flying time. And as Joe had already noted, Selfe was still learning how to economize on fuel. If they had concluded that there was not enough fuel to return to England, then their choice was to ditch in the North Sea or attempt a forced landing in the Netherlands. Prospects for survival in an emergency dinghy in the North Sea in January were dim.

It was a terrible choice, but as captain it was Joe's to make. His urge to press on regardless, when flying with Gerry Roberts, had likely given way to caution while flying with Robin Selfe. A forced landing in the Netherlands, if successful, offered at least a better chance of survival, and perhaps even the possibility of evasion and eventual return to England.[6] In preparation, Joe took the precaution of releasing their bomb load. To this day, at least two bomb craters, about two metres deep and five metres across, are evident in the wooded area northeast of Lievelde. Although the site is now overgrown, at least two and possibly three craters at the edge of a small wooded area are visible in air photographs taken in 1945. AT122 carried three bombs: one one-thousand-pounder and two five-hundred-pounders. The crater locations indicate that the bombs fell in a line running more or less north-south, with the closest crater just under two kilometres directly north of the crash site. It seems from the nature of impact that at least some of the bombs were armed.

The aircraft was by this time difficult to control, but not out of control. Joe had abandoned his position in the nose and was kneeling just behind Selfe as they searched for an opportune place to land. With the moon approximately three-quarters full, they could distinguish between forest and field at low altitude, even if it was snowing. Now close to the ground, they could see a flat field with no apparent obstructions. It appeared to be the best choice in what was now a desperate situation. Although one can be instructed in forced landings, one cannot practise them. There was only one chance to get it right. Selfe gave it his best attempt, but the circumstances defeated him.

The aircraft approached from the southeast on its final descent, clipping the tops of the trees before crash-landing near the northern edge of the field. It was still oriented in the general direction of its approach, and so must have completed a near U-turn after releasing its bomb load. This is consistent with recollections of the aircraft being heard to pass nearby more than once, but in any event the time between bomb release and final descent cannot have been more than a few minutes. Those final minutes, again according to local accounts, occurred after curfew (eight o'clock in the evening), and probably very shortly after. A little over two hours had elapsed since takeoff.

AT122 had come down east of Lichtenvoorde, in Holland, somewhat less than twenty miles south-southwest of its prescribed track, and about forty miles short of Münster. They had probably lost some time on the way, climbing or descending to escape icing and turbulence, but their time over Lichtenvoorde would still have had them within schedule to reach their target within the prescribed time period. Those aircraft that did reach Münster managed to do so between 2000 and 2030. So Jacobson and crew almost certainly couldn't have reached Münster, or even thought they might have. If they had, they would have released their bombs over visible flak concentrations, as did most other crews.

Photographs taken afterwards, although grainy, reveal that the aircraft had sustained severe damage when it hit the ground. (See pages 342 and 343.) The tail boom broke loose from the main fuselage on impact and is lying on the ground. Lying to the left of the aircraft is what appears to be a section of the fuselage, possibly the part behind the rear gunner's cage (it may be the same piece of the fuselage that is piled in front of the workers dismantling the aircraft). Possibly the pilot's canopy area is missing. The port engine dug into the ground, the propeller blades are bent, and the port wing appears to have broken off. All this is consistent with police descriptions of the aircraft as "totally destroyed," and with other witness recollections of the aircraft lying in several pieces. The aircraft may have gone into an unrecoverable sideslip on final approach, as Hampdens were known to do. Or it may have stalled when it clipped the treetops, coming down at a steep enough angle to cause the tail boom and the end of the fuselage to separate on impact and fall back on either side of the aircraft. There is no indication that it skidded on the snow after the initial impact.

In the event of a Hampden's forced landing, the air observer was to evacuate his forward cockpit and sit behind the pilot, as Joe had already done. The wireless operator and gunner were to move forward and brace themselves with their backs against the main spar, facing backward. In at least one witness account, the crew was found "two by two," indicating that they had indeed assumed forced landing position.

None of the accounts indicate that anyone was wearing his parachute, ready to bail out. Nor is there any indication that anyone attempted to bail out, although under the circumstances it seems unlikely that he could have. In icing conditions, the latches on Hampdens stick and render escape hatches inoperable. Joe had written on more than one occasion about the observer's poor prospects for emergency escape from a Hampden. Perhaps by the time the need to bail out was inevitable, it was no longer possible.

None of the crew except the pilot would have been strapped in. There were several large and heavy unsecured items inside the aircraft, including ammunition drums, and the batteries were positioned behind the crew in their assumed positions. Any of these items coming loose on impact would have pitched forward into the men. The impact was almost certainly great enough to have caused severe internal, skeletal, and spinal injuries, and at least one of the crew suffered a fatal head wound. If death was not instant, it must have come soon. The doctor who examined the scene the next morning asserted, decades after the event, that he might have been able to save some of the men if he had arrived on the scene earlier. But as they were dressed in their heavy flying suits when he inspected the aircraft the next morning, he might not have been able to observe the full extent of their injuries. Several veterans of 106 Squadron later came to believe that the aircraft had come down in a blizzard, and that the crew had frozen to death, possibly trying to wait it out before emerging. The basis for this speculation is unclear but it seems improbable. Aircrews were under instructions to set fire to their aircraft and destroy it if they came down in enemy territory. Presumably if they had been able to get out and do that, they would have.

Over seventy years after the event, it seems unlikely that more can be said about the fate of AT122 and its crew. Exactly why the fatal crash occurred can never be known. But F/Sgt. Joe Jacobson's part in holding Bomber Command's place on the front line that winter was over. He had held on to the end, unflinching, never wavering in his conviction of the war's rightness and purpose, or in his faith in the future.

Part Five

Failed to Return

I pray that our Heavenly Father may assuage the anguish of your bereavement, and leave you only the cherished memory of the loved and lost, and the solemn pride that must be yours to have laid so costly a sacrifice upon the altar of Freedom.

— Abraham Lincoln, letter to a grieving mother, 1864

War is the greatest of all agents of change. It speeds up all processes, wipes out minor distractions, brings realities to the surface.

— George Orwell, *The Lion and the Unicorn*, 1941

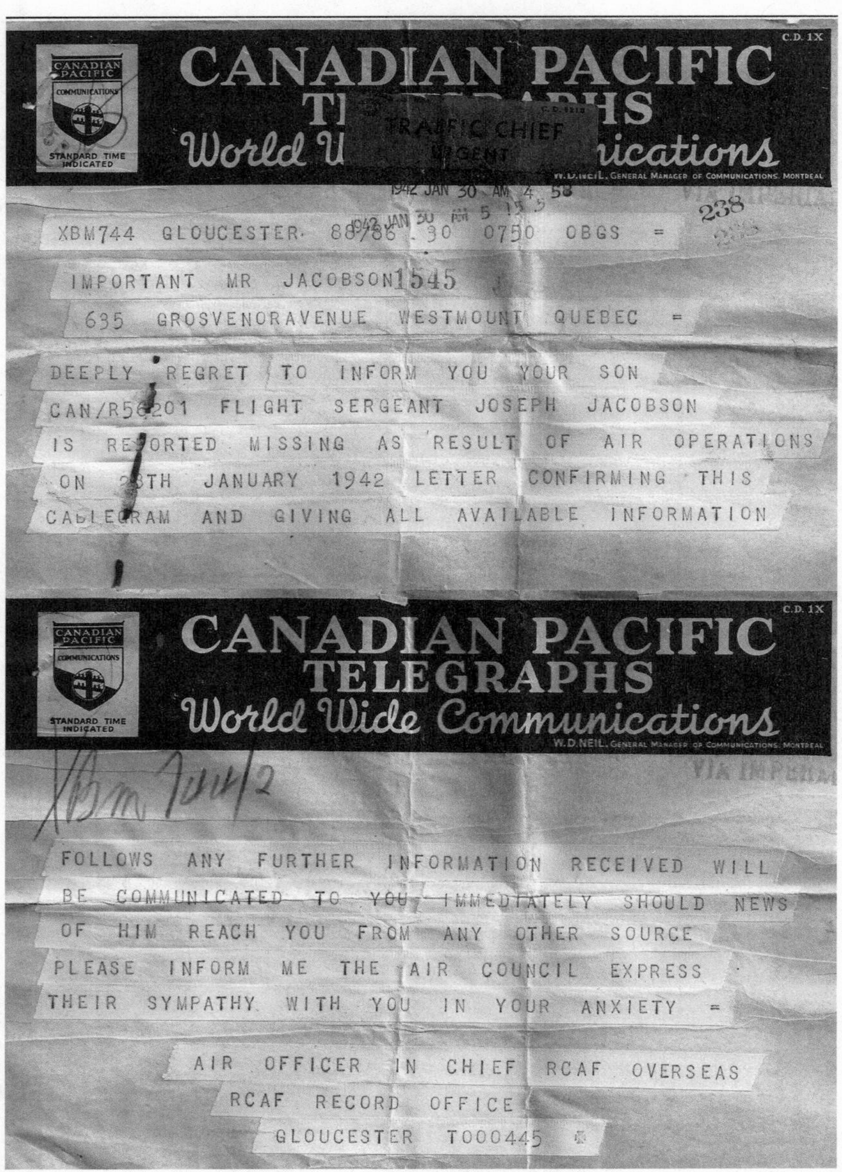

C.D. 1X

CANADIAN PACIFIC
TE[obscured]PHS
World Wi[obscured]mmunications

W.D. NEIL, GENERAL MANAGER OF COMMUNICATIONS, MONTREAL

TRAFFIC CHIEF
URGENT

1942 JAN 30 AM 4 58

1942 JAN 30 AM 5 15

238

XBM744 GLOUCESTER 88/86 30 0750 OBGS =

IMPORTANT MR JACOBSON 1545

635 GROSVENORAVENUE WESTMOUNT QUEBEC =

DEEPLY REGRET TO INFORM YOU YOUR SON
CAN/R56201 FLIGHT SERGEANT JOSEPH JACOBSON
IS REPORTED MISSING AS RESULT OF AIR OPERATIONS
ON 28TH JANUARY 1942 LETTER CONFIRMING THIS
CABLEGRAM AND GIVING ALL AVAILABLE INFORMATION

C.D. 1X

CANADIAN PACIFIC
TELEGRAPHS
World Wide Communications

W.D. NEIL, GENERAL MANAGER OF COMMUNICATIONS, MONTREAL

XBM 744/2

FOLLOWS ANY FURTHER INFORMATION RECEIVED WILL
BE COMMUNICATED TO YOU IMMEDIATELY SHOULD NEWS
OF HIM REACH YOU FROM ANY OTHER SOURCE
PLEASE INFORM ME THE AIR COUNCIL EXPRESS
THEIR SYMPATHY WITH YOU IN YOUR ANXIETY =

AIR OFFICER IN CHIEF RCAF OVERSEAS
RCAF RECORD OFFICE
GLOUCESTER T000445

The cable that every family dreaded, but so many received. (Canadian Jewish Archives)

Thirty

Requiem

The cable arrived in Montreal on Friday morning, followed by a letter from Joe's squadron leader at Coningsby:

> He was Navigator of an aircraft which left here on the night of the twenty-eighth of January to bomb a target in Munster, and I regret that he did not return. Although fair at the start, the weather became most unfavourable, and several other aircraft of the Squadron were forced to turn back owing to the thick cloud and severe icing conditions. No messages were received from the aircraft, and I am afraid there is nothing to indicate the cause of its loss. It is possible, however, that it made a forced landing, and that the crew, although prisoners of war, are safe....
>
> Your son had served in this Squadron for several months and had won for himself a reputation as a brilliant navigator. He had taken part in twenty-three raids over enemy territory, performing his difficult and dangerous duties always with skill and courage. He was very popular here, and we all appreciate the motives which brought him from Canada to help this country in her hour of need. I hope that it will be some small consolation to you that he has served us loyally and successfully.... (30 January 1942)

Percy and May received the news while spending a long weekend in St. Agathe in the Laurentians.

> Friday we received word that [Joe] was missing during regular flying operations.... at 8 30 AM I was called to the telephone. Long distance

from Montreal. Early morning calls usually denote disaster. Edith read the cable to me over the phone. It was a message that I had almost expected for the past two and half years. I never read in the paper or heard over the radio particulars of an RAF raid over Germany with the usual summing up of so many of our planes failed to return, without that fear in my heart. May tells me now she felt the same way. The shock did not find us altogether vulnerable. May stood up to the news like a major. Our first thought was to get home as quickly as possible. Then the question … what for? We telephoned Edith and Janet and they joined us … they stayed just the weekend. We remained until the Thursday. Thus May avoided the hundreds of telephone calls. When we came home there were many letters. However, we decided that this is no time for personal grief. The whole world is steeped in misery. Who are we to complain? Perhaps this attitude at the present time is all the easier because we have a firm conviction that Joe is alive and possibly a prisoner in Germany. This is bad enough to think about but as long as he is still with us … the main feeling I have at this time is absolute lifelessness, not all the time. Life's routine persists in both home and office. May, the first day she was at home went to her office.… I thank goodness had a pile of work to do. People of course have been most kind but we have been careful to make them understand that we want no sympathy, no pity. Possibly we overdo our gaiety when people are with us. There may be weeks of waiting before we know definitely about Joe. These weeks will be hard but I have a most remarkable wife, her courage and morale are superb. This attitude of ours about Joe still being alive is full of danger … we know it … but while there is uncertainty we are going to shut our eyes to the possibility of final tragedy. In a letter received from Joe written January 9th he mentions a friend that is missing and gave the opinion that the chances of his being a prisoner or saved are remote. Even this has not swerved us from our purpose not to consider Joe lost to us until someone advises us that he is actually dead. We will never give up hope of his being alive, while there is the slightest chance of this being so. May broke down only once to my knowledge as far as myself is concerned there hasn't been a tear. I know I have not yet faced the situation. The thing goes too deep. I dare not. Edith and Janet's morale is excellent. What they feel privately we know not but they are always gay when they are with us. I need a specific war activity, one that would absorb all my energies, these are times when I almost loathe my business. No husband and wife could be closer to one another than May, I know Edith and Janet have a deep affection for me … but I would give all I possess to have a talk with Joe. He would

> understand. I have many men friends, very good friends but no one who could rid me of this sense of being alone at times, to be honest this is only at times. Both May and myself in our younger days have suffered so much from emotional outbursts in our respective families that I am afraid we have gone to the other extreme, we hold ourselves in too tight. This may be dangerous. One thing is sure that May is one woman in ten thousand, ten hundred thousand, she is really so fine that I am ashamed of my own weaknesses. (PJD 8 February 1942)
>
> Joe is still missing. We feel that he is alive. We have not faced the alternative. May says that she will not give up hope until it is absolutely proved without a shadow of a doubt that he was killed in action. We believe we are leading normal lives. People have been most kind. They do not fuss over us. In years to come looking back on these days we may discover that we were not as normal as we thought we were.
>
> Last Sunday night a queer thing happened. A stranger (Alderman Goyette) telephoned me to say that he saw Joe's picture in the newspaper and he was positive that he was alright. Then he described how Joe had landed in unoccupied France and was being cared for by friends of the Allies. He said if the picture had told him a different story he would not have telephoned me. In any case it was a kindly act.
> (PJD 14 February 1942)
>
> This is his birthday. It is a hard day for his mother to go through. There is nothing to be done except wait. (PJD 17 February 1942)

During the wait, letters of sympathy and hope arrived from many parts of Canada and abroad. Duncan Hodgkinson's mother wrote from England:

> I hope by the time you get this our boys will have been found. I can't think anything else, they had done so many hard trips together, surely they must have thought just what they would do in an emergency such as this. But what I wanted to say was how Duncan used to speak of that boy of yours, cheering them up when in a tight spot & his rendering of songs etc. (5 February 1942)

Caught between hope and desperation, Dan and Monty scoured the country for news. In London, they made inquiries at the Red Cross, the Air Ministry, and RCAF headquarters, and the following week they travelled together to Joe's station at Coningsby. No new information was forthcoming. Dan wrote to Percy a week later.

One thing [Joe] said to me the last time we were together, if ever I am reported missing be patient for about four weeks and you will be hearing from me direct, which he gave me to understand was the usual time and custom for prisoners of war, so again I say have courage, whilst you have anxious days in front of you do not get downhearted.
(10 February 1942)

Yesterday morning we received a cable from England notifying us that word had been received from Germany that Joe had been killed in action. This was quite a blow because we felt that when the news reached us that Joe was missing there was a good chance that he had baled out safely in Germany or France. This was not to be. There is no wailing in this household. We do not allow people to be sorry for us. We tell them "go and be sorry for those fathers and mothers who have sons who are still with them" because they did not see the issues involved in this war with clear sightedness or did not care. Joe knew what he was fighting for. He did not fight for the British Empire. He fought for a way of life which we believe is the only one worth remaining on this earth for. This way of life has not been fully realized by our peoples but it is the one thousands strive for … a way of life which does not make the individual a slave of the state … he does not live for the state the state is there for him … this way of life is for the weak as well as the strong … the weak to be protected by our laws and law administrators … not to be subject to force of brute strength … this way of life will mean someday God willing that there will be no discrimination between white or black or yellow man … a full freedom of action of speech … a way of life which will not make one man master of another either politically or economically. Leadership there will be but leadership for the benefit of the many not the few. (PJD 22 February 1942)

Of course we cannot realize that anything has happened to Joe. There are times when the stab of our loss is felt and there is that awful and terrible bleak feeling of a finality that nothing on this earth can change. Hardly a day passes without something happening that inspires the thought I must write Joe about that. I know this happens to May too. Nevertheless in our hearts we do not believe that he has gone from this Earth. Our reason tells us that no mistake could have occurred, our hearts still beat with the hope that a miracle could have happened. We do not build on this the way we did when we heard he was missing. Then there was a real chance but we were not to be amongst the lucky ones. However, the feeling will not [go] down and can do us no harm. The hardest thing to bear is when the flood of feeling about Joe, our

> love for him, his love for us, gives way, as it must from time to time, to the deadly routine of ordinary living and the feeling that nothing is changed, not even ourselves. This feeling does not last too long, thank God, Joe is with us most of the time and when he is with us we are at peace. We want to keep with us until we die the great joy that filled our hearts when we received Joe's last letter. It completed us. We felt that he had said everything that was to be said. He knew that it might be his last letter to us and sought to make life as full for us as it has been for him. We knew how much we loved him and that we were loved by him with all his dear heart. We are not bitter. Life has been rich and full for us we are determined it will not become mean or thin.
> (PJD 7 March 1942)

Condolence letters lamenting the fallen son of a nation at war began arriving within days. Many invoked the values of sacrifice, dedication, and valour, and the hope that these virtues would bring both victory and a better world.

> I do trust that with time, you will be helped to see it as a high promotion for your brave, handsome son to the rank of a true hero, worthy of honour and lasting remembrance by his country, and of just pride on the part of his parents and family, until they meet him again.

> There is solace in the reflection that he sacrificed his life in the greatest cause in all human history, and that his noble passing must be a great and abiding inspiration to all who knew him …

> You can be proud of what Joey has accomplished in his short life – of his loyalty and bravery and of the sacrifice he has made for his King and Country. We hope that it will not be in vain.

> All of us will always remember him as a hero and a son worthy of his parents – one who gave everything to preserve all he held dear.

> Every person who cherishes freedom but more particularly every Jew owes you a debt of gratitude.

> I am firmly convinced that it is better to die fighting than to contemplate living in a world dominated by Hitler and his gang but how much easier it would be to do the fighting oneself than to have to sit back while the ones so dear to us do the job.

Several American friends of the family quoted Lincoln's famous Civil War condolence letter. Those who knew Joe on the playing field wrote of his character and achievements:

> I always admired his sportsmanship and his "grit" which he apparently carried with him in the Air Force in the same manner as he had always done on the playing field.
>
> I have a very vivid memory of that single incident in one of the last of McGill's championship football games when your fine boy made such a brilliant play and helped so much to win the game. Now, he has done a much more brilliant thing in a more deadly game.... he will be spared most of the miseries and disillusionments of life, having experienced its most vitally happy years.

Joe's older cousin Harris, then training in the army to go overseas, wrote:

> He knew the time had come when every decent citizen was duty bound to fight for all the things we believe in, he saw his duty and seeing it undertook it.
>
> I consider it a privilege to have known such a fine young man; I am proud he was my cousin; had he lived he most certainly would have made an important place for himself, as things turned out we who knew him will always carry his memory and mention his name with reverence.... he had ... a magnetic personality that impressed everyone who ever came in contact with him. (25 February 1942)

Clara Bernhardt, with two brothers now in the air force overseas, wrote from Preston:

> I *do* know how a mother feels about these things, and how hard it is to see the boys go. Yet underneath all the anguish, there is an intangible satisfaction too, that they are not content, as so many are doing, to sit passively back and permit someone else to do the job that must be done. (8 February 1942)

She attached a poem, "Missing," that she had written only a month before for another friend.

Clara Lettice wrote from Woodhall Spa:

> I feel it as much as though he had been my own son, because we had been so happy together all the time he had been with me.... It seems so hard to understand, why these troubles are sent. I am trying to take it,

as I know Joe would wish us, his memory will always be to me a source of strength and inspiration, and I am trying to draw on that to sustain me. I shall always have the happy memory of Joe at Xmas, when we had a few friends in to supper, and the lovely speech he made later in the evening. I gave them as good a time as I possibly could, and both he and Roger thoroughly enjoyed themselves. I shall always feel thankful I had the privilege of knowing two such perfect gentlemen, everyone who came in contact with them loved them … (4 March 1942)

In the latter part of March, Percy and May again spent a few days in Ste. Agathe in the Laurentians.

> We came home to find considerable mail. Mail about Joe still comes in. There were several letters returned. These were the letters sent to Joe and received in England after he was missing. The sight of letters that would never be read by him brought home to us like nothing has so far the fact that we will never see Joe again. (PJD 22 March 1942)

> Letters still coming in from the other side about Joe. May is brick but I think the fact that we will not see Joe again is beginning to sink in … as time goes on we will not find it any too easy … each warns the other not to indulge in self pity for a minute … to keep of good countenance and be no less brave than Joe was … but it is damned hard sometimes. (PJD 27 March 1942)

Adjutor Savard, whom Joe had met in London, visited the Jacobsons the day he returned to Canada.

> He told us as much as he could about Joe. We already know how popular he was but we were particularly pleased by his remark that he found Joe a man of culture with a keen intelligence. We mentioned the fact that we had received several letters criticizing some aspects of Britain's war effort from him and that we were surprised the letters were allowed to pass by the Censor. He told us that all of them did not pass the censor and that there was quite a batch in the files of RCAF in London.[1] (PJD 29 March 1942)

Three weeks later, Percy and May received a letter from Robin Selfe's wife Winifred, questioning the information from German sources via the International Red Cross that

> Sergeants Hodgkinson and Harding and two unidentified other occupants of their aircraft were killed.… What I can't understand is where

> Joey's and Robin's identity discs were. They are proof against breakage and fire. Also why use the word "occupants." Surely it is usual to use the word "body" when someone has lost his life.
>
> It is on these two points and the fact that the Germans are liars that I pin my hopes. I do hope this note on the letter has not distressed you. Forgive me if I have raised false hopes.[2]

Percy commented:

> There still seems to be a little mystery about Joe and one of his pals. Evidently neither [has] been completely identified. The Germans reported Joe killed but no particulars. There is of course nothing to build any real hope on. Silly of us to think otherwise. Of course we feel he is still alive, how could we feel otherwise. Different when you see a dear one die before your eyes. Then you know. There is a finality about that that brooks no argument. (PJD 22 April 1942)

The conclusion became more inescapable with each letter, yet the particulars on which it was based remained tantalizingly incomplete and inconsistent. The specifics of the German information received by the Red Cross and forwarded to the Air Ministry were never communicated to the family. But with each revelation that could be interpreted as offering the faintest indication that not all was yet known, their hope could not be entirely extinguished.

> Thursday morning during breakfast a telegram came from our Government stating that for official purposes Joe was considered as killed. January 28th was the date given. We both feel that no official proclamation can kill Joe. He is as alive today as ever he was. In any case whether or not the millionth chance occurs and after the war Joe is discovered somewhere in Germany, Joe will live. In a broad sense I do not believe there is any dead. Body is destroyed. No spirit does. Well we feel that about Joey and Peter. French and English papers have been printing Joe's last letter written before his flight January 28th. This letter is a eulogy of his French Canadian pal Roger Rousseau who Joe believe[d] had been killed but was taken prisoner in Germany. He said that Roger had done more to create good feeling between French and English than all the propagandists in the country. (PJD 30 May 1942)

Joe's family would learn nothing more of his fate, or how and where he met it, or where he was buried, until after the war ended. Hope diminished, but despondency did not, as Percy recorded many times in the following years.

Thinking what would happen after the war if Joe had been alright. I promised in one of my letters he would not have come into the business unless he absolutely wanted to.… I know that there are some who think that the fact there is no one to carry on my business is of serious concern to me. It is not. My business has been a means to an end … a living. I have no love for the business in the sense that some men have. I always wanted Joe to lead a fuller life than I have. A life with more freedom. There would have been a year of travel in Canada for him, then some sort of leadership in regard to rehabilitation, and possibly an outlet for that crusading spirit against injustice and privilege which was his great concern during the past several months. (PJD 27 June 1942)

A silver cross from the government came yesterday.[3] It was addressed to May but I have not given it to her yet. It has Joe's name and is in commemoration of his sacrifice for his country. It means that officially Joe is now declared dead. It is insane on our part to still desperately cling to the chance that the Germans either have lied or are fooled. But we still cannot help feeling that way although our reason gives such a conjecture thumbs down. Somehow, the last two weeks have been more difficult than the period immediately after our bad news. (PJD 10 July 1942)

Last night dreamt the first really vivid dream, of Joe since the day in January when he was reported missing. I saw him clearly, spoke to him and put my arm around his shoulders. I tried to hold him. Peter was there also. (PJD 7 August 1943)

For the life of me I cannot feel that Joe is not on this earth. I cannot understand why I should still be so sure that he is alive. My reason and my feelings are at war. I know his mother feels exactly the same way. Until we see the grave he is buried [in] or the war has been over for at least a year I am sure that this feeling will persist. In the meanwhile there is Joe's estate to be wound up. I have been putting this off and off. (PJD 12 September 1942)

Today was sent by the Government a form to fill out for settling of Joe's estate. This business, and there will be more of the same sort of thing for some time to come, is difficult for me because I am not yet reconciled to the fact that Joe has actually gone.… I do not take these matters up with May until the need arises. It will arise because in a few months the estate will be wound up and she will have papers to sign. (PJD 29 September 1942)

Of all the official correspondence that followed the first dreaded telegram, the statement of official presumption of death was the harshest. For the authorities, it was an administrative decision required to wind up the casualty's estate and calculate his family's entitlements. For the family, it meant that their country could no longer offer any hope for them. They were left to grasp whatever slim reed of hope they could find, without aid. Some families resisted the decision and refused to accept it, although they could do nothing to reverse it.

> Armistice day.... My own feelings mixed. I think Remembrance Day the better term. I am still not willing to count Joe as lost so did not or could not make the day as of special personal significance. Common sense tells me I am foolish to hang on to this thread of hope and I know that when the boys come home it will be harder than if I would accept the inevitable now. (PJD 11 November 1943)

> ... I find myself very much like the man who has become resigned to functioning in a somewhat crippled condition. Soon I may even forget I am a cripple in the sense of losing two sons. I do not grieve, I do not seem to be able to feel the reflected glory of being Joe's father which helped me so much the first year of his loss. (PJD 9 January 1944)

Joe's room remained exactly as he had left it. His mother could not bear to alter it, in case by a miracle he should return. A year later, May found Joe's first diary, from 1936, in his desk drawer. Neither she nor Percy had ever seen it, and its contents were both a stunning reminder and a revelation.

> Joe was then nineteen years old. We knew that he kept a diary of his war years but this came as a surprise to us. It is [a] diary of a sensitive boy and in it is a beautiful tribute to his mother and his home life. It is almost as if someday he expected we would find it and realize how much his home meant to him and how great a love he bore both of us. He said some very moving and fine things about me. He idealized me but the things he said about his mother are absolutely true. For a while back I have felt as if my heart was hard as ice. This discovery melted me and both May and I went on a jag, we broke down, I think it did us both good. We still feel that we must live in the present and not escape into the past that means death to our souls. But Joe and Peter are the present. Portions of Joe's diary refer to Peter. He writes sweetly about

> how they were just beginning to be fully companionable when Peter was taken. Peter after all was three or four years younger than Joe. He dwells on the details of Peter's death and his insight into our feelings and his concern for both of us moved us deeply. I have tried my utmost not to idealize Joe, to see him clearly with all his faults but this diary shows clearly that I need not worry. The lad himself was as lovely a character as no legend could exaggerate. He was so understanding, so appreciative so full of the highest ideals of service that we should be indeed happy and proud parents to have had such a lad. God Bless him. (PJD 14 February 1943)
>
> I wrote yesterday about our discovery of Joe's diary.… The diary is very much in the rough, is spasmodic but one things stands out clearly and that is Joe's awareness of life of his determination to taste every bit of his living. I think that the reason he wrote so much about his happy family life was so that in years to come it might serve as a reminder of his happy youth.… This trait of self-examination and sensitiveness to his surroundings is the more remarkable because he was not by any means an introvert. He took his pleasures gaily and with a whole heart. He was of excellent physique and shone well in every sport … He had beautiful coordination. He also did well in dramatics. He acted in the college play. He was beginning to make a good speech. His personality was vibrant with life and he had a tremendous charm.…
>
> And today February 15th a young refugee, German born, educated for the five years previous to the war in England, interned by the British on the outbreak of the war afterwards sent to internee camp in Canada, then released to go to McGill as Engineering student is occupying Joe's room.[4] (PJD 15 February 1943)
>
> Joe's great pal Gerald Smith is back from England.… Now he is starting all over again training for aircrew. Fine boy. We look upon him as a son. He has brought back with him some things of Joe's, his diary, letters received from us and other records. (PJD 27 October 1943)

Joe's parents knew that he had kept diaries in England. But their eventual return to Canada had taken the efforts of several people with shrewd foresight and substantial good luck. In the weeks before he was killed, Joe was already thinking about how to ensure that his diaries and notebooks would return home even if he did not. This would not be a straightforward matter. When an airman failed to return, his belongings were sent immediately to the Air Ministry for clearance before return to next of kin. Joe knew very well that the daily diary that he had kept since the previous February, his operational diary, and the notebook in which he had recorded his critique of the bombing campaign, would be impounded. He might also have suspected the same fate for the November and December notebooks that contained his political and philosophical musings. Mrs. Lettice later told Joe's parents that, after Roger went missing, Joe packed up his own papers with the intention of giving them to Monty. This he apparently did when he visited Monty in London the week before his final flight.[5] Monty in turn gave these to Dan Kostoris for safekeeping, who advised Percy that he had

> put it in a sealed envelope to lock it up in my Bank until such time as we can arrange with the Canadian Authorities in London to post it on to you. We have spoken to them about this and they have promised to deal with the matter when we write to discuss it with them. Of course, I take it that the Authorities will have to read through it before they decide to let it go as there may be something of a Military nature so if you think it advisable for that Diary to be left in my Bank sealed up until such time as you want it back … my personal opinion would be to leave it here … (12 February 1942)

Monty missed the first chance to get the diaries home. Joe had passed some of Roger's things on to Adjutor Savard, but he returned to Canada on short notice at the end of March. Monty learned of his departure too late to give him Joe's diaries as well. So it was not until Gerald returned to Canada eighteen months later, that Joe's diaries and papers arrived home neither censored nor impounded. Whether Gerald was aware of the inspection procedures to which servicemen leaving Britain were subject, whether he just took a chance, or how he managed to avoid them, is lost in the mists of time.

> Yesterday, January 28th, was the second anniversary of the loss of Joe. I was home ill and spent the afternoon looking through his diary. It brought us together and I felt as if he was in the room with me.
> (PJD 29 January 1944)

> Peter [who had died of leukemia on this day in 1936] was unconscious of his doom. Joe was not. He planned for us. His letters, his diaries, his talks with Monty, all evidenced a supreme joy in living. He loved life. He did his best to get as much of living once he knew his sentence. His passionate desire to see all, know all was clear, also made it clear that he wanted to remain a part of our lives, he tried to plan for me a way of life … (PJD 13 March 1944)

Had another glance through Joe's diary and was again struck by his awareness of his chances of being killed. This diary of Joe's is very revealing of the inner man. It is very frank and very satisfying for me to have always with me. It is as if I carried around a part of Joe himself. This it really is. He mentions the fact that he always was afraid of the mere mention of death. But death faced at close quarters, as he faced it on several trips stripped him of his fear of it. Final pages of his diary he says, and I feel, honestly that this old fear of death has been effectively given its quietus. He also sums up his life and is satisfied it has been a full and happy one. (PJD 18 April 1944)

Read again some parts of Joe's diary. This referred to his numerous flights over Germany. It covers the last half of 1941 … Joe's last half for ever … that is if the millionth part of hope which we still hold fails … when we overrun Germany we may find some remarkable instances of reported killed and missing being still alive … perhaps Joe might be … my reason tells me "no" but hope dies hard.

This diary of Joe's is sometimes sad, sometimes is very gay and is always honest. For an extravert it is remarkable because he does seem to strive for truth about himself. (PJD 10 September 1944)

We had a thread of hope that Joe might be discovered alive in Germany. This now seems impossible. There is a new organization founded with the objective of finding out as much data as possible about boys, like Joe, who have been given up for dead but with actual proof not available … so far.[6] Roger Rousseau's brother has telephoned us that Roger has landed at Halifax. He has been a prisoner of war for three years.… When [Joe] heard he was lost he made up his mind that this meant the end for Roger. This was not the case. Roger was saved and became a prisoner of war. Joe lost his life a few weeks after Roger was reported missing. A nephew of ours, Lionel Silver, also a prisoner of war, is expected home any day. I find no trace of bitterness on the part of May because of our, shall we call it bad luck. Her nature is indeed a beautiful one. (PJD 10 June 1945)

Last Wednesday I invited Roger Rousseau, Monty Berger, Gerald Smith and May for lunch at the Windsor. The three boys loved Joe. We felt warmed by their presence. We all talked freely about Joe.
(PJD 2 December 1945)

Late that year, the Jacobsons donated an annual scholarship in Joe's name to McGill University. And in late November they received notice from the RCAF, citing information from a Canadian Graves Registration Unit, of Joe's burial place in Holland.

> Yesterday we received from the Government Operational Wings and Certificate in recognition of "gallant Service rendered by your son Flight Sergeant J A Jacobson."
>
> These wings are given for operations against the enemy and we are proud to have Joe's well done job acknowledged. He is of course only one of thousands of our boys who did the right thing because in their hearts they knew it was the only thing they could do and maintain their integrity and respect for themselves.
>
> Last Wednesday March 13th was the anniversary of Peter's tragic death a death far more tragic and far more senseless than Joe's. Joe lived to enjoy something of life and he died a man. Peter was only a boy. Both were fine lads. God Bless them. (PJD 17 March 1946)

Near the end of January 1948, the RCAF sent Joe's flying log, which was part of his service estate, to his parents. Sometime later that year, the Commonwealth War Graves Commission inquired if the Jacobsons desired a personal inscription for Joe's headstone in the Netherlands. Percy supplied the following, which is duly inscribed:

> A Loving Son and Brother
> A warm friend
> His courage came not easily …
> He had it in need

Undoubtedly Percy composed it. He of all Joe's family would have been most aware of how Joe had managed to nurture and sustain his courage all through the period of his enlistment, training, and combat. Perhaps reflecting a lingering unwillingness to accept that Joe had not survived the first night he was reported missing, Percy supplied Joe's age at death as 24 years, as appears on his headstone in Lichtenvoorde General Cemetery. In fact he was twenty days short of his 24th birthday on that night.

After six years of reflection on Joe's life, Percy had returned to the enigmatic observation he had made in his own diary on 28 September 1940, when Joe first flew in training in Saskatchewan. Of all Joe's virtues, this was the one that Percy held in the highest regard: not simply raw physical courage but the moral courage of one's convictions. He had commented on that as the enormity of the Nazi extermination program was being revealed:

> I remember that Joe refused leave for the Jewish New Year and Day of Atonement because he felt that it was more important to pay some of his debts to the Germans than to celebrate the sacred days. He hated the Germans on two scores. What they had done to his people. What they were trying to do to the liberty which meant more to him than his life. He gave his life on both counts. I still owe a debt to Joe. I hope when my turn comes I will not repudiate it, even should it cost me my life. (PJD 20 December 1942)

That a father could feel indebted to his son's courage and sacrifice, indeed be humbled by it, was the ultimate gift. Whatever Joe might have achieved had he survived, his triumph of courage was what he did achieve. Nothing else could have given his father greater pride and satisfaction.

Joe's headstone, Lichtenvoorde General Cemetery, 4 May 2008. "A Loving Son and Brother. A Warm Friend. His Courage Came Not Easily … He Had It in Need." (Peter J. Usher photo)

Thirty-One

Holland

A bitter and exceptional cold spell hung over much of Europe in late January 1942, even attracting the notice of the *Montreal Gazette* on the 22nd. At Lichtenvoorde, a Dutch town of a few thousand near the German border, daily temperatures had been below freezing continuously since early January. The cold reached its greatest intensity before dawn on the 27th, when the thermometer fell to –27.4°C, the lowest temperature ever recorded in the Netherlands. The cold spell broke the next day as a warm front pressed in from the west, creating the catastrophic conditions that prevailed aloft on the night of the 28th.

That night, several people near Vragender, a small village northeast of Lichtenvoorde, heard a low-flying aircraft. As Bernard Nijland remembered the circumstances,

> On the night of the 28th, around 7PM, I went to Beneman's in Vragender to get salt, because we had to slaughter a pig which had to be pickled. It was extremely cold outside and there was blowing snow. You could not see in front of you. When I was back home around 2015, I heard a heavy creaking in the pine stand behind our house. Shortly before that we heard a plane come over very low altitude. I wanted to go take a look but I was not allowed by my wife. The reason being it was past eight o'clock and therefore dangerous.[1]

Hendrik Gunnewick recalled that on that same night, he and Beneman,

> who had a grocery shop with adjoining pub at Vragender returned home from a clandestine pig slaughter at Lievelde. Walking on the

> Schansweg they heard a noise from the air. They said to each other: "the Tommies are active again." Then they heard creaking in the firwood. Both men made off very quickly, as it was after eight o'clock, the curfew hour.

Others claim they heard the aircraft pass overhead twice. To the north, a few people heard bombs fall that night. Mr. Wegman, head of Air Warden Command Post, filed an incident report the next morning, stating that

> at least one bomb had fallen at around 2145 in a pine forest near the back road between Groenlo and Aalten.... No personal injuries reported. In addition there are two possibly unexploded bombs.[2]

Mr. Wegman, accompanied by policeman Ter Haar, investigated the next morning. They found evidence of two bomb blasts and several shattered trees. The blast had broken some windows in at least three farmhouses within six hundred metres. While conducting their investigation, Wegman and Ter Haar were told that a plane had been heard to crash the previous night. Following up on this information, they found that an aircraft had indeed come down east of Lichtenvoorde. They arrived at the site before lunch to find what they identified as a bomber, probably English, "completely destroyed" at the edge of a pine bush. They could see that there were at least two dead in the aircraft. Wegman went to the town hall to make a report, while Ter Haar stayed to guard the aircraft. At 2:30 that afternoon, the commander of the local occupation force arrived from Borculo and found that there were probably three dead in the aircraft. He ordered the aircraft to be placed under constant guard until the Wehrmacht arrived.

Wegman and Ter Haar were not the first ones to discover the aircraft, however. There are at least five accounts of individuals happening upon, or searching for, the downed aircraft. Theo Te Walvaart, of Lievelde, then about twenty-two years old, went rabbit hunting at about 8:30 on the morning of the 29th. He saw the plane with the RAF roundel on the fuselage, although he thought at first that it was a Dutch aircraft. He assumed he was the first person who came upon the aircraft because there were no footprints in the snow around it. Bernard Nijland, who had heard the aircraft the night before, also discovered the wreck when he ventured out in the morning. He may have been the second on the scene.

> I went to take a look and saw the plane, within it four dead flyers, of which the first one was missing half of his forehead. And so I ran away fast and almost had to throw up.

Mr. Klein-Gebbink, of Vragender, having heard about an aircraft that had crashed in the neighbourhood, went to the crash site with some others between 8:30 and 10:00 that morning. They found the wreck with the airmen still in it, but saw no sign of life. They also noticed oranges in the nose of the aircraft. Leo Paashuis and Joop Kruip, who lived in Lichtenvoorde, hopped on their bicycles to look for the crash that morning. As they recalled over fifty years afterwards, that was the first airplane they had ever seen. They saw four men, "two by two," all dead, heads bent forward. The Germans came along and ordered them to go away, but they stayed there until the bodies were removed from the wreck. After the Germans left, they returned to photograph the downed aircraft from a distance. Gunnewick and Minkhorst went to the crash site between 10:00 and 10:30 that morning, and saw from a distance a man, probably a German soldier, who gesticulated "Beat it!"

Still others remembered these events from their childhood, when interviewed sixty-five years later. Some recalled gasoline visible in the snow, some remembered the bodies in their flying suits, some remembered the Germans behaving disrespectfully toward the dead flyers, some claimed the snow was thirty centimetres deep. At least one person thought he had heard the engines cutting out, then coming on and revving up again before the crash, and also that the aircraft was in at least three pieces on the ground. Almost everyone recalls the event occurring on the coldest night of the year, although in fact the cold spell had broken the day before, and the temperature had probably not fallen below zero since the crash. Passhuis's and Kroop's photos show the aircraft bare of snow, and crop stubble sticking up through the snow. The snow cover on the field cannot have been deep.

Some time on the 29th, Dr. W. Hardy, Lichtenvoorde's general practitioner, was sent to investigate the scene, accompanied by two German authorities. He found four bodies in the aircraft. None had been thrown clear of the wreck, and none had escaped it after impact. Hardy determined that they had all died of injuries sustained on impact and that there was no evidence of injury from anti-aircraft fire. Interviewed many years later, Dr. Hardy stated that all four were in or near the cockpit. One had suffered a skull fracture and obvious brain injury. He added:

> I am of the opinion that if I had been there the same night, I could possibly have saved two of them, but because of the crash and loss of blood and severe cold they probably froze to death.

Dr. Hardy was also accompanied by Mr. A. Hummelink, a coffin-maker then seventeen years old. He had been ordered to make four coffins for the

Leo Passhuis's photo of AT122 on the morning of 29 January 1942, probably looking southeast, from over the handlebar of his bicycle, near Lievelde. (Courtesy Mrs. Leo Passhuis)

Leo Passhuis's photo of AT122 on the morning of 29 January 1942, probably looking northeast. (Courtesy Mrs. Leo Passhuis)

Belgian labourers dismantling the wreck of AT122 shortly after the crash. (AVOG Crash Museum)

dead flyers, but at first could make only three due to a shortage of wood. Hummelink, along with others including the town's gravedigger, returned to the crash site by horse-drawn wagon. They returned their cargo of three coffins, along with one body wrapped in a shroud and laid on a plank, to the mortuary at St. Bonifatius Hospital before dark.

When the bodies arrived at the hospital, the German authorities demanded their flying suits. The attending nurse refused this demand, and insisted that the flyers be buried in their battle dress as they had been found. No identification tags were found on the bodies. However, a number of personal effects were discovered during the crash investigation. These included a parachute bag, a tin box, a wristwatch, a comb, a couple of knitted gloves, a Player's cigarette case, a photo of one of the men with (presumably) his wife, a clasp, and a book: *The Rights of Man* by Thomas Paine. Apparently none of these items, which were all taken by the German authorities, served to identify any of the dead airmen at the time.

Three or four days later, conscripted Belgian labourers were brought in to break up the aircraft. The pieces were taken to the nearby railway crossing at Lievelde and loaded onto flatbed railcars destined for the Ruhr. There the remains of AT122 would be recycled into new armament that Germany could turn against its original manufacturers.

The copy of *The Rights of Man* that was found in the aircraft was Joe's. Perhaps he had taken it along as a talisman, or even to snatch a few minutes reading on the journey home. The wristwatch and knitted gloves were very likely Selfe's. As both Selfe and Hodgkinson were married, the photo of the couple could have belonged to either of them. Very likely the Germans destroyed the book and the photos, but kept the watch and gloves.

◉

Germany had attacked and occupied the Netherlands in May 1940, despite its neutrality, to facilitate an attack on France and eventually England. Hitler regarded the Dutch as Germanic fellow-racials, and he had no desire to enslave or eliminate them as he was already planning to do to the Poles. But the Dutch were a patriotic, religious, and largely conservative people, who did not see themselves as Germans and had no sympathy with Naziism. As the Netherlands had surrendered at the outset, most saw no alternative to accommodating the occupation and continuing their civic duties, however reluctantly. But there was widespread resentment when the Germans replaced the authority of the Queen with that of an Austrian Nazi, and sought to Nazify them through the media and the schools. Organizing for resistance, especially violent resistance, was a skill the Dutch people had not needed to hone for centuries. But many Dutch citizens engaged in small acts of defiance: flying the orange colour of the royal family, naming their daughters after Wilhelmina and Juliana, and listening to the BBC news.

By late 1941, all political parties had been outlawed except for the Dutch Nazi Party (NSB). But by that time, it was becoming apparent that neither the English nor the Russians were in imminent danger of becoming the next victims. There seemed to be less need to accommodate the occupation, and more hope that an Allied victory would end it.

The Germans exercised local control of the civilian population through the offices of the burgomeisters, the appointed mayors of municipalities. Traditionally the burgomeisters represented the Crown, and they were the senior local administrators, often responsible for supervising the police. Because the Netherlands had surrendered so quickly, its government had made no preparations for a prolonged occupation. The civil administration, with all its necessary records, thus came under the control of the occupiers intact. A system of identity documents to be produced on demand, and of ration cards, was soon put in place. In 1941, the German authorities began replacing burgomeisters, often with members of the tiny Dutch Nazi Party. The membership of the NSB consisted of at least as many opportunists as committed Nazi ideologues. Few had any training or experience for the job, and they were widely regarded with contempt by the citizenry.

In early 1942 the Germans were not yet ransacking Europe for food and labour, but they were tightening the screws on opposition, non-compliance, and especially harbouring or assisting enemy airmen. In response, non-co-operation and defiance were becoming resistance, and resistance was becoming organized. The more that courage became necessary, the more it was forthcoming. A key form of resistance was going underground. Tens and eventually hundreds of thousands of Dutch citizens, including some Jews but a much greater number of people who sought to avoid collaboration or labour conscription, would become *onderduikers*, literally, "underdivers." They had to find hiding places and false papers. A network began to form of people who arranged for and did the things necessary to protect their fellow countrymen. Many onderduikers went to the agricultural districts, where they were hidden in rural farmhouses for the duration. The churches, both Protestant and Catholic, provided moral and even practical support. But this form of resistance was not without risks. Failure to produce the proper identity papers was cause for arrest. Careless talk in public places could lead to betrayal, incarceration, and even execution. The occupation would become more harsh and cruel as the months passed. But at the beginning of 1942, rural municipalities in relatively isolated areas were feeling the yoke of occupation more lightly than the main cities. The flat, carefully tended landscape, criss-crossed by roads and railways, with only a few small patches of forest, offered little cover to conceal organized partisan and resistance activities. The Germans required only a modest occupation force to maintain control over the rural population.

In January 1942, the Lichtenvoorde area was patrolled by a small Wehrmacht unit in nearby Borculo. Several radar and searchlight batteries had been constructed in the area during the previous few months as part of Germany's Kammhuber line of air defence. The office of the burgomeister had been vacant for over a year. The previous occupant had retired, but had not yet been replaced. Meanwhile the town's employees, none of them members of the NSB, carried on with their work. There was no organized resistance network in Lichtenvoorde as yet, but a few committed individuals had already begun to hide and protect onderduikers, and the hopes of the citizenry rested with the Allies.

Such was the situation when, for the first time in the war, an Allied bomber crashed close to Lichtenvoorde, from unknown cause, killing all four of its unidentified crew. The news of this extraordinary event spread quickly, and seems to have galvanized a spirit of resistance among the citizenry. Some individuals had already acted in small ways with courage and conviction. Many more saw in this event the occasion to set aside their fears for personal safety. Sullen compliance became active defiance. So it was that the municipality of Lichtenvoorde arranged to honour the unknown men of AT122 by staging a funeral far removed from the simple military burial normally conducted by the Luftwaffe.

The funeral was held on Sunday, 1 February. The procession began on the hospital grounds, where each coffin was placed in its own horse-drawn hearse. Two of these were provided by the Catholic Church, with the horses wearing black hoods in the local fashion, the other two by funeral homes in Lichtenvoorde and nearby Groenlo. Two members of the local police force led the procession of the four carriages and a unit of about fifteen German soldiers from the hospital grounds down the Dijkstraat to the town's General Cemetery. Seven to eight hundred people followed solemnly under overcast skies and light snow.

Lichtenvoorde's small General Cemetery (for its non-Catholic minority) was, and still is, surrounded by a rectangle of tall trees. Many people climbed into these trees to get a better view. The graveside oration was given by Rev. Van Dongen, minister of Lichtenvoorde's Reform Church:

> How did these heroes fall and lose their weapons? We are standing here at the graves of four men fallen in the struggle for their fatherland. We don't know anything else. Their religion is unknown, it is unknown if they are sons of loving mothers, or if they are fathers of children at home, who ask their mother, where is father? All this is hidden from us. Yes, it is not even known if their relatives even know that they are missing. All this makes it impossible to say something about them. Except this one thing. That they have fallen for a cause which they know is a just cause.
>
> In similar fashion, friends and enemies are standing here at the graves around the remains of these fallen flyers. And both honour them in their own way. Both must have been convinced that these people fought for a cause which they considered to be a just cause. If we leave the correctness or incorrectness of their conviction aside, we can still determine this, that these men considered the centuries old freedom to be an inalienable right. That several of their comrades and who knows they themselves also knew to fight for a cause which centres around the principle of whether there will be freedom to preach God's word and to follow God's word in daily life. We thus stand at these graves as friends and enemies of these people, and we honour them in their fashion.[3]

Rev. Van Dongen read an elegy from the Old Testament and a song of victory from the New Testament. Wreaths were placed at the graves. The German soldiers honoured their fallen enemies with a military ceremony, firing rifle shots in the air. The coffins were lowered into the four graves dug the day or so before. Thus were the unknown airmen committed to the earth.

The horse-drawn hearses of the crew of AT122 at the head of the funeral procession on 1 February 1942, Lichtenvoorde. (AVOG Crash Museum)

The townspeople of Lichtenvoorde in the funeral procession, 1 February 1942. (AVOG Crash Museum)

The funeral service for the crew of AT122, Lichtenvoorde General Cemetery, 1 February 1942. (AVOG Crash Museum)

On the day of the funeral, the newly appointed burgomeister, NSB member Lamers, arrived at the town hall for his installation. He found no one there except two civil servants, who told him that a funeral for British airmen was under way. Lamers proceeded to the funeral. On arrival, he made a Hitler salute, to the astonishment of the townspeople to whom he was as yet unknown.

Two men secretly recorded these events on film. Albert Westerman was an important and influential person in Lichtenvoorde. His family owned a knitwear factory. Then thirty years old, he was one of the few people in town with a movie camera. He immediately resolved to create a visual record of the events, in the hope that at some future time the parents of the airmen the town was about to honour would be able to see the funeral. As he recalled many years later, the funeral was a protest, "to make a difference between good and evil, to show sympathy with the British airmen who had made a contribution to free us, we valued these people so highly."[4] Hiding in an attic in a building across the street, through a small window Westerman filmed the coffins being brought to the hospital, and the departure of the funeral procession three days later. Another local photographer, Mr. Wekking, was among those who had scaled the trees at the cemetery, and from that high vantage point he filmed and photographed the funeral.

The cost of the coffins, wreaths, and hearses amounted to 538.50 guilders, a significant sum in those days. The town submitted a bill for these expenses to the German authorities, which they duly paid. The newly appointed burgomeister was not amused by Rev. Van Dongen's oration. After the funeral, Lamers sent for his arrest. The next day, Van Dongen went to the town hall, where he provided notes of his speech, and was interrogated but let go. A few months later he was ordered to appear again before the burgomeister, who interrogated him again, and incarcerated him in a cell in the town hall. Van Dongen was sent to prison in Arnhem in August 1942, where he spent the next six months before being transferred to concentration camps at Amersfoort and Vught. He was released in March 1943.

The funeral at Lichtenvoorde was an exceptional if not indeed unique event during the years of occupation. With the burgomeister's office vacant, the town authorities, including the policemen who would later participate directly in the resistance, were relatively free to act. The nearby occupation authorities either could not or chose not to prevent the community from conducting the funeral. When local people had approached the aircraft and took photos the morning after the crash, they were merely waved away. A year later they might well have been shot on sight. The burial of the airmen would have been kept under strict control of the occupying authorities. Certainly there could have been no public funeral, much less an oration such as Van Dongen's. And indeed, there was no repetition of a public funeral when three other Allied aircraft suffered a similar fate near Lichtenvoorde in 1943.[5]

Rev. Van Dongen's funeral oration focused on the unknown identities of the fallen airmen. Why none was wearing his air force identity disc, in accordance with procedure, is unknown. The photos of the funeral clearly show four separate graves. Either at the time, or soon afterwards, they were marked with a single cross, labelled "4 Engelsche Vliegers." A photo taken shortly after the war ended shows three names on the main cross, with a smaller marker below for Harding alone.

How the Germans actually identified Harding's body, and how they determined Hodgkinson's identity, is unknown.[6] Possibly one or both had some other identifying items in their clothing. It appears that neither Selfe nor Jacobson did. At the end of the war, in order to determine the fate of its airmen lost over Europe, the RAF sent Missing Research and Enquiries Units, and Grave Registration units into the newly liberated territories. These agencies had more or less completed their work by late 1946. During that time, the Lichtenvoorde graves were exhumed, but the individual identities of Hodgkinson, Jacobson, and Selfe were not established as a result. In accordance with the practice of the Commonwealth War Graves Commission, where the individual identity of crews cannot be determined, their headstones are placed in alphabetical order. And so to this day, the three airmen are recorded as buried in a collective grave, and are identified on their headstones, left to right, as Hodgkinson, Jacobson, and Selfe.

When Percy and May Jacobson travelled to Europe in July 1950, they arranged through the Netherlands War Graves Committee to visit Joe's grave. It was then still a most unusual event in Lichtenvoorde to receive visitors from abroad. Burgomeister Waals met them at the railway station and brought them to his home for lunch. They met Ter Haar, the now retired policeman who had found the wreck, and Hendrik Leemreize, whom Percy described in his diary as an "underground worker of fame." Leemreize took them to visit his parents' farm, then to the cemetery to see Joe's grave, then to visit Albert Westerman, who showed them the film of the funeral, and finally back to the burgomeister's for supper. There they heard more accounts of the occupation years, and the lingering bitterness about the "Quisling Dutch," who went unpunished afterwards. The Jacobsons boarded the train for Amsterdam at 8:00 that night.

It had been a full day for them, and a deeply emotional one as the photograph at the cemetery reveals. May made no mention of her feelings in her diary, but Percy wrote:

> Ordeal for May when we were shown moving reel of Joe's funeral and burial … coming back in train May looked white my heart went out to her.… Tough day but lightened by goodness and kindness of all we met. (PJD 30 and 31 July 1950)

Both commented profusely on their hosts' bravery during the occupation and their generosity on that day.

Their visit was an important occasion for those in Lichtenvoorde who had begun the story over eight years before. Leemreize had subsequently sheltered a number of downed airmen and spirited them to safety. He had also taken on the task of caring for Joe's grave without knowing anything about him. Now he was meeting his parents. Westerman had dreamed that he would one day be able to show them the events he had secretly filmed, and on this day his dream came true. Not only had he survived the occupation, so had his movie film. According to their hosts, the Commonwealth War Graves Commission had initially suggested moving the graves to a common air force burial ground, but the town refused. These were Lichtenvoorde's graves to care for, theirs to remind them of what they owed to the dead flyers, and of what they had risked to honour those dead flyers and to protect and save the survivors who later parachuted down in their midst.[7]

Percy died the following year, but May, "the Jewish mother from Canada," returned several times in the early 1950s to visit the Waals, the Leemreizes, and her son's grave. And so May came to know Hendrik's wife, Anna, after they married in 1954, and their only son, Theo. She remained in touch with Anna for years afterwards, and left a small sum to the benefit of their son Theo. Over fifty years later, he still had the small gifts she had given him. In this way, Joe's mother also became part of the Lichtenvoorde story.

Stories have a way of changing and growing over time. Previously untold parts are added, some memories are triggered but others fade. So too does the evidence disappear from the landscape. The site of the crash no longer resembles the photos taken seventy years ago, although the bomb craters can still be seen in a forest that was once a field. Artifacts from the wreckage are displayed at the local Crash Museum, devoted to Allied bombers who met their fate in the vicinity.

About fifty years after the event, another element was recorded. Willem Geurink of Lichtenvoorde had been a member of the resistance, and had hidden people during the war. He was a neighbour of the Leemreizes, and knew them well. In 1993 he began setting down his memories of the occupation in a memoir and in a series of letters to his family. By then Hendrik Leemreize had died, but his wife, Anna, whom he had married some years after the war, was still alive. In his letters, Willem explained the importance of Joe Jacobson's grave to Anna, and why she continued to place flowers on it every year.

According to Geurink, Joe was shot down twice near Lichtenvoorde. The first time, he had parachuted to safety and was picked up by the resistance. He spent several nights at the Leemreizes in their concealed basement. Then Hendrik and some others took him halfway across the Netherlands to Baarle-Nassau near the Belgian border. There he was passed on to resistance people from Belgium. Only when Joe was shot down a second time, this time fatally, did Leemreize learn that the Belgian resistance had succeeded in returning Joe to England. It was for his role in saving Joe the first time, among other acts, according to Geurink, that Hendrik Leemreize had been decorated after the war, and this was why the Leemreizes had forged such a bond with the Jacobsons.

Could this story be true? There is no record of an Allied bomber being shot down near Lichtenvoorde before 28 January 1942, nor is there any record of successful evasion and return to England by airmen from that

Left: Hendrik Leemreize with May and Percy Jacobson at Joe's grave, Lichtenvoorde General Cemetery, 30 July 1950. (AVOG Crash Museum)

Below: The graves of the crew of AT122, Lichtenvoorde General Cemetery, probably early 1950s. (Canadian Jewish Archives)

part of the Netherlands before that date. Between Joe's diaries and his letters, there is no mention of anything remotely like this – indeed from those sources alone one can account for every day of his life from his arrival in England to his death in the Netherlands nine months later. There is nothing in the records of his operational training unit or his squadron that might support this account.

Even if Joe had come down a second time at Lichtenvoorde, how would Hendrik Leemreize have known it was him? Joe carried no identification and no one knew who he was. Leemreize is never mentioned as a witness to the crash, so only if he had gained admittance to the hospital and viewed the bodies could he have possibly recognized Joe. And although Percy and May both recorded their visit to Lichtenvoorde in detail, including their visit with the Leemreizes and seeing the film, they made no mention of this story. If it had happened, surely Leemreize would have told them about it, and surely Percy and May would have recorded it.

What then accounts for this story? Resistance people in the Lichtenvoorde area did begin assisting downed airmen the following year by sheltering and then escorting them to contacts in Belgium, whence the evaders would be passed along a chain through France to Spain or Portugal, as the more direct route via the Dutch coast was heavily fortified and guarded. Hendrik Leemreize was indeed prominent among those involved in *pilotenhulp*, as the rescue of downed airmen was called. He would escort groups of airmen by train, buying successive short-trip tickets so it would not appear that anyone was taking a long journey if asked for his ticket. But this system required more than just individuals finding and sheltering airmen. It required a trusted network of escorts and couriers across the country and into Belgium, and that was not yet in place in January 1942. None of the very few attempts to help downed airmen in eastern Netherlands before that time succeeded in returning them to safety.[8] It appears that the funeral was a pivotal event in welding a dozen or so key people in Lichtenvoorde into an effective organization that in the following years rescued dozens of Allied airmen. Yet no one talked about such doings at the time because no one knew whom to trust. Some in the network were betrayed and executed. By 1944, the occupation authorities regarded Lichtenvoorde as "Little England" on account of its efforts, but they were largely unable to break the network and it continued rescuing Allied airmen for the remainder of the war. Leemreize said little about his resistance work even after the war, although he was later recognized and decorated for his efforts.[9] So far as is known, however, there was no instance of a downed airman being rescued in eastern Netherlands and then crashing in the vicinity a second time, at any time in the war.

After fifty or sixty years, the details of events may be telescoped, conflated, or confused in memory. That in no way detracts from the importance of the Allied airmen's funeral on 1 February 1942 in galvanizing local resistance for the next three years. At least for some, the second coming of Joe Jacobson, born of a Jewish mother, has become a part of that story. And for the Leemreizes, Joe Jacobson was a symbol of wartime resistance. The specifics of what the Lichtenvoorde resisters were able to do at any particular time are less important than that they did indeed act with courage, selflessness, and at great personal risk during the occupation. The resisters succeeded in returning many Allied airmen to safety, and each in his or her individual capacity contributed to victory and liberation.

The crash of AT122 and the funeral honours for its crew that Lichtenvoorde insisted upon during the occupation are memorialized to this day. The story has been recorded in books, articles, and film, and recounted from time to time on television and in newspapers.[10] Every year on 4 May, Memorial Day in the Netherlands, the people of Lichtenvoorde gather in St. Bonifatius church by the hundreds for the town's remembrance service for both Dutch servicemen and civilians killed in the war, and for the RAF flyers who lost their lives in the vicinity. Those hundreds follow the same route to the General Cemetery as did the funeral procession for Harding, Hodgkinson, Jacobson, and Selfe. Following a brief ceremony, the town's children place flowers on the graves of the twenty-three Bomber Command flyers buried there. The people of Lichtenvoorde have forgotten neither their own resistance to occupation and oppression at a terrible time in their history, nor those from afar who died in battle for their eventual release from tyranny.

Thirty-Two

Epilogue

Nearly six years of war had left Percy numb and exhausted. The revelations of brutality and horror in Europe that emerged in the war's final days seemed beyond belief. Yet in Percy's eyes, too many of his fellow citizens remained oblivious and complacent. Percy had made periodic reference to his disappointments about local events during the war, not least about continuing anti-Jewish prejudice, and whether Joe's life was a sacrifice in vain. Had those six years of horrific struggle amounted to so little in Canada? It was now urgent to begin work on peacetime reconstruction, as Joe and Monty had so earnestly believed and fought for.

> My own feelings were mixed. I was glad … that is putting it mildly for the millions of people who could again feel with relief that their own were safe. I knew that I had in my thoughts rather feared the day when the realization of our personal loss would be … well I will leave it at that … I just felt lost for a while. I sat in Murrays drinking coffee for an hour, then walked along St. Catherine Street watching the crowds celebrate.… We closed our offices at noon. I went home to lunch in the usual way. Arranged to send some V Day flowers, red and white, to May whom I knew was feeling very much the same as I felt. We spent the afternoon quietly together.… Sounds a very trite description of one of the greatest days in history but my spirits were flat and I am not going to embellish this account with stuff that I did not feel.
> (PJD 7 May 1945)

Percy continued both his business and literary activities after the war, but rarely maintained his diary. In the summer of 1950 he represented Canada at the annual PEN International conference in Edinburgh after he and May visited Joe's grave in Holland. Percy had been in failing health and died the next year, surely in part of a broken heart. May survived Percy by twenty-five years. She wore Joe's operational wings as a brooch until her dying day. She treasured them as a tribute to Joey himself, above the Memorial Cross, which she had received in recognition of her own loss, and which she seldom, if ever, wore.

Monty Berger (whose father would soon become an air force chaplain) went on to an illustrious military career as an intelligence officer in a fighter squadron. Throughout the war, he continued to correspond with the Jacobsons, whom he held in high regard as they did him. Like them, he often recalled Joe's spirit for inspiration. Monty would write, on each anniversary of Joe's final flight, of the intensity of their bond during those few months in England, and their idealistic hopes for the new world they were fighting for. Responding to a letter from Percy about discouraging news on the political front in Canada, he said to the Pony Club:

> I remember saying in the early days to many people, and especially to Joe, "I begin fighting when this war is over." With 2½ years of war-weariness away from home, I find my resolve not weakening, but strengthening, and strengthening immeasurably. I have seen the elite of this generation go off never to return, and someone somewhere with fight, only if mental rather than physical, and with good heart, must carry on. (9 January 1944)

Monty never abandoned the idea of the play that he and Joe had discussed. They had intended it to be based on their own experience, but Monty now wanted to draw on Joe's character and outlook, based on his letters and notes, and to draw a moral from Joe's sacrifice. He hoped to complete it with Percy's assistance, when the duress of his wartime duties might allow.

> The message we want to get across … still stands, more indelibly clear than ever. It shines as a beacon light and cannot fail and its value as a guide does not less[en] for, alas, the gloom about is just as thick as ever … (29 January 1944).

Monty returned to journalism after the war with the *Montreal Gazette*, but later went into public relations. In 1965 he sought the Liberal Party's nomination in the federal riding of Mount Royal, but was defeated by Pierre Trudeau. The play never did get written, but neither did Monty forget it.

He talked to me about it sixty years later, when he gave me the Pony Club letters he had kept all that time.

Gerald Smith arrived in England in the spring of 1942 to serve as a radar technician. The next year he re-mustered to aircrew, and returned to Canada to train as a navigator. By the time he completed his training, the air force no longer needed new men from overseas. After the war, he became a senior manager in the women's retail clothing business in Montreal. Herb Ross enlisted in the United States Army. After taking basic training at Fort Bragg, North Carolina, he served in North Africa, India, and Burma. The three surviving members of the Pony Club remained in contact for the rest of their lives.

Joe's older sister Edith married soon after Joe was killed, and her husband later took over Percy's office furniture business. Janet married an American in 1948. After he died, she returned to Montreal and married Gerald Smith, who had recently become a widower. She visited Joe's grave for the first time in 2013.

Joe's cousin Lionel (Ray) Silver, an air observer in 10 Squadron, was shot down on the famous "Thousand Raid" on Cologne on 31 May 1942. He spent two weeks in the hands of the Gestapo before being turned over to the Luftwaffe authorities. He spent the next three years as a prisoner of war, chiefly in Stalag Luft III whence the Great Escape was mounted. In January 1945 he endured the long march westward that the Germans forced on their prisoners as the Russians advanced on the Eastern Front. He resumed his career in journalism after the war, and he was an active member of the Canadian Ex-Air Force Prisoners-of-War Association to the end of his days in 2001.

Every member of the McGill Redmen team who played in the championship game on 19 November 1938 enlisted within the next three years. Seven did not return. Those who survived took up the professions for which they had trained, or went into business. Many of them rose to prominence in Canadian life.

Roger Rousseau spent the rest of the war in a series of German prisoner of war camps, ending at Stalag Luft IV in Pomerania, where he was beaten and bayonetted. In the dead of winter of 1945, he survived the same forced march to the west that the Germans inflicted on all captive Allied airmen. He finally received an RCAF commission when he was repatriated to Canada in 1945. He went on to a distinguished career in the diplomatic service and was the chief of the Montreal Olympic Committee in 1972. He died in 1980.

All of the Hell Hooters became casualties. Aside from Joe and Roger, Mac Keswick was killed in training in 1941, and Jeep McLean was killed in action in 1942. Les Jupp and Cliff Chappell were captured in 1942, and Art Hunter in 1943. Les and Art spent the remainder of the war in German prisoner of war camps. Cliff was part of a spectacular escape from an Italian PoW camp to Allied lines in 1943. Over half of the seventy-four air observers who graduated from Rivers in February 1941 became casualties of the war, thirty being killed in action and another twelve taken prisoners of war. The casualty rate was much the same for all of the air observers who had arrived in England in the spring of 1941.

Henriette and Dan Kostoris were desperate to have their children back, and so the Jacobsons took Liliane and Yvette to New York in the summer of 1942 to sail to Lisbon. After a few days alone there, they were put on a flight back to England. Dan died in 1948, Henriette a few years later. Liliane married a decorated Canadian air observer, and they returned to Montreal after he was demobilized. Yvette moved to the United States after the war for her education, where she married an American and remained there.

Cecily Samuel graduated from the University of Toronto in 1942, and married a local doctor in August 1943. They later moved to Sault Ste. Marie, Ontario. Janine Freedman returned to Belgium after the war, and married a legal adviser to King Baudouin.

The Air Training Program eventually trained 131,553 men from all over the Commonwealth, of whom over 45,000 would learn the science of navigation and bombing at the several schools that were established across Canada. When the heavy bombers came into general service in 1942, the air observer trade was separated into navigators and bomb-aimers who were trained separately thereafter.

The issue of whether Canadians already serving in RAF squadrons should be transferred to the newly established all-Canadian bomber squadrons came to a head the week after Joe was killed. Some of Britain's senior commanders (and indeed some Canadians themselves) resisted this move. The problem was being solved by attrition, however, as there were less than a hundred Canadians remaining in 5 Group. Joe had been the last Canadian air observer in 106 Squadron.

106 Squadron retired its last Hampden about eight weeks after Joe was killed, shortly after converting to Manchesters. By May the squadron was entirely re-equipped with Lancasters, Bomber Command's highly successful workhorse for the remainder of the war. Wing Commander Allen had by then moved on, replaced by the charismatic Guy Gibson, who would eventually lead the celebrated dam-buster operation. Gibson had been earmarked for leadership by Arthur Harris, the newly appointed commander in chief of Bomber Command, who admired his courage and single-minded determination, his hatred of the Hun, and his impatience with men of lesser

commitment. Perhaps Gibson would have seen those same qualities in Joe, had he completed his tour of operations in 106 Squadron.

Joe was one of almost ten thousand Canadians killed in Bomber Command, or nearly a quarter of Canada's war dead in all services and about a fifth of all men killed in Bomber Command between 1939 and 1945. While they generally died clean-shaven and adequately fed, unlike infantry men, Bomber Command proved the deadliest of all the service branches.

Those who survived came home to a different country. Canada had gained a stronger sense of itself, and never again would go to war in Britain's footsteps. Economic depression had given way to modest prosperity. Canada was becoming a land of opportunity and hope. A few of the early Air Training Program graduates chose air force careers after the war, but far more went back to civilian life, where many made their mark in business, the professions, or politics. Anti-Semitism did not disappear after the war, but it was much less in evidence, and over the next few years anti-discrimination legislation would mitigate its worst effects. Canada was a better place to be Jewish in 1950 than it had been in 1940. Joe and the thousands of other Jewish volunteers, many of them in the air force, had surely played a part in changing the attitudes of their fellow citizens. Joe would have had the opportunity to take his place in the national life of Canada.

Bomber Command would eventually overcome the travails of 1941 and 1942, and go on to inflict enormous devastation to Germany's war machine and its cities. Bomber Command's strategic offensive soon became, and remains today, the most controversial aspect of the Allied struggle to defeat Nazi Germany. The controversy is both technical – relating to its military objectives and its effectiveness in achieving them – and moral. The former has become the province of military historians. The latter remains very much with us today, as the prospect of bombing one's enemy into submission has neither gone out of fashion in strategic planning nor lost its potency in mobilizing public support. Although it has not been my purpose to engage in either of those debates, Joey Jacobson's story sheds light on them.

In Britain, the bombing offensive was almost immediately disowned. Churchill made no mention of Bomber Command in his victory speech after VE Day, even though it was to that force that so many of Britain's best-trained men and so much of its industrial output had been directed for nearly six years. No campaign medal was issued specifically for the strategic air offensive, and "Bomber" Harris was ignored in the 1946 New Year's Honours List.[1] Harris himself came to bear the brunt of blame for area bombing, even though he was implementing the policies of his predecessors at Bomber Command and his superiors at the Air Ministry, the difference being that he managed to do so successfully, with Churchill's endorsement. Nor was Bomber Command much celebrated in postwar popular memory. The British public found the trope of plucky but improbable triumphs – Dunkirk, the desert rats, the dam-busters, and the Great Escape – more appealing than the planned, methodical de-housing of industrial workers and the merciless destruction by fire of cities like Hamburg and Dresden.

Joe would have had none of that. He had been entirely dedicated to the strategic air offensive, he supported its objectives fully, and he had no qualms about whatever damage it inflicted. He believed that winning the air war would require unswerving resolve and disciplined organization. He might well have been amazed at its subsequent effectiveness, which proved far beyond his dreams and imagination in those nadir months before he was killed. But defeating Germany was not simply an end in itself. For Joe, it was the necessary precondition for building a better world in a future peace. Even if he came to accept that he would not likely survive to see it, he never lost that dream, and never stopped thinking about how to achieve it. He had been a deadly serious warrior and a romantic idealist, courageous in both endeavours to the end.

Notes on Sources

Letters and Diaries

The letters and diaries of Joe Jacobson and his father Percy, and the letters Joe received from his friends, are held by the Alex Dworkin Canadian Jewish Archives (CJA) in Montreal. They are catalogued as the Percy and Joe Jacobson Collection (P0094). It includes 239 letters from Joe Jacobson, of which 139 were to his family, sixty-nine to his friends (mainly the three other members of the Pony Club), and thirty-one to others (of which twenty-five were to Janine Freedman); thirty-one letters from his family to Joe, of which twelve were from Percy and nine from May; sixty-eight letters to Joe from the Pony Club (most of them written by Monty Berger); and a few from other people.

The diary collection consists of Percy Jacobson's diary, 1939–45; May Jacobson's travel diaries, 1930, 1950, 1954; and six of Joe's diaries, of which two were written during his high school and college years (1936, 1937–39), one during his time at Manning Depot (July 1940), a daily diary in two parts (18 January 1941–27 February 1942), and an operational diary (August–December 1941).

The collection also includes four of Joe's notebooks (October 1941 through January 1942), dealing with various problems of the bombing campaign, reading notes, reflections on politics and squadron life, and the outline of a play, along with Joe's RCAF Flying Log Book (1940–41). Some related material, including correspondence, is in the CJA's Monty Berger collection (P0015).

The photos used in this book were (with the exceptions noted) held by the Jacobson family, some of which were subsequently donated to the Canadian Jewish Archives.

Joe and Percy corresponded with each other on a more or less weekly basis from September 1939 to January 1942. Percy kept a diary throughout the war, in which he recorded events both public and private, and reflections on them, every two or three days. Joe kept diaries intermittently in his late teens, a habit he resumed very briefly after enlisting. Upon completing his training in western Canada, he began a daily diary that he kept for the rest of his life. He began an operational diary (contrary to regulations) when he started his regular bombing runs over Germany, and soon began filling notebooks on subjects ranging from his critique of the conduct of the air war to thoughts inspired by his current reading material to fundamental questions about politics, religion, and the self-examined life. Joe also corresponded with his close friends on a frequent but less regular basis.

Virtually all of Joe's letters seem to have arrived at their destination, and subsequently saved by their recipients, with a few notable exceptions. According to his surviving correspondence, most of the letters he wrote home during his first month in England – at least three letters to the Pony Club and another three to his family – never arrived in Canada. But once the flow began, very few letters seem to have gone missing, although delivery remained slow and intermittent in both directions, and letters sent over several weeks might arrive all at once. Even airmail service, new that summer on a space-available basis, took at least two weeks. Although some of Joe's letters suffered the cuts of the censor's scissors, there is no evidence that any were blocked in their entirety.

However much Joe valued his incoming mail, whether from family or friends, very little of it has survived. Living as he did in cramped quarters while in service, he kept his possessions to a minimum. He saved none of the letters he received from his friends while in training or active service. A few of Percy and May's letters written to Joe before he left Canada survived; so also did those that they sent to Joe at Coningsby in January 1942, but did not arrive there before he was killed. They were subsequently returned to Joe's family by the RAF with his personal kit. Monty Berger was the keeper of the Pony Club's correspondence, and he generally ensured that the chain ended with him. He left Canada several months after Joe, so much of it remained in Montreal.

When Joe left Canada, he tucked his diaries in his desk drawer at home. How his personal diaries and notebooks from England found their way back to Montreal (save possibly one) is related in Chapter 30.

Newspapers and Periodicals (1936–42)

Canada

High school annuals: Westmount High, West Hill High; *Kitchener-Waterloo Record*, *Montreal Gazette*, *Montreal Star*, *Old McGill*, *McGill Daily*, *Regina Leader-Post*, *Saturday Night*, and *Westmount Examiner*.

United Kingdom

The Aeroplane, *Daily Express*, and *Sunday Express*.

Sources by Part

Preface

On servicemen's personal letters and diaries as sources, see the introduction to Richard J. Aldrich, *Witness to War* (London: Corgi, 2004), and the introduction to Audrey and Paul Grescoe, *The Book of War Letters* (Toronto: McClelland & Stewart, 2003), as well as Paul Fussell, *Wartime: Understanding and Behavior in the Second World War* (New York: Oxford University Press, 1989), 145, 291.

The changing character of Bomber Command memoirs is illustrated by the following selection (in order of first publication date):

Cheshire, Leonard. *Bomber Pilot.* London: Hutchinson, 1941.
Rivaz, R. C. *Tail Gunner.* London: Jarrolds, 1943.
Gibson, Guy. *Enemy Coast Ahead – Uncensored.* 1946; Manchester: Crécy Publishing, 2003.
Tripp, Miles. *The Eighth Passenger.* London: Macmillan, 1969.
Bushby, John. *Gunner's Moon: A Memoir of the RAF Night Assault on Germany.* London: Allan, 1972.
Peden, Murray. *A Thousand Shall Fall.* Stittsville: Canada's Wings Inc., 1979.
McIntosh, Dave. *Terror in the Starboard Seat*. Don Mills: General Publishing, 1980.
Renaut, Michael. *Terror by Night*. London: William Kimber, 1982.
Sawyer, Tom. *Only Owls and Bloody Fools Fly at Night*. Manchester: Goodall, 1982.
Johnson, P. *The Withered Garland: Reflections and Doubts of a Bomber*. London: New European Publishers, 1995.
Silver, L. Ray. *Last of the Gladiators*. Shrewsbury: Airlife Publishing, 1995.
Hewer, Howard. *In for a Penny, In for a Pound*. Toronto: Stoddart, 2000.

Death by Moonlight: Bomber Command, was broadcast on the Canadian Broadcasting Corporation network on 19 January 1992.

Part One

Lord Moran (Charles Wilson), author of *The Anatomy of Courage* (London: Constable, 1945), was Winston Churchill's personal physician.

On the situation and outlook of Montreal's Jewish community at the beginning of the war, see Gerald Tulchinsky, *Canada's Jews, a People's Journey* (Toronto: University of Toronto Press, 2008), particularly Chapter 9, "The Politics of Marginality," 283–327; and specifically for the Jacobsons, see Peter J. Usher, "Removing the Stain: A Jewish Volunteer's Perspective in World War Two," *Canadian Jewish Studies* 23 (2015): 37–67. For a novelist's perspective on inter-ethnic relations in Montreal at that time, see Gwethalyn Graham, *Earth and High Heaven* (Philadelphia: Lippincott, 1944).

I am indebted to Edith Low-Beer (née Jacobson), Janet Kwass (née Jacobson), Brian and Denise Infield (née Michaels), and Yvette Kale (née Kostoris) for background on the Jacobson, Kostoris, and Freedman families provided here and in Part Two. My thanks to Monty Berger, Gerald Smith, and Herb Ross for information on the Pony Club, and to Robert Willinsky for information on his mother, Cecily Willinsky (née Samuel). A retrospective on the 1938 McGill Redmen team appeared in *The Globe and Mail* on 11 November 2004.

Attitudes to enlistment in Ontario in the fall of 1939 are described by Jason Braida, "The Royal City at War: The Military Mobilization of Guelph, Ontario during the First 18 Months of the Second World War," *Canadian Military History* 9, no. 2 (2000): 25–42; and Ian Miller, "Toronto's Response to the Outbreak of War, 1939," *Canadian Military History* 11, no. 1 (2002): 5–23.

Information on the Preston Furniture Company is contained in the Percy Hilborn Papers in the Cambridge [Ontario] City Archives. For more on Joe's experience in Preston, see Usher, "Removing the Stain."

The crisis of late May is lucidly described by John Lukacs, *Five Days in London, May 1940* (New Haven: Yale University Press, 1999). For a concise account of Canada's war preparedness, see David Bercuson, *Maple Leaf Against the Axis* (Don Mills: Stoddart, 1994). On air force mobilization, see W. A. B. Douglas, *The Creation of a National Air Force: The Official History of the Royal Canadian Air Force*, volume II (Toronto: University of Toronto Press, 1986).

Information on Joe Jacobson's enlistment and subsequent training in Canada is contained in his service file (LAC, Service Files of the Second World War – War Dead, 1939–1947, RG 24/27825). On air force selection, see Allan D. English, *The Cream of the Crop, Canadian Aircrew, 1939–45* (Montreal: McGill-Queen's University Press, 1996); "RCAF Personnel History, 1939–1945," n.d., MS, DHH 74/7. For some consequences for Jewish recruits, see Peter J. Usher, "Jews in the Royal Canadian Air Force, 1940–1945," *Canadian Jewish Studies* 20 (2012): 93–114.

On the British Commonwealth Air Training Program (BCATP), see F. J. Hatch, *Aerodrome of Democracy: Canada and the British Commonwealth Air Training Plan, 1939–1945* (Ottawa: Department of National Defence, Directorate of History, 1983); and Douglas, *The Creation of a National Air Force*. For the progress of Joe's training at each school, I have relied on the BCATP unit daily diaries (LAC, RG24) for:

- No. 1 Manning Depot, Toronto
- No. 1 Initial Training School, Toronto
- No. 3 Air Observer School, Regina
- No. 2 Bombing and Gunnery School, Mossbank
- No. 1 Air Navigation School, Rivers
- Temporary Embarkation Depot, Debert

Accounts of initial training at about the same time are provided by Hewer, *In for a Penny, In for a Pound*; Silver, *Last of the Gladiators*, and also for air navigation training at Rivers, Jack Watts, *Nickels and Nightingales* (Burnstown: General Store Publishing House, 1995).

Personal characteristics of Joe's air observer classmates were obtained from LAC, RG24, Service Files of the Second World War – War Dead, 1939–47. Individual attestation papers provide information on place and date of birth, parents' place of birth, education, employment, father's occupation, and religion. Of the one hundred air observers who graduated in the late winter of 1941, forty-five were killed in service. Their files, along with information on two other individuals taken prisoner of war, provided me with a nearly 50 percent sample of Joe's class.

On air observer training, see *Initial Training Schools, Syllabus of Instruction*, n.d., BCATP Flying Training, DHH 181.009(D89A); W. G. Goddard, *History of Air Navigation Training in Canada*, 1945, MS, DHH 74/17; Hatch, *Aerodrome of Democracy*; C. G. Jefford, *Observers and Navigators and Other Non-Pilot Crew in the RFC, RNAS, and RAF* (Shrewsbury: Air Life, 2001); Thomas Ritchie, *An Air Navigator's Navigation in the Second World War* (N.p., n.d.) (Canadian Air and Space Museum Library); Royal Air Force, *Manual of Air Navigation*, Air Publication 1234, vol. 1 (London: H. M. Stationery Office, 1938) (amended and reissued 1940, 1941). On the course setting bombsights used in training (and on the automatic bomb sight described in Part Two), see Air Ministry, Air Publication 1730A, vol. 1, *Bomb Sights* (TNA, AIR10/2676). For personal accounts, see W. A. Hockney and M. D. Gates, *Nadir to Zenith, an Almanac of Stories by Canadian Military Navigators* (Trenton: Self-published, 2002); John Iverach, *Chronicles of a Nervous Navigator*, published by Mrs. Peggy Iverach, 1997; Silver, *Last of the Gladiators*, and Watts, *Nickels and Nightingales*.

For the details of Joe's flights during training and, later in this book, operations, I have relied on his RCAF Flying Log.

Part Two

On the convoy system generally, see Arnold Hague, *The Allied Convoy System 1939–1945: Its Organization, Defence and Operation* (St. Catharines: Vanwell, 2000). For specific details on the April and May convoys, see Hagues List, www.convoyweb.org.uk/hague; for individual ships, see variously the logs (TNA, ADM 53), movement cards (TNA, BT 389), and passenger arrival lists (TNA, BT 26) for *Duchess of Richmond, Georgic, Johan van Oldenbarnevelt, Laconia, Montcalm, Montclare, Nerissa, Pennland, Rajputana, Royal Sovereign, Royal Ulsterman, Vancouver Island, Wolfe*. Sailing details and passenger departure lists are in LAC, *Directorate of Movements 1939–48*, R112-386-6-E.

For the wartime occupation of Iceland, I have relied on Donald F. Bittner, *The Lion and the White Falcon: Britain and Iceland in the World War II Era* (Hamden: Archon Books, 1983); and James Miller, *The North Atlantic Front: Orkney, Shetland, Faroe and Iceland at War* (Edinburgh: Berlinn, 2003).

Letter extracts regarding the spring convoy and the Iceland stopover are in DHH 181.009(D283), *Censored Letters*, vol. 1, *Convoy Indiscretions in Canadian Mail*, ref c.7 supplement – Chief Air Advisor, A.I.1 (z) to HQ RCAF, 26 May 1941, and supplements. On the general atmosphere in Britain in 1941, see Angus Calder, *The People's War, Britain 1939–45* (London: Jonathan Cape, 1979); Norman Longmate, *How We Lived Then: A History of Everyday Life during the Second World War* (London: Hutchison, 1971); and for some views on the political situation, "Cato," *Guilty Men* (London: Gollancz, 1940); and George Orwell, *The Lion and the Unicorn: Socialism and the English Genius* (London: Secker and Warburg, 1941). On the Blitz, see C. Fitzgibbon, *The Blitz* (London: MacDonald, 1970); and Gavin Mortimer, *The Longest Night: Voices from the London Blitz* (Toronto: McArthur, 2005).

On the fate of the first air observer class, see R. V. Manning, "Graduation of the First Observer Course, BCATP," *The Roundel* 12, no. 8 (1960): 14–15, and for P/O Hill, his service file, LAC, RG 24/27747, and TNA, AIR 27/435, *42 Squadron Operational Record Book*.

An account of the history and operation of wartime postal censorship in Britain is provided in the *History of the Postal and Telegraph Censorship Department 1938–1946* (London: Home Office, n.d.) (TNA, DEFE1/3330). Information on the censorship of mail to Canada is provided in DHH

181.009 (D283), *Censored Letters* (4 vols.), and on the period March–June 1941, *RCAF Personnel in Britain*, A.I.1(z), Report c.7, General Summary, and Report c.10, General Summary, with supplements.

On the relations generally between Canada and Great Britain with respect to the air war, see B. Greenhaus, S. J. Harris, W. C. Johnston, and W. G. P. Rawling, *The Crucible of War, 1939–1945: The Official History of the Royal Canadian Air Force*, vol. III (Toronto: University of Toronto Press, 1994); W. S. Carter, *Anglo-Canadian Wartime Relations 1939–1945, RAF Bomber Command and No. 6 [Canadian] Group* (New York: Garland, 1991); *Report, Minister of National Defence for Air, Mission to United Kingdom, 30-6-41 to 24-7-41*, DHH 181.003(D132); and Douglas, *The Creation of a National Air Force*. For Canadian servicemen's views, see DHH 181.009 (D283), *Censored Letters*, and DHH 181.009(D1096), *Carbon Copy of Pamphlet Prepared for the Information of R.C.A.F. Personnel Proceeding Overseas from Canada*, RCAF (Overseas) Headquarters, London, 10 September 1942.

For details on No. 25 OTU (Finningley), I have relied on the unit's *Operational Record Books*, as well as the memoirs of others who were there at the time, notably Bushby, *Gunner's Moon*. Additional information on Joe's Canadian pals who trained in 5 Group is found in the *Operational Record Book* for No. 16 OTU (Upper Heyford), TNA, AIR 29/655. My account of aircrew training and of the circumstances of Operational Training Units in 1941 is based on information in TNA, AIR 2/4169, AIR 10/2315, AIR 14/1157, and AIR 20/1385. On the specifics of Bomber Command's perceived navigational requirements, its navigation training policies, and crewing issues in Hampden bombers, see TNA, AIR 2/4467, AIR 14/9, AIR 14/16, and AIR 14/64.

My description of the censorship system is drawn from *History of the Postal and Telegraph Censorship Department*; DEFE 1/332, photographs for official history; and DEFE 1/408, *Instructions for the Use of Postal Censors*.

I am grateful to Mark Connelly for suggesting a detailed review of the *Daily Express* and the *Sunday Express* (at the British Library) as a source for Joe's views during the summer of 1941.

Target for Tonight is preserved at the Imperial War Museum, London. For commentary, see S. P. MacKenzie, *British War Films 1939–1945: The Cinema and the Services* (London: Hambledon Continuum, 2001).

Part Three

The statement by Lord Trenchard is cited in Andrew Boyle, *Trenchard, a Man of Vision* (London: Collins, 1962), 470.

Of the many books that have written about the origins, development, and execution of the Royal Air Force's strategic air offensive doctrines, as well as the development of night bombing, I have relied especially on Robin Neillands, *The Bomber War* (Woodstock: Overlook Press, 2001); Richard Overy, *The Bombing War, Europe 1939–1945* (London: Penguin, 2014), especially Chapter 5, "The Sorcerer's Apprentice: Bomber Command 1939–42," 237–301; *The Strategic Air War Against Germany 1939–1945: Report of the British Bombing Survey Unit* (London: Frank Cass, 1998); and Sir Charles Webster and Noble Frankland, *The Strategic Air Offensive Against Germany 1939–1945*, vol. 1 (London: H. M. Stationery Office, 1961). Among the key documents provided in Webster and Frankland's Appendix (vol. 4) are the various Air Ministry directives to Bomber Command, and the Butt Report, referred to below. For how Bomber Command presented its air offensive to the public, see Mark Connelly, *Reaching for the Stars: A New History of Bomber Command in World War II* (London: I. B. Taurus, 2001). For Bomber Command's increasing application of scientific expertise to its operations, see Randall Wakelam, *The Science of Bombing* (Toronto: University of Toronto Press, 2013). For further details on bombs and bombing, see Karl Hecks, *Bombing 1939–1945* (London: Robert Hale, 1990); Roy Irons, *The Relentless Offensive, War and Bomber Command 1939–1945* (Barnsley: Pen and Sword, 2009); and J. A. MacBean and A. S. Hogben, *Bombs Gone* (Wellingborough: Patrick Stephens, 1990).

Detailed progress of the offensive is provided in Martin Middlebrook and Chris Everett, *The Bomber Command War Diaries: An Operational Reference Book 1939–1945* (Leicester: Midland, 1996). For an overview of Bomber Command's conduct of the air offensive during the first two years of the war, I have relied on TNA, AIR 8/423, AIR 8/440, AIR 9/131, and AIR 14/194, and on the monthly Headquarters Operational Record Books (AIR 24/229-241), including especially the nightly intelligence narratives and the daily strength returns (AIR 22/36-39) for 1941–42. For detail, I have relied largely on the correspondence files between the Air Ministry, Bomber Command Headquarters, and Group Headquarters, including conference minutes (AIR 14/1926–60). On the problems of navigation in particular, see TNA, AIR 14/66, AIR 14/450, AIR 14/498, and AIR 14/516. Most of these files include correspondence, memos, and minutes covering several months or even years, and must be read against related files. I have listed only the most important ones, and I have not cited the individual pieces within them except for direct quotes.

The most comprehensive sources on Hampden bombers are Harry Moyle, *The Hampden File* (Tonbridge: Air-Britain, 1989); and Chaz Bowyer, *Hampden Special* (Shepperton: Ian Allan, 1976). Technical specifications are provided in TNA, AIR 10/2168 (Hampden Pilot Notes), and details of operational problems in TNA AIR 2/1963, AIR 8/338, and AVIA 15/1967. Among the most useful observations by those who flew Hampdens are Bushby, *Gunner's Moon*; Gibson, *Enemy Coast Ahead – Uncensored*; and Chan Chandler, *Tail Gunner: 98 Raids in WWII* (Shrewsbury: Air Life Publishing, 1999). Details on the use of pigeons in Hampdens, and the RAF's pigeon service generally, are found in TNA, AIR 14/1405, AIR 20/1569, and AIR 20/4305. I am especially grateful to John Marshall-East of the Lincolnshire Aviation Heritage Centre for sharing his detailed knowledge of the Hampden bomber and its equipment.

On the social structure of the RAF, see John James, *The Paladins: A Social History of the RAF up to the Outbreak of World War II* (London: Futura, 1990); Francis Martin, *The Flyer: British Culture and the Royal Air Force, 1939–1945* (Oxford: Oxford University Press, 2008).

Joe's accounts of his sorties are supplemented by 106 Squadron's *Operational Record Book*, TNA, AIR 27/832, 836; RAF Coningsby's *Operations Room Log Book*, July 1941–February 1942, TNA, AIR 14/2433; 5 Group's *Operational Record Book* and appendices, TNA, AIR 25/109A, 115, 116; Middlebrook and Everett, *The Bomber Command War Diaries*; and the recollections of his pilot, J. G. Roberts, DFC, DFM, "Twenty Years in the Air," unpublished MS, RAF Museum 024027, and *Interview with W/C J. G. (Gerry) Roberts*, Catalogue 26580, Imperial War Museum. Bomb loads by aircraft and sortie (in addition to those recorded in Joe's operational diary) are given in the *Form "E" Summaries, No. 5 Group*, TNA, AIR 14/3188-93.

Details of operational casualties among Joe's comrades are taken from their service files (LAC, RG24, Service Files of the Second World War – War Dead, 1939–47), and W. R. Chorley, *Royal Air Force Bomber Command Losses of the Second World War* (Leicester: Midland Counties Publications, vol. 2 [1941], 1992, and vol. 3 [1942], 1993). Information on individuals taken prisoner of war is from *Liberated Prisoner of War Interrogation Questionnaires*, and *Evader and Escape Reports*, War Office, Directorate of Military Intelligence (TNA, WO 344; WO 288).

On meteorology in the early years of the war, and on icing as a flying hazard, see T. A. Fitzpatrick, *Weather and War* (Edinburgh: Pentland Press, 1992); C. G. Halpine, *A Pilot's Meteorology* (London: Chapman and Hall, 1941); R. H. Matthews, "Meteorology in Bomber Command during the War (European) 1939 to 1945," 5 Group, 1945, Manuscript, UK National Meteorological Library; Royal Air Force, *Manual of Air Navigation*; TNA, AIR 14/1941.

On the German air defence system, see Gebhard Aders, *History of the German Night Fighter Force* (English ed.) (London: Janes, 1979); and

Edward B. Westermann, *Flak - German Anti-aircraft Defences 1914–1945* (Lawrence: University of Kansas Press, 2001).

The monthly *Navigation Bulletins* are contained in BCHQ's *Operational Record Books.*

The *Report by Mr. Butt to Bomber Command on His Examination of Night Photos, 18 August 1941* is contained in Webster and Frankland, *The Strategic Air Offensive Against Germany 1939–1945*, 4:205–13. For Bomber Command's response, see TNA, AIR 8/440; AIR12/1218. The problems of navigation were continually discussed by senior air staff, whose views are recorded in TNA, AIR 2/4467, AIR 14/64, AIR 14/66, AIR 14/450, and AIR 14/498.

My thanks to Randall Wakelam for providing a copy of the Operational Research Section's Report No. 3, *Investigation of Raid on HULS - Night of 6/7th September 1941*, held by RAF Air Historical Branch, London.

My information on Canadian air observers in 106 Squadron is derived from the following sources: LAC service files (for individual movements among stations); TNA, AIR 29/655, *16 OTU Operational Record Book* (for movements to 106 Squadron; unfortunately, the *Operational Record Books* for 14 and 25 Operational Training Units do not supply the same level of detail); and TNA, AIR 27/832, *106 Squadron Operational Record Book.*

The mental and physical stresses experienced by Bomber Command crews are discussed by E. J. Dearnaley and P. B. Warr, eds., *Aircrew Stress in Wartime Operations* (London: Academic Press, 1979); D. Stafford-Clark, "Morale and Flying Experience: Results of a Wartime Study," *Journal of Mental Science* 95 (1949): 10–50; and M. K. Wells, *Courage and Air Warfare: The Allied Aircrew Experience in the Second World War* (London: Frank Cass, 1977).

For developments in the use of incendiary bombs for target-marking and fire-raising in the latter part of 1941, see TNA, AIR 9/132; AIR14/763. On the Berlin raid of 7–8 November and its consequences, see TNA, AIR 14/1926, 1928.

Part Four

Among the books that influenced Joe's thinking in the last two months of 1941 were Cedric Belfrage, *Let My People Go* (London: Victor Gollancz, 1940); Hewlett Johnson, *The Socialist Sixth of the World* (London: Victor Gollancz, 1939); Stephen Swingler, *Outline of Political Thought since the French Revolution* (London: Victor Gollancz, 1939); and Clive Bell, *Civilization* (London: Penguin, 1938).

The status of air observers, and particularly the question of whether they should be captains of bomber aircraft, had been debated within the

Command since before the war. See particularly TNA, AIR 14/1941, *Status and Future of the Observer,* 1 November 1941; AIR 14/753, *Present Status and Responsibilities of an Observer in Relation to Those of a Pilot*, 17 December 1941.

On mole operations, see TNA, AIR 14/753, *Mole operations*, 18 January 1942. For developments in the use of incendiaries, see TNA, AIR 9/132; AIR 14/763. The circumstances of Roger Rousseau's belated commission are on his service file (Library and Archives Canada, Military service file Roger Rousseau, J96092).

For details of the Munster operation of 28 January 1942, I consulted, in addition to the sources on operations cited in Part Three, the *Operational Record Books* of all of the squadrons involved. Weather conditions in England that day are based on the surface synoptic and upper atmosphere conditions available to Bomber Command that day (UK National Meteorological Archive). The Air Ministry's daily forecasts have apparently not survived. Weather conditions on the ground in the Netherlands are cited in Part Five.

Part Five

For much of the information in Chapter 31, I am indebted to Wim Rhebergen, of Hoevelaken, Netherlands, who has documented the fate of downed Allied bomber aircraft and crews in the Achterhoek district of the Netherlands. He arranged for and guided me on site visits in the area in 2005 and 2008, and granted me complete access to the documents, photographs, and interview transcripts he had collected in relation to the fate of AT122. He also provided me with a copy of Westerman's and Wekking's films and meteorological data for the Netherlands for the dates in question.

I am also indebted to Jan Geerdinck of the AVOG Crash Museum in Lievelde, Netherlands, for access to photographs, documents, and interview transcripts; and to Andrew Hodgkinson (Duncan Hodgkinson's son), of Devizes, England, for information relating to the fate of AT122.

For accounts of the events, see Henny Bennink, *Bezetting en Verzet* (Lichtenvoorde: Fagus, 2005); G. Nijs, "Neergestorte Engelse bombenwerper in de Besselinkschans 28 Januari 1942" [Crashed English bomber in the Besselinkschans] in *De Lichte Voorde – Lichtenvoorde tussen 1940 en 1950*, 31 (1995): 24–25; of other Allied bomber losses in the area, see Wim and Peter Rhebergen, *Vermist Boven de Achterhoek* (Naarden: Lunet, 1991).

Meteorological records for Essen, the nearest recording station to Münster in Germany, were provided by the UK National Meteorological Archive. Geographic locations are based on United States air photo 373_

CanON-022630-42, 1945, U.S. National Archives; Google Earth (2005); and *Topografische kaart van Nederland*, sheet 41B (Lichtenvoorde), scale 1:25,000, 2001.

I am indebted to John Marshall-East, Lincolnshire Aviation Heritage Centre, East Kirkby, for his interpretation of the extent of damage to AT122 based on the photographs reproduced in Chapter 31. I am also grateful for letters received from the Air Historical Branch (RAF), the Commonwealth War Graves Commission, and Marilyn Farias (Robin Selfe's daughter), of Bishops Stortford, England, in response to my requests for information relating to those events.

On the Nazi occupation of the Netherlands during the war, see Gerhard Hirschfeld, *Nazi Rule and Dutch Collaboration: The Netherlands under German Occupation, 1940–1945* (Oxford: Berg, 1988); Louis de Jong, *The Netherlands and Nazi Germany* (Cambridge: Harvard University Press, 1990); and Walter Maass, *The Netherlands at War: 1940–45* (New York: Abelard-Schuman, 1970).

My thanks to Wim Rhebergen (Hoevelaken, Netherlands), John Griffiths (Amsterdam, Netherlands), and Sietze Praamsma (Clayton, Ontario) for translating several of the above-noted documents from the original Dutch.

Correspondence between the Air Ministry and 5 Group with respect to requests to transfer Canadian aircrew to Canadian squadrons is in TNA, AIR 14/1941. See Connelly, *Reaching for the Stars*, on the evolution of Britain's popular memory of Bomber Command and the bombing of Germany.

Notes

Part One: Father and Son

Chapter 1: September 1939

1 *The Westmount High School Annual*, 1936, 92.

Chapter 2: Preston

1 Joe's Air Force medical board examinations record that he had 20/20 vision and did not wear glasses. He never mentioned his glasses again, or whether he needed them for map reading and log recording while flying.

Chapter 3: Enlistment

1 Also referred to as the Empire Air Training Scheme (EATS) or Joint Air Training Program (JATP) in its early years.
2 LAC, RG 24/27825, J. A. Jacobson service file, interview report, 11 June 1940.

Chapter 4: Toronto

1 In fact, the Non-Permanent Active Militia, Canada's part-time reserve force, to be mobilized as required for home defence, but not overseas service.
2 LAC, RG 24/27825, J. A. Jacobson Service File, Medical Board report, Toronto, 7 August 1940.
3 Of the six whose fate is known, one was selected for pilot training and succeeded, another was selected for pilot training but washed out and was reselected for observer training. Three (including Joe) were directly selected for observer training, and one for wireless operator/air gunner training. Of those six, five were subsequently killed in service and one was captured as a prisoner of war.

Chapter 5: Regina

1 MacLaren Keswick, who had completed three years of a forestry degree before enlisting.
2 He was navigating a three-hour flight across the dry prairie west and south to the American border.
3 The General Conduct Sheet recorded infractions requiring disciplinary action.

4 Dive-bombing was not in fact on the curriculum at bombing and gunnery schools. Generally associated with army tactical support, it was not part of the bombing offensive's tactical repertoire.
5 The photo in the *Montreal Star* was an outtake of the photo at the bottom of page 61 in this volume.

Chapter 6: Mossbank

1 The three air observers killed in this flying accident were on their last day of training in course 4 at Rivers. The affinity Joe felt for them is obvious, but he was almost certainly not actually acquainted with them as they were three courses and six weeks ahead of him. The closest they ever got to each other was at Mossbank, but Joe arrived there later the same day that they had left for Rivers.

Chapter 7: Rivers

1 This seems fanciful as there was no provision for it.
2 Joe's counterpart on outside wing for the McGill Redmen in 1938.
3 One of Joe's McGill Redmen teammates in 1938.
4 NAC, RG 24/27825, J. A. Jacobson service file, *Report on Pupil Observer*, 21 February 1941.

Chapter 8: Montreal

1 Joe's older cousin, sometime national slalom champion in the late 1930s.

Chapter 9: Debert

1 They were Mac Keswick, Cliff Chappell, Les Jupp, Art Hunter, Roger Rousseau, and "Jeep" McLean. All seven would be killed or captured.
2 Many Americans volunteered to fight in the Canadian forces while their own country remained neutral.
3 The Dick test consisted of an injection of serum to detect susceptibility to scarlet fever.

Part Two: Discoveries

Chapter 10: The North Atlantic

1 TC convoys were Canadian troop convoys, and HX convoys were merchant shipping convoys, originating in Halifax and destined for Britain, each numbered consecutively since the beginning of the war.
2 A Royal Navy battleship also serving as convoy escort.
3 This was Convoy SC28, consisting of thirty-four merchant ships and fourteen escorts, also en route from Halifax to Liverpool.
4 What Joe saw that day was most likely the flotsam and jetsam from the wreck of the *Rajputana*, an escort that had left Halifax with HX117 in March and was torpedoed near that location on its return run on 13 April. There is no record of a ship sunk on the 21st.
5 Classmates who had arrived from Halifax ten days before on the *Wolfe*.

6 Lionel had arrived in Iceland on 19 April, on the *Montclare*.
7 Joe also claimed that he wrote a letter to the Pony Club immediately upon arrival, but it too was never received. Joe believed this was because he had given it to a stranger to post, who had not done so. Had it been mailed, it might well have ended up in the RCAF's file of censored letters in London. As it seems not to have done so, Joe may have surmised correctly, although it was also the case that some mail wound up at the bottom of the sea.
8 Sgt. John Michaels of Westmount, and a graduate of Bishop's University, joined the British Army before the war while in London, and served in Palestine with the Royal Worcester Regiment. He was killed in action in Sudan on 7 April 1941, at the age of twenty-nine, and is buried in the Khartoum War Cemetery.

Chapter 11: The Blitz

1 Balloon barrages consisted of fixed arrays of balloons moored by heavy cables, surrounding factories and towns to deter low-flying enemy aircraft. An encounter between aircraft and cable could be fatal.
2 The Women's Auxiliary Air Force. By this time, women were widely employed in non-combat roles on every RAF station, in transport, radar, meteorology, communications, maintenance, and catering.
3 Later in 1941, Britain agreed to tax RCAF personnel serving in Britain at Canadian rates, and refund the amounts already levied.

Chapter 12: England

1 L. F. Stevenson to Air Intelligence, 19 and 22 May 1941. DHH 181.009 (D283), *Censored Letters*, vol. 1.
2 Joe numbered his first few letters to the Pony Club. The first extant letter to his family from England, dated 1 June, states that he had already sent at least three letters to them. These included, by his own account, the story of his trip across the Atlantic, one about London and the plays he saw, including some programs (both twenty-page masterpieces by his own account), and his first letter from Finningley. Apparently none reached its destination. Percy observed in his diary: "Joe's letters must have gone down to Davey Jones Locker" (16 June 1940).
3 Jack McIntyre extract, main supplement. A.I.1(z), Report C.10, DHH 181.009 (D283), *Censored Letters*, vol. 1.
4 Joe's spelling of names was not his strong point. He had by this time known Dave Davies for at least three weeks, and they would soon be posted to the same operational squadron.
5 Art Hunter, "Jeep" McLean, and Ken Fraser had been among Joe's closest friends in training in Canada. They and several other Canadian observers were now on operational training at No. 16 OTU at Upper Heyford. Some of them would soon be posted to a newly formed and nominally Canadian squadron.
6 Leading aircraftman, as Joe had been classified until graduating as a sergeant.
7 A week later, the secret of radar's importance in Battle of Britain was revealed in the English press.
8 Ack ack, variously mentioned by Joe as aak or aak aak, refers to anti-aircraft fire, also known as flak.

Chapter 13: Operational Training

1 TNA, AIR 14/1941, AOC-in-C Richard Peirse to Groups, 12 July 1941.
2 TNA, AIR 14/9, Air Vice-Marshal Arthur Harris to Air Ministry, 4 January 1940.
3 The Distinguished Flying Cross (for officers) and Medal (for men) were awarded for both specific acts of distinguished flying on operations and for consistently meritorious flying. Joe very quickly took on board the common but incorrect assumption that the decoration was automatically awarded upon tour completion.
4 In this case, "friendly fire" from British anti-aircraft gun crews who did not always correctly identify aircraft entering their range of fire.
5 This was unlikely in Wellingtons, impossible in Hampdens.
6 Joe did not say why, but a Wellington had crashed and burned nearby the previous day, killing one of its crew.
7 The broad inlet of the North Sea that separates Lincolnshire and East Anglia.
8 Most likely on the daylight-only cameras with which bombers were still equipped, but which would be of no use on night operations. Few operational aircraft were as yet fitted out with night cameras.
9 Although Jack had been posted to No. 25 OTU on the same day as Joe, like most of their classmates, he managed to get through his required flying time with fewer interruptions and delays. He was given a week's leave and directed to report to 106 Squadron on the 18th.
10 Sgt. James Cooper had graduated from the air observer course preceding Joe's and had arrived in Britain a month before him. He was killed in a flying accident on 3 June at No. 11 OTU near Bassingbourn, Cambridgeshire.
11 Sgt. Charles Davis was Joe's classmate throughout Air Observer School. He was killed in a flying accident on 19 June at No. 16 OTU (Upper Heyford). Sgt. Ed Grange was badly injured in a separate flying accident the same day at Upper Heyford. He was in the air observer course after Joe's, but they had shipped out to England at the same time. Grange would be killed in action in 1943.
12 P/O Robert George Mitchell had been Joe's classmate all the way through training in Canada (as had Milward). Arriving in England a few days before Joe, he had been assigned to No. 16 OTU. His Hampden aircraft vanished without a trace during a night raid on Hamburg on 17 July, three weeks after beginning operations at 50 Squadron.
13 Joe had received incorrect information (as sometimes happened in connection with casualties). His classmate "Pop" Miller (so nicknamed because he was then thirty-one years old) turned up alive and well at Joe's next station in August. He would be killed in action while navigating a Hampden in 402 Squadron on 12 February 1942, on the notoriously failed Operation Fuller, against German battleships running the English Channel under cover of foul weather.
14 If Joe kept a diary of his training flights, it has not survived. He did, however, keep a diary of his operational flights when he began combat in August.

Chapter 14: A Canadian's Estimate of England

1 "Censorette" was a patronizing nickname applied to letter examiners, generally middle-aged women with decent educations occupying the lowest level in the Censorship Department's hierarchy. The letter was sent by air, although the envelope itself is not in the Jacobson collection and presumably was not retained.
2 Postal and Telegraph Censorship Submission PO/57935/41, 7 August 1941. DHH 181.009 (D283), *Censored Letters*, vol. 2.

3 Air Commodore L. F. Stevenson to the Secretary, Department of National Defence for Air, 14 August 1941. DHH, 181.009 (D283), *Censored Letters*, vol. 2. Identification of both sender and recipient was omitted in this three legal-length-page rendering.
4 *The Lion and the Unicorn* was at the time Orwell's most widely circulated book. In it he characterized the English as deeply patriotic but also insular and quite uninterested in things foreign; as obstinate and "clinging to everything that is out of date and a nuisance … but they have a certain power of acting without taking thought." He likened the English to "a family in which the young are generally thwarted and most of the power is in the hands of irresponsible uncles and bedridden aunts … a family with the wrong members in control." He accused the ruling class of stupidity, incompetence, lack of imagination, and an infallible instinct for doing the wrong thing," yet at the same time "*morally* fairly sound … in time of war they are ready enough to get themselves killed."

Chapter 16: Preparing for Battle

1 By mid-1942 the process would take sixteen months.
2 Sgt. Stanley John Tyson, of London, Ontario, and P/O John Keith Dingle Williams, of Saskatoon, had trained with Joe from the beginning through graduation. Tyson was among those who had been confined to barracks with Joe in Regina; Williams graduated at the top of the class. They arrived in Britain a few days earlier than Joe, and were posted to No. 3 OTU (Coastal Command) in Chivenor to train on Beauforts. Tyson's aircraft went missing without a trace on a navigational exercise over the Atlantic on 31 May. Williams had been reassigned to a torpedo training unit in Scotland, where he was killed in a flying training accident on 30 June. Tyson is commemorated at Runnymede (the RAF Memorial for those who died in its service in the Second World War with no known grave); Williams is buried at Hawkhead cemetery, Paisley, Scotland. Sgt. E. R. Kennedy, and Sgt. J. F. MacMillan, who had attended ITS in Toronto with Joe the previous summer, were killed in the same flying accident at No. 21 OTU in the west of England, on 24 July. Both are buried at Long Lawford churchyard, Warwickshire.
3 Adjutor Savard later wrote *Les ailes Canadiennes Françaises*, a tribute to individual French Canadians serving the RCAF, published in 1944. Ernest Savard was a Montreal stockbroker, and head of a syndicate that managed the Montreal Canadiens. Jean-Charles Harvey was a journalist, author, and member of the Canadian Authors Association, known for his anti-fascist and pro-allied views, and his criticism of Quebec conservatism, clericalism, and anti-Semitism. B. K. Sandwell was then editor of *Saturday Night* magazine, and prominent in English Canadian intellectual and publishing circles. Both Harvey and Sandwell were associates of Percy. The Canadian journalists were on a tour lasting several weeks to report on Britain's wartime spirit.
4 *Daily Express*, 24 July 1941; *New Statesman and Nation*, 2 August 1941.

Part Three: Night Bombing

Chapter 17: Bomber Command

1 TNA, AIR 14/682, 23 September 1940 minute.
2 The Air Ministry drew a direct link between its gallant flyers and the heroic age of exploration in its publicity booklet, *Bomber Command: The Air Ministry Account of Bomber Command's Offensive Against the Axis, September 1939—July 1941* (London: Air Ministry, 1941).

3 4 June 1940 Directive, Air Ministry to Bomber Command, in C. Webster and N. Frankland, *The Strategic Air Offensive Against Germany 1939–1945* (London: H. M. Stationery Office, 1961), 4:113.
4 30 October 1940 Directive, Air Ministry to Bomber Command, in ibid., 4:129. The term "moral" was commonly used in relation to the desired effect of the strategic air offensive at that time. I have preferred to use the term "morale."
5 9 March 1941 Directive, Air Ministry to Bomber Command, in ibid., 4:133.
6 TNA, AIR 14/1960, Minutes of Conference, 2 June 1941.

Chapter 18: Initiation

1 Aak aak, also referred to as flak, was a common shorthand for anti-aircraft fire.
2 W/C J. G. Roberts DFC, DFM, audio interview, December 2003, reference 26580, Imperial War Museum, London; *Twenty Years in the Air* [typescript], 1989, reference 024027, Royal Air Force Museum, London.
3 Both aircraft were indeed shot down by night-fighters. Len Acres, a fellow observer, was killed and is buried at Gembloux, Belgium. Johnny Cook survived, but was taken prisoner of war.

Chapter 19: Confidence Affirmed

1 P/O James Paul Erly, DFC, of Toronto, had arrived in England in February. He, along with his classmate Rae Dunn, were posted to 106 Squadron at the beginning of May, the first Canadian flyers to serve there. His aircraft was downed by flak during an operation on Mannheim on 23 August.
2 These "special informed sources" were probably the *Intelligence Narratives of Operations* and *Intelligence Summaries* compiled at Bomber Command Headquarters and circulated to groups several times each month. These Command-wide summaries of operational debriefings were secret documents, not intended as propaganda, yet they suffered from the same defects.

Chapter 21: Confidence Tested

1 TNA, AIR 24/234, *Bomber Command Navigation Bulletin – August 1941.*
2 TNA, AIR 14/1218, J. M. Butt to W/C Duggan, 18 August 1941. The report was commissioned by Churchill's science adviser in July to determine the accuracy of bombing, and assigned to Mr. Butt, an economist in the civil service.
3 TNA, AIR 12/1218, *Investigation of Inaccurate Navigation during Operational Flights*, BCHQ to Groups, 13 September 1941.
4 TNA, AIR 27/832, *106 Squadron Operations Book Record*, 6–7 September 1941.
5 Fred Matkin had been with Joe on the *Laconia* and in operational training at Finningley.
6 Rae Dunn, one of the first Canadian observers to serve in 106 Squadron, was nearing the end of his first operational tour, this being his twenty-eighth sortie. His aircraft went down in Denmark after losing an engine. All were subsequently captured and taken prisoner of war.

Chapter 22: A Brotherhood Lost

1 Murray MacLaren Keswick, of Hartland, NB, was one of Joe's closest friends throughout training, a bond augmented by being confined to barracks for the same escapade

the previous September in Regina. They left Debert at same time, but Keswick got to Britain first, and was posted to No. 21 OTU and then to 149 Squadron a month before Joe completed his operational training. Keswick was observer on a Wellington when he was killed on the Berlin raid on the night of 7–8 September, at the age of twenty-two. He is buried in the Reichswald Forest War Cemetery in Germany.

2 Jack McIntyre, age twenty, had been posted to 106 Squadron from Finningley two weeks before Joe. His aircraft was shot down by a night-fighter. His body was never recovered and he is commemorated at the Runnymede Memorial. The other three men survived, but were taken into captivity. The Squadron's aircraft were unable to penetrate Hamburg's air defences that night despite clear weather.

3 "Lord Haw-Haw" was William Joyce, an Irish-American Nazi sympathizer who went to Germany to narrate regular propaganda broadcasts to Britain during the war. He was tried and hanged for treason in 1946.

4 John Donaghue, from New York State, was an air gunner in 97 Squadron. He would be killed in action in 1942.

5 The item, "A Jew in Hitler's Patch," which appeared on 15 July 1941, offered no support for its claim.

Chapter 23: Action and Inaction

1 Everett Littlefield, from Massachusetts, was then serving as an air gunner in 12 Squadron.

2 Lionel Shapiro was a war correspondent for the *Montreal Gazette* and *Maclean's*.

3 Mrs. Jacobs, a relative of Percy's, had invited Joe for the traditional breaking of the fast after Yom Kippur.

4 Joe is referring only to his close friends. In fact, the squadron participated in two raids during that week. One aircraft failed to return after being recalled due to fog. In the outcome it had overflown England entirely and the crew (including a wireless operator/air gunner who had crewed with Joe on two previous occasions) bailed out over Ireland, where they were interned for the remainder of the war.

5 TNA, AIR 24/235, *Bomber Command Navigation Bulletin—September 1941*.

6 This achievement was singled out among his consistently accurate bombing record in his DFC citation two weeks later.

7 The crew was not in fact credited for this sortie. The critical point of no return to count as an operational trip toward tour completion was latitude 4 degrees east (at the Dutch coast); if the trip was aborted for any reason before reaching this point, it did not count. This was Joe's second aborted sortie, so he had thirteen to his credit.

8 The real number was about ten, although it would reach twenty before long.

9 Joe is referring to F/Sgt. H. I. Popay, DFM.

10 One of which crashed near Hamburg with F/Sgt. Douglas John Carmichael, of Noranda, Quebec. He is buried at the Becklingen War Cemetery in Soltau, Germany.

Chapter 24: Questions and Doubts

1 The code name for the main electric power plant in Cologne.

Chapter 25: Winding Down

1 5 Group was not involved as its commander, Air Vice-Marshal John Slessor, with commendable foresight, objected on account of forecast conditions, and he was

authorized to send his aircraft to Cologne instead. The loss of thirty-seven bomber crews on this single night was the highest of the war to that point.

2 Roger Rousseau had been dispatched with a small force to mine Oslo Fiord in Norway the same night, from an advance base in Scotland. It was a tough assignment; unlike the Baltic coast, the Fiord was steep-sided and the German guns could fire on low-flying aircraft from above as well as below. Joe had also been detailed for the Norway operation, but was reassigned. 106 Squadron lost three aircraft in Norway that night, including that of F/O Bruce Gordon McIver, DFC, of Hamilton. He had enlisted around the same time as Joe, but took his air observer and operational training at other units, and was posted to 106 Squadron two months before Joe arrived. His DFC citation (awarded six weeks before he was killed) refers to his courage, persistence, skill, and bombing accuracy. His aircraft was last heard from on its return from Norway, off the coast of Scotland, but never seen again. McIver was twenty-five years old, and is commemorated at Runnymede.

3 13 November Directive, Air Ministry to Bomber Command, in Webster and Frankland, *The Strategic Air Offensive*, 4:142.

4 Ibid., 1:383.

5 By this time, Joe and Duncan Hodgkinson had crewed together with Gerry Roberts on fifteen sorties, and Sid Harding had been on six with them. Duncan and Sid were both Londoners. Duncan was married, with two young children.

6 Massey Beveridge was a McGill Redmen teammate in 1938. A fighter pilot, he was killed in action over France in 1944.

7 Referring to the number of crews lost on the Berlin raid.

Part Four: Holding the Line

Chapter 27: December Doldrums

1 W/C Robert Allen, DFC, DSO, had enlisted in the RAF in 1935 and completed his first tour in 1940 as a Hampden pilot in 49 Squadron. He assumed command of 106 Squadron in April 1941 and held that position for the next year, when he was succeeded by Guy Gibson. During his command, he led several of the squadron's most challenging assignments, including daylight raids on German factories and on battleships at Brest.

2 Dated "Sunday evening, 15 December," almost certainly misdated as Sunday was December 14.

3 Les Jupp, who had been injured in a bailout over England, resumed flying in 78 Squadron and was shot down on a raid on Mainz in August 1942. He spent the rest of the war in a prisoner of war camp. Tim Buck was the leader of the Communist Party of Canada.

4 Airgraphs had just been introduced by Canada's postal service. For the price of six cents, the sender could submit a single letter-size page to be microfilmed for air transport and enlarged to postcard size on arrival in England, where it would be forwarded by regular mail. The service was one way only, from Canada to the UK. Joe's parents also sent him airgraphs in December.

5 Of five other air observers who began around the same time as Joe, three appear to have experienced a similar situation, but completed their tours of operation a few months later.

6 Sgt. Jack Lloyd Gibson, of Edmonton, who was the navigator on the aircraft. Joe and Jack had begun their training together at No. 1 ITS, and although they completed

their air observer training separately, they had sailed to Britain together and found themselves on the same base when Gibson was posted to 97 Squadron in early October. Gibson, aged twenty-one, is buried in Coningsby. This was a costly operation for Bomber Command; six of forty-seven heavy bombers were lost. As Joe would soon learn, one of his classmates and friends, P/O Nicholas Frederick Durban, was killed in the same raid, his 7 Squadron Stirling bomber shot down by German fighters off the French coast. Durban, of Portage la Prairie, Manitoba, has no known grave and is commemorated at Runnymede. He was twenty-three years old.

7 Part of a small, aborted, daylight intruder operation over northwestern Germany. The aircraft crashed in Holland, three of the surviving crew members were captured and taken prisoner of war, including Sgt. Ron Yearsley, WO/AG, who had crewed with Joe on the Hamburg raid on 31 October.

8 TNA, AIR 14/753, *Mole Operations*, 5 Group HQ to Stations, 18 January 1942.

Chapter 28: New Directions

1 F/Sgt. K. McKenzie, DFM, wireless operator/air gunner, age twenty, with whom Joe had flown on his second operation in August. Also killed on this sortie was air observer F/O Alexander James Fraser, of Ottawa. Fraser, age thirty-one, had enlisted a month before Joe, and had trained at different units. Joe probably never knew him. Although Fraser was posted to 25 OTU, he was not flying during the time that Joe was there due to prolonged illness. He was posted to 106 Squadron on 2 January. On the very next day, his aircraft was lost without trace on a mine-laying operation off the Frisians. The crew is commemorated at Runnymede.

2 Three officers from RCAF Headquarters in London had embarked on a whirlwind inspection tour of nineteen stations in England the week before.

3 TNA, AIR 14/2433, *Operations Room Log Book, RAF Coningsby*, 15 January 1942.

4 TNA, AIR 14/763, Bottomley to Peirse, 25 October 1941.

5 Fourteen Canadian observers were posted to 106 Squadron between May and October 1941. Up to this point, seven had been killed in action, two taken prisoner of war, and three moved to other squadrons earlier on. Miller had been taken off regular flying to serve as a station officer at Coningsby. Joe was now the last of the original fourteen still in action. Three newly posted Canadian observers had begun operations in January. Each was killed on his first sortie.

6 Mrs. Lettice later told the Jacobsons that after Roger went missing, Joe had at first put all his private papers together in another room for Monty to take home, but that Joe had taken them away in his valise when he moved to the aerodrome (4 March 1942).

7 The RCAF had no role in the matter at this point in the war, except to forward Air Ministry approval to Ottawa for pro forma ratification.

8 It appears to have been routine practice in the RCAF to promote flying personnel by one grade after the first year of service. The promotion had been backdated to 1 October, but Joe had only just been formally advised of it. Roger was similarly promoted effective the same date.

9 One on an operation on Bremen on 21–22 January, the other gardening the next night. The navigator of the second was Sgt. Stewart Alexander Morrison, of Montreal, who had been posted to 106 Squadron a month previously. Joe would not have known him until his arrival there. This was his first operational flight. Morrison's aircraft was lost without trace and the crew is commemorated at Runnymede.

10 F/O Arthur John Benning Monk, of Winnipeg, was killed on 11 December during a mine-laying operation off Brest. He was posted to 144 Squadron, another 5 Group Hampden squadron, in July 1941. Aged twenty-nine, he has no known grave and is commemorated at Runnymede. F/Sgt. Donald Louden Henderson, of Winnipeg, was reported missing on 11 January from operations on Wilhelmshaven. He had volunteered to take the place of an air observer who was ill that night. Henderson was posted to 408 Squadron, an early RCAF Hampden squadron then still attached to 5 Group, in July 1941. Aged twenty-eight, he has no known grave and is commemorated at Runnymede. Both had been Joe's classmates during their air observer training in Canada.
11 Joe seems to have heard that Moe Usher, then serving in 35 Squadron, was reported missing, but this proved to be incorrect.

Chapter 29: 28 January 1942

1 Joe is referring to Percy's letter of 29 December, the last he would receive. F/Sgt. H. I. Popay and F/Sgt. D. A. Hammatt were awarded bars to their DFMs in January.
2 When Joe wrote this letter, no news of Roger's fate had yet reached the squadron. In fact, his aircraft had been hit by flak around midnight of the 15th and crashed in Denmark, where all four of the crew were captured and imprisoned for the remainder of the war. In 1944, Réal Rousseau relied on this letter to pursue inquiries into the status of his brother's commission while he was still in Stalag Luft 4.
3 TNA, AIR 14/2142, *Intelligence Watch Diary, 5 Group*, vol. IV, 28 January 1942. The following morning at 0530, 5 Group reported to Bomber Command: "Frontal belt 9/10 cu tops 7000' with thin cloud up to 20,000'. Snow not of sufficient depth to obscure hedges." Why Bomber Command HQ wanted this information, and what was done with it, is not disclosed in the record.
4 Patrick, of Stettler, Alberta, is buried at Great Bircham Cemetery, Norfolk.
5 TNA, AIR 27/832, *106 Squadron Operations Record Book*, 28 January 1941.
6 That is what Lionel Silver, by then an observer with a heavy bomber squadron in Yorkshire, speculated when he wrote to Percy and May on 15 February after hearing that Joe had gone missing: "Anti-aircraft fire may have affected their engines, depleted their petrol supply or otherwise damaged the aircraft so that it would not be possible for them to keep aloft until they got back to England." As Joe's target was well inside Germany, Lionel continued, he had a better chance of landing safely and being taken prisoner of war. If so, he could be back in England before the war is over, as a friend of Lionel's who had failed to return from an operation four months previously now was.

Part Five: Failed to Return

Chapter 30: Requiem

1 Subsequently archived (DHH, 181.009 (D283), *Censored letters*), including Joe's letter of 22 July 1941.
2 Undated (first page missing), probably written in early April.
3 The Memorial Cross, also known as the Silver Cross, was awarded to the mothers or wives of servicemen who died in active duty.

4 Fred Haiblen lived with the Jacobsons for nearly two years while studying, and later moved to the United States. I am grateful to Janice Rosen and Janet Kwass for this information.
5 Joe's final daily diary, covering the period 18–27 January, and his last notebook of conversations with Monty and the outline of their proposed play, also with entries up to 27 January, must have been with his kit in barracks. Perhaps they were regarded as innocuous, as evidently they were released after the routine Air Ministry inspection along with the remainder of his belongings to Dan Kostoris as his designated next of kin. These items would also have been included in the bundle that Dan gave to Gerald to take home.
6 This would be the Missing Research and Enquiries Unit established by the RAF at war's end to locate and identify airmen lost over enemy territory.

Chapter 31: Holland

1 The interviews cited were conducted by Jan Geerdinck, AVOG Crash Museum, Leivelde, between 1971 and 2006, unless otherwise indicated.
2 Process-verbaal (report by Th. Wegman, Head of Air Protection), 30 January 1942, reproduced in G. Nijs, "Neergestorte Engelse bombenwerper in de Besselinkschans 28 Januari 1942" [Crashed English bomber in the Besselinkschans], in *De Lichte Voorde* 31 (1995): 24–25.
3 Quoted in ibid., 31:26, translated by Sietze Praamsma.
4 Wim Rhebergen interview, television documentary broadcast in the Netherlands in 1997.
5 Two Lancaster bombers (one from 106 Squadron) were shot down by night-fighters on return from an operation on Berlin on 30 March 1943. Each carried a crew of seven, all of whom (with the exception of one who survived and was taken prisoner of war) are buried at Lichtenvoorde General Cemetery. A Stirling bomber was shot down by a night-fighter during an operation on the Ruhr on 26 June 1943. One of the crew survived and was taken prisoner of war; the other six are buried at Lichtenvoorde General Cemetery. There is no evidence that the local resisters were able to provide assistance to the survivors in either case.
6 According to a newspaper account published in England in the 1990s, Duncan Hodgkinson's sister was quoted to the effect that a family friend had heard his death confirmed in a German radio propaganda broadcast shortly after the crew failed to return (information from Wim Rhebergen).
7 Although the CWGC did sometimes concentrate isolated graves into larger cemeteries, this was more common in Germany than in the Netherlands, where there are numerous local war graves. The CWGC has no record of such an attempt with respect to the Lichtenvoorde General Cemetery.
8 Two recorded attempts, in August and September 1941, led to the arrest and execution of the helpers and the capture of the airmen. In the second case, two airmen who survived a crash about twenty kilometres west of Lichtenvoorde were escorted by resistance men as far as Den Haag before being discovered and arrested.
9 Leemreize was awarded the King's Medal for Courage in the Cause of Freedom in 1947. He was one of about two hundred Netherland citizens upon whom Britain bestowed this honour.

10 Most recently in local television newscasts on the occasion of its seventieth anniversary in January 2012, and when Joe's surviving sister Janet visited his grave in July 2013.

Chapter 32: Epilogue

1 It took nearly sixty years to agree on and construct a permanent commemoration of Bomber Command in London. Queen Elizabeth II dedicated the Bomber Command Memorial in June 2012.

Index